SANCTUARY

MOMENTS IN HIS PRESENCE

DAVID STRUTT

malcolm down
PUBLISHING

First published in 2017 by Malcolm Down Publishing Ltd
www.malcolmdown.co.uk

British Library Cataloguing in Publication Data
A catalogue record for this book is available from the British Library.

ISBN: 978-1-910786-77-2

Cover image by Anthony Consiglio
Cover Design by Esther Kotecha
Art direction by Sarah Grace

Printed in the UK

Foreword

I've been looking forward to holding this book for ages now – ever since I heard David was beginning to write it! I always knew it was going to be good but the day he sent me the finished article I knew it would sit by my bed for the rest of my life! It is truly beautiful because it comes out of years of friendship with God and enjoyment of His word.

The day I first met David, many years ago now, I realised instantly that he was unlike anyone else I had ever known. At that time he was walking through an agonising 'valley of the shadow of death' as well as struggling with his own painful leg injury. The quiet faith of the man astounded me! When he later married Hannah, another person I greatly admire, I was delighted to ask them both to work with me at Beauty from Ashes. Our ministry supports people going through bereavement, loss, disablement or any kind of suffering, and David and Hannah definitely know how all that feels first hand! Their empathy and genuine love is so obvious as they listen to and pray with the people who visit us here, or help me to lead our healing retreats.

I think I would rather hear David speaking than any other preacher I know. Perhaps because he doesn't 'preach', he just chats about the God he loves and has grown to know so well over the years. And that is also exactly the way he writes. I love the way he uses the tiny, ordinary things of life to explain complex concepts, making them so easily accessible to the rest of us. Perhaps this is due to years of experience as a teacher?

Reading this book felt, to me, like discovering a fresh delight on each new page. Because David shows us how the Bible has impacted so many of his own memories of the ordinary small events of everyday life, he manages to bring the Scriptures alive in a very relevant and up-to-date way.

This book is definitely going to be my partner each morning as I enjoy my daily appointment with the Lord; and I honestly believe David's book is a 'must have' experience for everyone!

Jen Rees Larcombe
Beauty from Ashes

Introduction

I love reading the Bible! Each day, preferably early in the morning, I sit at my desk. I pray that the Spirit of God will open the Scriptures to me, and then I read! Sometimes I hungrily devour but, in all honesty, some days I struggle or get indigestion, or everything seems very quiet, but I have learned to persist. I have called this book *Sanctuary* simply because that was the title God gave me, in prayer, about five years ago. Sanctuary in Hebrew is *qôdesh*: 'a sacred place not for common use' or 'something set aside for sacred use'.

What follows is a collection of thoughts and insights from many years of reading, preaching and being inspired; notes that I scribbled on hundreds of scraps and placed in a box entitled, 'Sanctuary'. I knew that one day I would write this book for you and many others like you who, daily, place a great importance on coming into His glorious presence – to praise Him, to hear Him and to be healed and restored by the wonders of His love and faithfulness.

This book of daily reflections is not meant at all to replace your daily Bible reading but I do pray that, alongside God's living Word, it may stimulate, inspire and refresh you. Use it beside your own Bible and ask God, as I do, to *'Break open Your words and let Your light shine out; let ordinary people* (like me) *see the meaning'* (Psalm 119, *The Message*). Neither is it intended to be a theological tome but something that helps you go deeper into His love and aids you on your journey; I have only given chapter references so that you have to dig a little!

May I also say that, over many years, I have collected many hundreds of thoughts like a gleaner in a field and I apologise if anyone feels I might have 'borrowed' their thoughts. It is inevitable! They say there is nothing original in the Kingdom and I thank all those who have spoken God's word, written down inspired thoughts, prayed with me and nurtured and encouraged me. Bless you all! Thank you for your dedication to the King.

A practical suggestion . . . with the aide-memoire PREFACE:

PRAY before you

READ your Bible aided by these daily prompts.

ENGAGE with the Holy Spirit; He is willing to meet you.

FREE yourself of everything that might be a burden and a distraction.

ASK your heavenly Father to bring *fresh* understanding and to bring

CLARITY to your study today and to

EMPOWER you so that you may go out to share the treasure of God with someone.

———•———

The pages are arranged so you can coincide your reading with the date and the church festivals, or read *Sanctuary* at some other pace using the numbered days.

At the end of each day's reading, I have added a short prayer. This is not intended to be the fullness of what you might pray, merely a source of inspiration for further meditation.

I have the following 'borrowed' prayer pinned above my desk. If you aren't sure how to pray, try the Prayer of St Brendan. It is as beautiful today and still as inspirational as the day it was first written down about 1500 years ago.

Help me to journey beyond the familiar
and into the unknown.
Give me the faith to leave old ways
and break fresh ground with You.

Christ of the mysteries, I trust You
to be stronger than each storm within me.
I will trust in the darkness and know
that my times, even now, are in Your hand.
Tune my spirit to the music of heaven,
And somehow make my obedience count for You.

May God bless you and, as you read this, may you know His great hands enfolding you and His Spirit bringing you alive every day.

David

JANUARY

Day 1 – January 1st

New Beginnings . . . I used to offer my services, albeit informally, as a landscape planner. There is little more wonderful or profoundly challenging than to be asked to envisage a finished project when all that is before you is a plot devoid of history, or plan or purpose, let alone shape, form or plantings.

'*The earth was formless and void, and darkness was over the surface of the deep; and the Spirit of God was moving over the surface of the waters.*' (Genesis 1)

Imagine that. Nothing there! No thing except that which was a brilliant idea in the burning, creative heart of God! Imagine the glorious inspiration; Father, Son and Holy Spirit longing together. At the beginning of the year it might be good to see that you have that unrealised potential. True, you have a history, just as a garden plot has; things are buried beneath the surface that may well need to be picked over, prised out and consigned to a rubbish pile, but this is a fresh start! However amazing and wonderful God's earth is, remember He doesn't seem to have set out to create a municipal park (complete with *Keep off the Grass* signs). He was creating a home where the pinnacles of His creation, man and woman, would live and partner with Him in His passion for all things beautiful. Home! It's that personal. Him and you forever.

Thank God that He is the Lord of fresh starts, new moments, inspiring and creative perspectives. See the beginning of this year for what it is: a springboard opportunity into the deeps of your pilgrimage into God's goodness and faithfulness. We don't have to be Olympic divers, full of style, balance and skill, but simply ready and willing to take the plunge with Him and into Him . . .

'Beyond the familiar and into the unknown' . . . Amen.

Day 2 – January 2nd

'Better than life . . .' In Psalm 63 we come across these startling words: *'Because Your loving kindness is better than life, my lips will praise You.'*

Yesterday we looked at the very beginning of all things. Today we look at the ending (or to be more precise, *our ending*). Although we may be reluctant to think about it overmuch, our mortal life as we know it here on earth will cease. The statistics, as they say, point in that direction. I have officiated at many funerals and often read the words of Psalm 103 at the committal: *'As for man, his days are like grass; as a flower of the field, so he flourishes. When the wind has passed over it, it is no more and its place acknowledges it no longer. But the loving kindness of the LORD is from everlasting to everlasting on those who fear Him.'*

What a big *'but'!* But for His loving kindness there would be no trace of us after death. His loving kindness is better than life itself; it has always been and always will be. Dwell on that for a moment: *His loving kindness is better than life . . .* This remarkable but inferior shell of earthly life that God has made for us will wilt and crumple and then expire, BUT for those who trust and revere Him, His love and His kindness is better than life as we know it! What an overwhelming reassurance! There is more to come and nothing can come between us and the life that comes to us now and on through eternity by His loving kindness! That was God's plan: no death, and eternity with Father, Son and Holy Spirit in a beautiful place. A seamless, wonderful existence of unutterable splendour and kindness.

David wrote Psalm 103 in the Judean desert when he was instructed by God, through the prophet Gad, to go there. It was all about escaping the murderous clutches of Saul. In the barren desert, the future king contemplates the depths and the power of the love and kindness of God. Jesus went to the same desert, sent by the Holy Spirit; and in that place, as He dealt with the enemy's taunts, He realised fully, as the Son of Man, just how faithful His loving Father was.

As we reflect on these scriptures and the magnificently awesome love of God for us we can, whether facing the desert place, contemplating the ending of our days or just looking to another day, rest in the knowledge that God's care for us is better than life itself. What can we fear? Jesus said:

'Do not let your heart be troubled; believe in God, believe also in Me. In My Father's house are many dwelling places.' (John 14)

My Lord, my Master and my King! How safe I am in the immensity of Your love and faithfulness that took You to the cross for us. The victory of victories was won there, and Easter Sunday when You rose from the grip of death really does mean that You have the final say in *everything*! *EVERY THING!* How safe I am in Your love and faithfulness. Always and forever. Amen.

Day 3 – January 3rd

I am not sure how you feel about 'waiting'. It's probably not a glamorous or welcoming thought to be queuing for a train that is then cancelled amidst groans from the gathered masses. The word 'waiting' in Scripture has quite a different meaning. 'Hoping' also has a meaning beyond *hoping the next train will run on time.*

Psalm 130 goes, *'I wait for the LORD. My soul [my life] does wait and in His word do I hope.'* Those two words 'wait' and 'hope'. The Hebrew suggests an intimate waiting which is far from passive. *'I bind together with You; I twist together* [qâvâh] . . . *the core of my being entwines like a rope plait . . . and for His word, I patiently tarry* [yâchal].'

'My soul waits for the LORD more than the watchmen for the morning.' Anyone who has ever spent a wakeful night, maybe waiting with a little fear and anxiety, will know what it is to long for the morning light to glimmer in the night sky. With the light of dawn

comes security and peace. That was how it was for the watchmen on the city towers and ramparts; and the psalmist writes, *'more than that do I wait for the coming of the Lord . . . for His word.'*

Dear Lord, may I learn to tarry for You, not seeking to persuasively wring out a word from Your Spirit, but really longing and thirsting for Your Presence; in that place I will, I know, hear You speak words of life. Amen.

Day 4 – January 4th

'My heart is not proud, nor my eyes lofty.' (Psalm 131)

David's psalm here has the most beautiful descriptions of contentment in God; utter childlike reliance and peace on the Provider who knows all things and for whom nothing is beyond His great reach. So often we come to the Lord, heads full of worries, or earth-bound limitations, or maybe with great visions of what we believe will be. And then quite suddenly the Spirit of the living God whispers, *'Shush, my little one . . . don't fret. You concern yourself with great and difficult things but I am here for you . . .'* There is something delightfully *simple* about the words of this psalm. It speaks of a man who really has come to the end of himself. These words reflect so many of the words of Jesus who encouraged us to come to Him in childlike faith.

Lord, there are so many things in my head today. They whirl around me, stripping me of my peace. I choose to set them aside now and to focus on You and Your graceful, loving care for me. Amen.

Day 5 – January 5th

We continue today . . . *'Surely I have composed and quieted my soul; like a weaned child rests against his mother; my soul is like a weaned child within me.'* (Psalm 131)

What a stunning picture King David paints for us! The child is weaned. This is not a clamorous child seeking sustenance at the breast. The child *is* weaned. The new-infant life-passage of constantly demanding and receiving provision is over. I will never doubt again the Provider's ability to succour me, in all circumstances. I have grown so far and all is well. I will not fear. I am content to be held – more than that, to be held against the breast and the beating heart that once produced such urgency in me. I am at rest. The Comforter is near. That is enough.

'*There was reclining on Jesus' bosom one of His disciples, whom Jesus loved.*' (John 13)

Dear God, I can hardly believe this; You are as near as that to me. You feed me and You comfort me. How can I doubt Your love for me or Your willingness to bring me through all things? Amen. So be it. I love You.

Day 6 – January 6th

'*A tranquil heart is life to the body but passion* [qin'âh] *is rottenness to the bones.*' (Proverbs 14)

The sort of passion that is spoken of here is most definitely negative! There is the healthy, God-speaking passion that we have spoken of in the last readings but this is a consuming desire to hold, most likely driven by fear of loss. It might describe a jealous spouse and that level of emotion is destructive to trust and is the opposite of tranquillity. Far from describing the *shâlôm* of the weaned child in Psalm 131 it conjures up an image of anxiety: if you go away, will you ever come back to me? Can I be sure? It consumes and destroys.

Jesus came and stood in their midst and said to them, '*Peace be with you.*' He showed them the wounds in His hands and His side, and the disciples rejoiced because they saw it was the Lord. Again, He said to them, '*Peace be with you*' (John 20).

Father, I thank You that Your loving faithfulness to me means that I need never fret or be anxious. Fill my heart with the tranquillity of Your Spirit. Forgive me for my times of false longing when my heart has raged after the wrong things, and heal my bones where they need Your touch. Amen.

Day 7 – January 7th

'And he [the prodigal son] got up and came to his father. But while he was still a long way off, his father saw him and felt compassion for him, and ran and embraced him and kissed him.' (Luke 15)

Jesus told this story. It is a story, a parable, intended to convey something of our heavenly Father's love for us. He seems to have deliberately chosen to describe a father whose love and affection for the son who came back having blown it, as outrageous and over the top. He is the running father who hitches his robes up and risks social ridicule by behaving like this towards his errant son. Everyone knew the lad was a rude and arrogant young man – and yet the father cannot resist welcoming him back and forgiving him. There is nothing grudging in the father's love; no 'well let's see how it goes'. He embraced the lad and kissed him.

Sometimes we need to be forgiven and sometimes we need to be reminded of the enormity of the Father's love for every one of us who decides to make our way back to Him. Clothes in tatters, not very clean and in desperate need to know again the unconditional embrace of our Father in heaven who watches down the road for the day we may turn back to Him.

Dear Father, I cannot believe You watched for me while I went away and broke Your heart with my errant ways, and yet You did. You come running to greet me and rain kisses on me, such is Your delight to have me back. Thank You for Your lavish love to me when I didn't deserve to have You even look in my direction. Amen.

Day 8 – January 8th

'The Spirit of the Lord is upon Me to . . . set free those who are oppressed.' (Luke 4)

The story of the father running after the lost son is central to the ministry of Jesus yesterday, today and forever. When Jesus stood and read from the scroll in the synagogue, He was, quite shockingly for some ears, ushering in a new season of God's Spirit's activity on earth through His earthly mission. It was a provocative thing to do. He was declaring for all who could hear, 'I am the One', and, not surprisingly, it raised a few eyebrows and the ire of the religious leaders.

Those who believe understand His 'mission statement' but it is good to reflect on it afresh as we cast our eyes around our world and see those who need to be set free – our neighbours, our work colleagues, and our family members. Jesus came to set them free. The truth is we do not see people clearly, at least not as Jesus did. He really *saw* that people around Him were oppressed (some translations say 'downtrodden'), despite all the outer frippery and the distractions of worldly fulfilment. He saw their deep need and spoke to them of kingdom love and compassion.

Today and every day we can ask afresh of the Holy Spirit, 'Come and anoint me for Your ministry, to set the downtrodden free.' The crucial point to understand is that there is no Division II when it comes to the Holy Spirit. The very same Spirit in Jesus is *exactly* the same Spirit that fills you and me. We don't get a watered-down, second-rate, earth-weary Spirit; it is Himself! The unrestrained fullness of Him. Breathe in that truth today.

Father, thank You that You long to fill me afresh more than I ask You to. You do not forget how much You want to equip me. Forgive me that I don't remember to appreciate You and to thirst for You. Come to me today, I pray. May I also declare, *'The Spirit of the Lord has anointed me to . . .'* Amen.

Day 9 – January 9th

The kingdom of God grows like a seed. Ever watched your seeds growing? It happens slowly!

'The kingdom of God is like a man who casts seed upon the soil; and he goes to bed at night and gets up by day, and the seed sprouts and grows – how, he himself does not know. The soil produces crops by itself; first the blade, then the head, then the mature grain.' (Mark 4)

As children, we grew mustard and cress on cotton wool so that we could watch the tiny seed swell and the roots push outwards. Usually it happens in the darkness and to look would be to disturb and probably cause damage that might never be repaired. I have learned to be patient in matters of the Kingdom. We shower droplets from our streams of Living Water, not necessarily even knowing where or how they land, and then we wait before the Lord of the harvest. It would be great if we always saw the entire process of a disciple coming to faith but it's not normal to have that awareness. For me, as I look back, I recognise how many droplets had to nurture me before the day when I invited the Holy Spirit to take my life. Thank God for all those people who faithfully spoke of God's love and faithfulness over many years.

Father, thank You for the witness of countless folk who spoke nutritious words to my spirit over many years. I praise You that You are the Lord of the harvest and that You never let words of Life fall to the ground without achieving Your ends. Bless You for Jesus, who opened the gates of glory and welcomed me in. Amen.

Day 10 – January 10th

'Why do You stand afar off, O LORD? Why do You hide Yourself in times of trouble?' So begins Psalm 10.

I often feel like shouting, as in the pantomime theatre, *'He's behind you!'* The truth is that it can seem as though God doesn't care in the silent times; *where is God?* It is so difficult to pray and sometimes even to believe, and at such times it seems as though the enemy's taunts become even louder and more vicious.

My advice is to make sure that you have done everything you can possibly do to clear up anything left undone . . . and then wait. Don't fall for the trap of blaming God. Even if heaven is silent, keep telling yourself testimonies from days gone by. I know it seems silly doing this but something happens as we remind our souls of God's hand in our life at an earlier time; our focus changes to one of giving glory to God. David speaks to his soul, so many times:

'*Why are you in despair, O my soul?*'

At the toughest time of my life I had not a clue what God was doing as *everything* seemed to be going wrong. My wife was very ill and I was struggling with physical difficulties and a great deal of pain after considerable surgery. One day I prayed for a man with the same problem as I was suffering from and, would you believe it, he was immediately healed! My immediate reaction was to feel hurt, left out, passed over and frustrated with God's inaccuracy! Surely I should have received *some* of the blessing! But then I began to praise God for what I had seen Him do. The Holy Spirit spoke to me about all that was happening in our lives and completely changed my understanding. I found my 'repose'. It didn't happen overnight, but I persisted; 'God has been good and I will praise Him,' I told myself over and over.

After a very long rant, the psalmist, finally, has got it off his chest and suddenly says, '*The LORD is king forever and ever.*'

My Father, there are days when You seem a long way off. I know You are there but only in my head do I know this. I understand now that You led me through that time to deepen my faith that I might learn to stand. When all about me everything falls away, I will still praise You, because You are worthy. Amen.

Day 11 – January 11th

'The unfortunate commits himself to You; You have been the helper of the orphan . . . O LORD, You have heard the desire of the humble; You will strengthen their heart, You will incline Your ear to vindicate the orphan and the oppressed.' (Psalm 10)

It is extraordinary how many times of late we have been approached to provide ministry and counsel to those who are afflicted in the journey of life and suffering from oppression of one sort or another. Sadly, in these present days, families break up, relationships tumble and things can become very unpleasant. It is extraordinary how the very worst side of people emerges under those circumstances and the enemy loves it and stokes the fires of hatred and bitterness.

When we become involved as supporters, I immediately think of some of the prophets of old who quietly looked to God and trusted Him to bring through resolution. It is their position of 'repose' that impresses me.

The humble, or perhaps *the afflicted*, will constitute the clear majority of those who will make a path to our door. You may be helping such a person, or perhaps you are one of them. You don't have to be parentless to be an orphan; the term describes many people who find themselves alone. I know that as a young Christian I emerged from that state and I am far from being an orphan now; I often describe myself as a 'very little boy with a great big Dad'! We can't presume on God to fight all our battles but when we are genuinely oppressed by injustice; I think this psalm, and others like it, can speak powerfully into our lives.

I recall once thinking that God often takes the aggressive, attacking stance and uses it for His purposes, rather as one might do in judo. It is the out-of-balance rush that He takes and uses to trip someone up. I have seen it happen so many times and it is there in the Psalms. How many times do the psalmists speak of their enemies digging a pit or trap and then falling into it?

If you are in an unpleasant situation, or know someone who is, sit quietly before the Lord and ask Him what He would do to break the stranglehold of unpleasantness and destructive high emotion.

Father, thank You for the encouragement You give to us in this psalm. Help me to quieten my hurts and to come before You to see what You have to say about the way out. Help me, in this time of deep trial, not to fall into the same trap. I will not rise to the bait but rather rise early to ask You to guide my day. Give me peace in these days, O Lord. Amen.

Day 12 – January 12th

There are times when what is happening on the world stage just doesn't make sense. It seems the wrong people hold the power and that they wield it with cruelty and with blatant disregard for every protest. How are we to make sense of it, other than the obvious: that we live in a fallen world that is groaning in anticipation of the coming King?

I have always had a deep fascination with the prophet Habakkuk, who lived in such a time. The Babylonians were incomparably powerful and cruel. Their forces were described as a vast killing machine. The prophet observed that all around him, in his own country, there was corruption, violence and law-breaking. Nothing made sense. He longed for his own land to be filled with a people whose hearts sought after God. God tells him that He will do that but, first, He is raising up the Chaldeans to 'sweep through like the wind, and then pass on.' God promises that the enemy will be punished for what they do but, make no mistake, it is He who is doing it. Habakkuk is, not surprisingly, dismayed. He cannot come to terms with God using an evil force for His ends.

'Your eyes are too pure to approve evil, and You can not look on wickedness with favour. Why do You look with favour on those who

deal treacherously? Why are You silent when the wicked swallow up those more righteous than they?' (Habakkuk 1)

Then God speaks to him of what will be; He speaks graphically of the corrupt, the idolaters, and the contemporary low life but, in the middle, comes God's declaration that *'the earth will be filled with the knowledge of the glory of the* LORD, *as the waters cover the sea'* (Habakkuk 2). This is what will be! At the end of this chapter describing just how dreadful everything is through God's eyes, the prophet finishes with these words: *'But the* LORD *is in His holy temple. Let all the earth fall silent before Him.'*

There is something about that verse that sends shivers down my spine. As we look around in the present day at all that appals us and seems incomprehensibly grim and disturbing, listen to the voice of the One who sees all things and will not be thwarted in His dealings with mankind. *'But the* LORD *is in His holy temple. Let all the earth be silent before Him.'*

Holy God, I only see in part the evil that surrounds me. You see it all and I feel it must pain You to watch the mess we are in. Have mercy on us, Lord. Your heart is to have the earth full of the knowledge of Your glory, that I know, and I know it will be so but spare us the sort of disaster that the prophets spoke of. Spare us from long, dark seasons where there is no light. Fill my heart with the repose of understanding fully that You *are* in Your temple. I fall silent before You, my Lord. I fall silent in awe of You, Mighty God, Everlasting King. Amen.

Day 13 – January 13th

I suggest that you read Habakkuk, if you haven't done so already; it's a gem and has spoken into my life in many personal situations. There is the most wonderful declaration from the mouth of Habakkuk when he begins to understand that he must accept what God is going to do. He comes to a place of repose, even in the face of impending doom and destruction. It is all frighteningly real and yet so beautiful; no place here for quasi-faith. He begins,

'I heard and my inward parts trembled, at the sound my lips quivered. Decay enters my bones, and in my place I tremble. Because I must wait quietly for the day of distress, for the people to arise who will invade us.' (Habakkuk 3)

One can almost quake with him such is the weight of the prophetic word he is carrying. Imagine knowing that that is descending on one's country (before anyone else does, one assumes!). I sit in amazement at this man of God who then turns to his unshakeable faith in God. The passage of three 'thoughs' follows: though the fig tree should not blossom . . . though the yield of the olive should fail . . . though the flock should be cut off from the fold . . . But he finishes with a tumult of profound praise,

'Yet I will exult in the LORD, I will rejoice in the God of my salvation. The Lord GOD is my strength, and He has made my feet like hinds' feet, and makes me to walk on my high places.'

I can add little of worth to that so I will just say it once more: 'He makes me to walk on my high places.'

My God, You are an amazing God; that in the midst of great trouble and distress You come to a man when all seems lost and You fill his heart with such love and wonder. I want also to walk on my high places in days of impending loss so I ask You to build me up in Your goodness that I may also lead others onto *their* high places at times when otherwise, they would be lost in the dark valley. Great God of my heart, I worship You. Amen.

Day 14 – January 14th

While on holiday a few years ago, we drove through the Highlands of Scotland and then stopped for a break. Sitting with a bowl of soup, I looked across the gangway where an elderly couple were eating lunch and quite suddenly I felt God say, 'I want to say something to that lady.' I don't find that easy to do where strangers are concerned and I prevaricated. If I am brutally honest, I said, 'Oh, Lord. But I am on holiday . . .' Then, just as I decided to cross the enormous space between us they gathered their belongings to go. I let them go with deep remorse. I had failed. 'Oh, Lord,' I said, under my breath, 'please give me one more chance to speak to her. I am sorry but I was frightened and far too selfish.' A little later, after we had finished, I saw the lady on her own in the shop so I went straight to her. I didn't even know what Jesus wanted to say but I knew He wanted to speak to her. So, I said, 'Hello. Please excuse me for interrupting you but I am a Christian and it seems that sometimes God wants to speak to us. I feel He wants to say something to you. May I share it with you?'

Far from receiving the hostile reaction I imagined, she smiled and said simply, 'How lovely.'

I spoke. 'God wants you to know, *"He sees your struggle."'*

That was that. So simple.

She smiled again; laughed even. 'Well,' she replied, 'I am struggling on two counts today. I left my stick in the car and my husband has gone to fetch it because I cannot walk safely without it.' She hesitated and then added, 'But we have just come from the infirmary in Inverness where they told me I have cancer and there is nothing they can do.'

With tears in our eyes, I put my arm round her shoulders and prayed for her. I never saw her again.

'Then she called the name of the Lord who spoke to her, "You are a God who sees [El-Roi]" . . . therefore the well was called Beer-lahai-roi [the well of the living One who sees me].' (Genesis 16)

Lord, thank You that You see me. You have always seen me. You know my every thought; You know my words before I speak them; You know my thoughts, worries and fears today. Speak to me today and bless those who receive unsettling news. Amen.

Day 15 – January 15th

Where we occasionally holiday there is an island in the distance which is clearly visible one day and yet the next it may be wrapped in mist and cloud and quite obscured. It was there, of course, all the time; just not visible to me.

And so it was, later in Hagar's life, when miserable, dejected and hungry in the desert she thought that she and Ishmael, her son, would surely die. She couldn't *see* God in her circumstances. She was so upset that she set her young son down in the shade at a distance because she couldn't bear to see him when he died. What a forsaken situation to be in. But as an Egyptian maybe she hadn't reckoned on the God of the Hebrews whose name was also that of her son by Abraham. *'Yismâel' (Ishmael)* or *'God hears'*. He was there, just as the island was yesterday, but surrounded by clouds or perhaps by her own fears, doubts about her worth and full of her unhappiness.

'She . . . lifted up her voice and wept. God heard the lad crying; and the angel of God called to Hagar from heaven and said to her, "What is the matter with you, Hagar? Do not fear, for God has heard the voice of the lad where he is" . . . Then God opened her eyes and she saw a well of water.' (Genesis 21)

Father, sometimes my eyes are closed, perhaps by my lack of faith, but it is so wonderful to know that You are present and hearing my cry. I call out to You today, as Hagar did, when the going was too tough and the future looked desperate. I pray for friends engaged in exhausting journeys of body, mind or spirit. I call You by Your name El Shâma, the God who hears me. Thank You. Amen and amen.

Day 16 – January 16th

It's wonderful as we read the story of Abraham, Sarah and Hagar in Genesis. In many ways they were folks just like you and me – pilgrims on a journey with God. They made mistakes, doubted, and failed to understand quite how great God was and how very firmly He had established His covenants with them. One of the many wonderful things in this story is that there are so many new names given. Even God was given new names as we have seen!

Abram (High Father) was given the name Abraham (Father of a Multitude). I have often joked that he and his wife Sara (Sârai) got the 'ah'. God's name was woven into theirs as they trusted Him and ventured forth into the impossible. Sarah was given the new name meaning 'Princess'. God often calls us by names that call out the faith in the people He loves. He often announces such followers in advance giving them names that describe not so much what they shall be called but what they shall *be*.

'Behold, the virgin shall be with child and shall bear a Son and they shall call His name "Immanuel" which translated means, "God with us."' (Matthew 1)

Father, I wonder if You have a name for me? I wait before You now, asking, *What shall I be called and what shall I be?* Speak to me as I tarry in Your presence, I pray. Amen.

Day 17 – January 17th

Thank God that we don't have to be perfectly formed before God uses us! Do you ever feel that maybe God cannot use you until . . .?

Certainly, it can be true that God calls us to release something to Him before He in turn brings His blessing to bear on us, but quite often it is the potential He sees and encourages us with. Remember Peter after he declared that Jesus Christ was the Messiah?

'And Jesus answered and said to him, "Blessed are you, Simon Barjonah, because flesh and blood did not reveal this to you, but My Father who is in heaven. I also say to you that you are Peter (Greek: Petros), *and upon this rock* (petra) *I will build My church."'* (Matthew 16)

God didn't intend to use only Peter but others, too, as *petra* is plural, but the real point was that He gave him a new name! The name Simon meant 'reed' and maybe it conferred notions of being unstrong, bendy, and possibly unreliable when the pressure was on; so, He called him 'Rock'. How wonderful that was! It is so beautiful that despite the obvious weaknesses that Simon was still capable of displaying at times, Jesus saw Simon Peter in His Spirit, as heaven recognised him.

Take heart. God delights over you and has a destiny planned for you!

Father in heaven, despite the boundless enormity of Your family, You know each one of us by name. You know our days, even our potential perversities, but also our glory in Jesus both to come and right here, today. Thank You! Amen.

Day 18 – January 18th

While Jesus was on His way to Jerusalem He met ten outcasts of society. They were the untouchables as they had leprosy. They called out to Jesus, pleading for Him to have mercy on them, such was the reputation Jesus had for healing people. It doesn't say that He healed them only that He told them to show themselves to the priests. The account unfolds that one came back and that one was a 'foreigner' – a Samaritan. He loudly shouted the praises of God and fell at the feet of Jesus, thanking Him, such was his gratitude that the crippling power of his dreadful disease had been broken. Hallelujah! When Jesus responded, He asked where the other nine were. 'Were ten not cleansed?' He enquired and went on to point out that it was the 'stranger who was not a Jew' who gave glory to God. It's a strange business but I do wonder if the other nine went to the religious leaders who were very much struggling with the healing ministry of Jesus and somehow put the 'fear of God' into the nine to prevent them acknowledging their healings. We cannot know but, for sure, it was the non-religious man who went on his way with Jesus' words echoing in his ears.

'*Stand up and go; your faith has made you well.*' (Luke 17)

Jesus, I give You praise and glory today. I fall at Your feet as I reflect on all that You have done for me. May I never be the one who does not immediately return to bless Your Majesty for kindnesses freely and generously given to me. Amen.

Day 19 – January 19th

We often comment in our house that the behaviour of a football crowd, generally, is far more exuberant than worship in many churches! Psalm 95 speaks of worship.

'*Let us shout joyfully to Him with songs. For the LORD is a great God and a great King above all gods . . . Come, let us worship and bow down; let us kneel before the LORD our Maker* (Hebrew – accomplisher). *For He is our God* (Ĕlôhîym – great, magnificent God), *and we are the people of His pasture, and the sheep of His hand.*'

I imagine the sheer vitality and resounding praise in the days of the psalm writers! How refrained we can be, although nowadays we might try to explain that it is 'refined' not refrained! The words used are quite specific; the worship word is 'prostrate' – '*Come let us prostrate ourselves . . . let us kneel before the Lord.*'

Throughout Scripture we find men and women freely expressing their worship – whether it be the Samaritan man freed of leprosy, or Abraham when God established the covenant with him (Genesis 17). We find men and women dancing, shouting and generally raising the roof at the greatness of God. I vividly recall a night when the Holy Spirit overwhelmed me with His love; without a thought, I fell to my knees before Him. Almighty God. My Saviour.

Dearest Lord, my magnificent King. I am on my knees with praise today. I give You the worship that befits a King. It is right to give You thanks and praise. Amen.

Day 20 – January 20th

Today is one of those perfect out-of-season beach days. As I sit writing, I can hear the children's cheerful voices; see the colourful kites flying against the cloudless blue sky, and somewhere in the background the heckling and ridiculing of politicians in 'Prime Minister's Questions'! It sounds like a game but it isn't. What must it be like to be promoted to be effectively the head of the land? I would hate to sit on that front bench!

I find myself thinking about Joseph, a man who stood before the governors of Egypt as Chancellor of the land, in order that the flock of God, the Hebrew nation, might be saved. He was rapidly promoted from Pharaoh's dungeons when the gift of dream interpretation was valued by the leaders as God's saving grace to Egypt. *You shall be over my house,* the Pharaoh told him. Israel was made welcome in this foreign land in days of drought and famine and, thus, they were saved from catastrophe. Joseph was belittled, scandalously abused, falsely imprisoned for *years* but he eventually told his estranged brothers, *'Do not be grieved or angry with yourselves, because you sold me here, for God sent me before you to preserve life'* (Genesis 45).

A man who can truly set aside his own desires, tragic conditions of life, anger, resentment and hurts and simply know peace – that God is behind it all – deserves our most serious attention! Not least because is he not in some strange and profound way a prophetic messenger sent to declare the sacrificial ways of the Messiah Jesus? He is functioning in the grace-bringing, saving ways of God who, without regard for Himself laid down everything. Throughout Scripture, the prophetic unveiling of Jesus seems to happen repeatedly, like the waves on the shore. Each wave comes closer . . .

'So Israel set out with all that he had, and came to Beersheba, and offered sacrifices to the God of his father Isaac. God spoke to Israel in visions of the night and said, "Jacob, Jacob . . . I am God, the God of

your father; do not be afraid to go down to Egypt, for I will make you a great nation there.'" (Genesis 46)

Father of all, You are the Great Sustainer and I stand in awe at the strength You give to Your children in tough times. I think about Joseph and just marvel. What a heart he had! The truth is I do not have to imitate anyone but *trust* that whatever I may be called to do You will provide. You are my strength and my shield. Amen.

Day 21 – January 21st

'O sing to the Lord *a new song'* (Psalm 98)

It is so good sometimes not to set out to plumb the depths in Scripture but instead simply to respond to the simplest injunction. Sing a new song today! If you feel you cannot sing, shut the door. It is between you and your Father in heaven – the wonderfully appreciative audience of One! Maybe you cannot even think of any words? How about, 'My Lord, how I love You!'

The amazing thing about worshipping God in this way is that when we haven't the words, the Holy Spirit gives them to us; and when the tune won't come, He provides. Sometimes I laugh at my own inhibitions and put out of my head the notion that God is scoring my entertainment value as though I was on *X-Factor* – and I realise He is gazing into my heart's desires anyway and He smiles with delight!

The 'sing' word David uses in this psalm is *'shîyr'* which means 'to sing like a minstrel'. I used to think 'court jester' when I learned that, but it isn't. It's to be like a minister, 'a minstreller' of worship, and so I often move around and be myself before Him – I have even been known to laugh and smile!

O Lord, it's so good to let my singing rise before You today. It's the best I can do but I know You will perfect my worshipping heart. I want to surrender it to You so that I may fully and freely express my love for You. Hope of my heart, You alone are worthy of my praises. Amen.

Day 22 – January 22nd

I am in an idyllic place today, here, near the beach. As I am in a wheelchair I am a little limited for getting out and about but in my heart, as I sit typing, I might tell you, there is no limitation! Being reduced to a level of 'incapacity' means all sorts of things depending on your personality; for me it is frustration at not being able to do practical things. My children once laughed at me when I adapted a crutch handle to hold the garden hose so my plants would still be watered in the hottest of summers when it was beyond me to weight-bear. 'Dad,' they said, good humouredly, 'couldn't you just sit and read a book?'

I think of many people who struggle with very great infirmity, much more than mine, and I marvel at how they adapt and survive. More than survive – they thrive! Learning to re-invent oneself before God is very important in certain seasons. I think of Jesus who left everything behind and re-invented Himself as the Son of Man. It would have been so easy on many occasions to just resume His glory and supernatural capacity to do anything He wanted – stones into bread in the desert to put the enemy firmly in his place, or skipping all the suffering of the cross by going back to glory from the Mount of the Transfiguration.

'Let us run with endurance the race that is set before us, fixing our eyes on Jesus, the author and perfecter of faith, who for the joy set before Him endured the cross, despising the shame, and has sat down at the right hand of the throne of God.' (Hebrews 12)

God, You turned Your back on glory, for our sake, to bring us home; strengthen me to see things a different way – to understand the joy of heaven. As much as I want to linger in the places and times of shining radiance, show me how to descend and journey with You in the valleys. Amen.

Day 23 – January 23rd

One of the wonders of God's unfathomable ways, which I will expand on later in the book, is that it is often in the place of greatest testing, the season we least wanted to *ever* visit, that God quite suddenly and astonishingly ushers in deep, deep understanding of His nature and His dealings with us. In the Scriptures, there is a Hebrew word that crops up now and again in the Old Testament that means a variety of things: *'âbar'*. To me it signifies a crossing over, something of a momentous point in a journey, a time when you just *know* that God has changed the atmosphere. *We can't manufacture it; God does it.* When Abram received the covenant of God, His fire passed between the offerings that Abram had been instructed to set out.

'*It came about when the sun had set, that it was very dark, and behold, there appeared a smoking oven and a flaming torch which passed between* [âbar] *these pieces. On that day, the LORD made a covenant with Abram.*' (Genesis 15).

Thus writes the psalmist (Psalm 92) in the place of spiritual or physical exile, isolated in despair of being far from home and God:

'*Deep calls to deep at the sound of Your waterfalls; all Your breakers and Your waves have rolled over* [âbar] *me. The LORD will command His loving kindness in the daytime; and His song will be with me in the night.*'

My Father, I know You allow me to navigate the deeps, the dark places, and the desert experiences. In those places my natural inclination is to ask You to lift me straight out of them but my inner person, the person You are transforming, cries out, 'Lord, let the treasures of the darkness be mine in this moment. Christ of the mysteries, I trust You to be stronger than each storm within me.' Amen.

Day 24 – January 24th

Continuing with the theme of our God who mysteriously transforms the dark experiences, I think of all those who have been suffering and then God has moved, either in mind, body or spirit, and transformed the situation. On occasions, a miracle of physical healing, a stunning transformation of a sick body; and on others an equally remarkable profound change in the understanding of the situation – a deep call from Father in the midst of very choppy seas. It is not ours to choose, although we can ask; indeed, I think we always must ask, but let our prayers be wise: *'Father. Would You come to fill this season, we pray? There may be something of infinite worth that You desire to bring, something that may be of far greater worth than a physical healing moment. We ask that You would do what You see as right for us now; meet us at our point of real need, we pray.'*

I notice that Moses in his forty years in the wilderness was *'pasturing the flock of Jethro his father-in-law, the priest of Midian; and he led the flock to the west side of the wilderness and came to Horeb, the mountain of God. The angel of the* LORD *appeared to him in a blazing fire'* (Exodus 3). Not only was Moses looking after someone else's sheep, he was at the rear of the wilderness with them. That is down and nearly out however one might view it . . . and then God moves, majestically and in a history-changing movement. His fire blazes in where, of all places? A bush!

Dear Lord of the Fire that burns so brightly in the darkness, come to me and those I love; those who are in the very back of the desert, hot and weary; those who feel they have hit the buffers – come and blaze, I pray. Amen.

Day 25 – January 25th

'So Moses said, "I must turn aside now and see this marvellous sight, why the bush is not burned up." When the LORD *saw that he had*

turned aside to look, God called to him from the midst of the bush and said, "Moses, Moses!"' (Exodus 3)

Burning bushes were not, apparently, very uncommon, such is the heat of the desert. Not an attractive concept if you don't like very hot weather! What attracted Moses was the supernatural nature of the conflagration; the fire burned brightly but the tinder-dry bush was not immediately consumed – in fact not at all! It was just burning fiercely!

There is the most wonderful childlike curiosity about Moses' reaction: *I must go and see what's going on here.* If I am honest, my reaction might be, 'Oh, no, we might soon have a major fire on our hands. Let's try to put this out!' But if you have ever witnessed the supernatural you will know that there is an almost irresistible draw to watch, to see and to understand. We can learn from Moses' reaction; be curious! Get closer to the Fire. If something remarkable is happening, God will call you by your name! Suddenly Moses finds himself responding to the commanding voice, *Take off your shoes . . . Honour Me, the Holy One.*

I recall once leading a session on a retreat. It was evening after supper and a classic time for a few folks to doze but, as I taught, I felt my excitement grow. Then I distinctly felt the atmosphere change. Others noticed. God had come! I led the meeting nearer to the Fire; encouraged people to draw near, to receive prayer. The talk was abandoned and people were healed and mightily blessed!

Almighty God, I praise you for the astonishing ways You meet with us at the back of the desert and in the most unlikely places; through fire-laden bushes and hushed and awed rooms. Come close to me, I pray, in all I do, to transform my ordinary and mundane moments into holy ones, and the dirt under foot into Your Holy ground. Amen.

Day 26 – January 26th

This morning the piercing rays of dawn's sun shone over the twigs of winter trees against a dark sky that swelled with the threat of a storm, but it seemed as though the bright light would win and the day would be glorious.

I am reminded of Psalm 110 in which David seems to be writing prophetically, I believe, of God speaking to His Son. My interpretation of verse 3 goes:

'Your people will freely give themselves as joyful sacrifices to You in the day of Your strength. In the splendour of Your holiness, shining light in every direction as the dawn breaks, the dew of Your youth is going to be upon them.'

In the midst of winter days, we can feel a little lost. The news is bad, the battle seems to be wearying, the weather chilly and damp, and we wonder if the new shoots of spring will soon break forth. So it is in the spiritual realm. A new day will break with overwhelming beauty and the followers of Jesus will see in their spirits, 'The dawn is coming! The day of God's power and full force is nearly upon us! Hallelujah! We welcome the King! We welcome the King!'

Lord Jesus, today I want to tell You how I feel about the stuff of life. If I am honest, sometimes it is dispiriting but I know that a day of awesome power and glory is coming as You take back that which is Yours. I offer myself to join that joyful throng as the King is revealed in all His splendour and power. O come, Lord Jesus, come and take Your rightful place in our hearts! Amen.

Day 27 – January 27th

Today we worship the Lord. I woke early with a song on my heart, 'He is my rock and salvation!'

'My soul, wait in silence for God only, for my hope is from Him. He only is my rock and my salvation. My stronghold; I shall not be shaken.

On God my salvation and my glory rest; the rock of my strength, my refuge is in God. Trust in Him at all times, O people; pour out your heart before Him; God is a refuge for us. Selah.' (Psalm 62)

Sometimes King David seems ahead of his time! He is like a new covenant believer. He had learned to trust and in these few verses he expounds some really helpful points:

- Wait before God – don't rush in with all your thoughts and petitions!
- Speak to your inner person, 'Hush, now. We are going to listen.'
- He is the safe place. Rock often means a 'crag': a secure nook in the rock, safe from view, safe from the battering of the elements. Any climber will tell you the value of spotting a crag, a cleft.
- He is the only One who will save me! And listen – *on God my glory rests!* This is not the only place in the Psalms where David speaks of his glory. It is clear that he is not referring to God's glory but instead, astonishingly, the glory of God that he, David, carries. This is the heavy glory of God, the *kâbode*.
- 'Pour out your heart before Him . . .'

What can we say?

My Father, it is *Your presence* I seek. I love Your presence. I want to be known in heaven as a lover of Your presence. My soul, I love the presence of the King. I will wait for His presence – no one else will satisfy. Your presence, Lord. Holy Spirit, I invite You today. I bring You my adoration. Like sweet oil at Your feet, I pour out my worship before You. Amen.

Day 28 – January 28th

In a holy dust-up between the religious 'prophet' Amaziah, at the time of King Jeroboam II, and Amos the shepherd, an amazing conflict happens that has encouraged me so much over the years. You may want to read this short book as it is only nine chapters. If you do you will find it a remarkably contemporary message. There was greed amongst merchants and traders, political intrigue, and what can only be described as crass religious arrogance. Amos is told in no uncertain terms that his presence is no longer required! As far as the leaders are concerned, he is *persona non-grata*. It would seem that Amos only actually prophesied over a few days. Here is what he says to Amaziah:

'I am not a prophet, nor am I the son of a prophet; for I am a herdsman and a grower of sycamore figs. But the LORD *took me from following the flock and the* LORD *said to me, "Go prophesy to My people Israel." Now hear the word of the* LORD.' (Amos 7)

It is outrageously wonderful to know that if God your Father chooses, He can, in a moment, take you from the most menial humdrum of tasks to extolling the wisdom of God even to the most influential people! I love it!

My loving Father, forgive me for the days when I have doubted that You wanted to put words in my mouth that might shape or influence the progress of Your kingdom. Forgive me my fear. Lift from me, I pray, anything that would speak to my spirit untrue thoughts and somehow diminish me before You. I am Your child. Thank you. Let me be a spontaneous and accurate hearer of You. Amen.

Day 29 – January 29th

There is a fascinating series of thoughts around the words 'bless' and 'to be blessed', the well-known words which have been spoken and sung in many forms:

'Bless the LORD, *O my soul, and all that is within me, bless His holy name.'* (Psalm103)

The fundamental meaning of the Hebrew word used here, *'bârak'*, is 'to kneel'. It speaks directly of humility or, perhaps, paying homage. It trips so lightly from our tongues; 'bless', we say. There is a softening of the meaning very often as we translate from Hebrew. Why don't we say, 'Kneel before the LORD, and all that is within me, kneel before His holy name'? There is also a word-connection with 'drinking'. Camels kneel to drink and the word is closely associated with the drinking place of these creatures that take deep draughts of water to ensure their survival in desert places.

The word for 'all that is within me' signifies our core place, our very centre. I like that. I don't want to simply be blessing God in a superficial way that costs me little. He deserves the homage of my deepest being. I recall being in a meeting many years ago, when the Holy Spirit seemed to be saying, 'Go out into the aisle and kneel before God.' I didn't find it easy, fearing that everyone's gaze would be on me and that I might be thought 'strange' or even 'exhibitionist'. I did go and the atmosphere of the meeting changed at that moment. I cannot explain it except to say that the Holy Spirit does love to catch us up in praise of the Father. If we cannot physically kneel, we can still do the equivalent in our spirit-person.

Father, I want to practise the presence of God and to bring You my deepest affections and my most profound worship. I kneel before You today. I am not used to doing this but I know that if I am obedient to Your Word of truth, You will value my praise. I wait here, bowed before Your Majesty. Amen.

Day 30 – January 30th

Some of us have had the mixed blessing of being on state benefits of some sort or other. For me it conjures up images of being unwell for a long period of my life. King David wrote and sang:

'Bless the LORD, O my soul, and forget none of His benefits; who pardons all your iniquities.' (Psalm 103)

The word is better translated 'kindnesses' and I find this so helpful as I read this psalm.

So, may I suggest: 'Kneel before the LORD, and forget none of His kindnesses; who forgives all of your perversity.'

I feel I can more fully and wonderfully respond to that. Goodness, if I start to list all of God's kindnesses to me . . .

Dear Lord. Thank You! What a small and totally inadequate phrase that is. And as for my perverse ways . . . where would I be without Your loving kindness? Amen.

Day 31 – January 31st

Dom John (later St John of Bosco) was a 19th-century priest who lived and worked among the agricultural communities in Italy. He was called by God very early on in life, in the rough and tumble of the playground, to minister to his friends and locals who didn't know Jesus. He said that it wasn't enough for these people to be loved; they had to *know* they were loved. He was an evangelist and he is remembered on 31st January. It was God's *love* that came to him first – before the call to go out came. He loved God and God honoured him.

'Because he has loved Me [says the Lord], therefore I will deliver him; I will set him securely on high because he has known My name. He will call upon Me, and I will answer him; I will be with him in trouble; I will rescue him and honour him. With a long life I will satisfy him, and let him see My salvation.' (Psalm 91)

FEBRUARY

Day 32 – February 1st

In my Bible, I use a sticky note each day to mark which psalm to read next. On the yellow paper are hand-written the words:

'Blessed is the man who has made the LORD his trust.' (Psalm 40)

Occasionally the gum expires and I rewrite it on a fresh one! Life is like that – you need to replenish your capacity to stick! It reminds me every morning that the trusting act of opening my Bible to read is a blessing to me. I do it because I love the Lord and I love His word; He is worth it and I trust Him. It honours Him to say, simply, at the beginning of each day, 'I want to spend time with You, my Lord. I chose to make You my trust this day.'

The idea of blessing in that context is not complicated. My grandchildren have choices first thing in the morning. They can sit on Grandpop's lap for a story or a catch-up moment, or not. They can find other things to do, if they choose. There are the conkers from yesterday's walk to inspect; maybe there's a TV cartoon to watch. Am I pleased when they choose to sit with me? Yes, I am! I am blessed by it and from that moment our day together will be different. I won't sulk if they don't but the day won't be as full. I hope it's a mutual feeling!

The word blessed in Hebrew is *'esher'* and is best translated and most often translated as 'how happy'. *Esher* means being prosperous and well-looked after – blissfully happy even! Fundamentally it indicates *enjoying a full relationship with God.*

Understanding this also helps me when I say to people, *'Oh, be blessed today.'* It's a mini, two-second prayer for them, and much more than saying, 'Have a good one.' So today I say to you, 'Be blessed of God.' I hope your trust in Him will grow today.

Dear Lord, You are the One who prospers us and You alone can fill us with that sense of 'all is well'. *Really* well. My trust *is* in You today. Without You, I know I would be lost; in You I am found. I am known. One who cares for me and wants me to be blissfully content in my life is surely for me and will watch over me. I am truly blessed! Amen.

Day 33 – February 2nd

Home again, after a spell away. It was well-timed but not planned that way. The house is surrounded by scaffolding for the decorators who are tackling the high gables and upstairs woodwork. At least, that was the plan – until we started to examine the edges of the roof and realised that it was in poor shape and, tempting as it was to cover it up and put the gutters back, we had little choice but to go ahead with a new roof! So we are surrounded by lovely, chirpy, very skilled builders who seem to be knocking in about 12,500 nails each day! Yes, I know, peace be with you also!

The reason for mentioning all this is that I can see there is a spiritual equivalent. In our lives, we patch things up in order to survive and carry on. Sadly, through hurt, disappointment, perversity or any number of life events, the rot can set in, usually somewhere out of sight. Behind the equivalent of the old gutters, under that leaking tile near the chimney – the one that we couldn't readily reach to fix – we sort of know there *might* be a problem but we hope there won't be . . . sooner or later there is and we have to stop, admit it, and fix it.

I wonder if you have a problem like that (not on your house) – one that keeps resurfacing under certain circumstances and, when it does, it affects you very deeply. Many years ago, while in pastoral and counselling training, a problem kept popping up deep in my spirit that I found difficult to deal with. It made me fearful and tearful. It always occurred around talk of death or serious illness. To cut a long story short, it was enough of a problem to seek and receive some very loving and discerning prayer ministry. It related to an event from about 15 years previously, when, as a young boy, I saw an unfortunate and tragic event as a woman took her life in a particularly violent way. As I was prayed for, far from being smoothed over as though Jesus was a champion plasterer covering the cracks, the Lord put His finger on this point of extreme pain and all the shock and the anguish of that event came out of my inner person. I went through the physical shock as I was ministered to. It had been buried for *15 years!* I was healed and freed from nightmares and fears of death so much so that I went on to become a bereavement counsellor!

The sword of the Spirit is like that. Sometimes God does perform the most amazing micro-surgery!

'For the word of God is living and active and sharper than any two-edged sword, and piercing as far as the separation of soul and spirit, of both joints and marrow, and able to judge the thoughts and intentions of the heart. And there is no creature hidden from His sight, but all things are open and laid bare to the eyes of Him with whom we have to do.' (Hebrews 4)

We need never fear. If there is a problem, our Father will send in His wonderful Holy Spirit theatre team. If it is something we would rather not admit to, deal with it! Do you think for one second He doesn't know already? So often I have seen deeply wounded people be restored in this way. It is truly miraculous to see the enemy's claws peeled from someone's inner being and watch the healing take place. It is truly glorious to behold!

As I speak, there are some bits of old, woodworm-eaten roof timbers being hurled over the scaffolding and into the skip! Hallelujah!

Father, Son and Holy Spirit, You are an amazing and skilled therapist, surgeon, counsellor and friend. I want to trust myself to Your tender health check in the coming days. I invite You to do that. If there are bits of rot in my timbers would You expose them through the Holy Spirit's work in me? Let loving friends who really know how to partner with You be there for me. Oh, make me whole, I pray, in body, mind and spirit! Amen.

Day 34 – February 3rd

'Jesus was saying to those Jews who had believed Him, "If you continue My word, then you are truly disciples of Mine; and you will know the truth, and the truth will make you free."' (John 8)

As a counter to this, they began to speak of their history effectively as Abraham's progeny to point out that they couldn't need liberating as they weren't prisoners to anything. Because of sin they were, of course, unaware captives – of sin – they just thought they weren't. 'Is that a drip I hear from my roof? Could it be leaking? No, it cannot be; I have tiles on my roof. It must be the birds tapping . . .' Ever had a conversation like that with yourself, or perhaps the Holy Spirit?

Jesus' reply was very straightforward, as if to say, 'Look, a drip of water is a drip of water. Don't kid yourselves with your ideas of security.'

'Truly, truly, I say to you, everyone who commits sin is the slave of sin.'

You can read on in the account to see how it developed but the synopsis is that they had deaf ears to the notion that *it is the Son who sets you free*. Only the Son. There are grave dangers in relying on *anything else* to set you free. I do warn folk about dabbling in this or that for healing and wholeness. Beware that even Satan can appear like a shining one, and he does, and he leads folk astray. He induces a false sense of well-being but eventually, what seems attractive at first, leads to darkness.

Continuing with the roof analogy, we can well see that it might be possible to plug the leak. Many have done that but in the middle of the night, when you hear the drip, may I recommend that you ask the Master Roofer what might be going on?

Father, I know that there are gaps in my shingles, that when the wind blows my inner person creaks and groans in the night. I *feel* vulnerable. Maybe I have some things to sort out today. I invite You, the Holy Spirit, to cast Your penetrating gaze over this house of mine and speak truth to me. I need You. If You speak, I will take note. I trust that if You don't bring anything to light today, I am genuinely free and I won't go poking around but live in that lovely truth. Thank You, Lord Jesus, that You have set me free! I am so grateful for all You did for me on the cross of Calvary. Amen.

Day 35 – February 4th

'Come to Me, all who are weary and heavy laden, and I will give you rest.' (Matthew 11)

Literally: *'all who work to exhaustion'*.

There are so many ways to feel weary, heavy laden and to work or live to exhaustion, that I won't try to list them here. Suffice it to say that you can become mighty weary apart from straightforward toil; sickness, depression, as well as the pressure-cooker worlds of work and family, which may all contrive to bend your back under the load.

Naaman was a man with a great set of credentials – brave, valiant and a successful military man – but he also had leprosy (2 Kings 5). When an Israelite servant girl told Naaman's wife that the soldier could be healed through the ministry of the great prophet Elisha, he eventually ended up at Elisha's door. (It's a roundabout story but that's it in a nutshell).

It is a story about *surrender*. When Naaman arrived at Elisha's door, one of those wonderfully prophetic moments happened that is guaranteed to wind up and annoy any un-surrendered man! The prophet of God didn't come downstairs to greet him. He sent his servant with a message. I always imagine Elisha in the middle of his 'quiet time' (I don't think he is reading his morning paper!), but his relationship with God was such that I think he *was* reading the news – God's news. 'A man will come to you today who is rather arrogant and full of himself and his own ideas of importance, and we will bring him to the truth, Elisha. We will make him well, in more senses than one.'

43

'Elisha sent a messenger to him, saying, "Go and wash in the Jordan seven times, and your flesh will be restored to you and you will be clean."'

There is an interesting Hebrew word here for 'clean': *tâhêr* which means 'bright or sound or uncontaminated'.

Naaman's response was to remonstrate that Elisha hadn't come out to perform a miracle, and then he poured scorn on the quality of God's chosen river. His own servants got it straightaway and tried to persuade him, interestingly, saying that *if he had asked you to do some great thing you would have done it.* Brave servants! (NB: Often the people closest to us speak the truth even if we don't like it!).

So, he went and was completely restored.

It is a story that is really worth a study. How laden in wisdom it is!

Father, we praise You for Your desire to heal us and make us whole but we also see from this that You are to be Lord of our lives, surrendered lives stripped of pomposity and self-importance. Speak to me today of the things You would have me bathe seven times in Your river. Amen.

Day 36 – February 5th

In the same Naaman story (2 Kings 5) there are some interesting bit-part players. The king of Israel, approached in the first instance by Naaman, with a referral from his own king, is clearly terrified out of his wits and way beyond his competence to cope. He is convinced that this great warrior and the king of Aram are spoiling for a fight! At that point it is difficult for both men. Naaman has stepped out of his own comfort zone, followed the young girl's advice, and gone to . . . who else would you go to? The king!

It is a lovely story of how God puts the true power in the hands of the men and women He trusts to wield it well: the servant girl, an Israelite, the spoil of war and in slavery to an Aramean family; and Elisha the prophet, a bald man who was probably not much to look at but he had inherited twice the anointing of Elijah. The other character in this is Elisha's servant, who doesn't come out of it over well and ends up cursed with sickness. We should never be surprised to bump into people, even people of faith, who become corrupted and are in it to meet their own deep needs. It's very sad but it does happen. Maybe they need to bathe!

The main thrust of the story comes when Naaman is healed and stands before Elisha (he comes downstairs this time) and tries to persuade him to accept gifts. Elisha will not. (Never touch God's glory). Naaman declares before all his associates and staff, *'Behold now, I know that there is no God in all the earth, but in Israel.'* Wow!

I rather think that this is significant not just for Naaman himself but also for the relationships of the two countries. God is a Master Diplomat!

If you ever have the opportunity to pray for someone of 'high-standing', do it without fear or favour. You never know what God is doing!

Dear Lord, I stand in awe of Your ways. Make me not only clean but also a trusted friend who, through Your grace, sees what You are about. Give me courage to pray and speak words of faith on those days when something is rumbling in the heavenly places. Let it all be for Your glory! Amen.

Day 37 – February 6th

The account of Jesus being cross-examined by the Roman Governor, Pontius Pilate, is another such story of Glory meeting earthly power. Pilate was no fool. You didn't become a Roman leader without having proven your ruthless ability in battle and in managing men. He was a hard case. And yet we see him deeply questioning who Jesus really was in a way that few others had done. Perhaps he had heard things about the Lord beforehand and was challenged (John 18). 'Are You the King of the Jews?' he asked. Jesus gave an extraordinary reply that seemed to satisfy Pilate.

"*'My kingdom is not of this world. If My kingdom were of this world, then My servants would be fighting so that I might not be handed over to the Jews; but as it is, My kingdom is not of this realm." Therefore Pilate said to Him, "So You are a king."*'

Jesus then seems to read something in that response that deserves a reply of more depth. It feels like someone reeling in a fish . . .

'*You say correctly that I am a king. For this I have been born, and for this I have come into the world, to testify to the truth. Everyone who is of the truth hears My voice.*'

What a stunning response! *Everyone who is of the truth hears My voice . . .*

Pilate could have replied at any point, 'You are totally mad! No wonder they want to be rid of you' or 'Don't give me that rubbish. You think I am daft?' But he didn't. We were thinking about God the Master Diplomat – but He is also a fisherman – *the* Fisherman.

Pilate's final declaration, that he found no guilt in Jesus, and his ensuing efforts to get Him released, speak volumes. Pilate was a man caught between a rock and a hard place. Social unrest and the wrath of Caesar, or executing this man whose authenticity and steady calm had drawn him. Maybe the first selfless character he had met in his long career in the Empire.

We can only guess at the nights Pilate laid awake pondering it all, particularly in light of the events of the following Sunday morning.

Lord Jesus, even when You were speaking truth and justifying Yourself, You were calm. Your trust in the Father's will truly takes my breath away. Even then, You are seeing this powerful leader as a vulnerable man and holding out eternity to him. May the Holy Spirit give me that same sense of not being diverted from the Father's will in *my* life. May I, likewise, *fish for men.* Amen.

Day 38 – February 7th

I have a lovely picture on my desk; it's glued to my blotter where I pencil down my best, significant, early morning thoughts and people's names for prayer. It depicts an elderly man embracing a very small child in the middle of the night. It's not clear whether it is a boy or a girl, but it is clear the moment is one of great distress. The sense of comfort is huge. The grandfatherly man's hands are massive compared to the child's head. It is a wonderfully sensitive and intensely spiritual work of art. If I could discover who painted it, I would probably have used it on the cover of *Sanctuary*! It is all the more special as it was given to me by Prue Dufour when my wife was dying. Prue died not long after sending me the card.

Underneath I have pencilled:

'When my anxious thoughts multiply within me, Your solace and compassion delights and comforts my soul.' (Psalm 94)

The psalm is very beautiful and has spoken to me and many who have come for prayer in times of trouble and have sat with it. It is also special because of Prue, whose life was committed to those who were approaching the end, or struggling, and she left a huge legacy through all she did. Her simple action of sending that card to me, despite her circumstances, but knowing I would be deeply moved by it is so precious.

Dear Lord, sometimes we can bring such comfort through the smallest action. You take a seed and grow it into a tree, but we have to respond and carry the seed to a field where we let it fall. Teach us to be 'First Responders' in the Kingdom, sending messages of comfort and encouragement, arranging practical help and by praying, *'Thy Kingdom come on earth as it is in heaven . . .'* I rather think that we will discover that the overwhelming beauty of heaven that will seize our hearts will be *Your loving kindness.* May Your Kingdom come in my heart, my thoughtfulness and my hands, today. Amen.

Day 39 – February 8th

I once knew a lady who had very serious arthritis. She was more or less confined to bed. Our team visited her several times as she asked for healing prayer but nothing changed. One day, a member of the group had a picture; it was very vivid of a little girl shut in a cupboard. Quite appropriately the picture was offered as God does often speak to us in this way. The lady started to cry, then she wept, and then she sobbed, heart-felt heaving of the soul. After a good period of time she quietened and even smiled. 'That was me,' she explained, 'my mother often did that to me when she couldn't cope. I hate her,' she added, bluntly and fiercely.

Her mother, long since dead, was still a point of very great pain to her. We spoke of the deep need to forgive those who have hurt us. We told her that sometimes when we just cannot do it, we can ask God to enable us because we want to do it but we cannot find the way. She began to express this willingness and gradually her inability to say the words melted as the Holy Spirit enabled her. It was a glorious time of release and we then finished by, once again, praying for healing. Within a few days I saw her again, not in her home, nor her bed, but out pushing a trolley in the supermarket.

'Fear the LORD and turn away from evil [grief]. It will be healing to your body and refreshment to your bones.' (Proverbs 3)

Father, thank You for this dear lady who was resurrected by Your healing touch on her body, mind and spirit. It is wonderful to see Your risen body beckon people out from their graves. My Lord, may I partner with You in many resurrection moments. Amen.

Day 40 – February 9th

We looked at the life of Joseph a few weeks ago; the extraordinary story of how God not only used him but somehow managed to protect his heart from harbouring unforgiveness and resentment.

'Watch over your heart with all diligence, for from it flow the springs of life.' (Proverbs 4)

There are various characters in the Bible who lived like this. I am thinking about David who was irrationally hated by Saul. David was anointed to be King as a very young man, and as he matured he must have known that he might manage to make a better job of it than Saul. Saul suffered from depressive seasons when he felt persecuted and he blamed David. David, meanwhile, on the run from Saul's men, was so full of honour towards Saul that it is quite overwhelming and inexplicable, except for the fact that he knew how safe he was with God and had no need to try to topple Saul. When he was in the back of a cave hiding from Saul and the man himself walked in to answer the call of nature, David could have stabbed him and dealt with the problem. But he didn't. He did sneak close enough to cut off the corner of Saul's robe, which was a clever move as he was then able to say, 'I am no threat to you; look, I could have killed you but I didn't.'

He did it again, taking Saul's spear and a jug of water from Saul as he slept (1 Samuel 24). David was troubled by this stirring inside him against the 'Lord's anointed' – what he referred to as 'the stretching out of my hand' against him. Such was David's reverence, not so much for Saul but for God. This is so important; reverencing *God's ways* in difficulties.

David spoke to Saul and explained how he could have harmed him but didn't:

'When David had finished speaking these words to Saul, Saul said, "Is this your voice, my son, David?" Then Saul lifted up his voice and wept. He said to David, "You are more righteous than I; for you have dealt well with me, while I have dealt wickedly with you."'

Saul continued by blessing him and his coming kingship of Israel.

Father, I see in David's behaviour that he models so well how conflict may be resolved. And You honoured David for his reverencing heart. May I see Your way in conflicts; not to get *my* way but to accept that You are Lord and King and that conflict resolution is Yours to bring about and Yours alone. Amen.

Day 41 – February 10th

A dear friend of mine has died very recently. Her funeral will be soon and it will be a great celebration of her life now that she has gone to be with the Lord. She was 101 years old!

When she was in her 80s she came to faith in the Lord. She had always believed and been a churchgoer of sorts but in Australia, far from home, she went to a meeting where she heard the gospel preached and it went to her heart; she realised she needed to repent, be forgiven her sin and made new. At 85 she was baptised! Praise God for her new life in Christ and thank God for the man who obediently spoke the words put on his heart by the Holy Spirit's bidding.

I recall a similar elderly lady (Enid, she was much younger – only 94) who asked me to take her funeral when the day came. We talked about it and in particular the meaning of a *Christian* funeral. Now you need to know that Enid had been a faithful churchgoer all her life. We spoke of the death of Jesus. She paused and said, 'Do you know, I have always thought that it was such a waste of a good man's life.' No one had ever told her why Jesus died. I was shocked. When I explained, she immediately invited the Lord into her life and surrendered herself to Him. She was visibly made new. Her sense of sin being lifted from her was immense. She kept saying, 'Why didn't anybody tell me?' In the following months, Enid couldn't wait to go to heaven, indeed she became quite impatient to the point of feeling a little rejected! That's transformation for you! Then the day came quite suddenly. From quite good health she passed on within minutes. How I praised God for her and thanked Jesus at her funeral!

'Then He said to His disciples, "The harvest is plentiful, but the workers are few. Therefore beseech the Lord of the harvest to send out workers into His harvest."' (Matthew 9)

Lord Jesus, the Harvester of Souls. Wake me up to Your call to go out; to speak of You and of Your redemptive death on the cross that sinners might repent and find new life in Your Resurrection Spirit. God, we bless You for the harvest; send us out, I pray. Amen.

Day 42 – February 11th

Have you ever thought, 'If I was God I would want this or that project to happen through me, right now'? It's possible to think that with an absolutely God-honouring heart and not at all from selfish motives.

'David said to Nathan the prophet, "Behold, I am dwelling in a house of cedar, but the ark of the covenant of the LORD is under curtains."' (1 Chronicles 17)

He had a desire to build a temple for the Lord and felt uncomfortable that he had a grand house. Nathan said to go ahead for the Lord was with David. But that night God spoke to Nathan and told him that David was not to build a house for Him to dwell in. God speaks of how He took David from the pasture and had looked after him and the people, and had never asked for a house to dwell in.

God then speaks this astonishing word: *'Moreover, I tell you that the LORD will build a house for you.'* He explains that He will establish the house, the kingdom, and the throne through David's son and it will be established for ever . . . so speaks Nathan to the king. (Really, it is worth reading this chapter.)

David had been a man after God's heart and accomplished so much but he had blood on his hands from warfare (1 Chronicles 22) so he merely started making provision for the house in vast quantities of gold, silver, bronze and iron, timber and stone; the craftsmen were also recruited.

It seems to me that, given David's incredible worshipping heart and his desire to honour the God of Israel, it is remarkable that he was able to let go of the vision, and generously pave the way for his son to fulfil it! How many men can do that? *Son, I can't do this. It's been a life-long vision of mine but I so want it to happen that I have provided for you to do it . . .*

There is a fascinating moment in this story that you may have spotted. *'Then David the king went in and sat before the LORD and said, "Who am I, O LORD God, and what is my house that You have brought me this far?"'* and then follows an extraordinary realisation of all that God has done to establish His kingdom on the earth.

Sometimes in life we have to come before the Lord, with all our aspirations set to one side and just hear Him. It is what I call going from the *horizontal* (dashing hither and thither to make things happen) to the *vertical* (coming before the Lord and hearing Him). I commend it to you as an appropriate response if projects don't seem to be *flowing* as they might do or, preferably, at the outset! It might be a small aspiration or a considerable one. That doesn't matter.

Lord, sometimes I am found wanting as I dash to and fro aspiring to do great things for You. None of them are wrong in themselves but they need to be accomplished by You, and in Your time and in Your way. Give me the grace to sit before You and to hear what You may have to say. Sometimes I need to reset my satnav. I am willing to do so today, in Your presence. Thank you, my Lord. Amen.

Day 43 – February 12th

David commanded all the leaders in Israel to help his son Solomon. The land and all its inhabitants have been given into David's hand, and now there is peace on every side. So, he speaks to Solomon before the gathering and before God and says:

'Now set your heart and your soul to seek the LORD your God; arise, therefore, and build the sanctuary of the LORD God, so that you may bring the ark of the covenant of the LORD, and the holy vessels of God into the house that is to be built for the name of the LORD.' (1 Chronicles 22)

What a prayer!

Holy Lord, over the centuries You have done so much to create a people after Your own heart, to bring You praise and to delight in fellowship with You. The prayer of David still holds true for me today. I want to build a house here within me, where Your presence will be pleased to come. Fill me with Your glory, through the Holy Spirit's presence. I arise and seek You. My heart is set. It is Yours. Amen.

Day 44 – February 13th

How tempting it is to look at everything we have around us, all that we own and think how much *I have*. In one sense we do, but I learned many years ago to hold onto everything with a very light touch; it really is all the Lord's and not ours.

Many years ago I owned an Austin Mini. They were notoriously easy to break into and start and, sure enough, one morning there was a space where the car should have been. I was furious! The theft of the car dominated my thoughts all week and nearly crushed me.

Five or six days later I read this scripture and came to my senses (just as I was about to preach on stewardship!). Apart from the fact that it was *only* a car, it wasn't mine anyway. It was not my responsibility (other than looking after it well) and so if it went missing . . . I told the Lord if it was His will for us to not have a car it was OK. I really meant it! Almost immediately I received a call from someone a few hundred yards away to say they had heard on the local grapevine that my car had gone missing and that there was a blue Mini outside their house. The car was fine. Someone had taken it to save walking home it would seem!

'Blessed are You, O LORD God of Israel, our Father forever and ever. Yours, O LORD, is the greatness and the power and the glory and the victory and the majesty, indeed everything that is in the heavens and the earth; Yours is the dominion, O LORD, and You exalt Yourself as

head over all. Both riches and honour come from You, and You rule over all, and in Your hand is power and might; and it lies in Your hand to make great and to strengthen everyone. Now therefore, our God, we thank You, and praise Your glorious name. But who am I and who are my people that we should be able to offer as generously as this? For all things come from You, and from Your hand we have given You.' (1 Chronicles 29)

And so, David offered towards the building of the Temple.

Father, it is such a wonderful truth and so liberating to realise that, as our Father, You promise to undertake to meet our needs if we keep close to You and are faithful in all things. What a relief. Forgive me for the way I have viewed my comparative wealth as mine. It is Yours. What a Father You are. Amen.

Day 45 – February 14th

I am a great fan of wild birds in my garden. Coincidentally there is a buzzard calling high above, echoed by the call of three young ones. The parent is teaching them to soar. However, I don't feed buzzards, as a rule. Each morning on the way to my desk for quiet times, I fill the seed hoppers. The birds sit in the tree beside the feeders and the branches twitch with anticipation! One robin is always first and will feed in front of me if I don't retire straight away! Then the place turns into the Paridae equivalent of Gatwick airport. In one minute I can count thirty birds coming down to seek nourishment. It's a ritual for me and, in return, I am treated to this amazing display.

Do you know one thing that has never happened? The birds have never lined up outside to ask if I can really afford to feed them! The robin may come and sit glaring by my desk if I happen to forget but not one bird has ever challenged my ability to provide for them. They just come down and feed. When they have a nest, it is quite extraordinary how much food they will consume to feed their young. When it runs out, I top it up.

'And do not seek what you will eat, and what you will drink, and do not keep worrying. For all these things the nations of the world eagerly seek; but Your Father knows that you need these things. But seek His kingdom, and these things will be added to you. Do not be afraid, little flock, for your Father has chosen gladly to give you the kingdom.' (Luke 12)

As is so often the case, Jesus turns everything on its head; the things we feel matter and consume our time and energy and even our devotion – pah! No; prioritise. The God realm first, please. I don't think Jesus means to not bother about basics or fail to conduct ourselves in a mature and thoughtful manner – but we can be carefully careless and then let go.

Father, Jesus reflects with His words the economy of heaven. The kingdom and its values of care, compassion, and love of the Father and His ways are all that really matter. I should know this by now as You have taught me so many times how faithful You are. I am sorry. I think of the birds in the garden and how they come to feed, hungry and trusting. I am hungry for You, Lord, today and I am trusting. Amen.

Day 46 – February 15th

Thinking of garden birds made me reflect on a very special moment a decade or more ago. It was only days after my late wife died. I am sure you will know for yourself that God often speaks through every day things, events and, in particular, nature. The phone rang and a friend spoke – someone I didn't know very well but we had met through a local church and I knew she was quite prophetic.

'David,' she said, hesitantly, 'I know this will sound really odd and, under the circumstances, I didn't want to bother you.'

I encouraged her to tell me what she felt God had said.

'Robin,' she said. 'Just that . . . Robin.'

I thanked her and that was the end of that. It was post-Christmas and I have to admit I thought *she has one too many Christmas cards around the place!*

It was a bright, chilly January morning and I went out in the garden and stood warming my face, close to a shrub that my wife and I had planted years before. I became aware instantly that something moved immediately to my right; it was no more than twelve inches away. I turned slowly to see a robin sitting right there; I could easily have touched it. Then something happened that I have never known before or since: the robin sang right in my face. He kept singing in my face. I was overwhelmed and I rather think he must have seen the tears rolling down my cheeks.

The thing is with the prophetic of God, you either get it or you don't. You have that sort of ear or you don't. God spoke volumes through that tiny creature that day. Don't tell me that He doesn't care when we are caught up in loss or sadness.

'Now as He approached the gate of the city, a dead man was being carried out, the only son of his mother, and she was a widow; and a sizeable crowd from the city was with her. When the Lord saw her, He felt compassion for her, and said to her, "Do not weep." And He came up and touched the coffin; and the bearers came to a halt. And He said, "Young man, I say to you, arise!"' (Luke 7)

Jesus, You know each and every loss among Your people. More than that, You feel it. You feel for each one. Compassion seizes You in the guts. Forgive me but that, Lord, is what it says in Your word! That's how You really are. You fully know its every consequence. How You love. You weep with us but then, in Your power and Your splendour, You tweak something to tell us You are there. Sometimes it is a big tweak and other times less. Thank You for them all and please open my ears and eyes to hear and see You. Thank You for that robin and all the people who have received the touch of Your love through that story. Amen.

Day 47 – February 16th

The Hebrew word, 'chûwl' is an interesting word.

'What ails you, O sea, that you flee? O Jordan, that you turn back? O mountains, that you skip like rams? O hills, like lambs? Tremble [chûwl], O earth, before the Lord, before the God of Jacob, who turned the rock into a pool of water, the flint into a fountain of water.' (Psalm 114)

This is our God! The psalmist here is celebrating God who went before them out of Egypt and led them through the wilderness. And you wondered about my robin story! Just imagine seeing the rock struck!

I think God takes great pleasure in showing us His awesome ways. We just ask and expect.

In Psalm 29, which I would just like to say at the outset ends with the words, *'The LORD will bless His people with peace,'* we read of a God of glory who thunders and whose voice smashes the tall cedars, and hews out lightning. He shakes the wilderness, makes Lebanon skip like a calf and . . . makes the deer to *chûwl. Chûwl* can mean 'to give birth' and it is often translated so but I rather think that here it means 'to dance' or 'writhe'! *'He makes the deer to dance!'* That is the other meaning. If you have seen ponies turned out on fresh pasture in the spring, or watched the antelope after the rains in Africa, you will know why I suggest that. And the earth dances and writhes also.

Why are we so surprised when the great God we love makes us *feel* things? I have certainly trembled and been shaken before the Lord when He comes close. He is an awesome God! He is *so many* things which is why it is so remarkable that at the end of all of this, the last line is: *'The LORD will bless His people with peace.'* The word used for 'bless' there is *bârak*, meaning that God chooses to kneel down to us to bless us. O, my Lord. Such tenderness!

Father of might and terrifying power, how we limit You (in every direction). You smash the trees with Your breath and yet we also see that You are infinitely gentle, choosing to reach down to us as children and scoop us up in tender arms. I am so blessed by this. Amen.

Day 48 – February 17th

For the next few days we are going to be thinking about Elisha and his exploits including the Siege of Samaria. It might be worth reading it all first (2 Kings 6 and 7).

Bearing in mind what we focused on yesterday, it might be good to be honest with God about our faith and where it has yet to be stretched. The stories we are looking at are simply wonderful so perhaps ask the Lord to stretch you! It is astonishing to be in the presence of someone who God uses to be truly prophetic. They will come through with things that are so accurate and incisive that you really do know you are in another realm to the one you normally inhabit! Elisha was like that. It appears at times that he is so convinced of God's capacity to cope that he is laid back. I am sure he isn't – most very prayerful people are not – they just have quiet, powerful faith to move mountains.

So today we look at a well-known passage from the Gospels (Mark 11). You may recall that Jesus had cursed a fig tree. Peter remarked on passing it that it had withered. (We'll talk about the fig tree later because it is a remarkable prophetic moment.) Jesus answered them, presumably as they gazed at the sad, dried-up tree:

'Have faith in God. Truly I say to you, whoever says to this mountain, "Be taken up and cast into the sea," and does not doubt in his heart, but believes that what he says is going to happen, it shall be granted him. Therefore I say to you, all things for which you pray and ask, believe that you have received them and they will be granted you.'

That seems clear. Off we go . . .

Lord, I know my horizons need to be stretched. I don't want to have a mind-over-matter head; I want to be so filled with the Holy Spirit and with a deep knowledge of Your ways that I can walk with You on this journey just as the disciples did. Strolling under the open heaven of Father, as they did. It must have been amazing to be with Jesus – but the truth, is I am too! Amen.

Day 49 – February 18th

To understand Elisha is to appreciate that from the moment Elijah left him, he expected to receive twice the anointing. He immediately demonstrated that he had received at least as much as he struck the waters! It is interesting that Elijah told him he had asked a difficult thing. Difficult for whom? For God? Surely not. No, it was going to be difficult for Elisha to walk under that level of anointing. He would have to stay sharp and very open to the holiness of God. Isn't that what Elijah meant when he said, *'If you see me when I am taken from you it shall be so'* (2 Kings 2). Others might have stood around and *not* seen it. Elisha did. His eyes were wide open. His 'antenna' was up and working. I am not being facetious here. Prophetic people are tuned in. They have exercised and tried and refined their faith in action.

The youthful prophet who lost the axe head in the river when cutting trees to create a shelter had lost a valuable thing (2 Kings 6). Axe heads were precious, often handed down from father to son. This was borrowed. What is the first thing you do with an axe before use? Stand it in water to swell the shaft which makes the head firm. It takes a while – maybe overnight. I am guessing that he was a bit impetuous and the axe head flew off! Oh! How do we know he was impetuous? They wanted to move base but Elisha was not that keen and it appears they had to plead with him to join them. Perhaps they should have asked him first?

Whatever, Elisha sees that gravity can be reversed or water made momentarily denser than iron, so he throws a stick in that changed the 'atmosphere' and the axe floated to the top. You get the impression that Elisha might be just a little annoyed when he tells the lad to, *'Take it up for yourself.'* Maybe I am wrong and Elisha never lost his cool with impetuous youngsters (as I used to do . . . frequently).

Father, we prepare ourselves for this journey with Your man, Elisha. As we do, would you open our senses in a new way to Your promptings in the next days so that we may be alert to Your presence in all things. Amen.

Day 50 – February 19th

The first story (2 Kings 6) involves a supernatural 'spook'! Elisha was aware of every conversation in the enemy's camp. It made the king of Aram really twitchy as he thought there was a mole on his staff, but one of his servants told him the truth: *'My lord O king . . . Elisha, the prophet who is in Israel, tells the king of Israel the words that you speak in your bedroom.'* Such a contemporary story! Move over CIA!

Long story short – the king of Aram decides to encircle the city of Dothan where Elisha was and so eliminate him. Elisha's servant opened the curtains one morning and rubbed his eyes in disbelief because the city was surrounded with Aramean mounted cavalry and chariots. *'Alas, my master!'* he cried. *'What shall we do?'*

Elisha (is he laid back, or is it my imagination?) tells him not to fear and speaks that memorable phrase, *'for those who are with us are more than those who are with them'.* Ho! Elisha prayed for his man to see the supernatural reality which he then did see! Chariots of fire and horsemen surrounded Elisha. Just imagine being with this great man of God – who then prays for the enemy to be made blind. While they cannot see, he goes to them and explains that they are in the wrong place and he will do them the kindness of leading them to the right one. He takes them to Samaria where the king of Israel is situated – right in the heart of the Israelites camp. *'Shall I kill them?'* asks the leader of Israel, who is then told by Elisha to provide a massive banquet for them all instead. The Arameans are so overwhelmed by the treatment that they leave Israel alone for a long season. Praise God!

An extraordinary story by any reckoning, but one that does make me consider present crises and how we approach the resolution of war or even disputes closer to home. I think it's fair to say that we don't ask God for His supernatural Spirit as a key player at the Ministry of Defence, although sometimes the accounts of individuals in our own time do show that God is still willing to intervene in mighty and miraculous ways when called on by His children.

My Father, what an amazing God You are! You thrill me. Open our eyes in these days to see Your solutions when all seems locked up and unsolvable. There is nothing new under heaven. Bring on the Elishas, we pray. Seat people in high government who see with Your eyes. Amen.

Day 51 – February 20th

Later (we are not told what the interval is between these stories but we assume that the king has changed and the previous goodwill is now lost), the king of Aram has Samaria in lock down in the middle of a long siege.

It is a desperate situation and, again, it makes us reflect on contemporary situations where innocent populations are trapped in appalling wars. It was so bad that a donkey's head sold for eighty shekels among the Israelites. I am not sure what the going-rate is for the ingredients for donkey-brawn but it's probably a great deal less. As for dove dung, well, read the story for yourself!

The king of Israel was pacing the walls, a man whose heart had lost trust. Under his robes, he was dressed in sack cloth when a woman cried out asking him to intervene. In modern parlance, he replied, 'If God won't help you, how do you suggest I am to help you – perhaps from the local supermarket or from the wine merchants?' but then he draws back from his sarcasm and asks, 'What is the matter?'

In a moment of astonishing and heart-breaking revelation of the depths of the tragedy, the woman declares that she and a friend are in dispute as they killed and ate her own son and now the friend will not reciprocate. They are in the pits and the king, hearing this story, beside himself with anguish, tears his robes and vows to have Elisha's head by the end of the day. Quite why is not clear. There was clearly an expectation that the prophet would save them or, perhaps this was the second instalment of an unknown story. The king sends a messenger to the prophet but Elisha sees him coming from the king in his spirit's eye and tells the gathered elders to barricade the door. The royal messenger's take on the situation is that 'this evil is from the LORD' and they do not intend to wait any longer. (I am not sure what they are hoping to do . . .)

Elisha's response is to prophetically speak the end of the siege into being. By this time tomorrow barley and flour shall be freely available at sensible prices at the city gate (my wording).

Let's leave the story at that point and reflect for a moment today . . . As we pray, I wonder where we see ourselves in this story? I am also aware that you may have, just as I do, situations that are completely locked up. They may have long histories with a lack of resolution – effectively under siege.

Our Father, who art in heaven, You alone know how to break the siege in my situation. I have failed. I have tried so hard. Forgive me that I have not sought You as much as I might have done. Nothing is beyond You. I will sit quietly before You now and wait for You to speak of what You would do. Amen.

Day 52 – February 21st

The royal officer we heard of yesterday came from the king of Israel, and when he heard Elisha's bold, prophetic declaration that the siege would end within twenty-four hours does not have the faith to believe it.

'If the LORD should make windows in heaven, could this thing be?' (2 Kings 7)

Elisha, ever to the point, declares that he will see it *but he will not eat of it.*

If you have read ahead, you will know that the Lord did not need to open the windows of heaven, as such. The answer was just a few yards away. It needed to be made a little more accessible to the besieged folk inside the city walls.

I put it to you this way because, sometimes, we imagine that God will have to 'open the windows of heaven' to answer a prayer and we, having made it nearly impossible for ourselves to believe it, then do struggle to believe it! I remember many times when God answered prayer in the most extraordinary ways but not through the channels I had thought and had indeed 'ruled out'.

When my family grew from two children to three we had to face the fact that we needed a new, larger car. In those days carry cots were casually laid on the back seats, or worse, but even so we could not fit the youngsters in the car. I told my seven-year-old son that we needed to pray for a new car in the absence of any finances; the idea of going out to buy was too far-fetched! We prayed and during this bedtime moment my son paused, climbed out of bed and reached down for one of his favourite Matchbox toys – a blue Volvo estate car, declaring, 'We will have one of those!'

'Ah, bless,' I thought wondering how to lower his expectations without damaging his little faith.

A week later, as I drove out of school, I saw a friend who I had not seen for a while and paused to speak. 'Hello, David,' she said. 'Oh, I do love these Austin Travellers. I ought to try to get another one. I regretted getting rid of mine.' So I explained that I might be selling it and would let her know.

'OK,' she continued, 'I really must get rid of my car; it's far too big for me.'

'What have you got?' I enquired, not thinking that the Lord of all provision was about to make a move.

'A great big blue Volvo estate,' she replied . . .

Admittedly I did have to do quite a bit of work to sort out the car but we swapped cars and that was that! Within ten days a blue Volvo estate sat outside our house!

You see whilst God does sometimes open the windows of heaven, He frequently doesn't need to, and I hope that story builds your faith and gives an insight to this story of the siege of Samaria. I know we don't serve a 'God of parking spaces' and shouldn't expect Him to be there to meet our needs but it seems that He loves to treat His children sometimes! I should add that my son was very blasé about it and simply said, 'Well, Daddy, what do you expect; we prayed.'

'Truly I say to you, whoever does not receive the kingdom of God like a child will not enter it at all.' (Mark10)

Father, O Father, You are such a glorious family Man, a God of all faithfulness, particularly when life just will not add up. I thank You for the provision for my life and forgive me for the times that I take the basics, such as food, clothes and my home, for granted. Amen.

Day 53 – February 22nd

Now back to the story of the siege (2 Kings 7). Elisha had promised food and, as yet, there wasn't any. A few hours to go for the prophecy of plenty to be fulfilled. Outside the gate were four outcasts who were lepers and they were, to put it bluntly, quite fatalistic, saying to one another that if they stay put they will die and if they go into the city they will die, so they may as well go to the Aramean camp and they may spare food – or not. If they don't they die anyway, so what's to lose?

Without wishing to be too cynical, do you know that that is the fatalistic outlook of many in the world today? More than that, I have known many who have come to faith in our God on the same basis that those four lepers elected to wander down to the Aramean camp. 'Well, we may as well give it a whirl – there's nothing lost, so yes, you can pray for me . . .' The point is that they were all without hope, except maybe Elisha who had such a relationship with the mighty Jehovah that he could never be without hope. More serious philosophers have made similar points as the lepers did, albeit in more cerebral terms. 'First you live and then you die.'

'Whateverrr . . .' they say.

What they had not reckoned on was that, no, God had not made windows in heaven, but He had caused the Aramean army to hear the sound of a vast number of horsemen and chariots bearing down on them and they had fled. Really, just like that. They left. Went. Took nothing with them. Scarpered for fear of their lives being lost. Empty camp. The only noise being the gentle ee-awing and neighing of donkeys and horses.

'Forever, O LORD, Your word is settled in heaven. Your faithfulness continues throughout all generations; You established the earth, and it stands. They stand this day according to Your ordinances, for all things are Your servants.' (Psalm 119)

Dear Lord, what an amazing God You are! The ways You change circumstances to bring about Your salvation are many and wonderful. Show me how You desire to achieve 'holy pincer-movements' around my friends! Give me the quiet faith and the vision to see that when I pray in utter reliance on You, You will bring people to faith by pouring out Your love and goodness on them. Oh Lord, I commit to start praying for those I know who are sitting outside the city gates with no hope. Amen.

Day 54 – February 23rd

Within a short while the lepers became, at least potentially, the most enviable foursome in Samaria.

'They entered one tent and ate and drank, and carried from there *silver and gold and clothes, and went and hid them; and they returned and entered another tent and carried from there also, and went and hid them.'* (2 Kings 7)

Ho, ho! If only my mum could see me now! Look at me! Would you believe it? Just as well we took a chance (on Jesus), hmm?

When people come to faith they are often amazed. They can't believe it. I have often prayed for people who are healed which is so beautiful, but sometimes they are 'just' overwhelmed with peace! The wonderful *shalom* of God descends. 'I have never felt anything like this,' they declare. 'What has happened?' It's treasure time. They will never be the same again. Praise God!

Living God, I praise You that Your sheep hear Your voice. People recognise that You are *different*. You break the cycles of deprivation and isolation. Jesus had the same effect on people as He walked and talked; *we have never heard anything like this!* God, give me the faith to go out and be the emissary of heaven in the places where I live and work. To touch lives through the power of Your Holy Spirit on me. Amen.

Day 55 – February 24th

Suddenly something happens! The four lepers are overwhelmed by the goodies as they sit amidst all the Aramean spoil.

'Then they said to one another, "We are not doing right. This is a day of good news but we are remaining silent; if we wait until morning light, punishment will overtake us. Now therefore come, let us go and tell the king's household."' (2 Kings 7)

Years ago I remember a man called Alf who came to our church in a sorry state through alcohol, mental issues, poverty, etc. He had hit the bottom. He would venture in through the door, hover at the back and always leave. Later he became a Christian and was gloriously filled with the Holy Spirit one evening in a meeting. In a strange way, these four men remind me of Alf. As far as he was concerned he had found the gold! He couldn't believe that God was so good or that he, Alf, could be welcomed into a community. But here's the main thing: when he gave his testimony, he told us why he decided for Christ. It was because the people on the door always thoroughly welcomed him in. He had never previously been made welcome, that he could recall. He was outside the city gates and completely down and cynical – whichever way I go, I die.

He came one day, looking a little awkward and I asked him what was wrong. He replied that nothing was wrong but he had a favour to ask. I said, 'Ask away, Alf. What is it?' He said, 'Well, the thing is, I would like to be on permanent door duty welcoming people in, if I could. Would you mind?'

He couldn't understand why I laughed so much until I explained that 'welcoming' was not generally the job that people rushed to get on the rota for in churches. His reply was as if to say, 'I have such good news, I cannot sit on it, and everybody who comes in will be told how God met me at the door.' Alf became an evangelist at the door of our meetings. And no one walked by without being greeted!

'This day is a day of good news, but we are remaining silent . . .'

Father, thank you for the 'Alfs' of this world who cannot sit on the good news but are compelled to go out and share it. We, who have so much, fail to share; we can so easily remain silent. Fill our mouths with the praises of heaven for the Saviour by whom we were saved! This day is a day of good news. Amen.

Day 56 – February 25th

When the four men went back to the city gate (you can imagine the shouted conversation), 'No, really, we went down to the Aramean camp and there was no one there – just boxes of cornflakes and fresh bread and chocolate bars and dates . . . and freshly brewed coffee!' When the word reached the king of Israel in the middle of the night he immediately replied to his servants:

'I will now tell you what the Arameans have done to us. They know that we are hungry; therefore they have gone from the camp to hide themselves in the field, saying, "When they come out of the city, we will capture them alive and get into the city."' (2 Kings 7)

Fear and suspicion will abound at the first telling of the good news of Jesus' love. It will, really! There are so many fakes out there. TV advertising is full of wild claims and promises that cannot be kept (never mind those of politicians). In the eyes of the world 'there are no free rides'. But what happened? One of the adventurous servants (or perhaps personal hunger drove him) told the king that if he were to send five chariots out to investigate they would be no worse off than those left inside to perish! It's a little like the lepers who were left outside! The chariots went and pursued the Arameans as far as the Jordan and all they could see were their possessions strewn on the ground in their mad flight. It was ALL true! It really was a day of indescribably good news!

After the camp was plundered the flour and barley were sold at the gate *just* as Elisha had prophesied. Hallelujah!

Remember the royal servant who had challenged Elisha's word? He did get to see the food sale but, unfortunately, he was trampled in the rush of starving Samarians and so he never did get to taste it.

This is one of those gloriously interwoven stories that tells stories within stories and is so wonderfully contemporary! The word of the Lord expressed to Elisha was simply that the Lord would supply their needs. Elisha may have known the details of it but it's likely that he didn't. He simply caught that whisper on the wind of what the Spirit of God was going to do. One last question: in the entire account, where was Elisha? Unless I am wrong, he was in his room.

'But my heart stands in awe of Your words. I rejoice at Your word, as one who finds great spoil.' (Psalm 119)

Lord God, my heavenly King. This story is so beautiful. It speaks to us of Your great majesty and Your divine plans, Your delight at turning everything upside down and leading Your children through, not just into a new place but also to a place of deeper understanding. Speak to us of mission and ministry, prayer and the prophetic call of the Spirit to come close, be still and to understand You. Jesus, be glorified in me today. Amen.

Day 57 – February 26th

'Who is the man who fears the LORD? He will instruct him in the way he should choose. His soul will abide in prosperity, and his descendants will inherit the land. The secret of the LORD is for those who fear Him and He will make them know His covenant.' (Psalm 28)

David wrote those words. It's not one of the most poetical psalms but it speaks of a volume of experience of God's faithfulness. The word 'fear' has so many connotations that aren't very helpful. I prefer 'revere' because it seems to speak of the love which draws one in and calls us to be immersed in everything of God and nothing which might counter that. We don't revere God with religiosity but we do with our lives poured out before Him, knowing full well that to do wrong is to risk the beauty of being immersed in Him. It's an intimacy that is spoken of here. Unless you are crazy, you don't set out to crash an intimate relationship!

That's what the line is saying, *'the secret counsel of the friends of the Lord is for those who revere Him'*. That's very special! It is what the Lord promises us. It makes the hairs on the back of my neck stand on end!

It's actually a very gentle verse although it may not come over that way at first glance. Even 'instruct' has a beautiful meaning. It means 'to flow' as water does – it's a natural act, like a stick following the course of the river. It can also mean to shoot an arrow that then gives direction. That helps me to understand greatly. Sometimes God really does sweep us along with a prophetic word and, without really knowing it, suddenly we are at our destination, speaking something out or doing it! At other times, we might 'see' His arrow fly and we set off after it and gradually home in on what God is doing.

I rather think Elisha could have told us many things about these two ideas. He always seems to be still before the Lord.

Lord, I think it is so wonderful that You want to share the intimacies of heaven with us who love You and honour Your ways. Oh, that I would not sully that relationship with worthless things that have no consequence or beauty in my life. Teach me to be still before You to watch Your arrows fly. Flow me in Your gentle instruction. I really want to know what You are saying! Amen.

Day 58 – February 27th

Many years ago, I listened to Arthur Wallis speaking. I wrote in my Bible, 'God will have an exceedingly glorious house!' I can still hear him speaking those exact words.

Isaiah prophesies, *'I shall glorify My glorious house'* (Isaiah 60). It is the chapter which speaks of how God will gather all His radiant ones, hearts thrilling and rejoicing on the way to the Father's house. Everything, it seems, will be on its way to Jesus in a glorious parade! 'I will make gleam my beautiful family home,' God promises, in different wording.

It's worth pausing sometimes from the pressures of life, from all the busyness, just to reflect on where we are going. We are going to Father's House. It will be truly wonderful! Maybe read chapter 60 and then join me.

Father, Your beautiful house will gleam with the radiance of joyous faces who will have something of the Father's looks about them! They will come from everywhere to celebrate. There will be a signpost that we pass in this joyful procession: 'The City of God'. We will all pause in hushed awe when we see how beautiful it is. Maybe we will shade our eyes such will be the glory of the Lamb there; the Lamb that was slain. Bless Your holy name God; bless Your holy name. Amen.

Day 59 – February 28th

'Do not let your heart be troubled; believe in God, believe also in Me. In My Father's house are many dwelling places; if it were not so, I would have told you; for I go to prepare a place for you. If I go and prepare a place for you, I will come again, and receive you to Myself, that where I am, there you may be also.' (John 14)

I thought today we might begin with this well-known verse, often read at funerals and known as the 'words of comfort', which they are, but Jesus didn't speak those words at anyone's funeral! He spoke them over His disciples because *He was going to leave them.* One of the points about this verse, which we will come to at a later date, is that it is 'bridegroom talk'; the words spoken by a husband-to-be when he left his betrothed and went to build a house or add a wing to his father's house, that he might come back to fetch her when all was ready! *If I go and prepare a place for you, I will come again . . .* So, we must be asking ourselves, are we ready, because the house is exceedingly beautiful and those whose hearts have been melted, those who have been completely undone and perfectly restored in the likeness of the Son, will one day find themselves responding to the call, *'Come for all is now ready . . .'*

Father, the Scriptures tell us so many beautiful prophetic stories of what will be. Thank You. Thank You for Jesus who went to the cross that we might be completely cleansed of all that is not fitting for a lifetime in Father's House. Prepare my heart, Father, in which ever way You see fit. Let every single thing that is not of You be melted and dissolved by Your pure refining fire on me. Amen.

Day 60 – February 29th

This may well be one of the less-read offerings in this book! No matter.

After Jesus had spoken the words we looked at yesterday from John 14, there comes a moment of exchange between Jesus and Thomas. He asks the sort of question I might have asked:

"'You know the way where I am going." Thomas said to Him, "Lord, we do not know where You are going, how do we know the way?"' (John 14)

That's a reasonable question in anybody's book, isn't it? We may have guessed the answer but, the truth is, that is a question many people need to have answered. It may not be worded in exactly that way but there will be a moment when we must be prepared to be quite explicit.

'Jesus said to him, "I am the way, and the truth, and the life; no one comes to the Father but through Me."'

That is more of an answer than Thomas needed but I imagine Jesus read them all correctly, including the unspoken questions from the group.

How many times have you been asked an indirect question that might directly relate to your faith? 'You always seem to be so cheery? What is it . . . How do you cope . . .?'

When my wife died, I preached at her funeral. The Holy Spirit was on me in a powerful way and He carried me through (and changed a few lives on the way). People said, 'I don't know how you did that,' and I took every opportunity to explain that Jesus had come to take her home, that she knew she was heaven bound, that it was all through Him, and so to want to tell that story of His boundless love and faithfulness to her and to me, was a story that God helped me to tell. We had many interesting conversations. Always be ready and willing to share: 'Well, my friend; it's Jesus, actually.'

Father, thank You. Thank You. Thank You. Thank You. *'Tell out, my soul, the greatness of the Lord. Unnumbered blessings give my spirit voice; tender to me the promise of His word; in God, my Saviour, does my heart rejoice!'* Let my heart always leap to tell out the true story in all its appalling grit and utter perfection: Jesus is the Way, the Truth, and the Life. Amen.

MARCH

Day 61 – March 1st

I often think that this is the saddest sentence in the entire Bible:

'Then the LORD God called to the man, and said to him, "Where are you?" He said, "I heard the sound of You in the garden, and I was afraid because I was naked; so I hid myself."' (Genesis 3)

The first question I ask myself is, 'Did God *really* need to ask the man where he was?' I rather assume that God knew. He does tend to know these things. Nevertheless, He did ask and I assume that He asked because He wanted Adam* to admit where he was! It's not unlike the mother who calls out, 'What are you doing?' If you remember that, may I let you in on the secret – *she knew already!* Parents know these things.

I often quip that the first five pages of the Bible are the story of how it all went wrong, and the rest is the story of God in His relentless and passionate love for His creation trying to guide mankind back to the original plan. Had the Fall not happened, the Bible may have been about ten pages long!

What was the original plan which we mentioned back on January 1st? I suggested then that it wasn't to provide a municipal park, rather the most beautiful, perfectly eco-balanced, exotic place imaginable. This Paradise (and I use the word in its literal, non-holiday-brochure fashion) was *perfect*. Man and woman were to populate it and tend it and it would forever be blessed. Not just to *enjoy* beauty but also to *share* the most fulfilling love and worship of God that we can ever begin to imagine! Think of those days when you are caught up in worship and just never want to let go – like that *all* the time only multiplied by 77 and without even rehearsing it! I also believe that there, life was to be eternal. *They were never intended to die!* All they had to do was plant plants, reap crops, pick perfect peaches and there was nothing in it *at all* to spoil it. It never even rained! Really! The moisture came up out of the ground. There were no umbrellas in

Paradise. If you are struggling with all that it is because it did go wrong and we are left stunned and bereft – but, the spotless ones will see it in all His glory, one day; there *is* a way back.

The Fall, as it is so often accurately referred to, involved a fruit which wasn't intended for eating; God forbade the man that particular delicacy and he was warned in no uncertain terms not to eat, but they did and the rest, as they say, is history. I won't get into debates about the nature of this account; I do not believe it is the place to do so, but the *meaning* behind the story is there for all who have eyes to see. One glance at contemporary society will tell you that 'forbidden fruit-picking' is rife. As I watch, I also note that the higher the fruit is, the more bizarre its nature, the more offensive the flavour of it, man simply has to pick it and demonstrate for all to see that *he can do whatever he wants without regard for anybody.* That is adequate explanation for me. That *is* the story. Whether it be the 21st century or the 2nd, the story is the same – man says, 'I will do whatever I choose, the uglier the better, and I will have no regard for anything a parental figure might say . . . I do not believe there will be consequences because I believe *I am* the centre of the universe.' It is just that God says, *'I am . . .'*

To finish, I would like to say to all who feel sorrow at this state of affairs, who find they are crying out, 'I want to be found! God, I no longer want to hide!' there is an answer and His name is *Jesus.*

'I tell you that in the same way, there will be more joy in heaven over one sinner who repents.' (Luke 15)

Lord God, maker of heaven and earth, thank You for Your wonderful plan. I am truly sorry for my part in making a thorough mess of it with my sinful existence. Please forgive me for all my wrong. Thank You that You had such love for us that You gave Your one and only Son Jesus the Saviour, to die on the cross of Calvary to pay the price for us coming back to You and being found. I want to be found in You. Holy Spirit, come and fill me and make me new. Amen.

*The names are gradually introduced and that's a story in itself. Adam in Hebrew is Âdâm pronounced 'Awdawm' – 'man'. Eve's name comes later and is in Hebrew Chavvâh pronounced 'Kavaw' – 'the life-giver'. And, by the way, no 'apple' is mentioned!

Day 62 – March 2nd

When Jesus stood in the synagogue and read Isaiah from the scroll (January 8th), He made an extraordinary statement and each of us who believes needs to sit up and take note! This short series will explore 'our expectation' of what God may be doing, or wanting to do, in us.

'The Spirit of the Lord is upon Me, because He anointed Me to preach the gospel to the poor. He has sent Me to proclaim release to the captives, and recovery of sight to the blind, to set free those who are oppressed, to proclaim the favourable year of the Lord.' (Luke 4)

Generally speaking, as we grow up we are taught not to 'be pushy'; we learn to take a low view of ourselves; not always, but the trend might be said to be in that direction. There is humility and there is false humility, and when we come to thinking about the Holy Spirit's work in us, I am convinced that we need to know and celebrate *'Who we are in God'* and *'What we are called to be'*. These ideas will change and grow as God grows us as believers, but the bottom line is that we should be very wary of ever saying, 'Oh, no, really, I could never be that!' Think of Amos. He wasn't, and then he was! God did it!

As we listen to our Lord speaking about the Holy Spirit's work in Him: *'The Spirit of the Lord is upon Me to . . . He has anointed Me to . . .'* we need to understand that the same Holy Spirit is upon us in full measure to do the *same* works! *The same Spirit!* He was not afraid to speak the simple truth! Our Master was not bragging – it was Truth. I do believe that the church needs to dwell on this. If we are not seeing those same things happen in our midst now, we need to ask the Lord, 'Am I living in the fullness of all that God has for me to minister with at this time?' It's a very serious question to ask of God! It is so serious that I would put it near the top of the list of things that God calls us to do in these days! Other questions may flow from that one but don't be afraid to ask it.

The reason the listeners in the synagogue wanted to throw Jesus out was that they believed Him not to be speaking the truth! We believe differently, don't we?!

Heavenly Father, You poured out Your Spirit on Your Son, Jesus, that He might go out and start a revolution with Your love and power. Unless You tell me otherwise I am going to repeatedly ask You to send Your Holy Spirit on me. I will receive it and run with whatever You give me and, by Your grace, I will go out and change my corner of the world! I ask this in the precious name of Jesus. Amen.

Day 63 – March 3rd

I frequently come back to this moment in the synagogue; indeed, that verse from Luke 4 is pinned above my desk as a constant provocation to my spirit, and it is there for a good reason. My background and my nature is to think (very humbly, of course) that I cannot! The enemy comes along to what? Rob! Steal! Yes, that's right. He does not want you to become the person that God wants you to be and we need to be wise to his whispering and his filthy diminishing tricks.

It is put very succinctly in 1 Peter 4:

'As each one has received a special gift [charisma], *employ it in serving one another as good stewards of the manifold grace of God. Whoever speaks is to do so as one who is speaking the utterances of God; whoever serves is to do so as one who is serving by the strength which God supplies; so that in all things God may be glorified through Jesus Christ, to whom belongs the glory and dominion forever and ever. Amen.'*

As stewards of His *grace*; that means you didn't win your ability as a prize, you didn't earn it, it wasn't due to you – it was given to you by Him as a gift – yes, when you didn't deserve it. So, humility and boasting do not come into it. I am what I am and I do what I do by His grace. It's the way God chose to wire me. He may increase His grace to me when I am ready to walk in more gifting and I will do all I can to be a suitable vessel for His goodness, but it is His to do as He sees fit. When Paul speaks of the *spiritual gifts* he uses another word, not *charisma*; I am aware of that, but what Peter writes is a wonderful gold standard: glorify God. It's that simple; do it and you won't go wrong!

Sovereign Lord, You have poured out Your Spirit on us that we may go out in Your name and bring a kingdom revolution; where Your love and power would endlessly touch lives and restore Your children. Speak to me of what I have not yet stepped up to receive. Sharpen my spirit person to understand Your grace gifting. Let me walk in humility and truth, just as Jesus did which enabled Him to say, *'The Spirit of the Lord is on me to . . .'* Amen.

Day 64 – March 4th

The presence of the Holy Spirit in a man or woman is the most potent equipping one can ever know. Jürgen Moltman wrote that 'the Holy Spirit is the unrestricted presence of God in which our life wakes up and becomes wholly and entirely living and endowed with the energy of His life in us.' Wow! Praise God. The enemy will do all he can to dissuade you of that truth. Believe it! Sadly, even churches can, on occasion, do all they can to silence a man who is full of the Holy Spirit and truth.

In the Scriptures, it is clear that when truth is spoken in the power of the Spirit nothing will prevent willing ears from hearing.

'And He came down to Capernaum, a city of Galilee, and He was teaching them on the Sabbath; and they were amazed at His teaching, for His message was with authority.' (Luke 4)

A little later we are told:

'And amazement came upon them all, and they began talking with one another saying, "What is this message? For with authority and power He commands the unclean spirits and they come out." And the report about Him was spreading into every locality in the surrounding district.'

I long to see that happen in the places where I live, work and worship. I wish I could tell you that every person I have ever laid hands on and prayed for has been instantly healed! I am probably, like most of us, still wearing 'L' plates so I don't always see this, but I have seen enough to know that God does mean faithful business with His followers! He is a generous Father.

Years ago I saw many healed through the prayers of others. I read about it and I thirsted for an encounter with the Holy Spirit through which He would unleash His power through me to those in need. I kept asking, 'Lord, why not?!' The first time I experienced this happened when a friend, David, with whom I was meant to be leading our Sunday service, was ill. His wife phoned to say that he would not be able to assist as all night long he had been in bed with a high fever. Something persuaded me to call on him on the way to the meeting. I dropped by and was met by a concerned wifely look when I asked to see him. I said, for no logical reason I can think of, 'I need to pray with David.'

I was led upstairs and as I opened the door I was met by a soggy heap of man who had sweat pouring off his brow and the bed sheet sticking to his over-heating body. Far from putting me off, I felt the passion and the faith rise in me and I declared, very simply, 'David, in the name of Jesus, get out of that bed!'

David looked at me, shook his head as if to flick it all from him and exclaimed, 'Phew! That feels better.' He leapt out of bed, dashed to the bathroom, hurriedly dressed and joined me in the car. He was truly healed. We went to the meeting and during the service we told what God had done. The healing power of Jesus broke out in that meeting that day and many were healed. Praise God!

God has the loveliest, Fatherly sense of humour. My prepared subject that morning was 'The healing Power of Jesus'.

Father God, how You long for us to long for You. I thirst. I cry out! 'Lord, more of You!' Send Your Holy Spirit and, I pray, please send Him now. Amen.

Day 65 – March 5th

The exciting episode I wrote about yesterday was not only foundational for me, in that God convinced me that He was pleased to use *me*; it also spoke to others and increased faith. That is how the Holy Spirit works; He is on a mission! The doubly curious and wonderful side of that day was the reading I had chosen for the service:

'And He got up and left the synagogue, and entered Simon's house. Now Simon's mother-in-law was suffering from a high fever, and they asked Him to help her. And standing over her, He rebuked the fever, and it left her; and she immediately got up and waited on them.
While the sun was setting, all those who had any who were sick with various diseases brought them to Him; and laying His hands on each one of them, He was healing them.' (Luke 4)

I still feel a smile rise when I read that nearly forty years later! Our God reigns! I so love that evening image: the courtyard lit by flaming wicks of torch light, as Jesus moves around the crowds accompanied by pleading voices and cries of joy and awe.

You may have been praying for a long time, really seeking God, without seeing a breakthrough personally or in your fellowship. I want to tell you today – *God answers prayers!* Keep praying! Let your heart be steadfast in Him!

'And an angel of the Lord appeared to him, standing to the right of the altar of incense. And Zacharias was troubled when he saw the angel, and fear gripped him. But the angel said to Him, "Do not be

afraid, Zacharias, for your petition has been heard, and your wife Elizabeth will bear you a son, and you will give him the name John.'" (Luke 1)

I always think of this passage when prayers *seem* to be unanswered. How old were Zacharias and Elizabeth? We do not know. We are told that 'they were both advanced in years'. I am not sure when you cease to pray to have a child, but I imagine some time before this history-changing event in the temple! God answers prayers. He is faithful. He never forgets. *Keep asking.* And I would suggest that you seek out the company of men and women of faith. Faith is 'infectious'. Whatever you do, don't let the enemy persuade you to hide away in a corner full of disappointment and doubt. He will try. The enemy has no ethics committee; he will try to give you a knockout blow while you are vulnerable. Worship God in every way you know how. It's a strange 'coincidence' that when I really worship, the Holy Spirit comes, and the more I worship, the more He comes! Hallelujah!

'If you then, being evil, know how to give good gifts to your children, how much more will your Father who is in heaven give what is good to those who ask Him!' (Matthew 7)

Father, thank You for this promise. I take You at Your word. I declare it is the truth. *My soul, I declare to you, we will seek the Father for the Holy Spirit's empowering!* Yes, I delight to give lovely things to my children so I believe You when You say this to me, Your child. I ask You again, 'Would You send the Holy Spirit on me, and, please, send Him now.' Amen.

Day 66 – March 6th

'My heart is steadfast, O God. I will sing, I will sing praises, even with my soul. Awake, harp and lyre; I will awaken the dawn! I will give thanks to You, O LORD, among the peoples, and I will sing praises to You among the nations.' (Psalm 108)

Those of you who were in the Boys' or Girls' Brigade will remember that word 'steadfast' we used to sing so often:

We have an anchor that keeps the soul;
Steadfast and sure while the billows roll;
Anchored to the Rock which cannot move,
Grounded firm and deep in the Saviour's love.

And I have a great fondness of that hymn; memories of the evenings gathered around the camp fire when we went away annually. Singing it in the open air makes me think of David thanking God and praising Him among the 'tribes' and 'communities', much of which, I assume, was out of doors. I love 'awakening the dawn'; being at my desk before light breaks. Maybe I am a little fanciful but I rather think God enjoys this little corner of the world having a voice that declares His goodness at first light. I think David did that also. I imagine Him dancing before the Lord, on good days and bad, calling out and singing, *'My heart is steadfast in You . . .'*

What really caused me to think is that the word used for 'soul' – 'I will sing praises with my soul' – is *kâwbôde,* which means 'glory' or 'glorious' or 'honour'! He is saying more than 'my soul', he is recognising the glory that God has put in him! *'I will sing to you, Father, with the glory that you have deposited in me!'*

Lord, High God of heaven, where the fullness of glory resides, I praise You this morning; this early-rising little piece of heaven sings to You because You are worthy. I look at the multi-coloured dawn which You have thrown across the sky today! O, my Lord, You are wonderful and I love Your wonderful extravagance! Amen.

Day 67 – March 7th

As you seek the Father for His grace gifting for you, that you might go out in His name to change the world, keep that injunction from 1 Peter 4 in mind at all times. Ultimately it is all about *love.* Loving others and loving God. It certainly isn't about you, your reputation or that of your fellowship. *Glorify God in everything you do.* It will keep you humble and it will keep you safe from criticism.

Psalm 106 tells us that when the people of God saw His amazing works to deliver them from Egypt, they believed in Him (easy in the day of the miraculous) and gave Him praise. However:

'They quickly forgot His works; they did not wait for His counsel, but craved intensely in the wilderness, and tempted God in the desert.'

What is going on here? In the midst of awesome works of God, the people were aware of the One who presided so majestically over their journey but, a little later, they quickly forgot because they were hungry and thirsty. In that moment of deep physical need, they forgot the centrality of love and worship. They forgot His provision; they forgot to enquire of God for His advice and wisdom, and they longed so much for their bodily needs that it became a lusting (that is what the Hebrew calls it).

Was God not still able to meet their every need? Of course, just as He does for you and me today. Why did it becoming 'testing' God rather than looking to Him? After things got worse and the people became involved in blatant idol worship it was only Moses who was able to stand in the gap as intercessor and prevent the destruction of the people. That is a scary albeit slow transition.

This is basic and we need perhaps to reflect on it. Remember it is always *God's face we seek and not His hand.* We seek the Provider not His provision. See the difference? One is worship and trust, and the other is an expedient move to seek to have a need met without much regard for how it happens. If you wonder why it matters so much, you might be able to recall giving someone a precious or expensive gift; that the paper is ripped off and then . . . and then . . . there is no acknowledgement of the giver. It hurts and it certainly does not encourage you to give again, does it? We excuse little children this lapse but not adults.

In my worship and prayer time I often thank God for all the small blessings I have but, also, I take the trouble to go back, way back, to the astonishing miracles: there is Ian, Maddy, Alison and another Alison, and Rebecca, Steve and . . . and . . . and . . .

I am not harking back or living in the past, but acknowledging that God is my wonderful Father and Provider and I love Him and I do not take anything for granted, ever. I thoroughly know that while He will never cease to be a graceful God, His grace to me could cease if I am not graceful – or go on hold for a season.

My loving Father, it is You I worship, and I worship You not because You do wonderful things for me or others to whom I minister, but because You are worthy of praise. Full stop. You alone. The Lord of heaven is enthroned on the praises of His people. I am one of them! *Be exalted, my God! Be lifted high!* Amen.

Day 68 – March 8th

'Truly, truly, I say to you, he who believes in Me, the works that I do, he will do also; and greater works than these he will do; because I go to the Father. Whatever you ask in My name, that will I do, so that the Father may be glorified in the Son.' (John 14)

Over and over Jesus teaches us to ask. Ask, ask, ask, He repeats. So how is that different from the people who longed in the desert and somehow tempted and tested God? I believe the key is the relationship; in those words, *'in My name'* and *'he who believes in Me'*. Previous to these verses, Jesus has been speaking of *'the Father abiding in Jesus'*. Elsewhere Jesus speaks of His constant abiding in the Father. He says that we are to abide in Him . . . The ultimate mutual abiding community!

'Abide' is a word that is central to all we are to be. It means, at its most basic, 'to stay'. It's often translated 'remain', which has connotations that aren't helpful. I used to tell my dog to 'stay' and he knows it means 'remain where you are'. It is so much more than that 'hang around'. I have heard that said in recent years: 'Hanging out with

Jesus'. Enough said. Each to their own. I believe that the fundamental idea of *living* in God's presence, loving to be caught up with Him and all of heaven in worship, constantly aware, ever-praising and being full of expectancy is more than 'remain'. It is vibrant. It is union, it is that tarrying that we spoke of; twisting together, binding and longing for more and more intimacy. That's a far cry from being demanding and somewhat petulant children!

Dearest God. Precious Jesus. Loving Holy Spirit, I need to say to You today that even if You apparently do nothing, on the days when I cannot see You, I will still praise You and remain a faithful dweller in Your house. My heart is steadfast in You, God. Nevertheless, I thank You for the millions of ways You have cared for me, answered my prayers and released Your power into those around me when we ask. If You never did another thing for me, just being found in Jesus would be *everything*! Amen.

Day 69 – March 9th

Occasionally there are news reports of fantastic finds in farm fields; most recently, Saxon hordes of coins and ornaments in Eastern England. You can see the disbelief and joy on the faces of the treasure seekers (not to mention the pound signs in their eyes!).

Jesus told several parables about things that were lost and found, or just found.

'The kingdom of heaven is like a treasure hidden in the field, which a man found and hid again; and from joy over it he goes and sells all that he has and buys that field.' (Matthew 13)

It is clear in some of these parables that Jesus intends us to be fully aware of the impact that discovering the kingdom of God will have on us. To ensure our gaining the kingdom, we will do anything! Jesus spoke of leaving family, he spoke to the rich young man of his wealth that would stop him finding eternity – He means us to understand that big life transactions will deeply affect us and call us to give up everything to gain Him. It doesn't mean that you *will* have to but it demonstrates the heart-attitude needed for kingdom business. We will want to give our all! Hold everything and everyone with a very light grip, I say.

This also has to do with 'abiding' and also to the followers who crossed the Jordan by God's mighty hand and then displeased Him so much. The simple truth is, if you are attempting to *abide* in God you cannot take much with you. It's total given-ness to God. Maybe you feel that's a little unreal. The answer to that is that it is simply reciprocating what God has given for you. May I suggest that whatever you give up to find the fullness of the Kingdom, you will never manage to out-give God. Not ever.

And so, we say today, Jesus, thank You for the cross. No one will ever give more than You gave up for us. As we approach the season of Easter, we recognise the selfless and relentless pursuit of Your desire to create a way back for each one of us. How easy it would have been to have diverted; diverted from being immersed in the Father's will. Father, Son and Holy Spirit we give You all the praise. Amen.

Day 70 – March 10th

Last evening I went to a meeting of a church ministry team. It was such a special occasion. I had asked everyone, in advance, to pray about how the influences in their lives had shaped their attitude to the ministry of healing that each felt called to. These people are not advanced in their ministry journey, in the sense that they might not all be moving in signs and wonders, but they were able to be very real. Several times while I was with them I felt the word 'authentic' come to mind. Honesty of heart before God is so important; realistic self-appraisal is a key to growth into God's plans for each of us. The world is full of spin and hype and the world is weary with it. Sadly, we also come across it in a few ministries. What is the point? Surely, the Lord sits back and waits for us to get to the end of ourselves and be real with Him?

At the beginning of the evening I felt led to mention in prayer the 'feeding of the five thousand'. It resonated with several people so, in conclusion, before we left, I read the following:

'Therefore Jesus, lifting up His eyes and seeing that a large crowd was coming to Him, said to Philip, "Where are we to buy bread, so that these may eat?" This He was saying to test him, for He Himself knew what He was intending to do. Philip answered Him, "Two hundred denarii worth of bread is not sufficient for them, for everyone to receive a little." One of His disciples, Andrew, Simon Peter's brother, said to Him, "There is a lad here who has five barley loaves and two fish, but what are these for so many people?" Jesus said, "Have the people sit down." Now there was much grass in the place. So the men sat down, in number about five thousand. Jesus then took the loaves, and having given thanks, He distributed to those who were seated; likewise also of the fish as much as they wanted.' (John 6)

When it was all over and everyone was fed, you may recall the Lord told them to gather the left-overs that nothing may be lost and, in another version, we are told there were many baskets full.

Let's be clear that Jesus had begun a major revival in the land. When 5000 men (and there may have been many women and children also) gather to hear you speak, it's fair to say something remarkable is happening, even if it was just because 'they saw the signs'.

Jesus challenges Philip with a question. He came from those parts so if anyone knew where to get food, Philip would. He does a quick mental calculation and says, effectively, 'Can't be done, Lord.' But Andrew comes with such an authentic, call it naïve, answer. It is, at one level, preposterous. Imagine the equivalent in a church council meeting: *'Well, here we are with a congregation that has grown by 1200 per cent in three years and we need to put up this new building, and estimates vary but we think it will cost at least 1.25 million pounds . . .' A little voice pipes up, 'Chairman, may I just say that I do have*

£6.50 that I found tucked in the glove box of my car . . .' That's the reality of the miracle that Jesus worked that day. Imagine how the man with the small sum would be ridiculed (although, of course, we would be far too polite to say so; our rising eyebrows would say it all!).

And all I could see in this group last night was a dozen faithful pilgrims holding out their five loaves and two fish in authentic worship of the Lord. It's impossible to raise them to a place where they will be able to minister to the needs of a community of numerous thousands, in the natural . . . and yet the Lord lifted the bread and then the fish and there was enough. They were *all* satisfied. It wasn't a trick whereby they *thought* they had eaten sufficient; their needs *had* been met.

Lord Jesus, I know You do not measure our offerings by their earthly proportions; You see with heaven's perspective. You have a glory filter! You see through heaven-tinted spectacles. Come and multiply what I offer to You today and make the small crumbs I bring gloriously sufficient. Bring the abundance of heaven to play upon the offerings of my heart. I am sincere: without You it cannot be done; with You everything is possible! Thank You that the desire of Your heart is to partner with me. Holy Spirit, be a multiplier in me today, I ask You. Amen.

Day 71 – March 11th

On the fireplace in my study is a stone jar. It has a wax-sealed lid and the label reads 'Pure Nard: £18,500'. It is, however, empty; a prop from a retreat last year. Remember Martha and Mary? Oh, and Lazarus was there, washed and tidied having been recently raised from the tomb. He was something of a celebrity and people wanted to see him. But this moment is family and friends gathered for supper.

'So, they made Him a supper there, and Martha was serving; but Lazarus was one of those reclining at the table with Him. Mary then

took a pound of very costly perfume of pure nard, and anointed the feet of Jesus, and wiped His feet with her hair; and the house was filled with the fragrance of the perfume.' (John 12)

The story is well known. Some grumbled about the waste but Jesus was very blessed and stood up for Mary and her gracious ways.

I can become engrossed in these moments; the interplay of very different characters and *the Presence*. We know little about Lazarus except the obvious – a life changed in the most remarkable way. Stories abound that he became an evangelist for the Lord, and travelled widely. Martha, busy, to make a special evening for Jesus. Was it a special celebration perhaps; a Resurrection Party? Amid the buzz of conversation and laughter Mary quietly breaks the seal. This is a precious thing, maybe even an heirloom; such things were saved for family burial rites. Judas watches. Then Mary kneels at the feet of her Lord and begins to pour out the precious ointment, wiping it with her long hair. Long hair unpinned, scandalously, some would say, for that moment. The most extraordinarily extravagant and prophetic anointing ever; pouring, spilling out worship. No wonder Jesus is deeply moved.

Somewhere in this I can also see the anointing of Mary's hair: once the sign of a fallen woman perhaps, but now redeemed and radiant, made holy; a token of the highest honour. *This is what I was; but I no longer am thanks to You, my Lord.*

And so we say, Father, this is what I was but am no longer. She owes no more than I do. Released, chains broken, shame lifted, and now a precious Friendship restored. Thank You, Father. Forgive me if I am stingy in my worship; why do I hold back when You didn't? You gave all for me. I long to bring You more. Holy Spirit, enable my worship, I pray. May costly fragrance fill this place as I give You my all. Amen.

Day 72 – March 12th

I am reflecting again on the meeting of our ministry team; of the stories that were told. One, in particular, was so very precious; everyone recognised that as she quietly told her tale of loss. Everyone was still. Words of terrible, sad loss. But what moved us so was that God had walked her through her very personal time of rending pain not just *after* the loss but *before*! God in His loving kindness and faithfulness had gently prepared her and, as He did so, there came a surrendering. *Your will be done, Father.*

Later, the story continued, came an extraordinary filling of the season, a new awareness almost, of the ways of God in the days of this season. The resurrection Spirit of Jesus was present so much that rather than limping through, this dear person went on to minister to others out of the richness that God had brought to her through her loss in those days! That is the resurrection power of Jesus, who flips on its head, death and loss, filling it with His hope and an overwhelming sense of His peace and comfort. Of course, loss still hurts – but this has a different quality.

'Blessed are the poor in spirit, for theirs is the kingdom of heaven. Blessed are those who mourn, for they shall be comforted.' (Matthew 5)

My Father, I thank You for this woman and her utter trust in You at a time when it would have been so easy to turn inwards and to become self-absorbed with loss and grief. Her eyes were focused on You. And You were there for her. Your resurrection Spirit transforms before our eyes until quiet, trusting joy comes. Bless you, Lord. Amen.

Day 73 – March 13th

When I trained as a counsellor there was a phrase that was never ever to be used: 'Don't cry.' To say that is to deny a person their space, it is to devalue feelings and, however kindly meant, can shut down any possibility of a conversation. It's a pointless and quite unproductive thing to say. Most often it demonstrates our own inability to stay with another's pain.

Remember Jesus meeting the mother as the funeral procession for her son reached the city gate in Nain? We looked at it a while back. What did Jesus say to her? That's right: *'Do not weep.'* How can it be that the Son of God, who should know all things, can say, 'Do not weep'?

There is something in the *knowing of Jesus* that creates an environment around Him, a *holy context* that makes it permissible to speak such things because *He Himself is the Healing Presence.* The words make sense! In the reverberating atmosphere of the Easter Sunday graveyard the angels said to Mary, outside the tomb of Jesus, *'Why are you crying?'*

If one knew nothing of this man it would be possible to construct an assumption about Him that He was considerably hard of heart. He is not. There are no equations or analyses that can explain this. He knew He was about to raise Lazarus from the tomb but, even so, as He stood with the weeping Mary, grieving deeply for her brother, we are told simply that *'Jesus wept.'* This statement should, I think, rivet us to the spot.

'Therefore, when Mary came where Jesus was, she saw Him, and fell at His feet, saying to him, "Lord, if You had been here, my brother would not have died." When Jesus therefore saw her weeping, and the Jews who came with her also weeping, He was deeply moved in spirit, and was troubled, and said, "Where have you laid him?" They said to Him, "Lord, come and see." Jesus wept. So the Jews were saying, "See how He loved him."' (John 11)

The Son of God is made man; wholly God and wholly man. I wonder if those things that had to be, that revealed the Father's glory, when the Father had to stay His hand and allow events to run, actually grieved Jesus on occasions, such was His capacity to identify with us in His obedience. I feel it is not only the Son of Man who weeps; it is also the Son of God. God has profound emotions. God weeps over our pain and grief. *See how He loved Him.*

My Father, I see something happening here. I cannot quite know it. The rhythms of heaven are breaking into my consciousness . . . The Father stays His hand despite the pain. He suffers the pain. He *really* does. And then I remember that as Jesus hung on the cross so that the world might be saved from itself, I also realise that right there, there in the blackest darkness ever, *the Father stayed His hand.* For me. Amen.

Day 74 – March 14th

The compassion of Jesus, a concept we may speak of lightly, is a very profound matter. Throughout Scripture we see the compassion of God shaping so many events. Many characters are blessed of God as they faithfully express His compassion. It is pivotal to all He is and who we *must be* in Him. Sometimes, inevitably, it becomes complex when God, who knows our destination, and is taking us there, might *appear* to not hear us in our distress. (It may not even be distress; a desire will do.)

I think of the rich young man in this context. We read:

'Looking at him, Jesus felt a love for him and said to him, "One thing you lack: go and sell all you possess and give to the poor, and you will have treasure in heaven; and come, follow Me."' (Mark 10)

The question the young man asked at the outset was, *'Good Teacher, what shall I do to inherit eternal life?'* This man is on a journey into God! You don't march up to Jesus and ask that unless you are either trying to trick Jesus, as others were want to do, or you are after life-changing truth. I believe the latter. He called Jesus 'good' which the Lord remarked upon, pointing out that only God is good. Jesus is drawing him out. 'Is *that* what you are after?' Jesus seems to be saying: 'I hear you . . .' After repeating the commandments, the young man confirms he is on the journey and is faithful. 'Since I knew how, I have done this,' he affirms but when Jesus gives him a call to deep faith, his face falls and he went away grieved because his wealth was great.

It's important to note that we do not know the end of this story. He may have wrestled with it, come back and become a deeply committed follower of Jesus. Or not.

What I see in this exchange is the God at work who is set on us reaching the destination He has in mind for us. We are apt not to do that, sadly, and pastorally it is not easy to send someone away with a 'When you have done what I have asked you, come back and talk some more' moment. We need to, though. We have a propensity to say to ourselves *I am sure it won't matter'*, sometimes with disastrous consequences. That is not love, nor is it true compassion. It is being soft-hearted and Jesus was not that!

Parents know this. 'I know you would like to eat a whole packet of sweets (every day this week), but you cannot.' Despite pleadings we do not do that, I hope, as it would be reckless towards our children's dental health and their well-being. That is love. We call it 'tough love'. It is not. It is love. Jesus, just like the Father and the Holy Spirit, always ministers to us in the way of LOVE. They know nothing else.

Father, I know this is true. There are times when I have been like a querulous child before You, manoeuvring and seeking to get my way. And sometimes You have kindly shown me things that I must do, the ways I must change, before the fruit of Your compassion and love can come through to me in full. God forgive me. I want to give You permission today, through the Holy Spirit's life in me, to speak to me if there are changes to be made. Lord, thank You that You know my destiny and You alone know how to prepare me. I surrender to Your ways. Amen.

Day 75 – March 15th

Sometimes, bearing in mind our thinking yesterday, it is difficult to bear the Lord's call to 'Stop!' Remember Peter, who, inspired by the Holy Spirit had revealed to Jesus that He *was* the Christ. 'Who do you say I am?' He had asked Peter. He had responded with truth and sincerity. It appears that within a few minutes Peter had managed to get it very wrong.

'And He began to teach the disciples that the Son of Man must suffer many things and be rejected by the elders and the chief priests and the scribes, and be killed, and after three days rise again. And He was stating the matter plainly. And Peter took Him aside and began to rebuke Him. But turning around and seeing His disciples, He rebuked Peter and said, "Get behind Me, Satan; for you are not setting your mind on God's interests, but man's."' (Mark 8)

Ouch! Ouch! and Ouch again! That must have really been a dreadful, stinging retort. He called me *'Satan'*! It is all to do with wisdom and, in particular, the wisdom of knowing your *destiny* in God. This must have been to Jesus just like one of the barbed temptations of the desert experience: *'All you have to do to stave off your hunger is to turn these stones to hot fresh-baked rolls . . . Mmm . . . can you smell the fresh bread coming out of the oven, Jesus?'* My words, clearly, but as I have said before, the enemy has no ethics committee. To have one of your closest friends come along and propose *exactly* the route you would, on a bad day, rather take – the road of less pain – how tempting! Why did Jesus turn around and 'see His disciples'? They were watching! It would seem that Peter might have been chosen to go and confront Jesus with their earth-bound, but genuine, remonstrations. Lesson One: Don't rebuke the Lord! Don't ever say *'I am not sure You know what You are doing!'*

Many years ago, I recall we were desperate for musicians to help lead worship. Out of the blue, along came a wonderful guitarist, who, musically, led remarkably well. Everyone said that this was such a tremendous answer to prayer. But there was something in my spirit saying, 'No!' At first I couldn't quite put my finger on it, but I knew this wasn't right for us. Finally, God spoke to me a word of real wisdom which I then employed in an extremely short but testing conversation. Sure enough, the person completely disappeared off the scene just as the Lord had said he would if gently pressed on a certain point. I, in turn, had to ask the Lord to show the others in the team why it had to be so. I needed my reputation restored! He didn't. That's leadership for you!

Lord Jesus, I am so grateful for the way You have applied Your wisdom to my life, even when, at times, You have put the brakes on, or even said 'stop'. I have looked back and seen why You did it and then felt grateful relief. Help me to hear You, and to spend time with You, before I dash forth. I know You save me from disasters and egg on my face, however sanctified! I recall that You did that even before I confessed You as my Lord. Thank You that You didn't just save me but You saved me from my potential mess-ups. Thank You. Thank You. Amen.

Day 76 – March 16th

'I waited patiently for the LORD; and He inclined to me and heard my cry. He brought me up out of the pit of destruction, out of the miry clay; and He set my feet upon a rock making my footsteps firm. He put a new song in my mouth; a song of praise to our God.' (Psalm 40)

When I was about ten years old my family holidayed in the Isle of Wight with my uncle and aunt. For some reason which I cannot remember, I persuaded my aunt to take a short cut back from the shops having bought bread and milk. It involved walking down a tidal creek and hence along the beach to where we were staying. Everything was well until we realised the bank was full of very dense brambles. We went nearer to the mud on the creek. It was fine; a little 'gloopy' but fine. I should point out that high heels were all the rage in those days and my aunt was wearing her pair purchased especially for the holiday. At any point on this mission we could have turned back – but we didn't. I kept reassuring that, 'It will be fine. Don't worry!' The gloopy mud turned to very thick goo, the sort that grabs at your feet and tries to suck you in. My valiant cries diminished. As we staggered across the mud the crusty loaf bounced several times and became more 'farmyard' than 'Farmhouse', I fear.

We arrived home none the worse for wear – at least nothing that a long period in the bathroom couldn't put right. So much for short cuts! We can be so like that in our journeying with the Lord. Sometimes, being in the mire is our fault and sometimes we are entirely innocent (and sometimes, probably most often, somewhere in between.) How good it is to 'stop', to come before the Lord, and ask, 'Is this the moment I turn back? Should I be here?' People say this of business enterprises; in the light of financial disasters, such is the power of the vision in the mind of an adventurer that the temptation is to carry on, despite all advice and signs to the contrary! Perhaps you have been in that situation and are shouting, 'Amen!' Perhaps you are in one of them right now; perhaps you need to stop wading through the creek . . .

Father, You are such a good guide. You know every place I put my feet. You see the muddy places long before we get there and, if we listen, You will steer us by another path. Help those who are in it up to their knees and speak to them of Your care and compassion. Like King David in this psalm, may they cry out to You. Place their feet upon a rock and put a new song in their mouth. A song of praise to You. Amen.

Day 77 – March 17th

My aunt (yesterday) saved her precious shoes, just, by dint of holding them high above her head, and I was forgiven. It was one of those stories that went into family history. A tale to laugh at whenever we gathered.

'Then He poured water into the basin, and began to wash the disciples' feet and to wipe them with the towel . . . When He had washed their feet, and taken His garments and reclined at the table again, He said to them, "Do you know what I have done to you? You call Me Teacher and Lord; and you are right, for so I am. If I then, the Lord and the Teacher, washed your feet, you also ought to wash one another's feet. For I gave you an example that you also should do as I did to you."' (John 13)

It is not recorded how the disciples replied. Peter remonstrated, misunderstood and then recanted but I rather think the others might have been a little mystified. If you have ever washed someone's feet you will know that it is very special experience.

Many wash feet and more; carers and nurses wash bodies as a matter of routine. Personally, I have to say I find it moving to wash feet, and moving to receive. Why was this example that Jesus gave so very remarkable that the phrase 'foot-washing' has passed into common usage?

I think we understand the spiritual significance of this moment – the Lord turned servant – and also the precedent He set us but do we *really* understand this?

To wash feet, as the giver, you have to come low. You generally have to kneel. Servants alone went that low in Jesus' day, and not just any old servant. It was very much 'last in washes feet'. The lowest slave, the one who had absolutely no status in life whatsoever, would wash the feet of guests as they arrived. To fail to offer water for feet and oil for the head was quite insulting. So, you come low and then you wash the body's 'work horses'. Feet generally are not pretty. They carry all the knocks and strains of life and, I don't know about you, but I do not much like anyone inspecting my feet at close quarters. In Jesus' day, it is reasonable to assume that they might have had donkey dung or camel messes on them. It was quite a job and no wonder that the 'boy' did the job. The moment you achieved the tiniest promotion in the hierarchy of the household you would be pleased to hand the bowl on to someone else!

But there is something extraordinarily special about it. It is intensely personal and it also requires trust. Feet are precious. The mutual, 'I come low before you' and the 'I will let you come low before me' dynamic is powerful.

I recall being asked to see a church leader. I didn't know him but felt it was all a bit tiresome and, if I am honest, I thought the whole situation could have been avoided if he hadn't been quite so full of himself . . . I arrived and the Lord said to me very clearly, *'Wash his feet, My son.'*

A bowl was organised and I duly bathed his feet and we entered that 'low-low' dynamic. It was a very deep experience for both of us. After I had dried them, the Lord then said, *'Now clean his specs . . .'* which I did. We remained good, trusting friends and that twin dynamic of serving and allowing him to see clearly that the Lord might move in his life will be with me always. Bless God that He takes us to such profound places. He is so wise.

Father, You send us out to wash feet but not just to learn to serve. There are times when the significance of such a simple prophetic act can, just as Mary poured oil, touch us all deep within. Thank You for the 'token' acts You call us to that lead us and others into Life! Keep me sharp to the moments when You speak so. May I always be prepared to come low before You and others in my service of the Great King. Amen.

Day 78 – March 18th

Many are the ways of bringing proud men to heel and the judgemental to right-thinking. That's not a proverb; I just wrote it down. God also has a sense of humour.

I worked with a man once who was *so* full of himself and his ideas; without a thought, he would trample over colleagues and friends alike to reach his destination. I knew my attitude to him, a Christian, wasn't right but I felt justified. After all, he was obnoxious!

One day God spoke to me in my quiet time and deeply challenged me about my pompous attitude to someone He loved. Oh dear. I repented and told the Lord I would really make amends as soon as the opportunity arose. That was on a Friday morning. Early on Saturday the phone rang and it was the man himself. He had a bit of a problem and, knowing that I was a handy DIY-builder-sort, he said he thought of me immediately as one to ask. 'Sure,' I said, 'how can I help?'

When I arrived at his house, the gentle sloping drive down to his garage was awash with sewage. It was knee deep. He had three very young children, another one on the way, a long-suffering wife . . . and no toilet. The briefest inspection showed that the blockage was actually a major drain collapse. 'Anno Domini' had struck under his drive in no uncertain terms. It was a terminal case. We cleared the mess with buckets into another drain and then began to dig . . .

Later that night, under a flood light, we covered over the new drain pipes we had installed together and went upstairs for a ceremonial flush. You know what I am going to say, don't you? We became firm friends and came to hold one another in deep honour. And we laughed. A lot!

'If your enemy is hungry, give him food to eat; and if he is thirsty, give him water to drink; for you will heap burning coals on his head, and the LORD will reward you.' (Proverbs 25)

Father, I can be such an obnoxious prig at times. I thank You for Your wonderful ways and Your sparkling humour. Let me be quick to respond to You speaking when I am out of order. Forgive me for all the things I think every day that aren't right for a child of God to be thinking. Make me like Jesus, I pray. Amen.

Day 79 – March 19th

I am not very mobile these days and moving things other than my own body around can be a strain and, at the moment, I am on crutches. We had a delivery and drivers, being under the huge pressures that they are to meet targets, are inclined to drop and run at our front door, especially if no signature is required. I don't blame them. Living in the country, we never go to the front door. A parcel could lay there abandoned to a mildew-laden death. The last 'drop and run' resulted in having to drag a large sack of bird food (remember the birds?) from the front door to the back. Bearing in mind our house has scaffolding (yes, it's still there – steel poles everywhere) and I am on crutches, it was some effort amidst a garden obstacle course. For some reason in the midst of this I suddenly thought of the Greek word 'rhuomai' (pronounced *roo-om-ahee*). It means 'to rush' or 'to draw' or 'to carry' or even 'drag'.

'For He rescued us [rhuomai] *from the domain of darkness, and transferred us to the kingdom of His beloved Son, in whom we have redemption, the forgiveness of sins.'* (Colossians 1)

My brain works very laterally, I appreciate that, but this verse describes so wonderfully how we are rescued by God. I doubt that we are dragged like a sack, rather, not unlike being dashed into A and E on a trolley, I suspect we are rushed with all haste.

When a person believes and comes to God in repentance, a very definite change takes place. It is as though they go to live in a new country – a new planet, even. We go from dark to light and chains to freedom. It's a sublime picture. I imagine the Father, Son and Holy Spirit rejoicing together, full of heaven's joy and beaming with delight. *Another one! Glory!* The verse, wonderful as it is, doesn't quite convey the fullness of the miracle God performs. Not only does He rush us but it also says that He transfers us *(methistemi)* indicating carrying away or even perfecting an exchange! What a wonderful image! He rushes us through, the exchange has been done on the cross, the debt is paid, and all is now sealed. We are *His*!

I have an image of a delivery being received by a dear elderly man. It has been long lost in transit but now it has arrived. He clasps it to his chest in His great arms; His eyes beam, His mouth is wreathed in smiles and tears of joy run down His cheeks. *'This son of mine . . . he was lost and has been found!'*

Father, we cannot guess at the pleasure it brings to You to see a long-lost loved one swept into the kingdom. You have told us there is rejoicing in heaven. I am in wonder. How You love us. I am lost for words so I fall at Your feet in thanks and praise that You found me. Amen.

Day 80 – March 20th

'Therefore bear fruits in keeping with repentance, and do not begin to say to yourselves, "We have Abraham for our father," for I say to you that from these stones God is able to raise up children to Abraham . . . And the crowds were questioning him saying, "Then what shall we do?" And he would answer and say to them, "The man who has two tunics is to share with him who has none; and he who has food is to do likewise."' (Luke 3)

The so-called 'fruits of repentance' preached by John the Baptist electrified his listeners to the point of clamouring for guidance as to how to make it *real*. When an evangelist speaks, that is the effect: *change!* How we need evangelists to step up in these days; men and women who can really stir hearts for the Lord, to convey that the King means *business* with this fallen world. Rise up!

John Wimber used to say that when people become Christians they expect to stroll down to the dock and find a sleek cruise liner but they are shocked to find a grey battleship. Forgive me if I slightly misquote that great man of God. The point is that although God sweeps us into His kingdom and there is celebration and delight, we also take on a beautiful robe of responsibility. We are from that moment sons and daughters of the King! *'Battle stations!'* becomes the cry.

I remember well the first time I 'drew my sword' and realised that we are part of an elite 'snatch squad'; snatching folk from death and bringing them into the kingdom of the Son. It wasn't pretty, but I tried my best and eventually won through partnering with the Holy Spirit. What a joy it was.

Dear Lord Jesus, I long to be on active duty for You. I hear the call to arms. Equip me, I ask, and send me out into the fray that I might carry the Good News of hope and life to those I meet. Let all that I am in You attract them. May my simple witness make them *homesick* for heaven and for You. Amen.

Day 81 – March 21st

'And as you go, preach, saying, "The kingdom of heaven is at hand." Heal the sick, raise the dead, cleanse the lepers, cast out demons. Freely you have received, freely give.' (Matthew 10)

I recall when I began to work specifically as a pastor to the elderly folk; at the end of my first week I went to see a lady, Yvonne. She was confined to bed and was also suffering from an angry inflammation right down one side of her face. She was such a dear soul, very forgetful and sometimes a little muddled. I asked her whether her face was being properly treated.

'Oh,' she sighed, waving her hand dismissively, 'they have tried everything – creams, lotions and tablets – and nothing has done any good.'

I asked very gently if she would mind if I said a prayer for her. 'Ooh no!' she said, 'do!'

So, I prayed a simple prayer. 'Lord Jesus, I believe You want to end this suffering that Yvonne has endured, so I speak to this infection now in the mighty name of Jesus and I say, "Be healed."'

103

That was it. Very peaceful, hushed tones, heartfelt.

On Monday morning I dropped by to see her and, to my surprise and joy, her face had nothing but the faintest blemish on it. She was healed! 'Yvonne,' I said, beaming with joy, 'your face is better!'

'Is it?' she asked me, looking strangely puzzled. 'Was there something wrong with it?'

'You had a . . .' I stopped, and smiled. I knew this was going to be between the Lord and me. My first prayer and a wonderful healing in my new job and the dear lady couldn't remember it! I made her a cup of tea and went out praising God quietly and chuckling.

Father, I love the mystery of Your ways. You bless me and make me smile. You love all people and You do wonders in our midst. Thank You for Your healing touch for this lady and so many like her. May we be aware of the elderly and infirm and understand that You want to move in their lives also. Bring to mind, I pray, those I might visit, whether for a miracle or a cup of tea . . . or maybe both. Amen.

Day 82 – March 22nd

'And the seventy returned with joy, saying, "Lord, even the demons are subject to us in Your name." And He said to them, "I was watching Satan fall from heaven like lightning. Behold, I have given you authority to tread on serpents and scorpions, and over all the power of the enemy, and nothing will injure you. Nevertheless do not rejoice in this, that the spirits are subject to you, but rejoice that your names are recorded in heaven."' (Luke 10)

When you see a healing or a deliverance and someone is set free in body, mind or spirit (or all of them) it is natural to rejoice and be excited! The next verse after the one above tells us,

'At that very time He rejoiced greatly in the Holy Spirit, and said, "I praise You, O Father, Lord of heaven and earth, that You have hidden these things from the wise and intelligent and have revealed them to infants. Yes, Father, for this way was well-pleasing in Your sight."'

Jesus, we are told, was jumping or maybe dancing for joy before the Father! Bubbling over! I suspect it was the advent of the day of revelation which thrilled Jesus so. Whatever prompted His exuberance, take note that our real joy is to be joy of knowing that you are the Father's children. Healings come and go. Your Royal Residency does not. You have been bought at a great price and dressed in royal robes. We are not to be scalp-hunters looking for the next spiritual high. (Forgive me for saying so if you find that offensive in any way.)

He also tells them something of awesome importance when He tells them that He saw Satan fall. He is not referring to a time while they were out ministering; He is stating a truth from before time: Jesus watched Satan fall from heaven. He knows what the enemy is like and He knows His limitations and His future. *He cannot touch you*, he told them.

My Father, I love to jump for joy when I see the power of Your hand at work. I will always be thrilled to see the kingdom of God come near but, on days when I am not dancing on the mountain tops but down in the valleys, I am so glad to be Your child. Amen.

Day 83 – March 23rd

There are moments when Jesus uses His very sharp prophetic gifting, coupled with His deep awareness of His immediate environment, to produce extraordinary insights that cause us to wonder and be amazed.

'Jesus saw Nathanael coming to Him,' (brought along by Philip), *'and said of him, "Behold, an Israelite indeed, in whom there is no deceit!" Nathanael said to Him, "How do You know me?" Jesus answered and said to him, "Before Philip called you, when you were under the fig tree, I saw you." Nathanael answered Him, "Rabbi, You are the Son of God; You are the King of Israel." Jesus answered and said to him, "Because I said to you that I saw you under the fig tree,*

do you believe? You will see greater things than these." And He said to him, "Truly, truly, I say to you, you will see the heavens opened and the angels of God ascending and descending on the Son of Man."' (John 1)

It is clear from the conversation between Philip and Nathanael prior to meeting Jesus, that the two were used to being entrenched in the Scriptures. We will never fully understand this moment but I wonder if Nathanael was sitting reading Genesis 32 when Philip came by. Perhaps he was reading of Jacob, the 'deceiver' – the 'tricky one'. Why else might Jesus choose to speak of him having 'no deceit'? I notice also the cry of the evangelist in Philip's voice: 'Come and see!'

I wonder about how Jesus sees us in those moments when little is apparently happening to us (from our point of view, at least), but God is watching and valuing our every move. Never belittle the value of the times when you are *'just having your quiet time'* or *'just praying'*; I suspect there is no such thing in our Father's eyes! Notice also how God makes us look and wonder at what is in store for us: *'you will see . . .'* Jesus said. We rarely know for sure. There is just that 'hint'.

There is an engaging local belief that Philip, Nathanael and Jesus, being of similar age, were all subject to the dreadful time of the 'slaughter of the innocents' when Herod was determined to purge any possibility of a new 'King of the Jews'. Many children were hidden from the death squads by desperate mothers and fathers. The custom goes that Nathanael was hidden under a fig tree. Maybe Jesus was not 'seeing' Nathanael that day; maybe He saw him thirty years previously, as a tiny child, guarded by the Great Father, that his destiny might be fulfilled. It may or not be so but this story brings home the capacity of the Lord to see us and more: to read our heart intentions towards Him.

Father, it must have been wondrous to be around Jesus during His earthly life! To have been awed by the simplest of conversations: a word here to that one and an encouragement to this one. But I remember today that *I am* in the presence of the Lord in the same way! That fills me with wonder. May I hear His asides, even the tiniest 'hints' as I go through today; a comment about the person I am speaking earnestly with, or even the lady in the post office who processes my parcel. I will live in a new awareness of the King! Thank You! Help me. Amen.

Day 84 – March 24th

On a similar theme as yesterday's one, I am struck by how Jesus really *sees* people. He challenges us to look beneath the superficial.

'Turning toward the woman, He said to Simon, "Do you see this woman? I entered your house; you gave Me no water for My feet, but she has wet My feet with her tears and wiped them with her hair. You gave Me no kiss; but she, since the time I came in, has not ceased to kiss My feet. You did not anoint My head with oil, but she anointed My feet with perfume. For this reason I say to you, her sins, which are many, have been forgiven, for she loved much; but he who is forgiven little, loves little." Then He said to her, "Your sins have been forgiven."' (Luke 7)

This passage is electric! Jesus challenges the gathered religious folk by speaking to layer after layer of their perceived place of 'well-being'.

'Simon, do you see this woman?' What a question! Of course, I see her! 'No, I mean do you *really* see her, Simon? Do you see the intricacies of her life? Do you know why she is doing to Me what she does? Do you *see her love*? Do you even begin to know how much she has been set free from and forgiven? Do you understand the grace on her life and begin to know her heart-felt gratitude?'

We are not accustomed to the social etiquette at the time of Jesus. We may fail to see that Simon may have been slightly offensive in his treatment of Jesus. Maybe he needed to be, pressured by the sullen ill-acceptance of the onlookers who were intensely irritated by this man who challenged them so. Added to which, this woman made an entrance, perhaps inviting herself in through the open door after the synagogue meeting. She went as far as to let her hair down in their presence . . . unthinkable. It was a veritable cauldron of possibilities; none of them particularly edifying. Hence the question of Jesus: Simon, do you *see* this woman? She may be all sorts of things in your eyes, My friend, but in Mine, the God of compassion and justice, speaking as the One who favours those who have not, and know it, I need to say that you offered me no water . . . no oil . . .

How very careful we need to be to see people as Jesus sees them. Whilst this is something of an obvious statement, let me put it another way: *How many children would continue to die of disease, famine and starvation if we could see them as Jesus sees them? If we truly feared the Lord, how many wars would cease in the blink of an eye if we could see . . . How many neighbours would cease to be uncared for if . . .*

Father, I read this passage and I know that I also do not see. And it doesn't always suit me to see; to see as You do. I would have to stop what I was doing and attend; give of myself in ways I never imagined possible. Father, it is not just my eyes that need to be healed, I realise also it is my heart. This precious woman blessed You because she moved towards You with all that she had. She did not hold back. How very threatening that is to me when I allow myself to 'see' her. Heal me, Lord, I pray. Heal my eyes and my heart. Amen.

Day 85 – March 25th

Jesus not only sees but He also listens. God is the archetypal listener. Jesus asked the less-than-obvious question that we would fail to consider, so fast are we to jump to conclusions. It is because He sees and He listens and He knows our deepest need.

'Look at the birds of the air, that they do not sow, nor reap nor gather into barns, and yet your heavenly Father feeds them. Are you

not worth much more than they? And who of you by being worried can add a single hour to his life?' (Matthew 6)

We become used to treating this as nothing more than rhetorical questioning, but pause to think. Is Jesus asking you a question that demands of your deep places? These are very real questions for every one of us.

Do you see the birds?

I see the birds, Father, and I do know, I think, how much more I am worth . . .

How much more are you worth, My son?

I am uncomfortable with Your gaze, Father . . .

Why would you be uncomfortable to consider for one moment your worth to Me?

I don't know, Father. I am sorry. I have never known such love as Yours. This world has not taught me such love. I realise that I am a beginner.

As we press into these very personal 'conversations' we appreciate that they were not intended to be entirely rhetorical. The answers to the questions of Jesus take us to profound places very rapidly! Surely, we do need to know why we worry, why anxiety can rule our lives and how great is the Father's love for us.

Dear Jesus, precious Saviour, You ask me questions that I hardly dare answer. You look into me and know the answer but, rather like the question to Adam, *Where are you?* You want us to be fully cognisant of the truth. You ask me questions in order that I may know myself *and* also know my being in You. Never cease to ask me questions, my Lord, that I may grow and become more and more like You each day. Amen.

Day 86 – March 26th

Jesus crossed over the Lake of Galilee and came to His own city, Capernaum.

'And they brought to Him a paralytic lying on a bed. Seeing their faith, Jesus said to the paralytic, "Take courage, son; your sins are forgiven."' (Matthew 9)

The word used here to indicate *forgiven* is literally, 'being sent forth' or perhaps 'being sent from you'.

An extraordinary story; did you notice what Jesus observed? *Their faith!* He saw their faith. It may have been the faith of the friends or, perhaps, He knew that they had asked the paralysed man, 'Do you want us to take you to the healer?' in which case it was *all* of their faith; we cannot know for sure.

Jesus then makes an outrageous statement: that this man's sins are being sent from him! He holds back from speaking *the* word. He looks around listening to that which is barely spoken: *Blasphemy! This cannot be tolerated!*

So, Jesus spoke to them of their inner (evil) thoughts and challenges them. He speaks straight to the unspoken question, and the sword moves swiftly dividing marrow from bone. *'Which is easier, to say, "Your sins are forgiven," or to say, "Get up, and walk"?'*

This is surely the most brilliant Father at work in a gathering within a larger crowd; simultaneously easing a man from his chains of body and spirit, growing and rewarding the faith of the man's friends, and demolishing the pretentious hearts of those who look on and inwardly curse. This is a rhetorical question, we assume. No one dares to respond aloud. They might have responded in the silence of their hearts, 'Of course it is easier to *say* the words of forgiveness . . .'

'But so that you may know that the Son of Man has authority on earth to forgive sins . . . Get up, pick up your bed and go home.'

We cry out in admiration and love for the One who speaks wisdom and truth without fear of any man. It is as though Jesus calls out through the centuries, *'Who will dare to take on the Lord of Lords and the King of Kings?'* and our spirits rise to the cry.

'But when the crowds saw this, they were awestruck, and glorified

God, who had given such authority to men.'

Lord of Lords and King of Kings, we worship You. You are truly Master of all You survey. Everything is in Your hand. We see how You bring truth and wisdom to bear and ask that You would teach us Your ways that we might 'do all things justly, love kindness and walk humbly with You, our God'. Amen.

Day 87 – March 27th

'Truly, truly, I say to you, he who believes has eternal life. I am the bread of life.' (John 6)

Although bread is central to westernised life, it does not have the significance it once did. For better or worse, we have so many alternatives as staples (and many of them from countries where they can ill-afford to export them!). It is worth reflecting on the very essential nature of bread as it is so often used as an illustration, that to fail to understand what Jesus and others were alluding to would be to miss the root of the spiritual point being made.

In the times of Jesus, it was not said that a man worked to make a living, rather *a man worked to eat bread.* We have the expression still, *earning a crust.* Life was referred to as the 'eating of bread' and fellowship as 'the sharing of bread'.

Remember this? *'He who eats My bread has lifted up his heel against Me,'* Jesus said, speaking of Judas, and taking the words of King David:

'Even my close friend in whom I trusted, who ate my bread, has lifted up his heel against me.' (Psalm 41)

There are strong emotional terms surrounding bread that are lost in English. A Middle Eastern villager described his community as, *'We are a people who eat bread'* – a simple statement effectively stating that *we are poor and have little else to eat.* Bread to us is *life.*

There are so many scriptures that refer to bread: the little boy who offered to Jesus his bread rolls, the Lord's prayer asks for *bread for today*, not food, and the story Jesus told to illustrate the extravagance of the kingdom tells us that the prodigal son thought that his father's house had bread and enough to spare. What incredible luxury among hired men!

Most remarkable of all, after they had eaten a meal together we are told, *'And when He had taken some bread and given thanks, He broke it and gave it to them, saying, "This is My body which is given for you."'* (Luke 22)

Jesus was saying, quite simply and emphatically, *I give you My Life. Take it.*

Here is the blessing that Jesus most likely spoke. There is little reason to suppose He did not. He wasn't blessing the bread as we often think; He was blessing God the Giver of Life. As we thank God for the body Jesus was willing to have broken on the cross, for us, we say, Blessed are You, O Lord our God, King of the Universe, who brings forth bread from the earth. Amen.

Day 88 – March 28th

I am fascinated by the calling of Jesus to His disciples. I am drawn to observe *how* He called them. It seems that if we, in our turn, are to make disciples of the Lord, as we are told to, we need to note how He accomplished it.

We don't know why Jesus ended up at Simon Peter's house.

'He got up and left the synagogue, and entered Simon's home. Now Simon's mother-in-law was suffering from a high fever; and they asked Him to help her. And standing over her, He rebuked the fever, and it left her; and she immediately got up and waited on them.' (Luke 4)

It is such a lovely picture, especially the thought of Simon's mother-in-law, healed of her sickness, determined to scurry around to put a good meal on the table for this most extraordinary Rabbi. It is possible that Simon was at the synagogue and invited Jesus, even asking Him to attend to his ailing relative. It is also possible that Jesus invited Himself, such was the open-door custom after a synagogue meeting. What we do know is that Simon observed all this. He *saw* the Lord ministering to her. When we observe, it tends to be an 'external' moment. It need not necessarily impress deeply on our heart, only the mind. It's reasonable to assume the same of the evening that followed. Perhaps Peter watched from a doorway:

'While the sun was setting, all those who had any who were sick with various diseases brought them to Him; and laying His hands on each one of them, He was healing them.'

What strikes me about this, in the context of Simon's journey to full discipleship, is that Jesus was quite natural around him, or perhaps we should say *'supernatural'* around him. Jesus continued with His ministry to those that had need in a naturally supernatural manner. There is no record of Him preaching to them. Nothing else is recorded about anyone's reaction except that, the next morning, they all wanted more of Jesus.

I learn from this that far from being dramatic about the power of the Holy Spirit to heal, it should be a natural part of our supernatural lives. We also should not necessarily expect onlookers, or even the person concerned, to be transformed by these precious moments!

I recall once being on holiday on the canals when we cruised by a man beside his moored boat and something checked in my spirit. I took note and slowed, calling out, 'Are you OK?' He and his wife were far from OK. They had a sick baby and were a long way from help, deep in the Midlands countryside. He asked me if I had a thermometer. I stopped and moored, and took my extensive first aid kit and went to him. The baby was limp with a high fever and the mother, bathing the child with cool cloths, distraught. I told them where they would be sure to find a doctor but it would involve a taxi ride and probably a long wait. This was before the days of mobiles. Even an ambulance was not at all straightforward without a phone. I had nothing else in my kit that might help. 'Perhaps you would allow me to pray for your baby,' I asked, wiping the thermometer clean on a swab.

'Oh, yes,' the mother cried out, 'pray!'

So, I prayed and, as we watched, the baby started to wriggle and look more baby-like and less like a damp rag doll. He cried a little, then opened his bright eyes and gurgled at us! I know my mouth was hanging open in surprise and I am sure theirs were also. I briefly thanked Father God for His immense goodness.

The point of this story is to illustrate that we don't need to make a great commotion about healing the sick and, sometimes, we have to trust God to take the person on his or her own journey when we, ourselves, are departed and are only a memory. I guarantee you that that couple will never have forgotten that moment when the kingdom of God came close, and as for that little life? Who knows?

I entrusted them to the Father and went on my way.

Lord Jesus, help us to be wide-awake to those moments when the Holy Spirit nudges us *this one* or *that one!* Thank You for the opportunities You give us to allow others to have an encounter with You, the risen Lord. May I be willing to quietly step out in faith, to bring Your healing to those in need that You may be glorified and they, in turn, are caused to turn their eyes to You! Amen.

Day 89 – March 29th

Travelling onwards with Simon, as he journeys into his own full, radical encounter with Jesus, we find the Lord teaching the crowds by the Lake of Galilee. The crowds press in until Jesus asks Simon to put his boat out a little way from shore to act as a floating pulpit where all could see and hear.

'When He had finished speaking, He said to Simon, "Put out into the deep water and let down your nets for a catch."' (Luke 5)

It clearly states in this passage that the men were cleaning up after a fruitless night of work. They can't have been in a good state of mind to be asked to start again, especially if their breakfasts were overdue, but Simon is clear that, despite these things, *'I will do as You say and let down the nets.'* Make no mistake, this is a hard word of Jesus! How easy it would have been to make excuses.

The story is well known. The catch was massive, so much so that they needed assistance to land it for fear of the boat rolling over under the excessive strain. The Lord rarely does things by halves! On taking in the awesome nature of this spectacular event, Simon *'fell down at Jesus' feet, saying, "Go away from me Lord, for I am a sinful man!" For amazement had seized him and all his companions because of the catch of fish which they had taken.'*

Jesus comes to them all in the ordinary stuff of life bringing the stupendous, holy, sacred moment that changes them all forever. A fisherman doesn't need telling twice that the Lord of Lords has commanded the fish to jump into the net! It is unthinkable in the natural, and Simon is, at once, on his knees asking for mercy. He has a *'numinous moment'*; the divine touch on his heart . . . *my Lord!* He is afraid of this new, mysterious friend who seems to be endowed with God-like powers. He witnessed it in his own house, he observed it in the courtyard, but this has gone way beyond all that! It demands a profound heart response. *My Lord!*

Jesus is so very wise as He calls us. He knows *exactly* how to bring conviction. It is like the iron particles we used to scatter on a piece of paper as children, to then watch with delight as a magnet is introduced below. Everything in us lines up. Heart change is inevitable and overwhelming!

My Lord! I come before You today as one who is astounded by Your power, Your goodness and Your wisdom. Catch me up in those practical and down-to-earth moments that really change lives; no longer observing, no more wonderment in the head, but a radical encounter, deep in the heart. You also teach me to be obedient to *Your word,* as Simon was. 'Even though I have toiled on this one before, at *Your word,* my Lord, I will do this thing afresh.' Amen.

Day 90 – March 30th

'For amazement had seized him and all his companions because of the catch of fish which they had taken; and so also were James and John, sons of Zebedee, who were partners with Simon. And Jesus said to Simon, "Do not fear, from now on you will be catching men."' (Luke 5)

When Jesus says to me, 'Do not fear,' I have never said, 'I am not afraid!' He speaks it when I am! So, He speaks to them, *'Do not fear.'* They were afraid! It is interesting to guess at the source of their fear. Was it the 'too much' of God? Many a man has lost his heart to Jesus because of the outrageously generous provision of God: *too much love, too much care, too much health, too many fish . . .*

The men are told not to fear; Jesus has a plan. They are no longer to earn their living catching fish with nets; their life work will be to become 'fishers of men' (Matthew 5). It strikes me as so wise to take a person who is a profound craftsman in a particular field, or in this case a lake, and then put some heaven-spin on it and make the man fit to work in the kingdom. Simon, who knew how to observe the surface of the lake, the wind, the sky and every ripple, to understand the deeps and the treasure feeding out of sight, will one day be practising extraordinary discernment over men's hearts and listening to His Lord. Later, possibly as an old man, he wrote:

'So we have the prophetic word made more sure, to which you do well to pay attention as to a lamp shining in a dark place, until the day dawns and the morning star arises in your hearts.' (2 Peter 1)

Lord Jesus, I fall at Your knees today. Just as You were Master over the fish in the lake, so I confess that You are Lord over all; commanding and calling everything that is not, to come into being. I want to partner with You as You make me a fisher of men through the gifting that You nurture in me. Thank You that Your glorious provision will always be there for me also as I go out in Your name. Amen.

Day 91 – March 31st

I have pondered many times on what transpired when Jesus told the fishermen to follow Him.

'When they had brought their boats to land, they left everything and followed Him.' (Luke 5)

Did they literally leave it all and follow Him? Did they abandon the huge catch, possibly the most lucrative haul that had ever been made? Was it left on the rocky shore for the locals to share out among themselves? I think so. I cannot imagine taking this sacred piscine gathering and cashing it in! It doesn't sound right and, if they had, I think there might have been mention of it, to underpin the enormity of the miracle. I believe they left it all. Quite how they explained it at home, I cannot imagine. *'I may be away for a while; I cannot say when I will return; I have met a man called Jesus.'*

Sacrifice. Simply that. Jesus calls us to die to all that we are and all that might lay claim to us. Didn't Jesus say to a man, 'Follow Me,' and the man replied that he should be allowed to first go to bury his father?

'But He said to him, "Allow the dead to bury their own dead; but as for you, go and proclaim everywhere the kingdom of God."' (Luke 9)

That is radical discipleship. These are hard words! The call of Jesus can wrench us out of our slumber and every one of our assumptions. He says *nothing* comes before our service of the King!

At the heart of the kingdom is *obedience*; the call to arms – the great grey battleship awaits. It is weighing anchor and will wait for no man. Throughout the person of Jesus *'obedience'* is written. Obedience and honour and love of the Father's will. And so must our hearts be so inscribed. The hard words of Jesus? Yes.

My Jesus, so often I call You 'Lord' and 'Master', and that is right for that is what You are, but in my heart, I confess, that I hope that

You will not call me to radical following. I praise You for countless lives laid down with joy in obedience to You, such is Your call to men and women. As Easter approaches I am aware that I do not want to be counted lukewarm in my response to You so I offer myself to You afresh today – all that I am and all that I have. In Jesus' name. Amen.

APRIL

Day 92 – April 1st

I think Jesus was fun to be with!

'When they came to Capernaum, those who collected the two-drachma tax came to Peter and said, "Does your teacher not pay the two-drachma tax?" He said, "Yes." And when he came into the house, Jesus spoke to him first, saying, "What do you think, Simon? From whom do the kings of the earth collect customs or poll-tax, from their sons or from strangers?" When Peter said, "From strangers," Jesus said to him, "Then the sons are exempt. However, so that we do not offend them, go to the sea and throw in a hook, and take the first fish that comes up; and when you open its mouth, you will find a shekel. Take that and give it to them for you and Me."' (Matthew 17)

This story is extraordinary and I couldn't resist looking at it today! Imagine you owe the Inland Revenue a few hundred pounds and in your quiet time you feel God is saying, *'Look under the third flower pot on the right in your greenhouse . . .'* and when you go there, the money needed awaits you! Would that be a miraculous, fun-filled moment, or not? Jesus was fun. He had a terrific sense of humour and I believe *He still does* show the same with us sometimes. Usually, underneath the fun He is making a serious point. Look back a few verses and you will find Jesus being critical of the disciples' lack of faith when He had to step in Himself to deliver a boy of a troublesome spirit hanging around and causing the boy harm. When they asked Him why they had not been able to minister to the boy, Jesus said, *'Because of the littleness of your faith,'* (literally lack of confidence) *'for truly I say to you, if you have faith the size of a mustard seed, you will say to this mountain, "Move from here to there," and it will move; and nothing will be impossible for you.'*

He then continued with some very serious talk of His coming death. It would seem He was trying to build them up, to understand that what Jesus spoke, happened. He explained, on the third day the

Son of Man will be raised from death . . .

What better way to bring a lesson home than to demonstrate it with a seemingly light-hearted, prophetically-laden gesture which they would never forget? There is another layer in this also (there always is when Jesus is teaching!). His reference to sons or strangers in His question to Peter is, it seems, saying, *'Do you think I, as Son of God, should pay the tax to My Father's own house? As family, should I pay?'* It's a bit of a chuckle with Peter. So, He adds, but so as not to be a stumbling block to these guys, let's pay it.

But did you notice Peter is referred to as a son? *The sons are exempt.* Wow! My Lord, You called me a son of the Father! He then sends Peter out to throw the hook in the lake. Imagine Peter's jaw hitting the ground when he opened the fish's mouth! He is a fisherman himself and yet, once more, the Fisherman of all fishermen has revealed to Peter His awesome powers. It's a wonderful story with many layers and, as always it is affirming and life-giving. As Peter walked back to the house, I can imagine him thinking, *'He really shouldn't be paying this tax! He is the Son of God!'*

Father, this story makes me smile. We love jokes and good humour, and You made us in Your laughing, smiling likeness. Help me to lighten up in Your presence and see that sometimes You do things with Your children just for the sheer pleasure of seeing them enjoy the moment. We know that there are serious moments in life, sometimes grave moments, but in them all You ask us to be smiling, trusting, sons and daughters of the King who holds all things in His hand. Amen.

Day 93 – April 2nd

You may recall the story of Elijah taking on the prophets of Baal. It was a very serious turning point in a period of evil dominion over the land. It is no laughing matter but one can see a humorous side to some of the things the man of God speaks in the name of the Almighty. In his challenge to the prophets of Baal he speaks, *'How long will you hesitate between two opinions? If the LORD is God follow Him; but if Baal, follow him'* (1 Kings 18). We are told the people did not answer a word. That's not surprising; how do you respond to the simple wisdom of God? The battle of the oxen on the altars commenced and after a great deal of spectacularly ineffective mumbo-jumbo no fire descends on the Baal offering 'Go on,' encourages Elijah, 'shout louder! Perhaps your god is busy with something and can't give you attention, or perhaps on holiday – who knows, he may be having a snooze!' It is funny to behold! When Elijah's turn comes, he encourages them to pour no less than twelve pitchers of water over his own offering.

Elijah prays to the God of gods and the King of kings, and the fire falls consuming everything: stones, water, and the ox. It wasn't a good night for the Baal worshippers who had put their trust in a vain, dark idol.

We are meant to learn and grow as we see the prophetic moves of God at work. He does it not to show off but because *He is God.* He just is! The 'I am' wants to show us 'He is'. And He wants us to know we are His eternal children. It stretches us and affirms us, often in things we sort of knew already! He writes in **BOLD** for us!

Years ago I met some missionary friends, home on leave for several months, and the couple came to us for prayer as they had a dilemma: should they return? They really didn't know whether God was calling them to go back to the mission field. We talked and we prayed for some time. It still wasn't clear but they left trusting that God would guide them. As they were going out of the door, I felt God say to give them some financial support so I went to my desk and, pen hovering over my cheque book, asked, 'How much should I give them, Father?' It is really difficult to explain how God speaks but He does, and He said, *'Four hundred and fifty-six pounds, thirty-eight pence.'* Just like that. I smiled and wrote the cheque. I folded it and gave it to them, blessed them and they left.

A few months later we received an airmail letter. They wrote that God had not only confirmed for them their decision, taken in faith, but their faith in His provision grew so much that their increased confidence in God as Provider caused their mission to grow vastly as a result! The momentum behind this was simple. They had paid for their flights and taxes and all associated costs in US dollars and had just received their monthly credit card statement in UK pounds, with the exchange rate calculations completed on the day of transaction. It cost them £456.38.

O, my Father, You are wonderful to us! How can I worship You adequately today? I know so little of Your majesty and Your might. I am a beginner but I am so grateful to be Your child; the child of a *wonderful* Dad. Stretch me and affirm me that I might grow in trust and faith to go out in Your name, that others might come to know You also as Lord and King of all. Amen.

Day 94 – April 3rd

Today we play 'the worship game'. In my heart, it flows out of revisiting yesterday's story of those two missionaries; visualise our God who knows us that well. He sees every intricacy of our lives and takes delight in moving in every detail of them!

Your role in 'the worship game' is to try to out-praise God! It's simple: you try to give God more praise than is His due! I use Psalm 8 as one of my meditations for this. You can read the entire psalm but here is the phrase I focus on:

'O Lord, our Lord, how majestic is Your name in all the earth!'

The Hebrew word for majestic is 'addîyr'. It means a good number of words: wide, large, powerful, excellent, gallant, glorious, goodly, noble . . . So, the 'game' is to substitute any adjective you can think of that describes our heavenly Father.

That's it.

SANCTUARY

O Lord, our Supreme Lord, how _____ is Your name in all the earth. Amen.

Day 95 – April 4th

The world is crammed with wounded people. The church, I suspect, may also be crammed with wounded people.

'Above all, keep fervent in your love for one another, because love covers a multitude of sins.' (1 Peter 4)

Let's us try to make the translation clear, even if it costs a few more words:

Above everything else you expend energy on, never cease having affection and benevolence for one another as this will envelope and hide a multitude of offences.

That is so good! What it does not mean is that if someone has hurt you, you turn your eye away, pretend it did not happen and walk on with deep resentment smouldering in your soul whilst through gritted teeth mutter, 'Love you, bro.'

When my friends say daft things, as they are apt to do (I don't do that incidentally, not at all, you understand . . .) it is easy to be hurt or, in that way we can hardly help but do, we gradually crank up our objection to the point where we are wholly and permanently affronted. Have you ever found sleep elusive at night because someone has done something to wound you? The offence goes round and round in your mind growing on every circuit. It becomes a black, ugly monster!

I used to have a lovely black Labrador. He was such an amazing and anointed friend to me. Believe it – he was anointed and he loved prayer meetings! When he first came to us from a rescue centre I forgave him when he messed on the carpet. He wrecked a set of heavy curtains (and the pole) when he tore it all from the wall to present to me as a welcome home gift. I forgave him immediately, and I even lavished praise and thanks on him. I forgave him even when he stole food from the kitchen (not morsels but whole Sunday roasts). He smelled, some said badly, but to me it was that lovely homely aroma of oily Labrador fur – sort of digestives with a difference. My car smelled, some said, but I didn't notice. Each autumn the carpets were covered in black fur, but, as I vacuumed, I loved him.

Get the message? Unceasing love covers over a multitude of offences.

Next time someone forgets your birthday when you *always* remember theirs, love him. The churchwarden can't help looking chilly; love her. When your son borrows your treasured car and takes it for a trip through a barbed wire fence; love him. When people revile you, be blessed; love them. If they ever nail you to a tree to die; love them.

Father, we may jest, but the reality is that love turns the eye blind in the face of offence and the ear deaf in the event of insult. May my spirit be so proofed by Jesus that such things are like water from a duck's back. Fill me with Your love. I thank You that even when my sin was so offensive to You, You loved me. And when I could not come home, You died for me and then brought me home. Such love. Amen.

Day 96 – April 5th

'This is My commandment, that you love one another, just as I have loved you. Greater love has no one than this; that one lay down his life for his friends. You are My friends if you do what I command you. No longer do I call you slaves, for the slave does not know what his master is doing; but I have called you friends, for all things that I have heard from My Father I have made known to you.' (John 15)

What a remarkable passage this is and, if we are prepared to let Jesus speak to us, it has the capacity to *utterly change our lives*. It's not the idea of sacrifice *per se* that is so remarkable; it is the idea that we are *friends* of Jesus. I hope you have good friends. You probably won't have that many who are really good friends. If you are fortunate you will have a few. With friends, I share all. We laugh, we cry, we speak of our highs and lows, if there is need we do our utmost to help out. There are no secrets between good friends not least because we are *known*; our stories are known, our families are known, we are taken at face value. If we fall asleep in the middle of dinner it probably won't matter overmuch. We can be affectionate, but above all else, we do not have to pretend any more. The masks have no place here. I think highly of my few special friends. I value them and all they do. *I believe in them!*

When I consider that Jesus feels like that about me, it is quite a shock. Do you know that when Jesus calls you 'friend' He is proud to be associated with you? He is proud that you are His friend; that you bother to read about Him each day, want to talk with Him, that you have a desire to say to others, 'Let me tell you about my Friend.' When I flop down tired, He doesn't mind. If I oversleep today and miss my quiet time, He does not raise an eyebrow and cold-shoulder me. Instead, He shares His secrets with me in the car on the way to work. Wow! I am glad to be a friend of Jesus. Somehow it makes life *so* much easier. I am not a fearful, grovelling servant any longer. I don't have to sidle silently into the room, risking His wrath, whilst trying to find a good moment to say, 'Excuse me, but if You have a moment, my Lord, I have a friend of mine here in some significant distress; far be it from me to disturb You my Lord . . .'

Laughable? Not really, for that is how we can be, can't we? Be honest. Jesus says there is one condition for this relationship. What is His command? *'Believe in Me.'*

Dear Jesus, You call me friend. I believe in You. I really do. You have shared everything with me that the Father shared with You; such generosity of Spirit with Your friends. I can relax in Your presence. I honour You with my heartfelt praise, Friend of mine. I am so blessed to know You and, more, to be known by You. Amen.

Day 97 – April 6th

The Gospel of John records many of the most profound teachings of Jesus in the days leading up to His crucifixion (John 14 onwards). One particular point that Jesus emphasised has made a great impact on me; it seems to explain all that we are called to do in His name:

'O righteous Father, although the world has not known You, yet I have known You; and these have known that You sent Me; and I have made Your name known to them, and will make it known, so that the love with which You loved Me may be in them, and I in them.' (John 17)

These are the last teachings of Jesus before He was betrayed and arrested so it is reasonable to put great emphasis on them.

'I have made Your name known . . .' explains the Lord; *'I have declared Your name . . .'* in some versions. To declare someone's name clearly means more than to say, 'This is Jean' or 'This is David'; more than an introduction to the Father! Declaring His name is to make known *all* that He is. '. . . *and'* continues Jesus, *'I will make it known . . .'*

I doubt that He intended us to believe that He would continue to do this only through His remaining days on earth until He dismissed His Spirit on the cross. No! It means much more. *It means that through the Holy Spirit's work in us, we will continue to declare God's name!*

I recall the day I understood that. It was as though ministry in Jesus' name became much clearer for me: we are, no more and no less, *to declare the Father's name*; His character, His ways, in fact *all that He is* will be declared in our every action, our every word, our every kindness, and our every prayer and ministration. People we are with are to come away thinking, *So that is what the Father is like! Now I know!* What an awesome responsibility but, more, how that speaks into our expectation and hope of the Holy Spirit's work in us; the astonishing quality of love that God had for Jesus may be in us until *'I in them'*. We are to be *full* of Christ Jesus. No more, no less.

Father, I long to declare Your name! I know now that I am to be a herald: *'This is Your Father!'* No one will take much notice of me, see me or credit me; they will say, *'Now I know the Father!'* My Lord, take my life, I pray, and through the power and radiance of the Holy Spirit in me, make me a living declaration of You! May that also be a check in my spirit person on the days that I represent anything else but You. Be glorified in me, I pray. Let me be full of Jesus! Amen.

Day 98 – April 7th

Jesus was speaking plainly to His disciples that He came into the world and that He was leaving the world again and going to the Father. The disciples responded that they understood. No figures of speech. No misunderstandings. 'By this we know You came from God,' they concluded.

'Jesus answered them, "Do you now believe? Behold, an hour is coming, and has already come, for you to be scattered, each to his own home, and to leave Me alone; and yet I am not alone, because the Father is with Me. These things I have spoken to you, so that in Me you may have peace. In the world you have tribulation, but take courage; I have overcome the world."' (John 16)

I must admit, I do find it difficult to come to terms with this passage. Not that I don't believe it; I do! The prophetic knowing of Jesus is that He knows the end is near. He had been speaking of this for some time – not incidentally in 'figures of speech'; it seems it had been beyond the disciples to take it on board.

If you have ever had to say painful farewells, you will know what agony of heart it can be. I well remember the evening that our house group gathered, at their own request, to break bread with my late wife and me and to say goodbye, a matter of a week or so before she died. I had my doubts about them managing it without great upset. It *was* painful, as you might imagine. Everyone knew there would be no more meetings together this side of heaven. It was a very peaceful meeting where words were few, but the peace was great. And then the moment came when everyone rose to leave and one by one they hugged, spoke the odd word and left. Alison remained strangely 'other-worldly' is the only way I can describe it. She knew she was going back to her Father. She had total peace. She nodded a good deal and smiled. Words at that stage were too tiring. She was not really with us; somehow her spirit was already anticipating the joy of heaven's embrace.

That was tough but what I read in this passage was that far from being with friends whose faith would keep them with Him and for Him, He was prophesying their scattering and their abandonment of Him. He knew what was in the heart of man. What an incredible agony that could have been. Can you imagine that? But Jesus speaks those words, *'I am alone in this but I am not alone because the Father is with Me.'*

If anything in this world can prepare us for impossible things it is this. Jesus, despite everything, is *still* encouraging them. Despite their fickle faith, if that is not too unkind, these travellers would soon depart Him. But Jesus blesses with peace. Jesus speaks of the troubles ahead for them, as He knew all things, and then speaks the most reassuring words ever, *'Take courage; I have overcome the world.'*

Hear those words today. Set your most dire fears and worries before you, gather them up if you will and make them an offering to the Lord, and hear Him say your name, and repeat to you, *'Take courage; I have overcome the world.'*

Father, today I simply sit before You, in silent awe. Amen.

Day 99 – April 8th

This year I was asked to take a funeral and thanksgiving for a wonderful woman of God. She was quite young with young family. It was immensely sad. Yet, in a strange way, her shortened life in God had been an extraordinary testimony of how drawing close to the Father through all her troubles and her treatment had brought peace and a beautiful worshipping heart which, in turn, deeply affected her lovely family and many friends.

I find it quite daunting to take such services, especially when the person concerned is a friend. Whatever I say, I want it to be authentic and a genuine tribute to the person's journey with God, but also to try to make sense of it all before grieving relatives. It is a nearly impossible task to make sense of such adversity. I am not interested in being trite or simplistic. So, I sat at my desk as soon she and her husband asked me to officiate and I prayed, 'Lord, what would You have me speak on, come the day? It will be so difficult.'

The reply was immediate and clear. It was the most beautiful and succinct summary of all she had been.

'*So teach us to number our days, that we may present to You a heart of wisdom.*' (Psalm 90)

We all knew that she had presented to the Lord her heart of wisdom. There is no translation of this verse which makes any better sense of it. It is exactly as it is. The Lord is saying to us to be aware that every day counts in the kingdom; to value each one and so prioritise God and His ways that our hearts grow and grow until anyone who glimpses our inner places simply responds, *Wow; that is a Father-loving heart that only pursuit of the Lord can have brought about. How beautiful!* When people see such a heart they will yearn for it themselves. They will feel homesick for the Father also. They will crave what you found and want it for themselves, just like the man who found the treasure in the field. It will become a life-priority for them: *I must have that also* . . . 'I need to number my days before this Holy God.'

Father, so many days are spent in relatively trivial pursuits, where time is barely devoted to seeking You. We stress and we strain when all the time You are calling us, '*Come to Me . . . come to Me.*' May our hearts be after You this day, and always, that we will bring delight to You, and others may say, *'I yearn for a heart like that. If Jesus did that, I want Jesus.'* Amen.

Day 100 – April 9th

I have a note in my 'Sanctuary box'; it reads: 'The easy flow of grace amongst His children, crossing thresholds, calling out the outrageous in the gentlest of ways.' That's it. Oh, and a scribble below, 'M 11:25'!

In the context of our season of Pascal pursuit, although this is not an Easter reading, it brings home some wonderful truths.

'At that time, Jesus said, "I praise You, Father, Lord of heaven and earth, that You have hidden these things from the wise and intelligent and have revealed them to infants. Yes, Father, for this way was well-pleasing in Your sight."' (Matthew 11)

That will do for today. We will look at the verses following later. This passage seems to flow out of Jesus' great tribute to John which He spoke after John's own followers brought word from Herod's prisoner, saying, *'Are You the One?'* Jesus' reply was simple to John. He didn't say, 'You are right, my friend, I am the Messiah.' He said instead, *'Go and report to John what you have seen and heard: the blind receive sight, the lame walk, the lepers are cleansed and the deaf hear, the dead are raised up, and the poor have the gospel preached to them'* (Luke 7). Jesus knew that that was all that John, shortly to be killed at the request of an evil woman, needed to hear: *'Kingdom mission accomplished, John. Well done good and faithful Son of the Father'* (my words).

Why was Jesus so thrilled? He had just finished something of a Holy Rant against all those who were so full of themselves; so replete with their theologies and bent belief systems that He needed to shout it out: *Father, you have revealed it to the little infants!* The word used for 'infants' there is *'nēpios'*; it means a toddler who cannot yet speak. It is possible, at a stretch, that it could mean 'a very immature, young believer'. He is making the point that those of simple understanding 'get' the kingdom. It's not difficult! On another occasion, He says the 'prudent' don't get it! I always imagine that the 'prudent' are those who listen and stroke their long noses and say, 'Well, I am not so sure it's that easy, young man . . .' The word 'reveal' means *reveal*! Jesus has 'taken the lid off'; all is in plain view!

And that was well-pleasing to God! It was Father's good pleasure to see the young disciples, full of trust and the simple sincerity of faithful hearts, devoid of deep learning, going out and proclaiming the kingdom.

People just like you and me, I think. *'It's Jesus you need!'*

Father, I am simple of heart. I am not bursting at the seams with deep theology and learning. I hardly know how to speak, but I know a Good Thing when I see it! It makes complete sense to me! You love us and You want to reveal Your love to all mankind and You are sending little me out in Your majestic name to proclaim the Good News. Little me, with a great BIG Father. I will go! Here am I! *'The easy flow of grace amongst His children, crossing thresholds, calling out the outrageous in the gentlest of ways'* . . . Amen.

Day 101 – April 10th

The passage we looked at (Matthew 11) seems to journey from the effervescence of childlike trust to the weariness of adulthood in but a few verses; so Jesus is speaking now:

'Come to Me, all who are weary and heavy-laden, and I will give you rest. Take My yoke upon you and learn from Me, for I am gentle and humble in heart, and you will find rest for your souls. For My yoke is easy and My burden is light.'

This is such a well-known saying of Jesus' but often it is taken at face value and, whilst I am all for doing that, the context here is important. The inference, given that it follows the verse about childlike faith, is that it is not so much about the burdens we think about each day – salary, mortgage, rising costs, sleepless nights – as about our 'faith base'. He had just been speaking so critically about the cities where there was solid resistance to Him and to His teachings!

Surely this is a plea to the 'wise and intelligent'; those whose expectations of a spiritual life had so shrunk that the followers were mired in nothing but manmade religiosity and bookish knowledge. Read the entire chapter and you will see.

'But to what shall I compare this generation? It is like children sitting in the market places, who call out to the other children, and say, "We played the flute for you, and you did not dance; we sang a dirge, and you did not mourn." For John came neither eating nor drinking, and they say, "He has a demon!" The Son of Man came eating and drinking, and they say, "Behold, a gluttonous man and a drunkard, a friend of tax collectors and sinners!"' (Matthew 11)

One can almost hear Jesus say, 'You just can't win, can you?' Adults, when compared to the children who brought Him such delight, are so complicated and they don't know what they want! It's a very contemporary comment. One hears commentators on society lamenting the loss of morality and bemoaning the lack of integrity and wholeness in society today, and then in the next breath being utterly scathing and dismissive of any notion that there might be a spiritual problem! Try mentioning the restorative power of Jesus on some television channels and see what reaction you get!

And so, Jesus speaks truth for those who will hear: take My yoke upon you, not all that stuff you are dragging round. Abandon it! It doesn't work! You will find My spirituality is gentle and, in embracing it, your burdens will fall away . . .

It's really *very* simple. My Father loves you!

His final comment is to say, 'Wisdom is vindicated by her deeds', quoting Jeremiah. *The truth will come out in the end and you will see. One day you will see . . .*

Dear Lord, cleanse my heart of all those dusty, dry belief systems that have no place in my life. Show me what they are, if I have them, and break me free of the chains of captivity. I want Life in my life, Your Life. I want to be one of those little children again. Amen.

Day 102 – April 11th

'Come to Me, all who are weary and heavy-laden, and I will give you rest. Take My yoke upon you and learn from Me, for I am gentle and humble in heart, and you will find rest for your souls.' (Matthew 11)

I am sure that Jesus really does see us when we are labouring under mistaken yokes. We tend to turn this into thoughts of how we *work,* which is only natural given the analogy to a beast of burden. So often the yoke we labour under is not that at all. I think I have probably ministered to more people who are living under an onerous belief system than to those who need to 'change career', so to speak.

I recall the deep anger in a friend who was an intensely intelligent woman with a beautiful character – only that sometimes the anger would appear, almost irrationally, and woe betide anyone in range!

The story had started in childhood when a younger sister was born. She was also a lovely girl but not at all pretty and not at all bright. The girls' mother, who was very keen to avoid the younger sister being crushed by the older sister's bright character and brain, and the resultant praise that was heaped upon her was an attempt, at all costs, to play the achievements of the younger one up and those of the older one down! It was a sort of maternal levelling instinct and thoroughly understandable. The problem was that it became quite extreme; so much so that the older sister was effectively ignored! When she achieved 17 'A' levels and mastered the art of forging Picasso's paintings while walking on the tight-rope (I jest, but you get my drift), the response would come, 'Very good darling, but have you seen what your little sister has done? She has finally achieved her Maths GCSE on the fourth attempt; it's simply wonderful and she is such a clever girl . . .'

We talked a great deal about this and prayed but not much changed. It was a huge burden to bear, going through life feeling that no matter what she did, it would never be enough to gain the attention she craved deep down; attention that would satisfy this deep but not well-understood longing in her life. She became a Christian and that did certainly change her but not this deep, corrupted belief about herself. She was still driven to fury if not recognised. But by what?

One day, for no apparent reason we could determine, Jesus seemed to say, 'Enough!' and gave the heave-ho to a little, angry, raspberry-blowing, foot-stamping, unclean spirit that had hung around since childhood days! Nasty things! Glory, glory! You who are heavy burdened . . . you shall find what? Rest.

Father, I love Your yoke upon me. Your yoke never chafes; it is balanced, even under load. You fit me for what I can bear so when I feel out of balance I ask You, Holy Spirit, is this You? Or am I walking under some hurt or wound or some nasty little thing that is sitting on my shoulder and mocking me, and You in me. O, glorious God, cleanse me and I shall truly be clean! Amen.

Day 103 – April 12th

When I was a little chap in the first year of my primary school, I had a teacher called Mrs Pearson. She was adorable; grey-haired and very kind. I trusted her. One day my mother came to school and was in the classroom talking after school finished. I heard Mrs Pearson say, 'Do you know, I think David has got a hole in the back of his head where the sawdust falls out.'

My mother repeated it to me every time I forgot something. It stuck. I wasn't quite sure what it meant at age five or six, but I was bright enough to know she may well have said, *David is dim; like Noddy . . . wooden head.*

Some of you will be laughing (don't worry, it is quite funny) and half of you will be aghast (don't worry, it is dreadful – but it gets better). We all know that one has to be careful in what we say, especially to children. What was it James said? The power of the tongue is like a rudder on a great ship? *'And the tongue is a fire, the very world of iniquity; the tongue is set among our members as that which defiles the entire body, and sets on fire the course of our life, and is set on fire by hell'* (James 3). Phew!

Well I progressed quite well at school; not many prizes I will admit, and I found studying very tough, especially committing things to memory. I continued at university where I did really well and came out with a very good degree. But it was so tough. I could understand complicated scientific concepts but I couldn't *remember them*. Occasionally, I thought about Noddy or Pinocchio or whoever I was supposed to be, but I never made the connection until much later, in pastoral training, when I was learning Greek.

One day my tutor, a lovely godly man, scratched his head and asked why I struggled so to remember and I said jokingly, 'Oh, I have a hole in the back of my head where—' I stopped.

'Yes,' he encouraged, 'go on.'

So out it came and we stopped the lesson and prayed, and read Scriptures such as Psalm 139. I had God's truth spoken over me that day and, in the name of Jesus, these words so long imprinted on my inner person, were commanded to come off; that I would be free to only hear what my Father said about me. It was a wonderful release! I felt the crushed little David emerge from the hurt.

The truth is we all have garbage like this on board, much of it down to the power of the tongue. King David wrote that, *'My soul is among lions; I must lie among those who breathe forth fire, even the sons of men, whose teeth are spears and arrows and their tongue a sharp sword'* (Psalm 57).

As the Easter readings draw near, I am staggered at how many characters in the story have souls laden with poisonous rubbish (presumably from somewhere in their own damaged stories) and their words changed the course of history for bad and, of course, for good.

Lord Jesus, sometimes I do not realise the power of my tongue to heal. The words I speak in Your name are powerfully creative. They can edify, bring healing, a sense of destiny, break chains and lead people into *life*! They can also do damage which ricochets through a life, belittling and wounding. Lord, may I guard my tongue just as I guard my heart. If I have wounded may I know it and be quick to make amends. Amen.

Day 104 – April 13th

'On the next day the large crowd who had come to the feast, when they heard that Jesus was coming to Jerusalem, took the branches of palm trees and went out to meet Him, and began to shout, "Hosanna! Blessed is He who comes in the name of the Lord, even the King of Israel."' (John 12)

The ordinary folk who came out to greet Jesus as He rode on a donkey, fulfilling the words of the prophet Zechariah, were declaring the truth.

'Save us!' they cried, 'the One who saves!' amidst the shouts of recognition; this was the King! It seems perfect. Perhaps God has accomplished His earthly mission for recognition of the Truth . . .

On the sidelines stood those who were far less convinced and hostile to this 'impostor' figure to whom all the glory was being given.

'The Pharisees said to one another, "You see that you are not doing any good; look the world has gone after Him."' (Luke 12)

The crowds cried out, we are told, as the word had spread from the primary witnesses of Lazarus' resurrection from his tomb. No doubt others were there also; those who had received healing and blessing from the hands of the God-man, the carpenter from Nazareth. But how easy it is to sway people from their recognition of truth and sense and goodness; it is as easy in politics and social disorder and war today, as it was in the lead up to the Feast of Tabernacles. The insidious poison of the leaders driven by such common emotions – fear, jealousy, ignorance and prejudice – gathered pace as, together, they felt safe and convinced in their mutual disapproval, their opinions and narrow beliefs. The words they spoke to one another in secret were death to the King of kings as sure as the nails that were later driven into His hands and feet. Words are powerful. The things that flow out of our mouths in a moment of fear, when we dive for the safety of numbers and the security of familiar friends, can wield the power of destruction and isolation for someone else; someone who is on the outside. Jesus knew men's hearts. He must have heard all that was shouted that day but it seems He was not swayed in the least. A few verses later, we find Jesus ignoring the calls of the Greek Jews who wished to see Him:

'Jesus answered them, saying, "The hour has come for the Son of Man to be glorified. Truly, truly, I say to you, unless a grain of wheat falls into the earth and dies, it remains alone; but if it dies, it bears much fruit."'

Surely Jesus *was* being glorified, wasn't He? The roaring crowds? The palm waving? The fronds scattered on the stony road? No. Jesus' face was set like flint on the route to Calvary; on the glory that His father alone could bestow, and He in turn could bring to the Father.

How easy it is to be swayed by the approval of men. Our eyes must look higher, my friends; gaze on the Perfecter of our faith.

Lord Jesus, You model for me the path to true glory. It lies only through my death and my resurrection in You; no other seal of approval will do except that of the Father. May I know this so profoundly as I seek to minister to those around me. It is easy to seek the ready popularity of those who 'like' me and, equally, to avoid the harsh criticism of those who do not want to know You; who will not want to hear Your words of truth or to walk in the light. May I be found faithful unto the day, Lord God. Amen.

Day 105 – April 14th

Who can imagine that a self-invite to your home could change your life?

'When Jesus came to that place, He looked up and said to him, "Zacchaeus, hurry and come down, for today I must stay at your house." And he hurried and came down and received Him gladly. When they saw it, they all began to grumble, saying, "He has gone to be the guest of a man who is a sinner."' (Luke 19)

We looked at the destructive power of words, but what of the creative?

These words of acceptance changed Zacchaeus' life. He was a chief tax gatherer for the Romans; not a popular man even if he had managed to be straight. Truth be known, he was utterly despised by all and formally rejected by the Temple. The lure of wealth had corrupted him and lost him his faith. The astonishing thing is that this man who was culturally, socially and spiritually taboo territory was won over by Jesus saying, *I want to be with you.*

It's not easy for us to understand how far Zacchaeus was from being accepted. It is equally incomprehensible to appreciate what Jesus did. In our western world, it is not that significant for someone to join us at our supper table. It is quite special, but not overmuch. In the days of Jesus, to be invited to dine was to ask someone to join you in your domestic 'holy place'; the inner sanctuary of the home. When you were invited there, it was as if to say, 'I wish you to become a friend to me; come and fellowship with my family. This will be a beautiful and heart-warming experience.' Jesus, of course, turned it on its head and invited *Himself* into the tax collector's home! I imagine it was Jesus' way of saying, in effect, 'I know you couldn't dream of me accepting if you invited me to your table, so much so that you would not chance the rebuff by asking. But, Zacchaeus, let me take the hit; I really want to be with you. Come down from that daft hiding place. Hurry!'

If you were filled with wonder when you came into a living relationship with Jesus, as I was, you probably spent much time pondering *how did it happen?* To *me?* The impact of knowing that God wants to be with you is life-changing in the extreme. And so it was for Zacchaeus. Before Jesus even articulated 'the three steps to faith' with Zacchaeus, the man was falling over himself to put his life right. The *presence* of the Lord was enough. *'Half of my possessions I will give to the poor, and if I have defrauded anyone of anything, I will give back four times as much.'* My calculations may be awry, but I think he might have bankrupted himself in that moment! *The fruits of repentance!*

Jesus spoke the infamous words over Zacchaeus that day: *'Today salvation has come to this house, because he, too, is a son of Abraham. For the Son of Man has come to seek and to save that which was lost.'*

It seems to me that this speech of Jesus was aimed at the shocked, tut-tutting onlookers. 'You need to know that I *see* this man; do you *see* him? You cast him out, but look now; he *is* a son of Abraham. See him, if you will.' And doubtless, the Pharisees, who we are told, so diligently tithed a precise tenth of all they had, listened in uncomfortable awe. A half? He is giving *a half?* Such is the heartfelt desire in true repentance.

Father, as I picture this story, I see that winning souls is not always about words. Breaking through the walls of rejection, corruption and even great wealth is about scaling them with extravagant, outrageous reflections of the Father's heart, and letting the prisoners out. Give me wisdom, as You had, Jesus, to know when to call, 'Come down . . .' Amen.

Day 106 – April 15th

We will never know what prompted Judas Iscariot to act as he did. It is very profound. Was God on Judas' side, as many have argued? It is true that throughout the Bible the death of the Messiah was prophesied. Someone, surely, had to be responsible for the death of the Saviour. Perhaps we should turn our attention to slightly less unfathomable questions and ask, why did Judas decide to betray the Lord?

'Then one of the twelve, named Judas Iscariot, went to the chief priests and said, "What are you willing to give me to betray Him to you?" And they weighed out thirty pieces of silver to him. From then on he began looking for a good opportunity to betray Jesus.' (Matthew 26)

There are so many threads in the story of Judas, most of which we cannot know this side of heaven. Jesus spent three years with this poor man as a close disciple and, given that we often have considered Jesus' extraordinary insight, He must have known, but clearly did nothing. Was this the ultimate example of the Father staying His hand in order that the earthly mission of Jesus would be fulfilled? I rather think so. Was Judas one of the twelve who came back rejoicing having been ministering in the power of Jesus' authority? We must assume he was.

And what got into Judas? Why was his mind so corrupted? His later regret and the taking of his own life suggest that he had a profound conscience which, for some reason not known to us, was overridden in this tragic episode. What childhood anger against authority figures was at work in him, we wonder?

We do read in our newspapers stories of unfathomable cruelty; of crimes so despicably awful that we recoil from even contemplating them. People just do behave so. But I also know the power of the enemy to corrupt. 'Where are you, Adam?' Remember that moment in the garden?

I once met a man who had wilfully taken another's life in a terrible, premeditated attack. He became a very remarkable Christian. God loved him and found him and brought him home. Such is the love of God for you and for me.

Lord Jesus, there are some events that we just cannot fathom. We know that You are powerful to save and we know that part of Your selfless sacrifice for which You left Your glory and came to live among us, was to make this journey to Golgotha. It seems You knowingly allowed men to walk the dangerous path of turning against You in deceit, such was Your mission to bring the Father's love to mankind. This Easter, I pray that I may be able to understand the depths of Your love for us. Amen.

Day 107 – April 16th

'O that You would slay the wicked, O God; depart from me, therefore, men of bloodshed.'

Strangely, although you may assume that this is one of the imprecatory psalms, it is not; it is a verse from Psalm 139. That's right, our 'comfort' psalm, which begins: *'O LORD, You have searched me and known me . . .'*

Even more strangely, when people choose to read this psalm aloud, I have known them omit these verses, claiming they do not fit, that this portion is somehow arranged awkwardly and mistakenly in the midst of such beautiful writing! This is David coming to terms with the Almighty's utter knowledge of his every part, and the wonder of the Creator's brilliance. As he dwells on the fact that many reject His love and care he realises how he hates their rebellion! They can have no part in his life. David was not a Christian; apart from many other things he was God's anointed; His soldier and warrior. David knew what it was to fight evil men and have their blood on his sword. Although this may raise 'moral' or 'ethical' issues for us (as the imprecatory psalms also do) it was clear for David: hating

God and leading people away from Him was a profound crime and such perpetrators deserved death. We must be careful when we are tempted to 'leave out' certain passages. If we do, we are at risk of saying God was wrong. He wasn't. I suspect our understanding is at fault.

Whether we speak of Zacchaeus, or Judas Iscariot, or King David, or you or me, we have to face up to the truth that the depth of God's knowledge about us is far greater than our own knowledge of our own being. The thrust of David's psalm here is to say, whether high or low, east or west, God knows me. Even when I think parts of me are hidden in the dark, the light of God illuminates them and makes as bright day. 'Hidden from Me' is not a phrase that exists in God's vocabulary. Do you know that? When David cries out, 'Get off me, men of bloodshed. For they speak against You with deep machinations . . .' I believe that he may also be addressing the inner, unhealed parts of his own being that still rebel against God and long for ungodly desires. How many nights have we all, along with Zacchaeus and Judas, spent in turmoil, battling our inner selves, much of which is barely known to us? I can only speak assuredly of myself: many nights!

As we approach the Easter Passion, let us be honest about the achievements of our God nailed to a tree. They are immense! God has redeemed you from the parts that you cannot reach, even in your deepest searching. David thus writes, 'You . . . are intimately familiar with all my ways.' And Paul writes in his first letter to the Thessalonians: 'Now may the God of peace Himself sanctify you entirely; and may your spirit and soul and body be preserved complete, without blame at the coming of our Lord Jesus Christ' (1 Thessalonians 5).

Entirely! Every crumb of your being! God help us if He only redeemed the parts we know of! We may be surprised at the depths of corruption or dark complexity we discover in ourselves; surely, the

Good News of Jesus Christ is that He is not surprised! Not at all!

O my Lord, the realisation that You really do know me is too profound to absorb. Such knowledge is too wonderful for me. How can You still love me? I come to You now, as David did, crying out, 'See if there be any hurtful way in me, and lead every thread of my being into Your everlasting life!' Thank You for the cross, Jesus. Amen.

Day 108 – April 17th

The discovery that we are known can be a very remarkable one. It is a revelation which, during Easter, may take us through the cross of Calvary, into the grave and then out into the resurrection Son-rise of Easter Sunday. It is such a relief to understand that we do not surprise God by our depths. Time and time, we hear of Jesus: 'for He knew what they were thinking', 'for He knew what was in their hearts'. I say it again: the Good News of Jesus is that we are known. The masquerading and the dance of pretence are no longer necessary. *He knows!* Jesus was not surprised by Judas' betrayal, by Peter's broken promise, by Thomas' doubting or by Zacchaeus' inner man. The onlookers were shocked and mightily put out. For Jesus, it was not the revelation of the man's greed that mattered but His need to say, 'It's alright, Zacchaeus, you do not need to hide in that tree where you think I cannot see you. I have always seen you, didn't you know? And I am not shocked, so why don't you come down and take Me to your house. Your days of hiding in the sycamore branches are over. I will show you that My Father and I accept you, and when you know that, My friend, your heart will be restored! In that place of restoration, I have no fear for you. In the love of the Father all that is bent will be made straight again. I see goodness in you and I know that you will do all things well. I have no fears for you, My friend. Come, rest in My love.'

Who could not be changed by that? Is this not a startling revelation to our hearts? We long to be found – but we also dread it. Where are you, Adam? We burst out of the undergrowth crying out, 'My Father, I am here! I long to be found by You. No more hiding! I run to You. I am terrified, but utterly undone by Your goodness to me.'

'For He rescued us from the domain of darkness, and transferred us to the kingdom of His beloved Son, in whom we have redemption, the forgiveness of sins.' (Colossians 1)

My Father, *I understand now.* I understand why You went to the cross. Not only did You choose to pay the price for my sin, all of it, even the depths which I cannot even begin to fathom, but You wanted me to come out into Your glorious light. What a relief to know I can be found without being destroyed, humiliated or diminished. I am Your son. Safe to be real in Your grace and Your love. Amen.

Day 109 – April 18th

The Good News of Being Known has repercussions beyond marvelling at our own cleansing and restoration. The power of it may percolate through into our ministries as we go out in the name of our Lord. No longer will we try to drag unwilling converts into the kingdom; no more do we struggle to persuade people by the scintillating power of our clever words. No, we *call* them, whether by our love, worked out in deeds and blessing, or by the power of the Holy Spirit changing bodies, minds and spirits with the signs that make men and women wonder. Wonder? Yes, wonder. *'Who is this that knows me? Who is this that calls me?'* they will say. Their hearts will long: *I also want to be found! I have heard I can be known!'*

Remember the woman at the well? A despised Samaritan *and* a woman. Surely the Lord would not speak with her, would He? Her life had been very difficult and, depending on how you interpret this story, she has either been greatly put upon to the point of misery, or very unwise. Let us not judge her. But listen to her words to the Lord:

'The woman answered and said, "I have no husband." Jesus said to her, "You have correctly said, 'I have no husband'; for you have had five husbands, and the one whom you now have is not your husband; this you have said truly." The woman said to Him, "Sir, I perceive that You are a prophet."' (John 4)

Later we read, after Jesus had declared to this woman that He was indeed the Messiah, the One she had spoken of and hoped for:

'So the woman left her water pot, and went into the city and said to the men, "Come, see a man who told me all the things that I have done; this is not the Christ, is it?" They went out of the city, and were coming to Him.'

Even later, we read:

'From that city many of the Samaritans believed in Him because of the word of the woman who testified, "He told me all the things that I have done." So when the Samaritans came to Jesus, they were asking Him to stay with them; and He stayed there two days.'

This revival in Samaria happened because of the Ministry of Being Known! The woman was set free when Jesus made it clear that He actually knew *everything about her*! It would seem she was longing to be found!

If you read the story slowly, you will see that Jesus begins with a clear Kingdom proclamation: *'Whoever drinks of the water that I will give Him, shall never thirst; but the water that I will give him will become in him a well of water springing up to eternal life.'* He is reeling her in with his beautiful truth.

As He engages her attention, notice that the emphasis of Jesus is not on sin but on *truth*. He spoke to her a simple word, calling her to focus: *'Go, call your husband.'* We can only guess what this woman lived with: a life full of guilt and shame perhaps? Or a desperately sad life, full of grief and loss?

Nowhere in this story is there mention of sin or forgiveness. I conclude, for various reasons, that she was an innocent woman. I do really (see Luke 20). The fact that we are challenged by the possibility of her innocence says much about us and possibly about how we minister to those we meet on our journey. But the real point of this story is that Jesus *knew* her and it was His extreme prophetic gift used in a tender way which drew her and many others into the kingdom of light. You see, we *long* to be found. Jesus is the Great Finder.

Lord Jesus, I am overwhelmed by the revelation of Your insight into our deepest needs; our longing to be known and found. As I go forth to minister to a broken world there is much I must learn so I invite You, Holy Spirit, to come to me and soften my harshness. Lift from me, I pray, the need to be judgemental and fill me with a spirit of mercy and love and prophetic truth. Amen.

Day 110 – April 19th

To be seen; how wonderful!

'And He was teaching in one of the synagogues on the Sabbath. And there was a woman who for eighteen years had had a sickness caused by a spirit; and she was bent double, and could not straighten up at all. When Jesus saw her, He called her over and said to her, "Woman, you are freed from your sickness." And He laid His hands on her; and immediately she was made erect again and began glorifying God.' (Luke 13)

Such a wonderful story! Picture it. This day is like any Sabbath for this lady: shuffling in, looking at the familiar floor and then life changed, in a moment. I have often wondered if she knew who called her. Did He know *her* name? Had He seen her before? I often think in these stories, Jesus probably did observe these people over a period of time and, in particular, their hearts. There was no kerfuffle with a demon here; it does not say she had one! It tells us she had a sickness caused by a spirit and who knows the origin of that negative spirit?

Many years ago, a colleague had four lovely young daughters. I didn't know them but had heard a great deal about one of them,

Becca, who had very severe curvature or scoliosis of the spine. It was so serious that major surgery was anticipated. Initially she was to be placed in a body brace to try to ameliorate some of her worst symptoms. Becca, I was told, not surprisingly for a girl in her young teens, was extremely upset at the prospect. Her father knew I was a Christian and I had been very open that we had started to see healings happening in our services. One day he caught me just as we were leaving school and asked if he could bring her for some prayer. I replied that they were all always welcome to come. But he said, 'No, I feel we should come to your house. She is very shy about it all. We don't go to church, as you know. I don't really believe, if I'm honest. I don't know if she will come but I might drop the suggestion into a suitable conversation.'

I had barely got home and made a cup of tea when the doorbell rang and there stood Becca and her father. I welcomed them and took them to a quiet room away from the hubbub of my own family and spoke briefly about prayer; that it is Jesus we invite to come and not healing hands or anything like that. I asked if I might lay my hand on her head, and she agreed. The moment I touched her, she trembled and then very slowly and gracefully slid to the floor, supported by us. This was not something that I had seen much at that time and, truth be known, I was a little concerned, especially for her back.

I knelt and spoke to her reassuringly and continued to bless her. She just smiled when I asked her if she was alright. After about five minutes she made to get up. When she stood, she was barely able to speak and just hugged her dad, telling him quietly that her back had been moving around while she rested. I asked if they would be able to tell if her back had physically changed and was told, in no uncertain terms, that they would. David added, 'You have no idea how bad her scoliosis is!' Sparing her blushes, I suggested that they went to the cloakroom to see. When they returned they were just ablaze with happiness. Her spine was quite straight!

It is a remarkable story that changed the course of a girl's life – and mine, I might add. I was more and more convinced that we didn't need to work up a lather in healing prayer but instead rest in the deep knowing that Jesus *sees* us. Jesus had seen her, and she knew it.

Lord Jesus, I praise You for Your heart of compassion and Your spontaneous ways. You really set my spirit on fire! Thank You for this young woman's healing and for all You are doing in her life. Thank You again that You see us and know our every need. Glory to You, Father, Son and Holy Spirit. Amen.

Day 111 – April 20th

The so-called High Priestly Prayer sayings of Jesus (John 16), spoken after the Last Supper, are very remarkable and worthy of our closest attention. There is one moment, recorded by Luke, which really catches my spirit as I picture the scene. Remember that there had been several disputes between the disciples as to which one was the most significant. Really? Yes, really. They were just like us!

'And He said to them, "The kings of the Gentiles lord it over them; and those who have authority over them are called 'Benefactors'. But it is not this way with you, but the one who is the greatest among you must become like the youngest, and the leader like the servant. For who is greater, the one who reclines at the table or the one who serves? Is it not the one who reclines at the table? But I am among you as the one who serves."' (Luke 22)

There is so much in the Christian life today that is a far-stretch from this radical teaching. It was entirely radical then in religious circles and may I respectfully suggest it continues to be quite radical now.

I am among you as the one who serves. I have washed your feet as the youngest one would do; if you do that you will be the greatest, and if you serve at table and are prepared to clean up after everyone, yes, you can be a leader for Me. I have served you in this way. I have been your leader. Watch Me. I wonder what the squabbling disciples thought after that gentle, profound rebuke. But Jesus never leaves people down. He constantly affirms them; He holds out promise to grow us:

'You are those who have stood by Me in My trials; and just as My Father has granted Me a kingdom, I grant you that you may eat and drink at My table in My kingdom, and you will sit on thrones judging the twelve tribes of Israel.'

That is quite extraordinary. Imagine hearing that word, personally, for you, from the mouth of the Lord! It is a truly awesome moment and so easy for us, in our familiarity with these readings, to gloss over. After arguing among themselves, perhaps, as to who had the greatest reputation for miracles, what would one say? I can only guess that the events of that evening left the disciples' heads spinning, although of course, as we know, there was more to come. Much more.

Lord Jesus, as I contemplate all of this, I sense nothing but Your grace saturating every moment; grace and hope. Even in this moment of nearing an appalling time You are turned outward, giving and giving and still giving. You truly are the Servant King, and I worship You. Amen.

Day 112 – April 21st

The evening of the Last Supper moved on into the next day after the foot-washing and, far from concerns and affirmations of what was to be in the heavenly realms, the conversation moves on to profound earthly matters; the events that must befall them before that day at the banquet table.

'Simon, Simon, behold, Satan has demanded permission to sift you like wheat; but I have prayed for you, that your faith may not fail; and you, when once you have turned again, strengthen your brothers.' (Luke 22)

I find it difficult to imagine what Simon Peter felt on hearing this. It is interesting to note that Jesus calls him by his old name: Simon, the Reed.

I have had some roller-coaster evenings but I think this must have been like nothing else imaginable. Peter, unable to comprehend what the Lord is saying, speaks from his heart:

'He said to Him, "Lord, with You I am ready to go both to prison and to death!" And He said, "I say to you, Peter, the cock will not crow today until you have denied three times that you know Me."'

To analyse this would be to demean it. This is a total crisis for Peter. And, can we be honest? It could have been me, or it could have been you.

Lord Jesus, You see all things as they will be. I feel the pain of speaking these words to such an enthusiastic and otherwise loving and loyal friend. It is the beginning of the Father staying His hand that what must be will be and, as horrendous as the thought is, Peter needed this to happen to make him the man of the destiny You had prepared for him. Lord, You know all things and the thought shakes me. I trust You to bring me through my dark valley times. Amen.

Day 113 – April 22nd

I am always deeply moved by the prophetic of God throughout history as it points towards Jesus. It takes my breath away that men and women of God, who had no natural knowledge of what was to come (as we do, of course, retrospectively), were so moved by God as to make accurate prophetic utterances concerning the day of His coming and the indescribable significance of His life. Entire lives revolved around this sole mission. One such person was the elderly man Simeon, who we are told was devout and God-fearing, and that it had been revealed to him that he would not die until he had *seen* the Messiah with his own eyes!

When Jesus was just eight days old, his parents made the journey to Jerusalem as was the custom in the Law.

'And he [Simeon] came in the Spirit into the temple; and when the parents brought in the child Jesus, to carry out for Him the custom of the Law, then he took Him into his arms, and blessed God, and said, "Now Lord, You are releasing Your bond-servant to depart in peace, according to Your word; for my eyes have seen Your salvation, which You have prepared in the presence of all peoples, a light of revelation to the Gentiles, and the glory of Your people Israel."' (Luke 2)

What a story this tells. This man has longed before God, probably for many, many years. He prayed for the *consolation*, the *comfort* of Israel. This is the prophet's heart: to perceive what is lacking and to bring it before God and then to hear from Him. He knew he would actually set eyes upon the One. Wow! And in the Spirit, he needed no further prompting. He saw.

He spoke to the parents, Mary and Joseph:

'And His father and mother were amazed at the things which were being said about Him. And Simeon blessed them and said to Mary His mother, "Behold, this Child is appointed for the fall and rise of many in Israel, and for a sign to be opposed – and a sword will pierce even your own soul – to the end that thoughts from many hearts may be revealed."'

Imagine, if you can, the thoughts of His parents' hearts. They were simple, devout people effectively thrust centre-stage of the world's greatest-ever earth-shattering event. It is not an edifying prophecy to receive, at least in one sense, but it is God speaking His truth: *You need to know this . . .*

As we come to the Easter Passion, this good woman had to watch at the cross, and it is John again who records the moment of the sword's thrust.

'But standing by the cross of Jesus were His mother, and His mother's sister, Mary the wife of Clopas, and Mary Magdalene. When Jesus then saw His mother, and the disciple whom He loved standing nearby, He

said to His mother, "Woman, behold, your son!" Then He said to the disciple, "Behold, your mother!" From that hour the disciple took her into his own household. After this, Jesus, knowing that all things had already been accomplished, to fulfil the Scripture, said, "I am thirsty."' (John 19)

We can only guess at the savage loss felt by each of these women at that moment. God stayed His hand for you and for me that all might be fulfilled. In this moment, the purposes of God were 'filled full'. *Nothing* could be added or deducted now. The 'giving' of His mother to John, and John to His mother, was the last, ultimate sign of family trust.

Lord God, we stand at the foot of the cross watching the blood being shed for all mankind, but as we do so, *we* know that the power of the resurrection Spirit of God was to break out not long after. For these and so many people who suffer, not understanding the fullness of Your purposes in their lives, we pray, and like Simeon, we long before You for the fullness of the resurrection Son-rise on their lives. Thank You for Your unutterable devotion to us, Your people. We praise Your holy name. Amen.

Day 114 – April 23rd

In our final reflection on this side of Easter, I am pondering Joseph of Arimathea and Nicodemus; two secret admirers of Jesus who now step out into the light.

'And after these things,' (that Scripture had been fulfilled to every detail . . . 'not a bone of Him shall be broken' and 'they shall look on Him whom they pierced'), 'Joseph of Arimathea, being a disciple of Jesus, but a secret one for fear of the Jews, asked Pilate that he might take away the body of Jesus; and Pilate granted permission. So he came and took away His body. Nicodemus, who had first come by night, also came, bringing a mixture of myrrh and aloes, about a hundred pounds weight. So they took the body of Jesus and bound it in linen wrappings *with the spices, as is the burial custom of the Jews . . . they laid Jesus [in the tomb].'* (John 19)

We can only surmise what went on in the minds of these two men. Was it perhaps the depths of their loss that caused them to set aside any further risk to themselves? It seems to me that in this hour they rose up 'to be counted', we might say. It is a strange phenomenon, the world over, that persecution brings out courage and strength. It is also clear by their absence that the disciples were not able to perform these ritual tasks for their Lord. It says many things about some of the characters but for these two, they served their Lord in the only way they now knew. The grave linens with which they so carefully bound the Messiah were soon to be left, cast aside, startlingly empty. Jesus had no place for them, in life or death.

Lord Jesus, when I really stop to think about each of the characters in the accounts of Your crucifixion, I realise how little I know. As these two men lovingly placed Your body in Your borrowed tomb, I wonder what was in their minds. God of Hope, You do not disappoint. You are ever faithful and You do what You say You will do. You are the Accomplisher of all things. I pray today that in those places and times of desperation I may be to others a sign for You; a living signpost of hope. Jesus, You are the Hope of my heart. Amen.

Day 115 – April 24th

Jesus died on the cross to save mankind from sin. But what does that really mean? St Paul, writing in Romans, tells us:

'Therefore, just as through one man sin entered into the world, and death through sin, and so death spread to all men, because all sinned . . . So then as through one transgression there resulted condemnation to all men, even so through one act of righteousness there resulted justification of life to all men. For as through the one man's disobedience the many were made sinners, even so through the obedience of the One the many will be made righteous.' (Romans 5)

I have taken two verses there and joined them since Paul in the intermediate verses expands on his theme. Now, remember Adam? *'Where are you?'* God called to him, knowing that there had been a very fundamental shift in their relationship. This is basic to understanding the death of Christ on the cross of Calvary. We might say that in that moment of disobedience with the forbidden fruit, however you choose to understand that, there was a change of disposition; man was *disposed* to view God very differently (and also disposed to view sin differently as well). Man, in effect said, *'I heard what You said, God, but I have chosen to go my own way. I don't need You.'*

The nature of sin that Jesus dealt with on the cross was our fundamental disposition to God. Jesus, through the shedding of His own blood, by His once and for all sacrifice, effectively rehabilitated man to God. He put the entire human race into the place of redemption. He undid that very foundational problem of the immense gulf between us and God. We can be back where God intended us to be before that Garden of Eden cataclysmic mistake. That is why the curtain in the Temple was torn in two. *Everyone can enter renewed union with the Father* through Jesus' death. That is finished. Jesus cried out, *'It is finished.'* Make no mistake, the universe experienced a shattering shift on that 'Good Friday', Passover weekend!

'And behold, the veil of the temple was torn in two from top to bottom; and the earth shook and the rocks were split. The tombs were opened, and many bodies of the saints who had fallen asleep were raised.' (Matthew 27)

What a fulfilment! That is some 'finish'! It was possible now, through the redemption for man, to live without sin! Yes! And before Jesus physically was resurrected, He went down in spirit to Hades and made a proclamation there also: *'It is finished!'* I imagine He declared. The Battle of the Ages is won! He effectively took back the keys of hell from the evil one. Hand them over! 'It is finished.' The Fall is undone! It was a momentous weekend in the heavenly realms.

But note well, the change in history wrought on the cross does not lead to some sort of universal salvation. Whether we receive that offer of being saved *is up to us.* Salvation is based on our own personal decision. We will be barely conscious of, or changed by what Jesus did unless we personally receive Him. It's no good just knowing about Jesus, or even being moved by the tragedy of His death; we must meet with the Lord, profess our personal sorrow for going our own way, and agree to change. Our old rebellious person must die! He must become the *Lord of His new life in me.* Remember my dear friend Enid (February 10th), who had all her life gone to church but no one had ever told her she needed to make a personal response to the offer of forgiveness and new life?

Father, sometimes we become so myopic. We see redemption in terms of our own lives only. Redemption was truly amazing and You are a truly amazing God to us, Your creation! All of that happened so that the great desire of Your heart might be fulfilled; that we might have our destiny brought back in line with Your wonderful first choice for us. Yes, my Lord, I run to You this day and accept Your grace gift of new and eternal life in Christ! Fill me with Your Holy Spirit, afresh today, I pray. Amen.

Day 116 – April 25th

Probably, we are all familiar with what is likely to be the most well-known verse in Scripture:

'For God so loved the world, that He gave His only begotten Son, that whoever believes in Him shall not perish, but have eternal life. For God did not send the Son into the world to judge the world, but that the world might be saved through Him.' (John 3)

This is the heart of the Good News. God loved us so much that He sent Jesus. There is a piece of punctuation that crops up there and whilst not right or wrong (there was none in the original Greek) it can trip us up. It can be explained by a different wording: *God loved the world that much that He sent His only begotten Son . . .* in other words: *That's how God loved! Yes! That much!*

We can alter the sense, especially with our over use of the word 'so' in modern idiom that we do not realise what John is trying to say to us: 'You want to know how much God loved us? I will tell you all, He loved us *that* much!'

Then follows an important sentence that is often missed:

'He who believes in Him is not judged; he who does not believe has been judged already, because He has not believed in the name of the only begotten Son of God.'

If you don't believe then you *are under judgement.* Make no mistake, before you believed and gave Your life to Christ and made Him Your personal Lord, *you also were under judgement.* The world is under judgement! People need to be told this. Judgement is not something that God will do one day; it is in place right now. Let's read the next verse:

'This is the judgement,' (or the ruling), *'that the Light has come into the world, and men loved the darkness rather than the Light, for their deeds were evil.'*

Jesus' death brought a mighty change. The Light came and those who turn to the Light will have that existing judgement lifted from them the moment they turn to the Saviour. It is a gloriously great Good News, and if you think I am being robust about it all, it is because God is. Jesus is. The Holy Spirit is. So are John and Peter and Paul and many others. It is the Truth, my friends.

My Lord Jesus, I see now that I was in such a dreadful and precariously dangerous place before You called me. Thank You, Holy Spirit, for speaking to me of my deep need for salvation. Thank You that the Saviour Jesus opened the gates of glory and made it possible to be welcomed in. May I go out to tell others that what You did for me may also be theirs by Your grace and loving kindness. Amen.

Day 117 – April 26th

'All the nations will be gathered before Him; and He will separate them from one another, as the shepherd separates the sheep from the goats; and He will put the sheep on His right, and the goats on the left. Then the King will say to those on His right, "Come, you who are blessed of My Father, inherit the kingdom prepared for you from the foundation of the world."' (Matthew 25)

This will happen as surely as you are reading this book! Everyone gathered! Imagine that. As an aside, do you know what? At that moment, *everyone* is going to believe! There will be no exceptions! Jesus spoke about sheep and goats because people really understood that analogy. It is slightly lost on us. In the Middle East, you knew the difference! A sheep is a sheep. There does not exist a sort-of-sheep, not as one might legitimately be confused by a mule and a horse. Sheep were infinitely more valuable than goats and when separating the flocks, which often happened because both were out at pasture together, there was a time of clean separation. And note that the goats who went 'Baaa, I am really am a sheep,' received short shrift from the shepherd. There's a judgement in place: sheep are this, and goats are that. So they understood this when Jesus spoke of the kingdom; God meant business. Whether sheep or goats, they *all* came face to face with the shepherd and his crook.

What does the King say to the sheep? *'Come, you who are blessed of My Father . . .'* A translation of 'blessed' in that context might be 'spoken well of'. Through the redemptive power of the Great Shepherd, we who once looked like goats are transformed. We not only *look* like sheep, we *are* sheep, through and through. We have been changed. The Father speaks well of us; perhaps as He surveys those on His right He says, 'To me, they look just like Jesus . . . inherit the kingdom that has been prepared since . . . page 1, Genesis chapter 1, verse 1.'

Father of the flock, I thank You that You transformed me. You didn't tinker with my head, or just give me a hope; You totally changed me. Thank You that You went after me all over those rocky slopes in my goat days. I was foolish and lost but You brought me home. Thank You that the promise of the kingdom is and will be fulfilled by Your grace and Your faithfulness. Amen.

Day 118 – April 27th

If you are discouraged sometimes by the world we live in, it's worth reading the Parable of the Tares Among the Wheat. Tares are like wheat but not wheat; rather akin to wild oats and oats. Wild oats are no use as they produce no fruit to speak of.

'The kingdom of heaven may be compared to a man who sowed good seed in his field. But while his men were sleeping, his enemy came and sowed tares among the wheat, and went away. But when the wheat sprouted and bore grain, then the tares became evident also.' (Matthew 13)

Not surprisingly the workers spotted this annoying extra crop and questioned the farmer, so he explained what had happened. They wanted to clean the fields of these rogue plants but the farmer said, 'Let's wait, otherwise you are likely to disturb the healthy, desirable plants as you uproot the others. At the end, we will get rid of them.'

Whether sheep and goats or tares and wheat, there will be a separation in the end but, meantime, it is painful sometimes watching how ungodly behaviour and dreadful evil seems to prevail. It's an interesting thing that wild oats always grow faster and a little taller than the real oats. They stand out. They have learned, in biological terms, that to be successful they must drop seed before the harvester rips them up. Watching evil succeed, and make no mistake it does, at least for now, is incredibly frustrating and often sickening. But I do believe that the Father in His great love stays His hand. Some of the goats or tares will become sheep! His heart is that not one should be lost. I know. You and I would just go, 'Bam!' Finish! Fortunately, the Father is much kinder and more merciful than any of us. But it reminds me of the psalmist who wrote:

'For the wicked boasts of his heart's desire, and the greedy man curses and spurns the LORD. The wicked, in the haughtiness of his countenance, does not seek Him. All his thoughts are, "There is no God." His ways prosper at all times; Your judgements, are on high out of his sight. As for all his adversaries, he snorts at them. He says to himself, "I will not be moved."' (Psalm 10)

But the psalm finishes beautifully speaking of this man's end but, more significantly, making reference to the things that are close to God's heart, saying that God hears the humble desire, He strengthens humble hearts and 'brings justice to the poor and the oppressed'.

Great Father of mine, You are so wise and kind when I would be harsh. I will content myself that You do know what You are doing. Meanwhile I will serve the weak and the poor and the downtrodden as a reflection of Your heart to them. At the end, Lord, vengeance is Yours, not mine, and I remind myself that I am here by Your great grace. Amen.

Day 119 – April 28th

I remind myself today of those wonderful words of the prophet Jeremiah speaking words of truth as he looked forward in his spirit towards the day when the people of God would return from their terrible experiences in Babylonian exile.

'They shall be My people, and I will be their God; and I will give them one heart and one way, that they may fear Me always, for their own good and for the good of their children after them. I will make an everlasting covenant with them that I will not turn away from them, to do them good; and I will put the fear of Me in their hearts so that they will not turn away from Me. I will rejoice over them to do them good

and will faithfully plant them in this land with all My heart and all My soul.' (Jeremiah 32)

And God continues to speak through the prophet as to how He brought this disaster on them but the future is one of permanence and establishment in His goodness.

Father, thank You that we live in the goodness of that covenant which is still being worked out and yet to fully come. In my heart, You cause me to reverence You. I feel it! I do love to live in that place of reverencing You, but I ask, Holy Spirit, that on my lazy days when I do not make the effort to touch Your heart and delight You with my worship, that You would fill me afresh and cause me to run after You! Amen.

Day 120 – April 29th

'While they still could not believe it because of their joy and amazement, He said to them, "Have you anything here to eat?"' (Luke 24)

The accounts of the immediate resurrection days are so delightful to read! I can look at them over and over because it fills my spirit with life! This expression from Luke speaks so much; they could not believe it for joy and amazement! Life sometimes is like that – but not often! We can only guess at the desperation they had experienced. The beloved Messiah gone; a limp and bloodied body shrouded and laid in a tomb. The end. Total perplexity; what to do next? The urge of men, filled with utter numbing disappointment, to go back to their fishing boats. There was a great deal of fear also, I imagine; might the disciples be rounded up? They kept the doors locked and barred.

And then word rumbles around; something so remarkable has happened, but it is taking them to the extreme edge of their capacity to believe. The Lord has risen and has appeared to some of the women! And then somehow the story flows out and quite suddenly

Jesus is in their midst!

But is it Him? It appears to be, and in the verse above we see the shock and joy and disbelief, and the complete normality of a friend wanting food, all rolled into one. *Do you have anything to eat?* We can almost imagine Jesus saying, 'Come on guys, I'm famished!'

If you take my nudge and look at the Gospel accounts of these few days you will come up with your own favourite, moving moments. They are not without humour, either!

'And he said to them, "O foolish men and slow of heart to believe in all that the prophets have spoken!"' (Luke 24)

I can fully understand how the disciples had not dared to believe. Imagine if they had been expecting the resurrection: 'It's day one, today . . . day two . . . so maybe by the day after the Sabbath . . .' It is worthy of note that *nobody expected this.* The words of Jesus might be translated, *'O you sensory men, how un-hasty of heart you all are.'* Sensory? Yes, because it seems to me that Jesus might be saying, *'You can only believe what your senses tell you that you can believe. If you can touch it, see it . . . You are so un-supple in your thinking!'* And may I suggest that Jesus could level that at most of us. The radical supernatural moves of God do defy the senses and the sense.

I recall taking someone to a meeting where a miraculous healing took place when a blind eye was restored; one that was so instantaneous and utterly visible that the person I took said afterwards, quite simply, 'There has to be some other explanation!'

'Then He opened their minds to understand the Scriptures . . .'

'Then their eyes were opened and they recognised Him; and He vanished from their sight.'

'And He said to them, "What are these words that you are exchanging with one another as you are walking?" . . . One of them, named Cleopas, answered and said to Him, "Are You the only one visiting Jerusalem and unaware of the things which have happened here in these days?" And He said to them, "What things?"'

Is Jesus displaying a great sense of humour or is He showing them something profound? Throughout Jesus' earthly life, He was with His Father in the Spirit in a way that must have been unfamiliar to Him in the glorious place He left. He had to learn to recognise the Father's voice to Him on earth as Son of Man. Is He now showing the disciples that they also would need to recognise Him and listen for Him in a new way? I think so.

And finally, most movingly of all, the moment when Jesus spoke but one word – *'Mary'* – which defies all elucidation.

I can only suggest that you sit quietly and wait for the risen Lord Jesus to speak *your* name.

Lord Jesus, I am caught up in the midst of this helter-skelter journey that these men and women were travelling. I can hardly believe it either, for joy and for amazement. But it is not just history; it is also *now* as You appear in every imaginable way to Your followers and seekers today. O, my Lord of Lords. I worship You. Amen.

Day 121 – April 30th

Given the nature of the resurrection accounts in the Gospels, that Jesus moves among the disciples unexpectedly appearing and disappearing as He wishes, I realise I must expect the unexpected of the Lord in my life and in ministry. At that time, the risen Lord had but one body, a body that continued to be physical even though it was not His previous, Son of Man body as they had all known it. Normal bodies do not pass through doors and walls. John wants us to fully understand this and twice records the sudden appearance of Jesus in the room behind closed doors. The first occasion was Easter Sunday evening. He is very specific about the times.

'When it was evening on that day, the first day of the week, and when the doors were shut where the disciples were, for fear of the Jews, Jesus came and stood in their midst and said to them, "Peace be with you." And when He had said this, He showed them both His hands and

His side. *The disciples then rejoiced when they saw the Lord. So Jesus said to them again, "Peace be with you; as the Father has sent Me, I also send you."'* (John 20)

And again, He appears:

'After eight days His disciples were again inside, and Thomas with them. Jesus came, the doors having been shut, and stood in their midst and said, "Peace be with you."'

I value that He appears and speaks the *shâlôm* of God over them. That is what He chooses to do: speak peace.

The words of Jesus which I would also like us to focus on today are simple ones that speak directly to us. Thomas did not believe the accounts he had received from the others, stating that unless he saw for himself, indeed touched the wounds of Jesus, he would not believe. When Jesus does appear and Thomas is present, Jesus gently rebukes him and then speaks.

'Because you have seen Me, have you believed? Blessed are they who did not see, and yet believed.' (John 20)

And that, my friends, is for you and me. You are blessed today as you believe that the Lord is risen. Jesus says so.

My Lord and my God, these accounts are wonderful and startling. They speak to us of the ways of heaven; that death could not hold You down; that eternity beckons the Lord of Life, and us also who are sons and daughters of the everlasting King because we believe. May I be filled with the thrill and expectation of the eye witnesses and may this be the reality of my life in You, Lord Jesus. Amen.

MAY

Day 122 – May 1st

The account of Jesus meeting some of the disciples on the beach after His resurrection is surely one of the most beautiful, natural but spiritually super-charged stories imaginable! Seven of them had gone fishing and returned, as was their habit, in the early morning. There have been many things written about this passage, recorded in John's Gospel, theorising about why they went back to their boats. It seems that it may have been that they needed food for themselves and their families. It does not indicate that they had gone back because they were intending to adopt their profession again as a way of life. Simon Peter simply says, 'I am going fishing,' and the others said, 'We will come with you.' And so, the scene is set for a very remarkable meeting.

When they return to the beach, nets devoid of a catch, and a voice calls to them, *'Children, you do not have any fish, do you?'* they explain that it had been a fruitless night. The command came back across the water, *'Cast the net on the right-hand side of the boat and you will find a catch.'* (John 21)

Once again, we see Jesus meeting their needs and setting their spirits on fire with the most natural of miracles for a group of fishermen. The net was nearly splitting and we are told that, once again, the Fisherman and Lord of all creation had commanded the fish into their net. There were one hundred and fifty-three but John tells us, *'the net was not torn'*.

John recognises that it is the Lord; those words carrying across the water, surely spoke volumes. John speaks to Peter who flings himself over the side of the boat to reach the beach where the Lord sits by a charcoal fire with bread and fish prepared. This story is laden with many threads which may come to you as you pray over it, so today I am going to suggest that you do just that.

Holy Spirit, as I sit with this now and imagine this scene, speak to me, I pray, of all the little details of life-changing proportions that are scattered generously through this story for us to see. Bless God for the wonder of the Living Word. Amen.

Day 123 – May 2nd

'Jesus said to them, "Come and have breakfast."' (John 21)

What more life-affirming, non-religious, memorable word could Jesus have spoken to His friends than that one? I appreciate it does not say more than that in Scripture, but to me it seems that Jesus might have been saying to them, 'You have had a battering in these last days and I know you went out to catch enough food to keep yourselves, but I want to say, "Guys, I am still here for you. Nothing has changed. Look at all these fish! Wasn't that so simple? Abide in Me." Now let's eat together as we always have done, in this beautiful spot on this perfect morning. I so enjoy being with you all again.' Am I being fanciful, or do you glimpse that also?

I recall once after a particularly frenetic time in my own life, I went on a retreat and had a long time of prayer with some faithful partners. I had a strong image come to me of sitting with the Father. We were sitting on each side of a huge fireplace in an old cottage with oak beams and everything that was needed to create an extraordinarily friendly, homely and relaxed scene. The fire was warm and the chairs delightfully comfortable. Jesus came in and leant affectionately on the back of His Father's arm chair and spoke with Him. Father smiled in response. I had the feeling that I should get up and leave, not least to offer Jesus my chair, but He waved me to stay put and smiled.

There was a suggestion of getting a cup of tea (I know, it sounds ridiculous), and my immediate reaction was to jump up to go to the kitchen that I might wait on them and honour them. At that moment, an indescribable Presence entered the scene and said that I should stay with the Father while He, the Holy Spirit, fetched tea for us all! However silly that may seem, deep in my spirit I came away with a sense that Father, Son and Holy Spirit really do desire to 'partner' with us and not lord it over us as we so often feel they must surely do. I learned something that day about letting God look after us sometimes, and not always be rushing around after Him in a desperate 'must do or the world will fall apart' way. It was very affirming and did speak powerfully to my heart condition.

Father, as I reflect on this beach scene with You, and also my own personal vision, I realise with delight that You desire to partner with us and do homely things with us. *You are our Father! A real Father!* Holy Spirit, thank You for this revelation of how You all long to be with us; to enjoy our company and have fun. Lord God, I love You. Thank You that I have a place in Your home. Amen.

Day 124 – May 3rd

Try as hard as I can, I cannot help but feel that as Peter leapt over the side of his fishing boat to reach the Lord sitting by the charcoal fire, he may, even in mid-air, have suddenly thought, with a little trepidation, of what was to come.

'*So when Simon Peter heard that it was the Lord, he put his outer garment on (for he was stripped for work), and threw himself into the sea. But the other disciples came in the little boat, for they were not far from the land.*' (John 21)

Any of us who have made a real mess-up know that there is likely to be an uncomfortable moment of reckoning. As far as we know from Scripture, there had been no reference to the night when Peter denied knowing the Lord.

'*The slave girl who kept the door said to Peter, "You are not also one of this man's disciples, are you?" He said, "I am not." . . . Now Simon Peter was standing and warming himself. So they said to him, "You are not also one of His disciples, are you?" He denied it, and said, "I am not." One of the slaves of the high priest, being a relative of the one* whose ear Peter cut off, said, "Did I not see you in the garden with Him?" Peter then denied it again, and immediately a cock crowed.' (John 18)

This must be one of the worst moments in the history of men's encounters with God but, and it is a huge 'but', we know that God restored him and from that point Peter went from strength to strength in His love and single-minded service of the Lord. May I let you all into a profound truth? We all must discover the end of ourselves before we are truly born into new life in the Lord. We will always make mistakes, sin, and need forgiveness; all of that is covered in the profound redemptive power of the cross. But what happened to Peter is different; it seems to be a matter less about sin and more about self-realisation. We all need to know just how weak we are, how strength-less to do good, to be good and to live for the Lord, apart from His grace and power. We all go through a time of crashing to the ground and being lovingly restored to our feet. After that, I suggest, we have a different poise.

Lord God, how many times have I disowned Your rule and Your rights on my life? When I sin, I effectively turn to You and say, 'In this moment I shall say, "I do not know Him."' Forgive me, Jesus. I know what I might be without You and I know how powerless I am outside of Your empowering presence. I stand in Your grace, Lord. Your amazing grace. Amen.

Day 125 – May 4th

And so, breakfast over, Jesus speaks to Peter. It does not tell us here that He took Peter aside, or talked in private, it simply says that He spoke to him. The implication is that Jesus completed the restoration of Peter in front of his friends. I believe that needed to happen, for their sakes and most definitely for his. They needed to hear this precious exchange:

'So when they had finished breakfast, Jesus said to Simon Peter,

"Simon, son of John, do you love Me more than these?" He said to Him, "Yes, Lord; You know that I love You." He said to him, "Tend My lambs." He said to him a second time, "Simon, son of John, do you love Me?" He said to Him, "Yes, Lord; You know that I love You." He said to him, "Shepherd My sheep." He said to him the third time, "Simon, son of John, do you love Me?" Peter was grieved because He said to him the third time, "Do you love me?" And he said to Him, "Lord, You know all things; You know that I love You." Jesus said to him, "Tend my sheep."' (John 21)*

There are and will be many debates surrounding this most sensitive encounter with God. One assumes that Jesus asked Peter three times because he had denied the Lord three times. It's not an unreasonable position to adopt. The sin that Peter had committed against the Lord at His most vulnerable time, probably in His hearing, was immense. His restoration, however, began the moment the cock crowed when he wept. It is said by tradition that in Peter's life he could not hear a cockerel crow without weeping. We cannot know the truth of that but such was his regret that we recognise it may have been so. The conversation above is the final moment of restoration, which began in the courtyard when Peter wept.

It is worth mentioning that the Greek words used here for 'love' are different in the questions and the responses and it can be argued from that that we might understand more of what is going on in this moment. Others argue that the words were not available in the original spoken language. Whatever the explanation, it is clear that Jesus is challenging Peter's capacity to love his Lord more than others might. Jesus doesn't need to hear Peter say it; He knows all things! He asks Peter so that Peter may confess it, and hear himself doing so, and be heard by the others. Confession and declaration of truth are powerful weapons and can be used to defeat the enemy who might otherwise have plagued Simon Peter all his life – *'Remember, Reedy one, how you hid in the shadows and cursed and said, "I don't know*

Him.'" Such is the filthy, degraded nature of Satan. Such is the love of the Almighty Father that He will not leave us in that place of misery and shame. He raises us up! Peter's confession of love is enough for the Lord. He can work with that!

The most important point I take to myself from this is that whatever appalling hurt Peter may have caused in turning away in denial of the Lord, the mercy and goodness of God is that He did not do the same to Peter. Or you, or me.

Jesus, Your wisdom in all things astounds me. Your everlasting love, through which You express life-changing forgiveness, causes me to know that I can come out of the shadows and confess to You when things go wrong. You stand me on my feet and set me on the path of life once more. Thank You that You never look away to disown me. You are constant; always a faithful friend. Amen.

Day 126 – May 5th

I have no doubt that when John tells us that if everything was recorded there would not be enough room in the world to hold all the books, he really means that a very great deal was not set down! I suspect that the immediate post-resurrection period is one such time that would have been so full of excitement and amazement that it would be difficult to find the words to describe the events they all encountered, let alone the time to create records!

The Ascension of Christ when He finally left the disciples, promising to them the imminent baptism in the Holy Spirit, is an occasion where there are few words recorded considering what an awesome event they had witnessed. I suspect it happened quietly, and without fanfare, which is why it is recorded as it is. How else do you record the Son of God disappearing in a cloud?

"'But you will receive power when the Holy Spirit has come upon you; and you shall be My witnesses both in Jerusalem, and in all Judea and Samaria, and even to the remotest part of the earth." And after*

He had said these things, He was lifted up while they were looking on, and a cloud received Him out of their sight. And as they were gazing intently into the sky while he was going, behold, two men in white clothing stood beside them. They said, "Men of Galilee, why do you stand looking into the sky? This Jesus, who has been taken up from you into heaven, will come in just the same way as you have watched Him go into heaven."' (Acts 1)

This time I suspect the loss was not the same; the disciples felt quite differently. Anything could happen; they knew from recent experience! There are a few aspects to this often-overlooked moment in Scripture that we might reflect on:

- This is the moment when Jesus ascended to His throne and took His place in Glory at the right hand of the Father. It is a time to celebrate His Kingship! *For the joy set before Him He had endured all. Time for great joy in heaven!*
- This is the moment when the disciples become independent; not from the Lord but *in Him*! It is Independence Day!
- This is the moment when the disciples are poised for mission! It is the Festival of Mission, which is still ours to run with today!

Almighty God, such a day, the consequences of which have rolled across thousands of countries, and through hundreds of years and made billions of disciples. Lord Jesus, seated at the right hand of our glorious God, You are the Master. We worship You, Father, Son, and Holy Spirit. Come, Lord Jesus! Amen.

Day 127 – May 6th

The period of time after the Ascension must have been quite extraordinary, to say the least. Apart from the dozen or so apostolic meetings with the risen Lord, there were clearly many more besides. Paul writes:

'For I delivered to you as of first importance what I also received, that Jesus Christ died for our sins according to the Scriptures, and that

He was buried, and that He was raised on the third day according to the Scriptures, and that He appeared to Cephas, then to the twelve. After that He appeared to more than five hundred brethren at one time, most of whom remain until now, but some have fallen asleep.' (1 Corinthians 15)

Five hundred! That's quite a few witnesses, and amazing to think that in the environs of Jerusalem there were that number of people whose experience was an unforgettable moment when they each saw the risen Lord!

Jesus had instructed the apostles as to how they should go out into the entire world and make disciples through the preaching of the Good News, accompanied by miraculous signs but, quite how, must have been a mystery to them. It is Doctor Luke who gives us the clue. He tells us that the disciples were *to wait.*

'And behold, I am sending forth the promise of My Father upon you; but you are to stay in the city until you are clothed with power from on high.' (Luke 24)

This narrative is picked up again in the opening verses of Luke's Acts of Some Apostles. This time he adds a little more detail.

'To these [apostles] He presented Himself alive after His suffering, by many convincing proofs, appearing to them over a period of forty days and speaking of the things concerning the kingdom of God. Gathering them together, He commanded them not to leave Jerusalem, but to wait for what the Father had promised, "Which," He said, "you heard from Me; for John baptised with water, but you will be baptised with the Holy Spirit not many days from now."' (Acts 1)

It is clear that after that instruction they did stay there, and we are told that they were all of one mind and continually devoted themselves to prayer along with some of the women.

By then we can only guess that they were full of expectation for what might come next. After the events of the previous five weeks, I think it is fair to say they didn't know what to expect, but they were by now bursting full of resurrection faith and recent teaching from the Master! Can you imagine for a second, their electrifying experience of sitting listening to teaching from the *risen* Lord; the One who still had the nail-scarred hands?

What I take from this, and I hope you do also, is that our circumstances are not very different two millennia later. We, who believe, have all shared a distinct and life-transforming experience of the risen Lord, and we are embarked on the very same mission. And we are surely waiting for more, are we not? Our prayer meetings are filled with deep longings for our churches, towns and homes to be filled with the Lord's presence, aren't they? Or have we become small-minded, parochial believers, trapped in petty concerns about God's provision for this and that? I see that they were all together and continually devoted to prayer. They were '*waiting' on the Lord*! As I have reflected on this over many years, the heart desire that I catch from this Scripture is that, quite simply, they wanted Jesus back!

Father, You have promised *the* promise; *Your* promise; *Your* Holy Spirit. I come to You now hungry to 'have Jesus back'. Nothing else will do. No one else can be sufficient for the task. I long for You and so I pray, Lord Jesus, send Your Spirit on me now, today. I wait in anticipation of Your goodness and Your power! Amen.

Day 128 – May 7th

Waiting is so difficult, isn't it? Remember Christmas Eve when you were a small child? The longing for Jesus in those post-Ascension days must have been an agonising time, albeit run through and through with wonderful times of prayer and worship. I would love to have been there to listen to rich renderings of Psalms and Old Testament prophecy perhaps. I rather feel it was more like those precious days before the birth of a first child when you don't know whether it is to be a boy or a girl; but imagine waiting when you don't know when 'it' might arrive and you don't know what the 'it' is you are waiting for! When I was seeking God to be baptised in the Holy Spirit, I had *no idea* what He would do with me!

'It will come about after this that I will pour out my Spirit on all mankind; and your sons and daughters will prophesy, your old men will dream dreams, your young men will see visions. Even on the male and female servants I will pour out My Spirit.' (Joel 2)

And they would perhaps have remembered some of the Master's own words also:

'But when He, the Spirit of truth, comes, He will guide you into all the truth; for He will not speak on His own initiative, but whatever He hears, He will speak; and He will disclose to you what is to come. He will glorify Me, for He will take of Mine and will disclose it to you. All things that the Father has are Mine; therefore I said that He takes of Mine and will disclose it to you.' (John 16)

And so it was, early one morning, perhaps after they had been together all night long, when there was a strange roaring like a great wind blowing and it filled the entire house where they were together. And a flame came into the room and separated, and it seemed as though tongues of this fire were licking around each of them, settling on them.

They experienced in the midst of this that their mouths were making sounds they had never voiced before; the Holy Spirit had come and each was, without thought or knowledge, pronouncing the words of God! They must have been both ecstatic and bewildered. The crowds slowly gathered and they were bewildered also! *What was this?* The men were fluently speaking all sorts of languages and dialects and actually extolling the glory of God in languages they could never have learned. There were shouts in the crowd, *'They are drunk!'* which attracted much merriment. And then Peter stood up and fluently spoke his first sermon. The crowds were pierced to the heart and crying out, saying, *'What shall we do?'*

God had sent the promise of the Father, the Holy Spirit, and the world was never going to be the same again. Three thousand people were added to their swelling fellowship that day; the fruit of conviction and repentance before a holy God.

Father, I come low before You today. Holy, holy, holy, are You, O most majestic and powerful God who is faithful in every word. Thank You for Your Promised One; the gift of the Holy Spirit poured out on mankind. However bewildering, Lord, I know I can do nothing without You, so I pray, pour out Your Spirit on me and please do it soon. Fill me! Amen.

Day 129 – May 8th

'Blessed be the God and Father of our Lord Jesus Christ, who according to His great mercy has caused us to be born again to a living hope through the resurrection of Jesus Christ from the dead, to obtain an inheritance which is imperishable and undefiled and will not fade away, reserved in heaven for you, who are protected by the power of God through faith for a salvation ready to be revealed in the last time.'
(1 Peter 1)

So writes Peter, in the introduction of his letter. It is a magnificent summary of what God did for those three thousand people, and you and me. It touches so beautifully on some key areas of the Christian journey. We are saved through the redemptive power of the cross. It is not an 'experience' that we work-up through our thinking after deliberation about Jesus – 'on balance, I choose to believe this' – no, it is a deep work of transformation from God and we will never be the same again. But look carefully: *'you, who are protected by the power of God through faith'*! We have a huge part to play in the ongoing life in our Master as we work out our salvation; it is through *faith in His power.*

I do not become a Christian and then move to a life of pious holiness whereby I somehow keep most carefully to a religious way of thinking that I may be one day found clean! Jesus had some harsh words for the religious leaders who did that and mistakenly led others in that way. If you do that, you will find that you must isolate yourself from anything that might tarnish your polished reputation. Read the rest of that chapter and you will see that this is a *relationship* which will develop. It will go through trials (yes, really) and your faith, which is like gold, will be refined and purified by God's faithfulness as you travel by faith in the One you have never seen but believe in. Glory!

Father, I give You thanks for my life that You have redeemed from the pit. The precious blood of Jesus has set me free. I will go on with You in faith, whether I am dancing on the mountain tops in the joy of the Holy Spirit, or down in the shadowy valleys where I will cling to You, knowing that it is Your power and Your grace that will alone sustain me and bring me through. I will abide in You, my Father! Send Your Spirit on me, I pray, that I may be ever aware of Your presence in me, guiding me, shaping me and finally bringing me to glory! Amen.

Day 130 – May 9th

Like Peter's epistle, the letter of James is tremendous reading. You can take it all at one sitting if you are of a mind to do so. You may not, however, take it all in! He scatters jewels around, often without apparent regard for colour co-ordination as he jumps from emeralds to sapphires and then diverts to rubies. But be warned, the words of James can pierce your hard heart, if you have one.

'What use is it, my brethren, if someone says he has faith but he has no works? . . . If a brother or sister is without clothing and in need of daily food, and one of you says to them, "Go in peace, be warmed and be filled," and yet you do not give them what is necessary for their body, what use is that? Even so faith, if it has no works, is dead, being by itself. But someone may well say, "You have faith and I have works;

show me your faith without the works, and I will show you my faith by my works.'" (James 2)

Faith travels hand-in-hand with the expending of energy for the kingdom of God. Some say they love children and spend countless hours supporting youth groups; some place such value on listening that they train as counsellors; others believe in healing and offer themselves as members of a ministry team. Faith works itself out, through works. It is always amazing to read the Trustee reports written annually by many churches. The things people do in the name of mission! I love gardening and am happy there and express myself in worship readily in a garden but it is a very solitary expression of faith, however much energy I may expend thrashing around there!

It always amazes me when I consider the journeys Jesus and others made to take the gospel out into the highways and byways; miles and miles of hot dusty roads. The extraordinary thing is that when you partnership with the King in your endeavours for Him, somehow the energy to do, and the stamina to press in, does come to you. And afterwards, even when weary, there is an incredibly special feeling of 'completeness'. It is the wonderful economy of the Father's kingdom.

My Father, I hear You speak and come before You as one who is willing to be sent out. I know I shall come back rejoicing. Send us out in the power of Your love. May we who share Christ's body live His risen life; we who drink His cup bring life to others; we whom the Spirit lights give light to the world. Keep us firm in the hope You have set before us, so we and all Your children shall be free, and the whole earth live to praise Your name; through Christ our Lord. Amen.

Day 131 – May 10th

'Is anyone among you suffering? Then he must pray.' (James 5)

I admire the straightforward directive given here. There are so many injunctions 'to do' in James. He often speaks directly to 'you'; he writes 'you' over and over. His words are simple and challenging, almost as if he is having a conversation. There is no profound theology here: *if anyone is suffering then he must pray.* Did you take that in? The underlying meaning in Greek is: 'if anyone is undergoing hardship – pray'.

James' view is that such prayer will be answered! He takes the Lord at His word. '*My Father knows your needs,*' Jesus said.

James was known as 'camel knees' or 'old camel knees' by some. When his body was prepared for burial after his martyrdom, it is said that his knees were calloused and swollen from time spent in prayer. He was often to be found in the temple; a solitary figure, on his knees praying for the nation. This is a man I should deeply respect; he knows about prayer. The provision of God will not only meet your needs but also grow your faith in the process. If the church has truly followed all the injunctions in his letter it would seem that the needs might well be met by the church! It is glorious when a fellowship functions in such a way. I remember a new Hoover being left on our doorstep days after ours broke and we had no resources to replace it. There isn't enough space in this book to tell you how the Lord has provided through my life. I grew in faith by praying!

So, are you struggling or suffering in some respect? Then pray! I have been asked so many times to pray *with* people about problems or needs. There are some folk who, as they approach you after a meeting, will always say the same thing – effectively 'this thing in my life will not shift. Pray for me that it changes (or stops, or starts).' Sometimes it is right to involve others to help you through prayer, of course it is, and it would be ridiculous to suggest otherwise. But, sometimes, I have to say to people, 'So what has the Lord said about it?' and I will then be told what the Lord said. He said to do this or that . . . 'Have you done as He told you?' I have to enquire. 'Umm, not really, but will you pray with me?' And so it can go on, sometimes throughout an entire lifetime.

James, the man of authority, with knees worn out by petitioning the Lord, considered prayer was enough and what a lesson that is to us who believe.

And so I say to you, pray, and if you feel this is a tough line to adopt, pray some more. I really believe God will illuminate it for you, give you resolution and grow your faith in Him.

Father, I do pray, You know that I do. Show me how I pray; not how *to* pray but *how I do pray.* Show me if I am fervent, un-distracted, passionate, believing, full of hope and persistent. Or if I am flitting around, not listening, whingeing and anxious before You rather than pressing into Your faithfulness. It's so easy to spend time with You which isn't quality time. I don't want to kid myself. Holy Spirit, show me, I pray. Revitalise me in the risen life of the Son! I speak to my soul: *Receive life in Jesus!* Amen.

Day 132 – May 11th

It is strange how God guides. I wrote yesterday's reflection and, after completing it, went to my emails and there was one from someone extolling the wisdom of James!

'Is anyone cheerful? He is to sing praises.' (James 5)

How many of us would say to ourselves, on a Sunday morning, 'I am *so* cheerful today, you just wait until I get to church!' Why not? Bring a psalm or an encouragement or a testimony to build up others who might be struggling. Just ask someone: 'May I, at an appropriate point, share something that is on my heart?' So often the word that God gives to us will really speak to others. You may be carrying one of Father's guided missiles! The Holy Spirit knows what He is doing! You may not be in that sort of church; if so, I would suggest that when something is 'lit up' for you in your daily readings, jot it down and put it in your pocket. I cannot tell you how many times I have done that and then, in conversation, I suddenly realise it is a word for the person I am speaking with. How good it is to say, 'You know, God cares so much about this issue; when I was praying, I felt this was important for today so I wrote it down – I believe it is for you!'

Jesus, Your word is wonderful and You never speak a word to me that is pointless. It never falls to the ground without achieving its purpose. Help me to become a faithful messenger with my spirit and my pockets full of Your treasures. Guide me by Your promptings that I may know the addressee or, if it is for me, may I really catch what You are speaking to me! I praise You for Your infinite care for each one of us. Amen.

Day 133 – May 12th

In the verses we have been looking at from James' letter, we see him covering people in every state; three to be precise: struggling, cheerful and sick. Forgive me for being simplistic but is there any other way to be?

'Is anyone among you sick? Then he must call for the elders of the church and they are to pray over him, anointing him with oil in the name of the Lord; and the prayer offered in faith will restore the one who is sick, and the Lord will raise him up.' (James 5)

And for the sick, send for the reliable, the leaders and those who have faith to pray and honour this age-old church custom of anointing: the sacrament that is an outward sign of the coming of the Holy Spirit to the anointed one. I love anointing people and not only when they are sick. It is a sacred faith act. It's not magic oil. Throughout Scripture God ordains anointing for several different reasons.

I like to place a little oil on my thumb, rub it gently onto a person's forehead and say quietly, 'I anoint you in the mighty name of Jesus who knows all of your needs. May you meet Him now where you need His touch in body, mind or spirit.' It doesn't need to be a complicated prayer. I keep my hand there, in a comforting way, *silently* speaking words of encouragement to the person's spirit, *Peace be with you now* . . . and to myself, words of truth as a silent declaration: *The Spirit of the Lord God is upon me because the Lord has anointed me to . . . set the captives free . . . proclaim liberty . . .* Glory! And then I listen. Is the Holy Spirit telling me anything?

Dear Father God, Your ways are so precious. Catch me up now in the power of Your anointing and let me go out to heal the sick in Your name; to declare freedom to those captives and to proclaim liberty to the prisoners. Thank You that this is the year of the Lord's favour! Amen

Day 134 – May 13th

'If he has committed sins, they will be forgiven him. Therefore, confess your sins to one another, and pray for one another so that you may be healed. The effective prayer of a righteous man can accomplish much.' (James 5)

When I became a Christian I was mightily changed in the blink of an eye by the power of the Holy Spirit who simultaneously overwhelmed me with the love of God *and* brought me to my knees in repentance, such was the impact of His holy presence on me. I was a new man. Really! I saw life from a different perspective from that moment. I saw my crazy thinking in the light of God's truth. I saw my depraved actions in the gaze of His loving eyes. It wasn't pretty, I can assure you, but the point was that God showed me, not to crush me but so that I could be freed from the bags of junk I had been labouring under. But I am not perfect! I try my hardest but, make no mistake, I fail. Sometimes my feet wander off the path He illumines for me and, when that happens, I know it (even if I am stubborn and don't immediately change direction). I may not even know why I do what I do. To be able to share that with someone who is safe, who understands the profound value in confession and knows how to listen to the Holy Spirit for answers to deeply personal questions, and can then pray for release and healing is just wonderful! I cannot understand why we don't all rush to do it! Actually, I do know why we don't; the enemy, remember him (the one without an ethics committee), comes along and whispers, *Surely you don't want anyone to know that, do you?* Just say to him, very firmly, 'Yes, I do. I want to be healed and unashamed in my Lord's presence!'

Father God, Your word says that Your desire is to take our sins so far away from us as You deal with them, as though it is east to west. In other words, You want them lost and forgotten, dealt with by the redeeming blood of Jesus. May I practise the healing ways of confession. Put the enemy's lies out of my head that I may be cleansed before You, a shining vessel to be filled with Your goodness and Your power. Amen.

Day 135 – May 14th

Sin wrecks you! Let me say it again: *sin wrecks you*. I don't like speaking of him too much, but sometimes we need to; the enemy's intention is to wreck you on any convenient rock. He will bend your rudder given half a chance, stick barnacles over your smooth hull, and ask seagulls to poop on your gleaming superstructure . . . I could continue but I won't. Sometimes we invite him – yes, really – and other times he plays despicable tricks to make you limp if he can. We invite him by wandering off the path of God and into the enemy's bramble bushes. The blackberries look tempting but beware: thorns and snagging lay ahead!

So we turn to Psalm 32, one of King David's best 'sin psalms'. Listen to him, this great man of God who really knew what it was to experience the pain of a huge mess up:

'*When I kept silent about my sin, my body wasted away through my groaning all day long. For day and night Your hand was heavy upon me; my vitality was drained away as with the fever heat of summer. I acknowledged my sin to You, and my iniquity I did not hide.*'

But before we feel overwhelmed in gloom and despondency, let me tell you how this psalm begins!

'How blessed is he whose transgression is forgiven, whose sin is covered! How blessed is the man to whom the LORD does not impute iniquity, and in whose spirit there is no deceit!'

I have two questions to ask you: did David know the capacity of sin to really 'wreck' him? Did David know the joy of being forgiven and set free?

The answer to both is a resounding 'Yes!'

I learn from this that is does not matter what I have done, to remain unforgiven is a disaster to my entire being, and also that there is blissful joy in being forgiven when the secret sin is confessed. The psalm continues, 'I acknowledged my sin to You, and my iniquity I did not hide; I said, "I will confess my transgressions to the LORD"; And You forgave the guilt of my sin.'

Lord, it's difficult to understand why we would *choose* to remain in sin when we could be resting in a place of forgiveness and clear of any deceit. I will sit before You now, in the integrity of my heart, and trust You to tell me if there is anything in me that needs to be brought into Your light. If You say 'nothing' then today I will rejoice before You. If there are things, then I will come low before You and seek Your forgiveness as I turn away from my sin. Holy Spirit, would You guide me now, I pray. Amen.

Day 136 – May 15th

Before we move on from David's tremendous Psalm 32, I would like to make mention of a phrase I used yesterday: sometimes the enemy uses despicable tricks to make you limp, if he can.

You may recall that I mentioned some time ago a horrid tragedy that I witnessed at close quarters when a woman took her life in front of me. What I recall so vividly is that the result of that trauma clung to me like a barnacle to a ship's hull. It did so for years. You don't need me to explain that it was not my fault. I was an innocent bystander. Does the enemy like to use our hurts and traumas to limit our capacity to dwell peacefully in God's love? Yes, he does. Is it our fault he can do this? No.

Do you think God wants to release us from those wounds? All my experience says the Lord does and He will.

Isaiah wrote that the Spirit of God would anoint Jesus to 'comfort *all who mourn, to grant those who mourn in Zion, giving them a garland instead of ashes, the oil of gladness instead of mourning, the mantle of praise instead of a spirit of fainting'* (Isaiah 61).

This week a lovely man of God came to see me. He has such a right heart before the Lord and is full of the Holy Spirit and truth, but . . . he knew that something wasn't right. There was a recurring, niggling problem that kept him at less than full power and slightly off course – as though his rudder was bent.

We probed around and asked the Holy Spirit to shed His light, which He did. Never be afraid to ask the Holy Spirit to show you such things with a simple prayer: 'Holy Spirit, would you please show us what is happening here? What is the root of this?' Don't make it overcomplicated. Having prayed, listen. The rapidity and clarity of His answers tells me again and again that He certainly wants to bring us to a place of wholeness!

It transpired that in his childhood, this dear friend had been hurt, quite inadvertently, by an otherwise very loving mother. It had caused him great distress as a child. As he grew older, he learned to hide behind a wall that he had built to convince himself and others that he wasn't hurting at all. It's such a common barnacle but a pesky, nasty one that is so destructive, not least because much of our thinking develops in quite wrong mindsets as we hide and convince ourselves that all is well. It is even more difficult if we loved the person and they loved us!

If all this sounds very familiar to you, let me reassure you that the Holy Spirit was soon at work as the three of us homed in on this problem and asked the Lord to take care of it, which He did. We then asked Him to heal it and put something *good* back in place of the barnacle that had tried to chew the timbers. Let me stress that none of this was my friend's fault. The only part that was his to do was to make sure he had forgiven the unwitting mother who had caused so much hurt, so that the wound had no chance to fester and cause further trouble.

Holy Spirit of the Living God, fall afresh on me today. As I read this I might be aware that there could be a barnacle or two on my hull and maybe my rudder takes me off course sometimes. I can't be sure, but I know that if I come to You, the Spirit of truth, You can lovingly show me if I have built a wall that I hide behind. Give me peace that whatever I am feeling today can be sorted and, in Your grace, lead me to people who can pray for me. Bless You, Lord, You know it all and have watched over me as you knit me together in my mother's womb. It is not a problem for You! Amen.

Day 137 – May 16th

One of the greatest changes that God brings to us as we believe is that our entire status changes. 'Status' isn't a big enough word, but it will do for today. Jesus deals with the fundamental sin of mankind who chose to go away from God; He opens up the gates of glory and welcomes us into His kingdom but He also gives us a new name and a new relationship with Him, the Holy God, which will really enable us to recognise sin and temptation for what it is and say, 'No!'

'For all who are being led by the Spirit of God, these are sons of God. For you have not received a spirit of slavery leading to fear again, but you have received a Spirit of adoption as sons by which we cry out, "Abba! Father!" The Spirit Himself testifies with our spirit that we are children of God, and if children, heirs also, heirs of God and fellow heirs with Christ, if indeed we suffer with Him so that we may also be glorified with Him.' (Romans 8)

This is one of Paul's great conclusions as the Holy Spirit leads him to set down in this great book the reality of our transformation in the redemptive power of the cross of Jesus.

What were we before we were 'adopted' by the Father? We were orphans.

Orphans are adopted. Orphans are 'fatherless'. You can't be adopted if you have a father! The enemy tried to be our father but he cannot be: it's impossible; he is the father of lies so anything he says is utterly untrustworthy.

What are we now? We are now signed, sealed and adopted children of the Father, and we cry out, 'Papa', 'Daddy'! The word 'Abba' is not a formal or theological word; it is the word used by children for their dads. I recall a friend who went to share a Passover meal with some Jewish friends. Something shifted afresh in his spirit when he watched the father come home at the end of the day and the children leapt on him and play-wrestled him and repeatedly called out, 'Abba', 'Abba'. You can guess how he was caused to reflect! This is intimate. This will knock the stuffing out of any spirit of orphan-ship that you might still have lurking around! Cry out to Him, 'Abba!' My Daddy! My Father! It may not come naturally at first. This can be a big revelation to our spirits! God has drawn you that close. This is not the remote father who sniffs and looks down his nose at you, saying, 'I suppose you can live in my house . . . Go away and remember children should be seen and not heard.' This is Father. Our heavenly Father.

My Papa. My lovely Daddy. Yes, this *is* revelation to my spirit but if Your Holy Spirit is telling me this is so, it would be quite wrong to live in a different promise, a different time, under a different spirit. That would be to deny You! There are things in me that need healing as my image of 'father' may be a little adrift. So I ask You, Holy Spirit, to shine Your glorious light on the areas within me that need to be brought into line with Your truth about me now. I am Your child! I am Your child! I am Your child! All praise to Jesus for the depth of the blessing He wrought for me on the cross. Amen.

Day 138 – May 17th

As I walked by the log shed this morning, a tiny movement caught my eye. When I turned to look, under the wheelbarrow, right at the back by a pile of firewood, was a small brown and white spaniel! We live near popular woodland, so stray dogs are not that unusual; but hiding in the woodshed? Like Moses I turned aside to look!

She looked very frightened, or wounded, or both, so I left her there and went to see if an owner was to be seen. Sure enough, after a matter of minutes, a tearful lady emerged who was very distressed having searched in the extensive woods for two hours. It seems that while she was walking her normally obedient dog, three large dogs had chased her and she had taken fright and, very unusually, fled.

'For you have not received a spirit of slavery leading to fear again, but you have received a spirit of adoption.' (Romans 8)

It is an extraordinary thing which I have noticed again and again in ministry to distressed people, that many of our problems are rooted in fears. Fears of loneliness, imagined shame, guilt, poverty, inadequacy, losing partners, health or serious illness . . . the list goes on and on. The fears are very real but they are *not true*. The Good News is that Jesus says, 'Do not fear . . .' with very good reason; there is nothing to fear! It is said (and I have never counted so I cannot vouch for this) that the Bible says, 'Do not fear' or 'Do not be afraid' three hundred and sixty-five times – once for each day of the year! Maybe I should write that at the top of every page: *'Do not fear!'*

'There is no fear in love; but perfect love casts out fear.' (1 John 4)

The little frightened dog reminded me very vividly how we can be before Jesus finds us: on the run and looking for a safe place to hide. We want to back up 'under the wheelbarrow' so we can peer out and feel we are protected. But St Paul writes that we do not receive a spirit of slavery leading to sin *'again'*. *'Does that mean that* once *I did have a spirit of fear?'* Yes, you did! Anyone who has not been born again is frightened at some level. Frightened of being lost and frightened to be found. What a muddle! Even the most basic, profound fear – 'What happens when I die?' – afflicts many people. Imagine Eden, after it went awry, and all the fears that might have assailed Adam and his wife: Will it rain or be too dry? Will I get on top of that jungle of weeds? Will the wild animals leave us alone tonight? What happens if Adam dies? Is my fig leaf big enough . . .? I am not being facetious, but these all have their contemporary equivalence. Think about it!

These things don't *all* shift when we become Christian believers, but many will. Some old habits and ways of thinking stick, and doesn't the enemy do his best to make sure they continue to stick? He never comes with straight statements such as *God is lying to you.* Instead he asks, '*Are you sure He loves you? Are you sure you can trust this Father – remember what happened last time . . . Are you sure . . . Are you sure . . .'* And then the big 'If'!

'*He ate nothing during those [forty] days, and when they had ended, He became hungry. And the devil said to Him, 'If You are the Son of God, tell this stone to become bread.'* (Luke 4)

Get it? *If. . .* Our response needs to be the same as that of Jesus, '*It is written . . .'* The answer to the father of lies is '*It is written that I am an adopted child of the Father in heaven . . . so shove off!'* (My words, but you get my drift.)

If you want to know one single reason why I have written this book it is so that you can become so absorbed in the truth and utter beauty of Scripture, that you are so clear of your identity in Christ, and so know the intimate love of the Father for you, that you can always reply, '*You are not putting that one on me, evil one, it is written . . .'* I do not picture you as that little cowering dog in my woodshed; rather as someone who stands outside in the Light, boldly declaring to all who would seek to diminish you, '*I am a child of my Father.'*

Dearest Father, my precious loving Daddy, I receive the truth of this. Help me to abide in You, in Your word and in Your revelation to me. May my spirit wake up and become fully alive in the presence of Your Holy Spirit living in me. I will not live under the wheelbarrow again! Amen.

Day 139 – May 18th

It's time! No more talk of lost spaniels! It is time to look at that greatest of parables (at least in my book): The Prodigal Son. It is told beautifully in Luke 15. Perhaps you would read it, preferably several times, even if you know it by heart! Ask the Holy Spirit to open your eyes.

This is a deeply moving story with layer upon layer of truth within it and there are even entire, brilliantly written books devoted to it, but let us draw out a few points in the next days. We should perhaps call it 'The Parable of the Loving Father and His Two Difficult Sons'. It's not quite so catchy, I give you that, but that is what it is: the highly illuminating account of two boys going in completely different directions regarding their loving father.

The parable begins 'A man had two sons . . .' That should give us a clue as we interpret this. Jesus wanted us to recognise the two boys but the key actor on the stage is the father. Everything pivots around him. The younger son, through total and appalling disrespect for his father, demanded that the estate be divided up between the boys. In Jewish culture this was an unimaginable insult that effectively said, 'I wish you were dead.' The law stated that a father could hand over his estate at any time in his life but the transaction could not be effected until he died. We will come back to this later as it is very important in the story's meaning. He was a headstrong, wilful lad for whom the grass beyond the estate boundaries was much greener! Most of us have had those thoughts at different times in our lives, but he acted on his thoughts and spoke it out. Both sons inherited. They younger one took off into a life of carousing and high living; it was expensive and quite decadent. As happens, he ran out of resources for his lifestyle.

As often occurs, outside influences and a lack of personal wisdom combine (have you come across that?) and there was both a 'nil' bank balance and a disaster in the land when famine struck and crops failed.

He went to a Gentile farmer and got a labouring job. The man assigned him, a Jew, the job of managing pigs! That is how we know he was a long way from home. But it was demeaning and so menial and poorly rewarded that he was starving. We are told that he 'attached' himself to the landowner. In Greek, it means 'joined'. The pigs were being fed pods of the algarroba (in Arabic *kharrūbah*). It is a Middle Eastern tree, also known as St John's tree – a reference to what he ate in the desert, perhaps. It is usually animal fodder and the sweet seeds are rarely eaten by humans. But listen, Jesus says that he is eating the pods! Not the seeds. Imagine wanting to eat the sweet corn stalks after the seeds have been removed and sent to the factory. It is intended to signify how far he had fallen; feeding pigs with *kharrūbah*. He was longing to fill his stomach with pod*s*. That word 'longing' is a very strong word. Things are bad. He wanted to be a well-off pig. Jesus knew how to paint a picture of how far man can fall!

One day in his misery, he thinks, 'my father's hired men have more than enough bread to eat'; in other words, back at home there is real wealth, even for the servants. Let us recognise what is happening here. I do not wish to belittle this young man's spiritual journey but he does not immediately repent of his sins! He thinks to himself, at home there is plenty to eat; I am hungry so that is the place to go. *Then* he is caused to think things through, repent before heaven (God) and rehearse what he will say to his father.

'But when he came to his senses, he said, "How many of my father's hired men have more than enough bread to eat, but I am dying here with hunger! I will get up and go to my father, and will say to him,

'Father, I have sinned against heaven, and in your sight; I am no longer worthy to be called your son; make me as one of your hired men.'"

Notice he wants to be a *hired*man. Clearly he is not going back saying, 'I will be your slave . . . anything, father.' There is still money in his sights; perhaps he wants to repay his debts to his father; to put things right. He is thoroughly aware of his wrong.

Father, I see in this story how lost I was. I was starving to death away from You. I had gone my own way, full of intolerable arrogance, wilfully ignoring You. Help me to see the true glory of what You have done for me, and to become inspired to go out, possibly into the places where the sense of personal loss is so great that people will do *anything* to survive. Lord, have mercy on me that I may be intoxicated with justice, love and kindness and walk humbly with You, my God. Amen.

Day 140 – May 19th

When I was just turned twenty-one, I wasn't exactly eating *kharrūbah* pods, but I was in a dark place. Morally and in other ways I was not comfortable in my skin. I had had a good enough upbringing to know right from wrong. Don't get me wrong, when I wanted something I could develop plenty of momentum! But I just couldn't change, and whatever I tried seemed to end up in a mess.

'I am of flesh, sold into bondage to sin. For what I am doing, I do not understand; for I am not practising what I would like to do, but I am doing the very thing I hate.' (Romans 7)

So goes St Paul's slightly tongue in cheek explanation of why trying to live by rules and leaving notes on the fridge to be a better person, just doesn't work!

One day, after I had been a little (not a lot) honest with someone about how I had no direction and felt washed up, the young woman said, 'Have you ever thought about God?' That was the extent of her attempt to evangelise me! But, give God an inch and the Holy Spirit will take a mile (forgive me), *I did turn to God!* I can only recall that I pondered this question one miserable, wet, November night and, strange as it may seem, I gazed through the rain-streaked window at a church that was across the road. (This is completely true – no preacher's hyperbole here!) It was the Sunday evening service and people were scurrying through the rain holding umbrellas and disappearing into the church. The love of the Father is such that He will use *anything* to reach us!

I thought, why would all those people do *that*? In the next moment, I found myself 'praying'. My exact words were, *'God if You are there, I really want to know . . . it's important . . .'*

Within two seconds the Holy Spirit fell on me with a powerful, overwhelming sense of love. I described it to anyone who would listen afterwards as being in a shower, but not of water; I was in a deluge of love. The immediate effect of the purity and warmth of this love was to push me to my knees. I just 'knew' I was in the presence of a very holy God! And then the tears came and the profound sense of my utter filth and degradation before Him. It was painful. There was love pouring down and me unable to look up, is the best way I can describe it. Out of my mouth came a stream of repentance for all I had been and pleas for mercy. I knew that if I wasn't made clean, I would probably die; such was the power of this love. When the 'shower' stopped, I was at peace. Tear-streaked, but peaceful. What happened in that next moment was as if I turned and looked into myself and I absolutely knew I had been totally changed.

'So he got up and came to his father. But while he was still a long way off, his father saw him, and felt compassion for him, and ran and embraced him and kissed him. And the son said to him, "Father, I have sinned against heaven and in your sight; I am no longer worthy to be called your son." But the father said to his slaves, "Quickly bring out the best robe and put it on him, and put a ring on his hand and sandals on his feet; and bring the fattened calf, kill it, and let us eat and celebrate;

for this son of mine was dead and has come to life again; he was lost and has been found.'" (Luke 15)

My precious Father, what can I say? I live to worship You. I live to speak of Your goodness and love. Thank You, Jesus, for the power of the cross to make men and women new. Thank You, Holy Spirit, that You go out, even into the byways of the wet streets of south London, to bring home the lost. I praise You with all my being. Amen.

Day 141 – May 20th

When Jesus told this story, He knew exactly what He was doing. He knew how outrageous it would sound to His listeners' ears. The father came running?! A father running would need to hitch up his robes to do that and that was the most undignified way for a father and a respectable land owner to behave. Imagine the mutterings down the street as he ran. Everyone would have known about the son. What a disgrace! And they probably all felt pity and possibly a little ridicule for this man who watched . . . and watched . . . We can imagine the old men sitting beside the road talking, out of hearing, 'Waste of space, he was, little good-for-nothing.' But the father is vigilant; watching. And one day he sees a tiny, filthy, ragged man in the distance. He doesn't look young but maybe . . . Could it be? And with that, he runs as fast as his feet will carry him. It *is him*! It *is* my son!

As they meet, the father is so overjoyed that the young man's carefully prepared words of repentance are barely voiced. He hardly gets the chance to repent. The father sees his lost heart, the broken spirit and that is enough. *He must be restored*, is all that is in the father's heart. I will restore him. He has come home.

The best robe? Yes. The robe that would be kept reserved to dress one of high honour at table. And the signet ring that signified that he was indeed the father's son and an heir. The ring of promise and a future as if . . . as if what? *As if nothing had ever happened.* This young man is forgiven and welcomed into the house where a grand celebration is begun. Everyone who was anyone would have been invited.

'Blessed be the God and Father of our Lord Jesus Christ, who has blessed us with every spiritual blessing in the heavenly places in Christ, just as He chose us in Him before the foundation of the world, that we would be holy and blameless before Him. In love He predestined us to adoption as sons through Jesus Christ to Himself, according to the kind intention of His will, to the praise of the glory of His grace, which He freely bestowed on us in the Beloved. In Him we have redemption through His blood, the forgiveness of our trespasses, according to the riches of His grace which He lavished on us.' (Ephesians 1)

My Father, I sit at Your table in wonder and delight. This You have done for me? It is all Your grace. I do not deserve it but it delights You to lavish Your kindness upon me. I am overwhelmed by Your goodness. *'Amazing grace, how sweet the sound, that saved a wretch like me! I once was lost but now am found, was blind, but now I see.'* Amen.

Day 142 – May 21st

There are two very sad, lost sons in this story. It is quite deliberately created to be so. You probably know what I am going to write. Yes, the older son. The younger son repented and became a son again; his father never ceased being a father to either young men but the older one could not cope with the extravagant love of his father. You may say, 'But surely he wasn't lost, was he? Surely, he was at home?' We are told that the older son, the co-inheritor, returned to the house and he heard the celebration. He enquired of a servant as to what was going on. He answered very innocently:

'Your brother has come, and your father has killed the fattened calf because he has received him back safe and sound.' (Luke 15)

The father's heart is at peace. He has received the son back again.

He is celebrating with his friends. The older brother, sadly, is far from at peace.

'But he became angry and was not willing to go in; and his father came out and began pleading with him.'

Indignity is piled on indignity; the father came out to the son because he wouldn't step over the threshold to speak. The father is risking further embarrassment before all the hired staff, his friends and everyone at the party. Look, he even has to plead with the other son now!

There is an issue here which we must look at if we are to fully understand the story Jesus created. Everyone listening would have understood immediately, but we might not. The older son is at fault. Under Hebrew law *both* sons would have inherited when the young son went off! That father could hand over everything to the sons which would then fully become theirs at his death. He still had many rights over his estate while he lived which is why he could order the killing of the fatted calf, but the most important thing to note is that when the younger son went off the rails, the older son did what? *Nothing!* There is no record that he remonstrated, as he should have done as the main inheritor and the senior son; he should have bent the younger son's ear and said, 'There is no way you are going to do this to Dad . . .' but he didn't. And, by the way, the older son inherited two-thirds of the estate, which he would still be holding at this point. He was as guilty as the younger son but was hiding behind this outraged veneer of respectability. This is why the father said *all that I have is yours*. He didn't mean 'one day it will be yours'; it already was. The only difference is that the younger son had probably had to sell his lesser share (at a much-reduced price because the father was alive and well).

The father doesn't seem to care, such is his love. He wants the son to understand how absolutely momentous it is: *the boy has come home!* Sadly, there is a sort of legality about the anger of the brother.

"'Look! For so many years I have been serving you and I have never neglected a command of yours; and yet you have never given me a young goat, so that I might celebrate with my friends; but when this son of yours came, who has devoured your wealth with prostitutes, you kill the fattened calf for him." And [the father] said to him, "Son, you have always been with me, and all that is mine is yours."'

Do you notice the son's words? He is counting – *for all these years* – he is not sharing in the wealth and prosperity, he is *serving*; how does he hear the father's words? He speaks of *'your commands'*. He resents not being given a goat to celebrate with when, actually, he didn't even need to ask: *it was his own wealth!* He had inherited along with his brother. He is also quite judgemental . . . *'prostitutes'* he spits out! And finally, his anger reveals how he really feels: *this son of yours* . . . No longer is he 'brother'; the young man is 'your son'.

Throughout the painful tirade, the father remains calm and his speech is entirely of the heart. *Son . . . you have always been with me . . . all that I have is yours.*

We cannot know the end of the story. I rather think Jesus left it that way. We are meant to see where we ourselves fit into this wonderful parable. But who was this told against, I wonder? Dare I suggest that this is really a story about the older son? The reason it is so beautiful to us is that it describes the father's love, but the ugly side is that the older son's hard heart meant that he could not take the expected place of honour and co-host at the table where all would have been invited to welcome the one who was lost and found. It was an enormous insult to the father and the real tragedy is that he missed the feast.

Father, this is such a telling story from every point of view but, as we understand it, we appreciate the dark underbelly of humanity. I am sure that I have my inner rages against apparent injustice, so I ask You, my loving heavenly Father, that if You see anything in me that is not befitting for a son of the King, please show me. Amen.

Day 143 – May 22nd

'Son, you have always been with me.' (Luke 15)

Is it possible that the son had never really been with the father? This story is so clever! He had been *with* the father at home, but I do find myself wondering, did he *know* him? If he had known him, would he not have stood with his father, longing with him and taking shifts to watch down the road for the return of the prodigal?

If he knew the father's heart, surely he would have joyfully carried the robe out of the house ready for the father to drape around the younger brother's grubby shoulders?

It is often said that Jesus spoke this against the teaching of the Pharisees. I doubt it. Jesus said that he welcomed their teaching. It was when He found hypocrisy in their behaviour together that Jesus had so much to be angry about. The ones who properly taught the Law but then didn't do it themselves; those who made it more difficult for the repentant to come back into the Father's love. The Jewish Law was very strong on welcoming in the repentant ones and those who came back to faith, although you wouldn't guess it from their reaction to Jesus dining and spending time with the outcasts of society. These are the legalistic Sons who have always had everything in the kingdom but don't seem to understand that Jesus has come for the lost. So many of the parables of Jesus fall into this broad category of meaning.

But we can be like that sometimes: when new young Christians don't look like us, or worship and behave like us 'established ones'; I am sure we are capable of looking down our long noses when people with a 'track record' come into the kingdom. *'Do you know about him? His family . . . my goodness . . .'* We had some people like that come to an Alpha group once. They livened up things a little. They sat, always rather isolated, on a table on their own. The funny thing is, all of them 'got it'! They understood the kingdom love of the father while some of the others, mostly long-standing churchgoers who had been persuaded to have a 'refresher', asked me very intellectual questions that no one (including me) understood! They were most content with the comfortable rhythms of liturgy and knew well when to stand and when to kneel; they were simply prevaricating in the face of such outrageous love.

We can be so ridiculous! Father must smile at us and, sometimes, shake His head sadly.

'Or what woman, if she has ten silver coins and loses one coin, does not light a lamp and sweep the house and search carefully until she finds it? When she has found it, she calls together her friends and neighbours, saying, "Rejoice with me, for I have found the coin which I had lost!" In the same way, I tell you, there is joy in the presence of the angels of God over one sinner who repents.' (Luke 15)

Father, my heart is sometimes no better than the Pharisees or leaders who found it so difficult to accept the ways of Jesus. He is always right but it can be so difficult to fully *agree* in my heart where Your gaze rests. Forgive me, Father. Amen.

Day 144 – May 23rd

'How blessed is he whose help is the God of Jacob, whose hope is in the LORD his God, who made heaven and earth, the sea and all that is in them; who keeps faith forever; who executes justice for the oppressed; who gives food to the hungry. The LORD sets the prisoners free. The LORD opens the eyes of the blind; the LORD raises up those who are bowed down; the LORD loves the righteous; the LORD protects the strangers; He supports the fatherless and the widow. But He thwarts the way of the wicked.' (Psalm 146)

I ask you, don't you love our God whose whole Being is like that? What beauty! Isn't He worthy of all our praise? Are we functioning in His likeness today?

'*And by this we know we have come to know Him, if we keep His commandments.*' (1 John 2)

Lord Jesus, send me out in the power of Your love. May I be so cleansed and made whole that Your injunctions to live well are my natural mindset and first inclination. I want to be like You, my Father. Amen.

Day 145 – May 24th

The story of the Transfiguration of Jesus is surely the most beautiful and arresting moment.

'*He took along Peter and John and James, and went up the mountain to pray. And while He was praying, the appearance of His face became different, and His clothing became white and gleaming. And behold, two men were talking with Him; and they were Moses and Elijah, who, appearing in glory, were speaking of His departure which He was about to accomplish at Jerusalem. Now Peter and His companions had been overcome with sleep; but when they were fully awake, they saw His glory and the two men standing with Him.*' (Luke 9)

Matthew seeks to explain: '*His face shone like the sun, and His garments became as white as light.*' (Matthew 17)

Mark adds: '*His garments became radiant and exceedingly white, as no launderer on earth can whiten them.*' (Mark 9)

On reading these accounts, it seems that they were lost for words, desperately trying to describe the indescribable scene they had witnessed. We are so familiar with these passages and yet their struggle to comprehend what they had seen can so easily pass us by. When someone says to you, 'They were white but, no, like no white you have ever seen' or 'as white as light' or 'radiant' it is clear they are struggling to find superlatives adequate to describe it. Notice also 'they fell asleep'. This is all very remarkable. The presence of God is like nothing else in the whole earth.

'The glory of the LORD filled the house. The priests could not enter into the house of the LORD, because the glory of the LORD filled the LORD's house. All the sons of Israel, seeing the fire come down and the glory of the LORD upon the house, bowed down on the pavement with their faces to the ground, and they worshipped and gave praise to the LORD, saying, "Truly He is good, truly His loving kindness is everlasting."' (2 Chronicles 7)

The Hebrew word means 'bend the knee' or 'prostrate'. I think they were prostrated with their faces on the ground. I have only a few times, a very few times, experienced the glory of God and, I may tell you, there is no other possible place to be other than as low as possible before Him. The glory of God does that to men. That is why the worship in heaven is so incredibly wonderful. It is no-holds-barred adoration of the King of Kings. People don't quibble there concerning whether certain forms of worship are acceptable or the angelic hosts too loud; *everyone is 'face down'*.

On the mountain, heaven came close to that one little place on the entire earth because the Son of Glory was there; the Father wanted to speak, Father to God-Man-Son, for all who were present to hear. No wonder that much later in life, when Peter was being mightily irritated by the false prophets who were pervading fellowships, one can almost hear him roar out,

'For when He received honour and glory from God the Father, such an utterance as this was made to Him by the Majestic Glory, "This is my beloved Son with whom I am well pleased" – and we ourselves heard this utterance made from heaven when we were with Him on the holy mountain.' (2 Peter 1)

He calls God 'the Majestic Glory'. Peter, John and James heard the Majestic One. Moments like that change you, I believe. You will never be the same again. No wonder Jesus forbade them to speak of it. How would you speak of such a moment?

Father, sometimes I need to be woken up from my complacent

and very small thoughts about You, the Majestic Glory. Holy Spirit, touch my life with the reality of heavenly glory, not for the *experience* but because I need to be changed, so that when I go out others will see the after-glow upon me when I have been with You. That is the reality of my intimate times with You. Yours be the glory, for ever and ever. Amen.

Day 146 – May 25th

'*Peter said to Jesus, "Rabbi, it is good for us to be here; let us make three tabernacles, one for You, and one for Moses, and one for Elijah." For he did not know what to answer; for they became terrified. Then a cloud formed, overshadowing them, and a voice came out of the cloud . . .*' (Mark 9)

The Greek is clear there, they were terrified (*ekphobos*); a similar word is used to describe the shepherds at the announcement of the birth of the Messiah but not quite of such great degree: *sore afraid; exceedingly frightened.* How small we make 'our God'. Forgive us, Lord.

I was present once when a faithful saint died. At that moment, whether it was an angel or Jesus Himself, I cannot tell. It was a bright winter's day and the sun streamed through the windows. Then the Glory came. God's glory makes the sun look dirty. That is the only way I can describe it. The room was suddenly full of glistening silver-white light; the colour of the brightest lightening, but not flashing; constant. And I buried my face in the bed clothes such was the Majesty. I thought if I look up now, I shall be dead.

These things change you.

O, Majestic God. I cannot pray. The words will not come out. I am not at all surprised that Peter did not know how to respond. I come low before You, Majesty. Amen.

Day 147 – May 26th

One can only guess how Peter, James and John felt on coming down from that place of Transfiguration. These three, the chosen of the chosen of the chosen, had been party to the most wonderful epiphany; it was of unspeakable beauty. But they came down, as we all must, to life in the valley. God does give us wonderful moments but we are not meant to live there. He does it to equip us and change us that we might come down and be in the world, healing, influencing and bringing glory.

'And when the voice had spoken, Jesus was found alone. And they kept silent, and reported to no one in those days any of the things which they had seen . . . When they came down from the mountain, a large crowd met Him. And a man from the crowd shouted, saying, "Teacher, I beg You to look at my son, for he is my only boy, and a spirit seizes him, and he suddenly screams, and it throws him into a convulsion with foaming at the mouth; and only with difficulty does it leave him, mauling him as it leaves."' (Luke 9)

The other disciples had tried to cast the spirit out and could not. Jesus has a few seemingly frustrated words for them. Right in front of Jesus the boy manifested and Jesus cast the unclean spirit out and returned the only son to the father. It seems clear from Jesus' words that He was warning them to 'get themselves together' because He was soon to be delivered up. 'How long shall I be with you?' He asked them. It sounds harsh, but it was the truth.

Down in the valley again, we see that Jesus is hoping they will learn how to minister and He seems concerned that they were not always as able to do so as He would wish; set against that is the knowledge that the Holy Spirit had not yet fully come to them. It is a mystery. Even more mysterious, given this rebuke, is that the disciples then had a dispute about who among them was the greatest!

Matthew tells us that they asked Jesus privately why they had not succeeded when Jesus had. Mark tells us something which may be the answer. Jesus told them something we should each remember.

'And he said to them, "This kind cannot come out by anything but prayer."' (Mark 9)

In the fuller account of Mark, we are told that the man declared a spirit 'made his son mute' but note that Jesus rebuked the spirit and commanded it *'You deaf and mute spirit'*. The spirit made the boy 'deaf'. Had Jesus seen something the others had not seen? Had He heard from the Father in His Spirit, *Tell the foul thing he must listen to you! He is not deaf at all! Just hiding behind the lie . . .'*

I suggest that Jesus is saying, in His response to the disciples' question, 'In prayer you will hear *all* that My Father wants you to hear about *every* situation.' Jesus had discerned the exact nature of the unclean spirit. We need to learn to be listeners first and doers second. Effective prayer ministry just might be listening!

Father, it is such an encouragement to understand this. That when I pray, I will hear You and You will speak all I need to know. Cause me to pause, before I rush in, particularly as I pray for others. May Your kingdom come around me today. Amen.

Day 148 – May 27th

I had a lovely word from the Lord given to me by a friend while in prayer today.

'As the deer pants for the water brooks so my soul pants for You.' (Psalm 42)

'So lovely,' I said, 'so true.'

She said, 'Yes, but the thing is, I feel God is saying it to you.'

The greatest lie that the enemy can speak to you is that your Father does not want to spend time with you . . . and if He does want to, it must surely be grudging . . . or hurried . . . or while He does several other things all at once . . .

My Father, Papa, I should know that; I think I do, but I forget in the scrummage of life. You want me! How lovely! I will stop right now and be still. How refreshing that is. I will sit with that glorious truth. Thank You. Amen.

Day 149 – May 28th

It is an extraordinary thing that God does choose who He involves in things, and we have no choice but to accept it with good grace; we may be the recipient, or a friend who is left to watch, wondering 'why him?' or 'why her?'

'Jesus took with Him Peter and James and John, and brought them up on a high mountain by themselves. And He was transfigured before them.' (Mark 9)

It must have taken some time and I do wonder what those three men thought about as they scrambled up the dusty slopes. Perhaps they had nervous feelings, anticipating something not altogether pleasant. A good talking to . . . like waiting outside the headmaster's study, but for what? Ever done that? Then, after worrying yourself silly all night long, it turns out it was to receive a commendation for something you had done!

We can be like that with God. Indeed, we can *live like that* with God!

Sometimes our ideas of God can drift into the 'headmasterly' area: He wants to see me; I must have done something wrong! And if you went to the sort of school that I went to, it was probably because your hair dared to creep over your collar or your shoes weren't the right shade of black, or some such trivial nonsense! How different the words of Jesus. *'Let the children alone, and do not hinder them from coming to Me'* (Matthew 19). Imagine a headmaster like that!

But what of the other nine disciples, the ones who saw Jesus draw the three aside to climb with Him? Were they aware? Surely they must have been. The Master was missing and so were the three disciples, and of course they all reappeared together. One wonders what they said, given how competitive they were with one another. I suspect that Jesus was firm with them about His ways. I can imagine Him saying, 'It is the way it is, but not being included does not have connotations of disapproval in the kingdom.' We need to learn this in our churches and in our families. Being taken apart for a purpose tells you nothing other than our Father recognises us as individuals, with individual needs and dispositions. But make no mistake, gifting and leadership brings responsibility; we forget that so readily. *'From everyone who has been given much, much will be required'* (Luke 12) is a principle of God giving gifts to His children.

'Let not many of you become teachers, my brethren, knowing that as such we will incur a stricter judgement' (James 3); words which aren't often included in the small print when you join the preaching rota.

So, let us be wise in our thoughts, particularly with those who are visibly 'taken apart' for a journey up the mountain. Even the awesome encounter they had there came with an expectation of the men they would become, and for Peter, as we have discussed previously, that expectation must have been a gut-wrenching and crushing aspect of his night in Pilate's courtyard.

My Father, it is an awesome responsibility to serve You. Teach my heart not to fear being left out. No one is left out in Your kingdom. It is the family of inclusion. Teach my heart to pray and honour those who are taken apart for the journey up the mountain. Teach me to value and exercise the gifting You have given me. I have so much but I also long for more of You at work in my life. Amen.

Day 150 – May 29th

Korah and his partners found themselves in a pile of trouble when they challenged the leadership of Moses.

'They rose up before Moses, together with some of the sons of Israel, two hundred and fifty leaders of the congregation, chosen in the assembly, men of renown. They assembled together against Moses

and Aaron, and said to them, "You have gone far enough, for all the congregation are holy, every one of them, and the LORD is in their midst; so why do you exalt yourselves above the assembly of the LORD?" When Moses heard this, he fell on his face; and he spoke to Korah and all his company, saying, "Tomorrow morning the LORD will show who is His, and who is holy, and will bring him near to Himself; even the one whom He will choose, He will bring near to Himself."' (Numbers 16)

The question we need to ask is *what was going on in their hearts?* It's a dangerous thing to speak so when we do not know the Lord's heart; instead we speak out of some other ugly, natural place, out of our wounded story, with all its resentments and sense of injustice. It seems to fall into the same category as the moment the woman 'wasted' the precious ointment, anointing Jesus; Judas said it was a waste, as he spoke out of his particular distorted view, but note the disciples were indignant also. Judas was not alone.

Moses' life was poured out before the Lord, and the Lord knew him. He knew every detail of his rugged journey and He loved him and honoured him among the congregation. Jesus loved the extravagant gesture of the woman who worshipped Him without regard for the cost or personal embarrassment or discomfort. You will need to read the rest of Numbers 16 to discover what happened. Let us be wise about those who have been chosen to lead; if we cannot be deeply wise, let us be silent!

Father, thank You that You choose men and women to lead. You know them. You know their stories, their longings and their desires before You. They, too, are on a journey as I am and they will not be perfect either but, the thing is, they are journeying before You. Let my role be to bless what You are doing in them. Let earnest prayer for those who shepherd the flock be a high priority for my prayer life. I come low before You, Father. Amen.

Day 151 – May 30th

Above my desk I have a card pinned there to remind me (among many other cards bearing verses of Scripture). I confess that I do not know where this came from but it has caused me to pause many times. It reads, *'A Christian pastor is one who perpetually looks in the face of God, listens to Him, and then goes forth to talk to His people. The Holy Spirit makes him a sacramental messenger. He is the message as the unconscious glory abides.'*

If we carry any responsibility at all for another, which I think neatly includes every one of us, our greatest call is to pray for and listen to God for those we love and care for. If we don't do that, all we will bring is our best thoughts. If we do pray like that, all will surely be well and profoundly of the Lord. I found that when I did not set aside time to pray for those I worked among, my care for them became very dry, tiring, lifeless and routine. When I prayed, times were filled with the unexpected moments, with the electricity of heaven; the crackling and sparkling was often in our midst.

Another card reads:

'The Lord GOD has given me the tongue of disciples, that I may know how to sustain the weary one with a word. He awakens me morning by morning, He awakens my ear to listen as a disciple.' (Isaiah 50)

If you are being taught by the Lord, you are His disciple. I often repeat this verse to myself on waking, long before I get to my desk. I commend it to you as a way of life. It is true. It *is* the word of the Lord to you. Believe Him and trust Him to speak and, as you become used to His guiding voice, in His many forms, you will learn to thrive in Him. Be blessed.

Lord Jesus, You may have made my tongue anew to be Your servant. You have made my 'ears' anew to hear You. Train my heart to believe You. Thank You. I trust in Your promise and I will set aside time each day to listen that You might teach me, that I may then go out with Your word, to sustain the weary. Amen.

Day 152 – May 31st

Many years ago I served on a ministry team, and early one morning, on the day of a service, I prayed the Isaiah 50 verse which we dwelt on yesterday. Immediately, I had a picture of a sad-looking young man. It was very vivid. I knew I didn't know him but the picture was deeply impressed on my heart. I prayed, 'Who is this, Lord?' I felt the Holy Spirit was saying, 'He will come today.'

I arrived and looked for this young man and he wasn't there. I wasn't very surprised as these daytime services seemed to attract mainly older folk. The worship began and I was troubled; I looked again. No young man. Then the Holy Spirit prompted me strongly, 'He is outside. Go and bring him in.'

When I went outside, there on a bench was the young man exactly as he had been shown to me. I do mean *exactly*! I went to him. He was really down on his uppers; everything that could go wrong had gone wrong for him. As I listened to him, I asked God, 'What is the word that will sustain this weary child?' I felt the Lord say, to tell him what happened. So I sketched for him what had happened and how the Lord had told me to come outside, telling me he would be there; then to bring him in. The tears flowed down his cheeks as the reality of such a loving God struck him; a God who knew him and cared for him sufficiently to do that.

'Well,' he said, laughing through the tears, 'I suppose I had better come in then.' He later received much very caring ministry from the team.

What I didn't know was that he had been there the week before, in my absence, and sat outside, his feet frozen to the ground, quite unable to go in.

Don't you love Jesus?

'*A bruised reed He will not break and a dimly burning wick He will not extinguish; He will faithfully bring forth justice.*' (Isaiah 42)

God, the loving Father who runs down the road to us, I give You thanks today. Bless Your holy, generous, loving name. Amen.

JUNE

Day 153 – June 1st

'How blessed is the man who does not walk in the counsel of the wicked; nor stand in the path of sinners; nor sit in the sessions of scoffers!' (Psalm 1)

Have you noticed that in the first verse of this first psalm there are three stages of engagement with unhelpful and damaging things in our lives? First 'walk', then 'stand', then 'sit'. This teaching is so wise. Most of us sniff out someone who is seriously ungodly and is potentially damaging to our faith and our walk with God, but the point here is that these enslavements can happen *slowly* and *so* subtly.

I recall a friend who was employed by a well-known firm that sold double-glazing. Their high-pressure sales techniques weren't illegal but were they moral? I doubted it. The sales training wasn't even considering the genuine needs of the client, or even their realistic capacity to pay for very expensive goods. The target was 'getting their money' – a signature on the order documents! It wasn't pretty, and I recall having an earnest conversation about it all: 'Would you do this to your brothers and sisters in the church?' I asked him.

The psalmist is very specific in his descriptions: first you might walk with the morally dodgy; then you might stand with the guilty, the proven criminals; and, finally, you sit with those who 'mouth off'! The final stage might not sound as though it should come last but these are the ones who are so ensnared by their life practices that they actually laugh, sneer and brag at those who are more sensitive and less inclined to corrupt ways.

It so speaks of life. In affairs of the heart, we see people going through this walk, stand, and sit process. Gradually people end up where they would *never* have considered appropriate in their right senses at the outset but they become inured by the journey and pursuit of love and having their deep 'needs' met. How important it is when you sense a nudge in your spirit that something is not right in a friend's life, to respond in prayer. Pray without hesitation, 'Lord, open their eyes! Stop them! Do something to wake them up!' If you have the call to pray, you may also get the call to go and speak. Psalm 1 is a good basis for explaining your concerns! And what about our own lives? Take great care; what appears to be just a little off the path may be the beginning of something more difficult to back out of. The very last line of this psalm records that *the way of the wicked will perish*. It is saying, literally, 'The way of the ungodly or morally wrong will wander off and get lost.' My friends, do not get lost!

Father, this is so true! Lifestyles can slip. The pressures to depart from Your ways can be great. Oh, that I might dwell in Your teachings and that my spirit will gladly receive all that You have to say. If You admonish me, I will listen with joy, for Your care for me is so great and Your faithfulness knows no ends. Amen.

Day 154 – June 2nd

'But his delight is in the Law of the LORD, and in His law he meditates day and night. He will be like a tree firmly planted by the streams of water, which yields its fruit in its season and its leaf does not wither; and in whatever he does, he prospers.' (Psalm 1)

So continues the second and third verses ... What a contrast! One is slow death from being far from the ways of the Lord, and the other is flourishing and verdant and fruit laden. I know which I would rather choose! It is so easy to think that the ways of man will succeed and equally difficult sometimes to see how God can achieve what is needed. But God is faithful and deception is not!

Meditating on the word day and night (which is often taken to mean early in the morning and then late in the evening) is bound to soak you in the truth and goodness of God. Life gets difficult without a close walk. I have sometimes given what I believe to be good counsel to people, after it arose out of time spent with God. You might say that it was revelation for a particular situation. It has been vaguely received but the determination and impetus of 'project vision' has prevailed over God's word to pause and to dig in with Him. I like that word *'Selah'* in the Psalms. None of us knows quite what it means but 'pause' is probably about right. 'Pausing before God' is often so wise. My friend used to say it meant, 'Hmm, fancy that!' When we rush on, sometimes God brings us back to exactly where we started from, with a whole lot of wasted energy, frustration and disappointment in between. Hmm, fancy that! The tree fruits in the right season; did you notice that? I love that 'God timing', when through His wisdom everything comes along *just on time.*

My Lord, You are a good, good Father and You are worth spending time with to understand the way ahead, especially when You see it and I don't. Please cultivate my 'pause button' so that I know to stop and to sit at Your feet, trusting that time so spent will bless me and all I endeavour to do to bring fruit in Your name. Amen.

Day 155 – June 3rd

'Like apples of gold in settings of silver is a word spoken in right circumstances.' (Proverbs 25)

Many years ago, I was laying foundations for a new kitchen extension I was building. One Saturday morning I was due to have a delivery of ready mixed concrete delivered. We knew we could not pour it straight in and that it would have to be wheel-barrowed. I was assuming the driver would be good-natured and willing to wait. A friend who, crucially, was a builder, pointed out that he would probably not wait and that, as my house stood on a slight hill, I would have to build a temporary holding enclosure for the wet concrete, otherwise it would be overtaken by gravity. Well, I decided to trust in the good nature of delivery drivers as I had known so many kind and understanding ones, and made no preparations. You can guess, yes, on the day, I was poised with a gang of friends, shovels and wheel-barrows ready, when an exceedingly grumpy driver pulled up with his slowly rotating drum of concrete. I cannot repeat what he told me to do with my shovel when I asked him if he would release the load a barrow at a time. He pushed the 'deliver lever' and out poured the load and, miraculously, it stayed put as we shovelled madly to take it inside . . . for a few minutes, and then it slowly but surely began to slither down the road, threatening to fill the kerbside drains! Hastily we dragged some baulks of timber to form a bund around it and the day was saved, apart from a huge amount of scrubbing and cleaning of the highway! I apologised to my builder friend. I should have listened to good advice and, in my novice-state, been a little less headstrong.

Father, what a beautiful picture that is of those apples in settings of silver. It is so true; a good word is like glistening oil to my spirit. It brings life and no regrets. Give me an open spirit to good guidance and to Your wisdom in all things. Thank You that I am surrounded by good friends who care deeply for me and sustain me with their prayers. Amen.

Day 156 – June 4th

One scrap of paper in my 'Sanctuary Box' has a few words penned from a sermon: 'Faith never knows where it is being led, but it loves the One who is leading. A life of faith is not easy; we like *certainty* but the spiritual life of faith is not like that. We are certain of our uncertainty. We like control but we have none; what we have instead is *rest* in the One who has control, knows where He is leading us and delights in our faith.'

'*I am the Alpha and the Omega, the beginning and the end. I will give to the one who thirsts from the spring of the water of life without cost. He who overcomes shall inherit these things, and I will be his God and he will be My son.*' (Revelation 21)

Father, Son and Holy Spirit, I praise You that You go ahead of me. You know the beginning and the end and the east to the west. Nothing is beyond Your gaze or Your plan. Give me to drink from that water of life, I pray, that I might rest by Your bountiful spring and know that my all is safe in You. Amen.

Day 157 – June 5th

The story of a single life is as nothing to the history of a nation, in human terms, at least. As we read the Old Testament prophets and begin to understand what God did in the midst of His people over and over, it feels as though we need to draw further and further back to see the overview of God's plans; His relentless pursuit of a people who would worship and love Him in spirit and in truth. That view is, of course, the view that God *always* gazes upon, and more, but as national and international situations ebb and flow we need to trust even more that God has a plan. What concerns you? Is it in His hands or not? You are right, it is.

When the nudge of God came to Jeremiah he felt led to visit the potter's house where God said He would bring His word. It is beautiful that so often God speaks through the ordinary by illuminating it and giving it 'voice'. He saw the potter throw clay and begin to raise a pot. Part way through it was spoiled and the potter lifted it free and threw it again. God spoke!

"'Can I not, O house of Israel, deal with you as the potter does?'" declares the LORD. "Behold, like the clay in the potter's hand, so are you in My hand, O house of Israel. At one moment I might speak concerning a nation or concerning a kingdom to uproot, to pull down, or to destroy it; if that nation against which I have spoken turns from its evil, I will relent concerning the calamity I planned to bring on it. Or at another moment I might speak concerning a nation or concerning a kingdom to build up or to plant it; if it does evil in My sight by not obeying My voice, then I will think better of the good with which I had promised to bless it.'" (Jeremiah 18)

If the clay inspired the prophet and he has troubled to explain to us what he saw, so indeed it may speak powerfully to *us* as a prophetic illustration. If we have seen the potter's skilful hands coaxing a thing of beauty out of a chunk of mud, so we can see that God acts so. I have never made a pot but I do paint and, when I do, it arises from a vision of something I have seen in my mind's eye. Sometimes I feel very strongly the beauty of what I may bring forth out of tubes of colour and a blank canvas *before* it becomes reality. Sometimes it works and the vision becomes reality but at other times I have been known to pick up a turps rag and wipe it out of existence! There is *no point* in pursuing something that isn't right. It will never reflect the vision I have unless I can see it taking shape. This helps me to understand why God can threaten to 'pick up the rag' and yet, *in His mercy*, He has rarely done that; the vision of what may be remains in His heart. Thank God it does, otherwise where would we be? A filthy rag in the bin? Jeremiah was later told to buy a pot and, with all the leaders present, to smash it as an illustration that when the people would not follow God and be moulded by His hands, He would indeed 'pick up the turps rag'.

Father, Your vision of Your fulfilled creation as it will be one day is so beautiful. Thank You for Jesus who came and broke into the never-ending cycle of sin, failure and consequent separation from You. We stand before You now as ones who are washed in the blood of the Lamb; there by Your grace and Your mercy alone. May I share Your vision and be so burdened by the power of Your creativity that I go out bearing the Good News of Father's heart. I praise You, God, my Father. Amen.

Day 158 – June 6th

We gave our thoughts to the Ascension of Christ a while ago. Several mighty Scriptures capture the glory of the 'full-circle' of Jesus, as this does from Paul's hand as he speaks of Christ's attitude as a model for how we be should be.

'Have this attitude in yourselves which was also in Christ Jesus,

who, although He existed in the form of God, did not regard equality with God a thing to be grasped, but emptied Himself, taking the form of a bond-servant, and being made in the likeness of men. Being found in appearance as a man, He humbled Himself by becoming obedient to the point of death, even death on a cross.' (Philippians 2)

It seems here that this first passage describes what we might see as half of the circle; Jesus came down from heaven and died to overcome sin on the earth. I doubt if there are many among us who can begin to visualise what it meant to leave the Father's side and appear on earth as a man. *Jesus emptying Himself by laying aside His glory* – I know I cannot! I have heard people query the fundamental tenets of our faith, claiming it is too difficult to believe in the virgin birth of the Lord. By comparison with the idea of the High Lord of heaven coming to earth to reveal the Father's love, Mary conceiving through the power of the Holy Spirit seems straightforward to believe! But all these events are so profound that all we can do is to ask God to give us profound revelation to enlighten us further. *This is our Lord Jesus who came not as a free servant but as a bond-servant!* All glory to Him!

Lord Jesus, I stand in awe of You. Your majesty and Your devotion to the great vision of heaven's Holy One takes my breath away. Thank You that You came. You came for us. You came so the Father would not have to reach for that turps cloth; You stood in the gap and the Father stayed His hand. Almighty God, I worship You. Thank You for saving me! Amen.

Day 159 – June 7th

The second 'part of the circle' is described by Paul in the verses following yesterday's reading in Philippians 2.

'For this reason, God highly exalted Him, and bestowed on Him the name which is above every name, so that at the name of Jesus every knee will bow, of those who are in heaven, and on earth and under the

earth, *and that every tongue will confess that Jesus Christ is Lord, to the glory of God the Father.*

Paul doesn't mention the resurrection here; he moves straight to the exaltation of Christ to the highest place. Where is the highest place? Beside the Father at His right hand; the throne where One sits if that One is an equal with God. That is being *highly exalted*. That was the joy that enabled Him to endure the cross and the shame; it was the joy of the full circle; ascended once again to His glory place with mission accomplished. 'It is finished, Father, I have taken back the keys.' 'My beloved Son,' we can imagine the Father saying, 'everything is now under Your feet. Everything!' And the whole of heaven went wild with delight at those words. Notice all the places that knees shall bow to Him: heaven, earth and under the earth; in other words, *everywhere and everyone.*

Father, when I actually stop and fully consider the total wonder of Your word in Scripture, I feel I need a new mind to understand, but, bless You, You have given us renewed ones to begin to understand the glories of Your majestic ways. Open my mind, I pray, as Jesus did with His disciples. *Holy Spirit, I want to see and understand, and be filled with the glorious wonder of Your ways.* Amen.

Day 160 – June 8th

Above my desk, I have a verse from Psalm 119 (it is verse 74).

'May those who revere You see me and be glad, because I wait for Your word.'

It is a genuine prayer of mine. When people love the Lord and long for more of Him through teaching and sound revelation, and genuinely lead deeply honouring lives, I hope and pray that they will say, 'He is here with Your word.' Is there a higher honour? It is why the crowds flocked around Jesus. I do not believe it was solely because of the miraculous healings; we are told that people came to hear Him speak, saying wondrously, 'We have never heard teaching like this before.' It is a matter of wonder when a man or woman has spent time coming low before the Lord of Lords and knows what must be spoken out. It may make the heart glad to hear such words; it may also bring fear! Eventually, it brings joy, as it is just as if it is of heaven, which it is really! I don't claim to do this always, or even often, but it is my prayer that the children of God will hear, through me, the Father speak to them. Make it your prayer. You don't have to preach to hundreds or thousands; God may have called you to bring that gold apple set in silver to the person next door who He knows is in need of heavenly sustenance.

Holy Spirit, this word and exhortation is true! It is for me! I will practise waiting for Your word that I may go out slaking the thirsts and the hunger pangs of all who truly love You. May I be the nourishment of the Holy Spirit to all who know me. May they be glad when they see me. Hallelujah. Amen

Day 161 – June 9th

I am leading a funeral and a thanksgiving this week, for a dear man who has gone to be with his Lord. We are sad but we are also genuinely experiencing the joy of his homecoming. He has set down in great detail what he would like included for his services. He chose Psalm 49.

'I will incline my ear to a proverb; I will express my riddle on the harp. Why should I fear in days of adversity, when the iniquity of my foes surrounds me, even those who trust in their wealth and boast in the abundance of their riches?'

It is not an easy psalm to speak about as it is apparently very 'blunt'. The poetic rhythms and warm encouragement of Psalm 23 are absent here. He speaks of the wise, the stupid and the senseless; all those who eventually die like beasts of the field. They create expensive houses as if they are forever homes, they call lands after themselves, he reflects. Sound familiar? But there are lines of startling power and challenge:

'No man by any means can redeem his brother or give to God a ransom for him – for the redemption of his soul is costly . . .'

What incredible insight. It is direct and challenges right to the core of the gospel we seek to share. No man can by any means *redeem* his brother. And yet this dear friend of mine *is* redeemed! In Hebrew language and culture 'redemption' is a very important word. It means, in short, paying the price for something. If you have been redeemed as a slave, you are a free man. You mean that someone paid the price for my friend. It's already been paid? Up front? Yes, it has been paid, in full, with nothing left owing. 'It is finished!' cried Jesus from the cross. Payment in full for a man's life *is* costly.

The psalmist later declares, *'But God will redeem my soul from the power of Sheol, for He will receive me. Selah. Do not be afraid when a man becomes rich, when the glory of his house is increased; for when he dies he will carry nothing away; his glory will not descend after him.'*

It's so important that we don't get trapped in the culture of the present times; it is consumerist and leads to a mood which, I feel, is quite the opposite of contentment, satisfaction and peace. Our redemption stands apart from all that and is of infinite worth. That is the heart of God for us. The redemption of a man's soul is costly. God knows. He paid for it with every last drop.

Father, I ask You to set me apart from things that are distractions to my soul. They are worth *nothing*. I am surrounded by so many whose ultimate fulfilment rests in possessions that will fade and decay. Thank You that my treasure really is stored in the heavenly realms with You. Thank You for Jesus who thought my potential in Him was worth paying the ultimate price for. That is pure grace to me and it makes me sing and dance. Amen.

Day 162 – June 10th

I am holidaying near to a river where it joins the sea. Sitting typing, I can see the water and the sea shore. The source of the river is miles away up in the surrounding hills but down here the flow produces life – reeds and other waterside plants provide havens for wildlife. Ducks, swans, seagulls and even a cormorant feed on the abundant life in the widening stream before it mingles, blended for ever into the oceans. I wonder as I watch whether the source has any concept of its purpose in all of this. It cannot have, surely? It just does what comes naturally to water. It flows out!

Jesus stood on the steps of the Jerusalem temple and boldly declared,

'If anyone is thirsty, let him come to Me and drink. He who believes in Me, as the Scripture said, "From his innermost being will flow rivers of living water."' (John 7)

When we ask the Source of Life to fill us, we will overflow! We won't have to puff and blow and struggle or drill down . . . the Lord of Living Waters will cascade from us and we in turn become a source of Life. Others around us will get wet! There will be splashes and dancing droplets cascading around. And just as the source of the river in the landscape I am looking at has no knowledge of what the waters downstream are achieving, so it will be with us. We may never know what the Lord of Life may be doing around us or downstream but just as water is bound to wet, so is He, the Life-Giver going to give Life.

Dear Life-Giving God, I am thirsty today! I praise You that You have made a promise to me that Your streams of Life-Giving Spirit-Works will flow from me. Fill me afresh today, I pray, so much that I pour out over others without regard for my own filling or needs. Thank You that the Source is eternally abundant and generous, and I will never be thirsty again as I give away in Your name. Amen.

Day 163 – June 11th

I am also reminded as I write that the sounds of the waves never cease. Yesterday there was a storm and the waves crashed onto the shore. The rain lashed, the mist rolled in and it felt like winter, not summer! Today, there is nothing more than the background of sea on shingle; music rising and falling like a repeated ripple of skilled percussion. It calms me.

'You who are the trust of all the ends of the earth and of the farthest seas; who establishes the mountains by His strength, being girded with might; who stills the roaring of the seas, the roaring of their waves, and the tumult of the peoples.' (Psalm 65)

When I watch the sea and take in all the waves that I can see, then consider all the waves that I cannot focus on because they are too far out, and finally I dwell on the concept of vast quantities of water being pushed around the planet – roaring torrents in unseen places – and I think, how wonderful that all of this is held in Your hand. The pull of the planets, intricately arranged in space, to counter-balance one another; it is a God-breathed wonder full of untold power and yet You call it all to keep its place and You define its boundaries! Not one molecule of water can burst in spray without You knowing. Don't you feel small in this overwhelming truth of such a powerful God?

You are amazing, God! Father, open my eyes to the wonder of Your creation today. Let it be inspiration to my soul. May I, like the oceans, lift up my voice to You. Amen

Day 164 – June 12th

Yesterday, a man juggled skittles and rode a monocycle on the promenade. His skin was deeply tanned and he looked as though he might spend much of his life on the beach front. He appealed to passers-by as if to say, 'Look my way! Be amazed at what I do . . .' but most passed by, slightly awkwardly, perhaps wondering if they would have to tip their small-change into his hat. Not an easy life. People don't readily look your way if you do something unusual. At least, not look you in the eye. Kite surfers, far off – they hold attention. No one is embarrassed there; rather, every onlooker is held mesmerised. The antics over the water are punctuated by 'Ooooh' and 'Aaaah' or 'Wow – amazing!'

I wonder what it would be like here if Jesus came to the beach café, or maybe sat on the break-water above the shingle. Would people hurry by? Maybe. But I think that these children would come to Him, drawn by what? I can see that some parents would come; maybe those two with that very little child in a 'frog cast'. Why would they come? They would be drawn. The electricity, the crackle and fizzle of the Son of God on the beach, changing the atmosphere and saying the unspoken words, 'Come to Me . . .' They would come.

'And they were bringing children to Him so that He might touch them; but the disciples rebuked them. But when Jesus saw this He was indignant and said to them, "Permit the children to come to Me; do not hinder them; for the Kingdom of God belongs to such as these.' (Mark 10)

Father, great Gatherer of all, come to this beach, this street, this office. Send Your Holy Spirit to change the atmosphere and heal the place. May it fizzle for joy. Make it a place of blessing, I pray. Use me. Amen.

Day 165 – June 13th

As I look out of my study window I count myself fortunate that we live amidst trees on the edge of woodland. Against the backdrop of beech trees still in the first flush of that wonderful acid green is a rowan covered in creamy blossom. Each autumn it is covered in berries and the blackbirds and the thrushes come to feast. It is a delight. A few years ago, the big old tree looked as though it might be failing; only a few leaves came out and it looked very sick. Two things happened to change the course of its life: the first was that I discovered that, quite high up, someone had wire roped the three or four main trunks together, probably out of the best intentions, but the steel had cut deep into the trunks; the second thing was that after carefully teasing the binding out of the wood, I drenched the tree roots in feed. The next year it blossomed as if nothing had happened to knock it off course. I often look at that tree and think how it can be so with us. Certain things have the capacity to deeply wound us and cut off the supply of nourishment to our spirits. The life of Jesus in us, coming to us by abiding *in* Him is crucial to our lives in God.

Jesus often alluded to nature to make the point and I see that tree and immediately think of the vine in Jesus' illustration.

'I am the true vine, and my Father is the vine dresser. Every branch in Me that does not bear fruit, He takes away; and every branch that bears fruit, He prunes it so that it may bear more fruit . . . I am the vine, you are the branches; he who abides in Me and I in him, he bears much fruit, for apart from Me you can do nothing . . . My Father is glorified by this, that you bear much fruit, and so prove to be My disciples.' (John 15)

The teachings of Jesus are so simple, but deeply meaningful and everyone would have immediately understood the point He was making. He is always very graphic. However tempting it might be to see luxuriant sappy growth on a vine, or any fruit tree for that matter, to leave it there in order to have a big tree would be pointless; you would, of course, see little fruit. It is the fruit spur that matters, not the bushiness of a grand and verdant tree; and so with us. Equally, the notion that you could cut a branch and it would live, deprived of the sap of the vine, would be nonsense to His listeners. Vine prunings and olive tree trimmings made kindling and firewood for the oven. Everyone knew the reason there were trimmings and their ultimate fate!

It's painful to be pruned, sometimes. Just when things are going well, something might come along: an obstruction to progress, or a difficult person in a group that has been tasked to a particular project. Do you think the objective God has in mind is to achieve the end game, or to learn to live together in love and in ever-deepening relationships born of the Holy Spirit's life in us? I suspect the latter, and so we are pruned back for a season but, don't doubt it, next spring there will be much flower ready for a heavy harvest. It is tough to feel the vine dresser's knife upon us but welcome it; He sees a heavy crop in the making!

My Father, as a gardener I know that I must cut down to create strong growth, but it is so difficult to experience the same in my life. Give me Your wisdom to know when to pull back from producing abundant greenery that cannot be sustained or useful. Let me accept it joyfully even when I cannot understand what You are doing and it seems contrary to my logic. Amen.

Day 166 – June 14th

I am sure that you have noticed, as I have, that Jesus often commanded those who had received healing that they were not to tell anyone what had happened. It is curious and many explanations have been offered including that He did not want crowds of people looking for Him! If so, why feed the five thousand? It might be that He was seeking to keep 'under the radar' as far as the authorities were concerned but again, if that were so, why would He make so many appearances in the synagogue? One day, Jesus was asked to go to a young girl who was dying. Jairus, her father, who was a ruler of the synagogue, came to Jesus and fell at His feet entreating the Healer to come to his house. Before He arrived, someone came from the house with a message that the Teacher should not trouble Himself as the girl had died, but Jesus replied, *'Do not be afraid any longer; only believe, and she will be made well'* (Luke 8).

One can only imagine what was going through this dad's mind.

When he left his home, the girl was perilously ill; a message has come saying she has died, and now the Teacher says, 'Don't be afraid . . .' I have never had to cope with my children in such extreme circumstances but my heart goes out to him. That must have seemed like the longest walk ever as he accompanied Jesus back to the house. When He arrived, Jesus only took Peter, James and John into the girl's room. The neighbours were there already, beating their breasts and lamenting. Jesus, seemingly going against the flow, provoked ridicule and laughter when He told all of them present that she had not died but was sleeping.

'He, however, took her by the hand and called, saying, "Child, arise!" And her spirit returned, and she got up immediately; and He gave orders for something to be given her to eat. Her parents were amazed; but He instructed them to tell no one what had happened.'

I once met a man who, as a child, had been raised from the dead after a serious accident playing ball in the road. He said that he recalls how he revived. There was no sense of needing time to recover; he was completely well. Praise God these miracles do happen. But why did Jesus tell them to tell no one what had happened in the room? Did He want to slip away leaving them believing that they were mistaken; that the little girl had indeed just been sleeping? It would seem so. The disciples knew, but no one else did. I believe that Jesus quite often had huge compassion and understanding for the people He healed. He once took a deaf man away from the crowds before He restored his hearing and it would seem He did that out of respect for the person in the midst of a sovereign act of God at work in his life. Is Jesus simply pleased to see the outworking of His power in mighty ways without gathering acclaim? I believe so. It is also possible that He was saving the girl from the excessive curiosity which, one surmises, would surround such an event; it was certainly so with Lazarus after he was raised. How different this is to the way such healing events happen now with social media and so forth, and

I wonder if that speaks volumes about how we view ministry today? This is not a tut-tut matter or disapproval of the times we live in; it is of great significance, I believe. What we do should be 'unto God'; testimonies are wonderfully edifying but we need to be sure that there is no element of 'look at me'! Every miracle is entirely God's grace and not of us. Let us give God the glory whether the story is told or not told.

Lord Jesus, Your motives and Your inclination were so pure and wise. Everything the Father had was Yours and You moved in that knowledge with quiet abandon to Him, not needing the approval of men. I need to learn that and find the same state of faithful repose. Purify my motives and my longings, and may I have more of You in my life. I thank You, generous God. Amen.

Day 167 – June 15th

Among the greatest verses in Scripture must surely be those in Romans 5. Paul received extraordinary revelation about the ways and works of God.

'For if while we were enemies we were reconciled to God through the death of His Son, much more having been reconciled, we shall be saved by His life.' (Romans 5)

The word used to describe this reconciliation is *'katallassō'* which has a specific meaning in the New Testament; it means to be reconciled one person towards another. It does not describe mutual movement towards one another as we might use to describe a broken relationship where both sides make the move. You may think I am splitting hairs but I would suggest not. *God did not change.* He stayed exactly the same but He did something very, very remarkable, even while we were locked in enmity towards Him: *He* reconciled us to Himself through the atoning death of Christ. If you thought you did some small thing to bring about this cataclysmic change in your life, I have news for you. You did not! You did nothing. True, you were saved when you believed in what He had done, but you did nothing, and even the believing was the Holy Spirit's work. All you did was to realise it when you believed!

We will never understand *grace* unless we accept the extent of our lost-ness and the love of God for us who did it all when we were quite unable to even consider His goodness, His great mercy or begin to fathom the profound depths of Jesus' atonement for a world under judgement.

If you think I am being uncharacteristically theological, it is because I want you to know that everything you are and everything you do is because He went to the cross for you. God loves you and, when you have realised it, be grateful. Enormously thankful, for ever and ever. Understanding this will, I guarantee, immediately turn you heart to worship and praise.

God, Your love is amazing! When I appreciate the enormity of this verse it puts all my silly posturing into place. That You loved me *that much* while I was totally not interested in You, Your plan for me, or Your future for me. I stand with my hands empty, outstretched towards You. That is all I can bring. I offer You my devoted heart. Amen.

Day 168 – June 16th

Today is a special day for me so I can only look to Psalm 139.

'For You formed my inward parts; You wove me in my mother's womb. I will give thanks to You, for I am fearfully and wonderfully made; wonderful are Your works, and my soul knows it very well. My frame was not hidden from You, when I was made in secret, and skilfully wrought in the depths of the earth; Your eyes have seen my unformed substance; and in Your book were all written the days that were ordained for me, when as yet there was not one of them.'

Sometimes we can only sit and wonder at God's care and provision for us. As a biologist, I am aware of all the stages of cell division, the gradual process by which the 'programme' for our development shapes cells that might otherwise be one great amorphous 'blob', and then produces you and me. We are different and yet so similar. We are totally unique. You could search the entire Earth but you would not find anyone like you! And yet God knows each one of us in intricate detail and calls us by name. When I came into being, I imagine Him smiling and saying, *It is good, David.*

Father, the longer I spend meditating on this psalm, the more wonderful to me You are. My understanding of Your ways is so limited but I do know that Your thoughts about me are so precious. I am glad you like what You see and that there is nothing I can do to improve on it. You are intimately familiar with me and cherish me and I am Yours, O, my Lord! Amen.

Day 169 – June 17th

Several years ago I was leading a church for their 'weekend away'. They wanted to launch the healing ministry of the church and I had been given that theme to speak and train on. It was a very special time as the entire church had committed to being there. I may also add that in the six months leading up to the weekend in question, a small group of ladies had met every week to pray for me and for the weekend! What glorious faith! When I heard that, I was moved to tears.

After the Saturday morning session finished everyone made to move across to the dining room. As often happens, some folk hang back to speak or to receive brief prayer. I was beginning to think I might miss my lunch and headed towards the door! A young woman approached me and asked if we might speak as we walked across. I had noticed her silent tears as I spoke during the morning, so I was pleased to meet her. She explained that she had a lovely family with two young children but there was a great sadness in her heart as her first child had died at full-term. It was a 'stillbirth'. Somehow the memory was marring the good of the present and she felt it was time that she ceased grieving. I asked her if they had named the child, or had a funeral. They had not, she told me (which is a common problem and a source of great sadness to many). Asking the Holy Spirit to guide me in such a sensitive situation, I said tentatively, 'I wonder if we should ask God what the child's name is?' She looked at me, slightly curiously, and then immediately, and in a very loud voice said, quite involuntarily, *'Luke!'* I am not sure who was the more surprised! I said, 'Well, it seems that God wanted you to know!' and we both laughed. Standing in the middle of the car park (such good places for dedication services), we quietly offered little Luke to God in prayer. We asked Him to care for him and guard him until such time as Luke and his lovely mum could meet again.

It was a powerful moment which reduced both of us to tears, but a deep peace came to her from that moment.

I feel to tell this story today because I am reminded by Psalm 139 yesterday that there are many mothers and fathers who lose their babies. It is an incomprehensible grief. The words of that psalm can seem to jar. I say to you, *trust our Father.* What I do know is that *every single life* is precious to God. Not one escapes His care. One day there will be many happy reunions with children who have grown up in the Father's house. We will, I am sure, be very, very surprised.

'But the angel said to him, "Do not be afraid, Zacharias, for your petition has been heard, and your wife Elizabeth will bear you a son, and you will give him the name John."' (Luke 1)

My Father, Your name says it all – Father. A father has children and You have made it clear to us that everyone is precious to You, named by You and completely known by You. In my spirit, I know You hold these 'lost ones' in Your great arms. I pray today for all those who have lost babies, not just those known personally to me; that Your Holy Spirit would meet them and speak the truth of heaven concerning their grief and their little ones. Bring comfort, I pray, and may the truth of Your tender Fathering be a profound healing to them. Amen.

Day 170 – June 18th

Names matter. We have previously thought about some of the people in the Scriptures who have been given names by God. When you choose a name for a child, ask God if He has a name for the expected one!

I am always struck by the names and meanings of the names of some characters we come across. Remember Jacob? His name we are told meant 'Heel Catcher' or 'Grabber'. In the womb, the two twins borne by Rebekah, Isaac's wife, struggled with one another. Prenatal fisty-cuffs! When they were young men, the two twins, Esau, the oldest, and Jacob were deeply affected by various events. Not least we are told that old man Isaac *loved Esau* but Rebekah *loved Jacob*. They were, it appears, an early dysfunctional family!

There came the defining moment when Jacob deceived the old father as he approached his last days and, in doing so, the young man, egged on by his mother, stole the older son's blessing! It was not a clever thing to have done and ever after the two sons did not see eye to eye. Indeed, Jacob spent a lot of his life on the run from Esau, both geographically and also in his mind. The story is a long and involved one. Jacob was not only the deceiver but also through his life he was deceived by others, not least his super-cunning uncle. Deception became his norm! He was the archetypal conman but he was also conned himself. It would take an entire book to unravel the full story of Jacob and explain why God wrestled him all night long until He changed the man into the leader of His people.

Finally, the twins have to meet and the messengers come with news that Esau is on his way to the meeting – with four hundred men in tow! To say Jacob was anxious about the outcome was an understatement, but that night he wrestled with a man, we are told.

It is clear this was not a dream. Jacob, when all alone, was wrestled by God as God exposed to Jacob who Jacob really was! We are told that the wrestling went on all night and at dawn Jacob's hip socket was physically touched and thereafter he limped. The most powerful tendon in a man's body had been torn apart by God! Is this the God you believe in?

During the night-long struggle we are told that Jacob would not let go; he was very tenuous and demanded a blessing of this man who seems to have been Jesus. It was a strange theophany moment.

'Then he said, "Let me go, for the dawn is breaking." But he [Jacob] said, "I will not let you go unless you bless me." So he said to him, "What is your name?" And he said, "Jacob." He said, "Your name shall no longer be Jacob, but Israel; for you have striven with God and with men and have prevailed." Then Jacob asked him and said, "Please tell me your name." But he said, "Why is it that you ask my name?" And he blessed him there. So Jacob named the place Peniel [the face of God] for he said, "I have seen God face to face, yet my life has been preserved."' (Genesis 32)

This is an extraordinary and powerful story. The Hebrew word for wrestle seems to indicate 'down in the dirt'. God got down in the dirt with Jacob and demanded that he admitted his name. *Who are you? Admit it; what is your name?*

'I am the deceiver, the tricky one, call me what you will; the Heel Catcher, Grabber, Supplanter. God, You know all things' (my words). He has to own who he has become and *then* God blesses him. He gives him the name Israel: *'the one who wrestled with God'.*

God, may my name reflect who I am in You, not my troubled past. If my life has a meaning, or if I have a name that I should have lifted from me because my past is now redeemed in Christ, please let me know my new name. May I rest in who You have made me to be called by a new name, and may I journey on into that destiny that You have saved for me. But if I have never come to terms with who I am then I need to be challenged by You, and I invite You to deal with me as You see fit. Amen.

Day 171 – June 19th

'Therefore the Lord Himself will give you a sign: behold, a virgin will be with child and bear a son, and she will call His name Immanuel.' (Isaiah 7)

'And behold, you will conceive in your womb and bear a son, and you shall name Him Jesus.' (Luke 1)

'Behold, an angel of the Lord appeared to him in a dream, saying, "Joseph, son of David, do not be afraid to take Mary as your wife; for the Child who has been conceived in her is of the Holy Spirit. She will bear a Son, and you shall call His name Jesus, for He will save His people from their sins."' (Matthew 1)

Names are important. The names God gives speak of destiny, something we have lost sight of; although it needs to be reflected on, perhaps, that we choose names with great care. Often the names we give to our children reflect a deeper truth that we believe for them or, at the very least, an important association. But from the very first, the name of 'Jesus' as we know Him, was a very specific description: 'The One Who Saves', 'God with us', and to the shepherds on the hillside at Bethlehem, 'A Saviour, who is Christ, the Messiah, the Lord.'

Destiny. Even Zacharias, the father of John the Baptist, prophesied that his own son would be called *'the prophet of the Most High; for you will go on before the Lord to prepare His ways; to give to His people the knowledge of salvation by the forgiveness of their sins'* (Luke 1).

All heaven knew and in the time of preparation the constant cry was of 'The One who comes'. Names matter. They give us an inkling of what God foresees and I believe that can also be true for us if we care to ask Him.

God shapes our destinies even when we are unaware of it happening. My nan used to take me to a mission church when I stayed with her. I remember being prayed for as a very small child. Who knows what God was arranging? Later, and I am sure it was not a coincidence, I met a doctor, a lovely Christian man who, forty years after I used to visit, was serving as a practitioner in the same church mission. We suddenly realised it was the same place and, as we chatted animatedly, I could see he was greatly moved that, so many years later, those prayers of a previous generation of quite elderly ladies had been heard by the Lord.

It's a mystery but let us pray for our little ones. Let us listen to God for them and when we hear, prophesy over them. Let us post guard for their lives. It's a rough and dark world out there now for young ones.

Father, many of us have names that we have yet to hear; names You have chosen for us. Thank You for our children and grandchildren and the children of our friends. Teach us how to pray for them and to be lookouts over their lives. We pray that You will raise up a young generation of gospel-lovers to take Your word to those who are heartsick and desperately need to hear Good News. Amen.

Day 172 – June 20th

You may recall that we thought about the rich young man burdened by riches that held him back from whole-heartedly embracing the message of the kingdom. Just after that meeting Jesus spoke the following:

'And Jesus, looking around, said to His disciples, "How hard it will be for those who are wealthy to enter the kingdom of God!" The disciples were amazed at His words. But Jesus answered again and said to them, "Children, how hard it is to enter the kingdom of God! It is easier for a camel to go through the eye of a needle than for a rich man to enter the kingdom of God."' (Mark 10)

The listeners were all aghast wondering who could be saved if it was so difficult, and the reply of Jesus was that for men, yes, it was impossible; for God, nothing but nothing was impossible.

The eye of the needle was the name given to the tiny door built into the great city gate, which was opened after dark when the gates in the heavy fortifications were secured at night by heavy bars. It was a squeeze for a man so as a defence it was perfect. For a wealthy man arriving after dark, with a camel train of trading goods or personal possessions, it was quite impossible to enter intact. He could squeeze through himself but without his baggage. *The baggage stayed outside!*

Jesus did not say it is wrong to have riches or that a rich man could not enter; he said it is *hard* for that man. The rich young man had issues with his wealth.

I often think that it is difficult for anyone to embrace fully and joyfully the Good News with *any* baggage, let alone the considerable load and distraction of wealth. Doubtless we *all* come to the kingdom with baggage – that is not the difficulty; God can relieve us of our burdensome issues. The problem lies in not *wanting* to let go! Remember Jacob? Having complex issues with the load we carry and our reluctance to have them dealt with becomes our difficulty. Have you wrestled with God recently?

What might we arrive at the gate with? When ministering to people who are struggling I often do speak of the baggage we carry; for most of us it is not great wealth but, instead, hurts and wounding, hidden sin, our refusal to forgive, and wrong identities that, although harmful to our well-being, are now familiar and vaguely and strangely 'comfortable'.

It is a wholesome exercise to imagine ourselves arriving late at night outside the gate. It is shut and barred but, on knocking, the 'eye' is opened. We cannot squeeze through with our burdens attached. What is it that we need to lay down?

Lord God, we are foolish to consider even for a moment that our burdens are worth clinging to but I have become accustomed to my life being this way. Everyone knows me this way. Speak to me, I pray, of the issues that still weigh me down that You would ask me to surrender to You. I long to be set free and truly abandoned to You. I come to You, my Father. Amen.

Day 173 – June 21st

The account of the so-called Gerasene Demoniac seems to be a highly strategic and prophetic move on the part of Jesus. If we go to the very end of the story, we find this man, who had been truly set free by the Lord, *'proclaim in Decapolis what great things Jesus had done for him; and everyone was amazed'* (Mark 5).

It begins in the previous chapter when Jesus told the disciples that they were to go over to the other side of the Sea of Galilee and the story of the storm is well known. Jesus slept on a cushion in the stern. Bearing in mind that these men were seasoned fishermen, we should conclude that this was an exceedingly great storm otherwise they wouldn't have woken Him, declaring, *'Teacher, do You not care that we are perishing?'* What a question! The boat was being swamped and they were in serious trouble. Very fierce tempests do break over the Sea of Galilee whipping the relatively shallow waters up into sizeable waves, as happens on Lake Erie where sizeable modern-day fishing boats are frequently lost 'at sea'.

The important point is that in the midst of this storm, the bucking boat contains the Lord of Lords who is asleep. The disciples, far from feeling a snooze coming on, are terrified for their lives. When they awaken the Lord, He speaks to the storm, 'Hush, be still,' and after the wind and the waves died down He addressed the disciples saying, *'Why are you so timid? How is it that you have no faith?'*

I think we must conclude that Jesus is not saying, 'What storm?' as though they were children who became anxious out in a little row boat on a municipal park pond on a breezy day. He seems to be saying, *'Why didn't you exercise your faith?'* It must have been difficult to hear that (again) but Jesus has, on different occasions, challenged them about learning to dwell in the truth that God has given them all they need; they need to learn *to live it out*. And so it is for us. In a crisis, we should be the ones who live out our faith in the Lord's absolute ability to keep us safe; not be the first ones to panic.

I recall once flying back from Holland when the captain announced that he was going to climb very rapidly to try to avoid a large thunderstorm ahead. It was possible to look out and see this huge storm approaching like a mountain range in an otherwise blue sky. I was sitting with a nervous passenger who anxiously gripped my hand. I remember saying, soothingly, 'Don't worry, it will be fine,' but then a little thought grew saying, *'Tell it to go away!'* So, I spoke a quiet prayer and, gazing at the black clouds, commanded the storm to subside, that we might have a peaceful passage back to the UK. The plane which was climbing sharply and being buffeted, suddenly levelled out, the 'fasten seat belts' sign went out and the captain commented, 'Crisis over,' or some such words. I will never know quite what happened but I thought, why not? Why not command it to go? Jesus does teach us to exercise our authority as He did. I have seen the weather change so many times in answer to prayer, most memorably with several hundred children who prayed at a holiday week for the torrential rain to cease by midday. The rain ceased at 12 on the dot and we went outside in the sudden sunshine for our balloon release event!

Lord God, You are the One who rules the seas the waves and the winds. Everything is beneath Your feet and nothing escapes You. Teach us to be men and women of faith in the ordinary stuff of life that our ministry will be to bring Your peace in the midst of life's storms. Amen.

Day 174 – June 22nd

The ensuing clash with the demonised man (Mark 5) is another story we all know well. If you think these stories are of the order of 'fairy tales', think again. Men who are truly possessed can be frightening and immensely strong. Their behaviour, demeanour and strength are not 'natural', remember. He has broken his shackles and now lives in the graveyard where he cries out and gashes himself. It is not a pretty sight but the Lord immediately engages with him as the spirit recognises who He is and begs for mercy when Jesus challenges the unclean spirit within him.

The account which follows tells us much, as Mark is inclined to do. The story is set in Gentile territory for there were pigs being farmed there, probably for demonic worship in the pagan temples. The unclean spirit is challenged by Jesus, saying, *'What is your name?'* The answer, that it is *'Legion; for we are many'*, suggests that what is going on here is a battle between unclean Roman associations and the power of God. We cannot be sure but when they entreat Jesus, He commands that they come out of the man and go into the pigs which then rush down the hill and drown – about two thousand of them. We might feel sorry for the pigs but their purpose was as evil as the Canaanite worship of Idols we read about in the Old Testament – a detestable ungodly thing. No doubt word went around that the God of this man, Jesus, had smashed their demon worship! Jesus is clearing the way for *Life* to come! The ministry of Jesus seems to be much more than simply setting a poor deranged man free. It is strategic and it is prophetic. In His sights, He has the aim of setting the Decapolis free!

'Their herdsmen ran away and reported it in the city and in the country. And the people came to see what it was that had happened. They came to Jesus and observed the man who had been demon-possessed, sitting down, clothed and in his right mind, the very man who had had the "legion"; and they became frightened.' (Mark 5)

In his 'right mind' again. How wonderful!

Lord God, heavenly King, you send us out to minister healing in all its forms, bringing wholeness and life to those who are bound. Help me to see the strategy of Your ways in families, communities and in our towns. Show us who holds the power and seeks to compete with You for people's lives. Prepare us and equip us for all we need to be competent and gifted in, in Jesus' name. Amen.

Day 175 – June 23rd

In this series thinking about the Demoniac story in Mark, we turn to a later chapter.

'Again He went out from the region of Tyre, and came through Sidon to the Sea of Galilee, within the region of Decapolis. They brought to Him one who was deaf and spoke with difficulty, and they implored Him to lay His hand on him.' (Mark 7)

It's amazing when breakthroughs happen as it clearly had here. First, the one well-known and frightening man whose reputation went before him, who, when healed, then asked to be allowed to travel with Jesus.

'[Jesus] did not let him, but He said to him, "Go home to your people and report to them what great things the Lord has done for you, and how He had mercy on you." And he went away and began to proclaim in Decapolis what great things Jesus had done for him; and everyone was amazed.' (Mark 5)

Radically different from those moments when Jesus urges secrecy! The people were afraid of the power of Jesus and wanted Him to leave them. Jesus left, but left one man in His place – an evangelist, commissioned by the Lord Himself. It is clear that this man did exactly as he had been bidden to do; he went to tell everyone of God's power at work in his life! By the time Jesus returns a small revival is at work and they bring the deaf man to Jesus to be healed. It is a beautiful story of great sensitivity and Mark goes to lengths to explain, which we will look at tomorrow.

Without doubt the most powerful message will usually emanate from those who have personal, recent experience of transformational healing through a touch from the Lord. It is wonderful to see, particularly because such people are always devoid of all the jargon and religiosity and, frequently, are lost for words. I well remember a lady who was healed after we prayed for her and she brought quite a few people to our door, but then she was launched in her own ministry and began introducing people to Jesus in her own right! Wonderful!

Lord Jesus, I stand in amazement at the ways that You worked among those who needed Your touch. I see that it wasn't random but had direction, flow and strategy in it. When you returned to a place, so often the experiences of God had spread. May I see as You see, that how I spend my time and energy may be initiated and furthered by Your promptings, Your directions and Your touch upon those You send me to. Amen.

Day 176 – June 24th

'They brought to Him one who was deaf and spoke with difficulty, and they implored Him to lay His hand on him. Jesus took him aside from the crowd, by himself, and put His fingers into his ears, and after spitting, He touched his tongue with the saliva; and looking up to heaven with a deep sigh, He said to him, "Ephphatha!" that is "Be opened!" And his ears were opened, and the impediment of his tongue was removed, and he began speaking plainly. And He gave them orders not to tell anyone; but the more he ordered them, the more widely they continued to proclaim it. They were utterly astonished, saying, "He has done all things well; He makes even the deaf to hear and the mute to speak."' (Mark 7)

What a turnaround in Decapolis! The once isolated forbidding land now wants more of the Lord! This is a strange healing. I believe that what Jesus did, He did for a specific reason. Mark gives us details that are meant to illuminate this story for us. He took the man away from the crowd. Why? Could it be that the roars of excitement which might follow the healing of his ears might be too much to bear? That is what people say after periods of deafness when they are equipped with a hearing aid. They need a period of adjustment away from noisy throngs. How kind and thoughtful Jesus was!

Then Jesus breathed a deep sigh. Why? What does this tell you, perhaps, about how Jesus saw this man? What was in His Spirit for him, I wonder? His tongue was bound, and Jesus loosed it. Why was Mark at pains to tell us that? I remember praying over this Scripture once and I began to wonder if the Lord was telling me that it was because his previous strange voice, as he attempted to articulate words, had been the subject of much mockery. It is so easy to curse someone like that: 'You and your stupid voice!' Children still are very cruel to one another . . . as are adults, of course and, remember, disability isolates people.

We must be wise about this story; we don't know exactly why Jesus did what He did. He doesn't call us to *copy* Him; to begin a saliva-based ministry! He calls us to *listen* to the Holy Spirit. I am quite happy to know that I do not know everything about Jesus! He is a glorious Mystery Man and, one day, I hope to be able to ask Him face to face, 'Lord, why did You do that the way You did?' The one thing I learn from this story is that He treats us sensitively and lovingly as the unique beings that we are. His answer may well be, '*Because he needed that . . .*'

Lord, I stand in awe of Your ways. I am engaged by Your mysterious ways. You read each one of us and, in partnership with the Father, You minister His love, His wholeness and His compassion to His children. May I also be a lover and a listener, and see Your children set free? Amen.

Day 177 – June 25th

'Who is the man who fears the LORD? He will instruct him in the way he should choose. His soul will abide in prosperity, and his descendants will inherit the land. The secret of the LORD is for those who revere Him, and He will make them know His covenant.' (Psalm 25)

This is a wonderful verse from David's pen. When you know God and truly revere Him, He will direct your life, keep you in goodness, and bless your family. I don't think this was theory for David; it had been worked out and worked into his life by God. The last line is fascinating and always grabs my attention. 'The secret' of the Lord in Hebrew is *'sôwd'* meaning 'intimacy'. When you revere the Lord and His commands and statutes for your life He will do no less than share *intimacies* with you.

Have you longed to know what God is doing? Then revere Him. David doesn't say God will tell you *everything,* (you wouldn't want to know anyway) but, as we say, He will tell you on a need-to-know basis as you reverence Him with your life . . . which is overwhelmingly wonderful!

My Father, thank You for this amazing promise that, as we draw close to You and honour You with our lives and our worship, so You draw close to us and have secret conversations and share intimate thoughts with us. Thank You for the many times You have done this but I long for more. May nothing come between us, Father. Amen.

Day 178 – June 26th

'But the Helper, the Holy Spirit, whom the Father will send in My name, He will teach you all things, and bring to your remembrance all that I said to you.' (John 14)

There have been many times in my life when I have stood in awe of what God has done. I was asked, through a mutual friend, to go to see a teenage girl who was in very serious difficulty. Her mum explained that the girl, we will call her Sue, had had a tumour removed from behind her inner ear where it had destroyed the workings of her ear and the nerves, and was growing towards her brain. It has a long name but let's not get too medical! All was as well as could be afterwards although, clearly, she now suffered from a considerable hearing impairment. The reason I had been asked to visit the home was that, very unusually, the same had started on the other side. When I met Sue, I was struck by what a very special person she was and her steadiness in her young faith throughout all of this had sustained her. Naturally, I wanted to pray for healing and we spoke about how God does heal but we don't ever know that He will in any circumstance. This young woman's faith was open to whatever God might do.

Over several weeks, I saw her as the time for further surgery drew close and, each time we talked together, I encouraged her and we prayed. One evening, I had a very clear picture of Sue playing the clarinet. I had no knowledge of whether she played an instrument or not, but it was a very clear picture. The next time we met I told Sue and her mum what I had seen. They both were open-mouthed and quite tearful. It transpired that Sue had been learning the clarinet from a young age but had been told never to play again such was the delicate state of her ear.

I felt that God was saying, '*She will play again,*' and that was how we prayed in line with the prophetic lead that God had given us.

I will conclude this story by telling you that I had a memorable phone call from Sue after a year or so. I took the call and all I could hear was music. Someone was playing a clarinet!

Such was her astounding recovery from the growth, without further surgery, that the surgeons had finally sanctioned her to go back to playing again! God is *good*!

Sue's healing is a good example of how our heavenly Father not only heals the sick but also guides us if we are open to His prompting.

Quite often prophecy is an encouragement to the person concerned as God reveals some detail of their life to *us* showing that He is there for *them*! It also grows our faith in leaps and bounds when we understand what to pray for. Praise God.

Lord Jesus, sometimes I sense You longing to bring healing to the sick. It is beyond me to know why You do what You do, when You do, but I am thrilled to be able to play my part in Your great healing moments. I ask that more and more I will share encounters with Your amazing power that changes not just bodies but entire lives. Bless You, God. Amen.

Day 179 – June 27th

A few years ago, a dear older man came to me when I had little time to give to him, and confessed that one night he had been channel-hopping when he came across a porn channel. One thing led to another and he became beguiled by this insidious stuff. I was quite surprised because he looked such an upright and godly person. There are ways to bring wise counsel and ministry to people with all sorts of addictions and I really wanted to help him but time was pressing as I had another appointment due. I prayed, 'God, would You give me a word for this man to break this wide open and bring healing to him?'

To my surprise, I immediately thought of Jesus rising out of the baptismal waters of the Jordan and the words, '*You are my beloved Son, in You I am well-pleased*' (Luke 3). I suddenly understood that God was speaking this word to the man and that that word would stop him in his tracks! I repeated what I had seen and heard. The man wept deep tears of repentance and nodded. 'Yes, yes,' he repeated over and over, and, smiling through his tears, he left.

A week later I had time to see him properly and he told me his story. He was a co-minister of a lively church and was approaching his retirement. On the Saturday following our first meeting he was due to lead an outreach men's breakfast. He prayed about what to speak on and the Lord told him to tell his story because it would be powerful to change lives. So, very courageously, he set aside all personal pride and humbly told the story. He told me that an awesome hush descended over the room as he finished and he invited anyone who wanted to acknowledge this problem to come forward. He told me, 'Honestly, there was hardly anyone left seated.' He went up to each of the men who stood at the front, placed a hand on each head in turn and *spoke the same word over each man!* He said the effect was electrifying as the Holy Spirit swept in on the word and brought not only conviction but also a deep sense of God's love and acceptance of these 'lost' folk. Several men gave their lives to God that day when they experienced real love; the love of God that their hearts yearned deeply for. In the light of *that love* they immediately ceased to have or want any allegiance to corrupt titillation.

It's a strange story because at first glance it could appear that God was condoning what they had all been doing but, of course, God was not; not at all! God was touching the very deep need of the men for genuine love; a desire that is met by the enemy with skewed and horribly distorted imagery that means *nothing* but is powerful to addict and corrupt.

He also told me the reason that it had had such a powerful effect on him when we first met and I spoke that verse over him. At his ordination, many years previously, that very word had been repeatedly spoken over him. God is amazing.

My Lord, You are the real thing! Your word brings *Life*. In the light of Your majesty and love, who can stand? Align my heart with heaven, I pray, that only Your love and Your Fatherly approval will ever satisfy my inner longings. Don't let me ever be lead into temptation to believe that anything else will satisfy me. Amen.

Day 180 – June 28th

In the accounts of Jesus' wilderness experience after His baptism in the Jordan, Mark's account is the briefest of the three synoptic gospels; but He tells us something very important.

'*Immediately the Spirit impelled Him to go out into the wilderness. And He was in the wilderness forty days being tempted by Satan; and He was with the wild beasts, and the angels were ministering to Him.*' (Mark 1)

The word that Mark used here, in Greek, is '*ekballo*'; it means 'driven out', or even 'propelled out'. It is the same root from which we get the word 'ballistic'. The Holy Spirit forcefully sent Jesus out, Mark declares. Luke and Matthew speak of Him being 'led out'.

However forcefully Jesus was led there, we must reflect deeply on why the Son of God needed to go there and what it accomplished for Him. I have heard it said that it was so that we would look to His experience and know that whatever temptations He faced, He withstood them by the word of God. That is surely only part of the explanation. It is key to full understanding, to appreciate that Jesus lived His life on earth as the Son of Man *and* the Son of God. He came in His humanity for mission and action. It seems that what was happening to Jesus in the desperate experience of the desert was that it was His earthly ministry that was being 'ratified', not His status as Son of God, despite the devil's taunts which began, '*If You are the Son of God . . .*' It was His humanity which was being challenged by Satan. Jesus' relationship with His father was in no doubt; '*This is my beloved Son, in whom I am well-pleased,*' God spoke as Jesus rose from the waters of the Jordan. His new status was not in doubt either, as far as heaven was concerned. Surely, Jesus was sent there to set down the 'game plan' for the enemy! Satan must surely have been dreading such a God-made-man mission from heaven into his territory but he was being told in no uncertain terms, and he was desperate to challenge it.

Remember in the Garden when the woman was challenged by the serpent regarding the Tree of Life? He said,

'You surely will not die! For God knows that in the day you eat from it your eyes will be opened, and you will be like God, knowing good and evil.' (Genesis 3)

Satan was throwing down a challenge with a spiritual corruption attached; it wasn't because she was hungry that she ate! He was saying to her, in effect, there is a shortcut to being on a par with God . . . just eat, woman, just eat! And of course, this relates precisely to Satan's own fall from heaven and his ungodly motives for the rebellion. He wanted to be God!

The temptations of Jesus are spiritual challenges to His humanity: *If you are hungry, Jesus, one crook of Your little finger and this stone could be freshly baked bread . . .* As he becomes more desperate to persuade, he reverts to the original battleground showing Jesus the world and offering it to Him by a different means than the Father's will: *If you will worship me, it will all be Yours; just think You could by-pass the agony of the cross . . . why don't You slip back to heaven?* They are all challenges to Jesus to persuade Him to operate as the Son of God, and not as the Son of Man sent on a mission of obedience according to the Father's will.

It's important for us to understand this thoroughly otherwise we will as likely diminish its entire significance saying, 'Well, I am hardly going to be using my God-given gifts to turn a stone into a crusty loaf, am I?'

Beware! The temptations of Satan to man are still the same spiritually corrupt challenges: *Surely you will find this satisfies the craving of your body . . . or mind . . . or spirit . . .*

Nearly every *apparently* complex battleground we may fight on as we bring the Good News to the world will distil down to this relatively simple challenge to accept pseudo-wholeness or to find godliness by a corrupt route. It is not the truth, my friends; it is not the truth. What did Jesus say? *'But when He, the Spirit of truth, comes, He will guide you into all the truth'* (John 16).

Lord God, when I imagine You in the desert, with Your whole being ripped apart by hunger and thirst, You still cling to the Father's promise to bring You through. May I also know this devotion to the Father's ways and, in doing so, stay safe; free from entanglement with alluring sin, looking only to You for sustenance and fulfilment. Amen.

Day 181 – June 29th

At the beginning of the month we looked at the 'walk, stand, sit process' that leads to downfall in Psalm 1. In Psalm 15 we find another sequence that leads to steadfastness.

'O LORD, who may abide in Your tent? Who may dwell on Your holy hill? He who walks with integrity, and works righteousness, and speaks truth in his heart. He does not slander with his tongue, nor does evil to his neighbour, nor takes up a reproach against his friend.'

So, we have: 'he lives out a life of integrity; thinks truth in the heart; and doesn't speak or say wrong things against friends'.

But this man is not a doormat, for the psalm continues that he despises a disgrace and honours those who revere the Lord; he keeps his word even when it costs him personally to do so and he won't go back on his undertaking; he will lend money but never ask for interest, and he cannot be persuaded to do wrong to an innocent person. David finishes by concluding, *'He who does these things will never be shaken.'*

What a model for Christian living and church life!

Lord, I know I fall short and I am sorry. I come before You today and ask that my demeanour, my heart's thoughts, and my actions and words will be edifying to all who meet me, and honour You. Forgive me when I can so readily slip into a different mode. Holy Spirit, cleanse my heart, I pray. Amen.

Day 182 – June 30th

If you were gripped by the notion of the Divine Wrestler in the story of Jacob at the river Jabok, you may have found yourself reflecting on times when you have been taken apart by the Lord; when the tendons and ligaments of your inner person have felt at breaking point as God has pinned you down on the floor of your life. This is how God deals with those He loves! For those who believe that God is just a cosy character to call on when needed, take care; your journey with Him may not yet have begun. It doesn't matter how you describe the wrestling encounter – grapes being pressed, bread being broken, or in the words of Psalm 57, a 'collapsed' and contrite heart – it comes to the same.

'And he who falls on this stone will be broken to pieces; but on whomever it falls, it will scatter him like dust.' (Matthew 21)

Jesus spoke those words referring to Psalm 118 which speaks of Himself, *'The stone which the builders rejected has become the chief cornerstone. This is the* LORD's *doing; it is marvellous in our eyes.'*

I must be honest with you, I have not often heard preaching on that verse from Matthew. But it's clear, one way or the other, Jesus will 'get' you. His loving way, when you go with Him on the journey of surrender to Him, is that He will break you into pieces to make you a child He can work through; emptied of yourself and finished with running; to make you truly fit for His kingdom; to sit with Him at the banquet table. It prompted someone to say, *'He whom the Lord loves, He beats to pieces'* and if you think that sounds harsh, think of the words of Job, surely among the most sublime in all Scripture: *'Though He slay me, I will hope in Him'* (Job 13).

If you haven't read the book of Job, I commend it to you. It will make you weep, it will make you squirm, and it will certainly make you vow never to open your mouth to utter your best thoughts to anyone going through the mill of anguish. Listen to the words of this very great man of God when his deep troubles and agonies were finally lifted from him by the Lord after the darkest time imaginable.

'Then Job answered the Lord saying, "I know that You can do everything and anything You want and nothing can stand in Your way. You asked me, 'Who is this who chatters away with "wisdom" but actually knows nothing?' God, I say to You, I was totally out of order, talking about Your ways when I understood nothing. I talked about You when I should have kept quiet; You are too wonderful for me to even begin to comprehend. You told me to listen to You; to let You do the talking. 'I will ask the questions and You give me the answers.' I admit, I once heard of You by the hearing of my ears. What I heard was but rumour. Now my eyes see You, God; I retract all I said. I repent in dust and ashes before You."' (Job 42, paraphrased)

That's my attempt to communicate Job's position before the Lord after a long period when God broke this man before He lovingly put him back together and blessed him mightily. The Divine Wrestler; do we dare to say, *'I know God'*?

My Lord, my God and King; we think, in our thoughtless moments, that we have You understood, tabulated, tamed and befriended. O Lion of Judah, have mercy on me. All this makes Your love for me and Your compassion for me even more astonishing. I am ever grateful and I am hushed into silence before You, Majesty. Amen.

JULY

Day 183 – July 1st

We once travelled to another city to attend a conference and had been warned that local parking was difficult and that we might need to use the 'park and ride'. First on our list was to draw some cash for the day but wherever we went in the city centre we were met with double yellow lines, so we went to the park and ride to catch the bus. We discovered that we had just enough money to park, but not to ride. It was one of those moments when you turn out every pocket and find 6p, 3 euros and a trolley token.

As we stood by the bus searching ourselves for resources, a couple, already seated and waiting, came forward, just as the driver was beginning to look a little disgruntled at us delaying him, and offered to pay our fares! It was so kind of them; an act of immense understanding and generosity. We thanked them profusely and rode the 'park and ride' into the city and went straight to a cash machine. I had a feeling that these two people must be Christians and, you can guess what happened, at the first coffee break of the day, we met them. They, too, were delegates. We thanked them again and restored their kind payment to them.

Although our 'adversity' that day was quite nominal, definitely of the momentary, fleeting sort, it showed how, when we are on tip-toes and looking for opportunities, with our 'radar' scanning as we listen to God, it is possible to touch someone's life in a very real way. The fact that I am remembering and writing this, years later, demonstrates that their kindness impacted my life when our resources were exhausted. *We can change lives!*

'In those days, when there was again a large crowd and they had nothing to eat, Jesus called His disciples and said to them, "I feel compassion for the people because they have remained with Me now three days and have nothing to eat. If I send them away hungry to their homes, they will faint on the way; and some of them have come from a great distance."' (Mark 8)

Jesus fed the multitudes with seven loaves and a few small fish and everyone was content and there was a great deal left over; seven baskets full, in fact, the perfect number in heaven. We see here that Jesus, full of the generosity of heaven, meets the crowd's very basic needs and does so after three days of ministering to them! He tells His disciples, *'I feel compassion for them.'* We rarely know from these accounts how people reacted; we are left to imagine their response but I do wonder here, as the people went off to their homes, buoyed up by this extraordinary miracle, the perfect end to three astonishing days, whether it was the talk of the town. We cannot know, but I also wonder if any of these people were present at Peter's first sermon at Pentecost and might have been numbered among the three thousand added to their number that day. These things happen.

Father, thank You for Your incredible kindness and for the generosity of heaven. Show me how to respond, in the ordinary moments of adversity, with the same selfless extravagance, not because I am 'targeting' someone but because I am trusting that every single thing I do for another one has significance in Your kingdom. Amen.

Day 184 – July 2nd

Over the years, many people in different states of distress have made their way to our door. Sadly, quite often, the cause has been a relationship breakdown.

One such person was a young woman who was quiet and reserved. It was clear that she was desperately unhappy but it was all very much 'held in' and controlled. I recall thinking, there is much more in here but it is well sealed up, locked in the cellar of her days. She was the daughter of a very controlling father and she had then gone on to marry an extremely controlling man. It happens. We prayed, but not much changed except that I had a sudden thought of the king of Israel who went to Elisha. It happened when the prophet was ill and approaching the end of his life; this is in fact his last recorded act. The king was distressed because the army of Israel had been severely reduced by the Arameans in a ferocious attack.

'Elisha said to him, "Take a bow and arrows." So he took a bow and arrows. Then he said to the king of Israel, "Put your hand on the bow." And he put his hand on it, then Elisha laid his hands on the king's hands. He said, "Open the window toward the east," and he opened it. Then Elisha said, "Shoot!" And he shot. And he said, "The Lord's arrow of victory, even the arrow of victory over Aram; for you will defeat the Arameans at Aphek until you have destroyed them." Then he said, "Take the arrows," and he took them. And he said to the king of Israel, "Strike the ground," and he struck it three times and stopped. So the man of God was angry with him and said, "You should have struck five or six times, then you would have struck Aram until you would have destroyed it. But now you shall strike Aram only three times."' (2 Kings 13)

This is a strange little story that leaves us wondering quite what Elisha was doing. It seems a little unfair as he did not tell the king to keep beating the floor but I think he was looking intently at the king to see what was within him. It needed the ministry *and* some inner strength also to accomplish his mission. So, three out of six, was how the king presented.

I took from a basket in the corner my rod and staff and offered the young woman the rod; I explained that it was a weapon in the hands of a shepherd, to beat off attacks from anything that would come against the flock. I suggested that she might like to beat the floor! Despite the odd suggestion, she knelt down and with the gentlest of movements did so with a muted 'boomph'. I thought 'there is more in her than that' and knelt beside her and put my hands on hers. We raised it above our heads and brought it down with a mighty 'bang'! I nodded to her and smiled, whereupon she took the rod and began to beat the floor with such increasing vigour that we really feared for the plaster on the ceiling downstairs! I didn't keep count but it was many more than six times! She finished tearful and dishevelled but laughing!

It was as strange as the story of Elisha and the king, for in that moment this lady somehow accessed her 'cellar', her locked-up feelings. Her rage was very evident. When we prayed, it was quite different; ministry to her hurt past became possible. How often we keep our offences and our hurts locked up in a basement where we think they are safe. They are not. They are dangerous baggage.

Lord God, Your wisdom and Your perception of how we are made is so good. You know our every thought and in times of adversity we need that touch from You to set us free to fight. I pray for those I know and for myself, that You would shine Your light into our 'basement places'. I long for the Holy Spirit to set me free, as You promised He would. Amen.

Day 185 – July 3rd

Adversity comes to us in so many ways and what is an adverse circumstance to one need not be to another. We need to remember this as we seek to minister to those in need. I recall an extreme moment that made no sense as it apparently had no significance, to me. When that happens to us we really need the Holy Spirit to shine His light.

I went to visit a lady whose daughter was unbelievably upset, upstairs in her room. She was inconsolable. No one had a clue what was going on. The girl was nearing the end of the summer term at school and was about to go on a school trip abroad, so my first thought was, is she frightened to go away? But no, she was an outgoing girl with many friends and had been really looking forward to the venture. I knew the girl a little so, in the end, I broke with normal decorum and went up and tapped on the door. I was invited in and sat on a chair while the daughter, red-eyed, hair tangled and a 'soggy heap', blew her nose and stopped crying.

'But when He, the Spirit of truth, comes, He will guide you into all the truth; for He will not speak on His own initiative, but whatever He hears, He will speak; and He will disclose to you what is to come.' (John 16)

I asked her if she knew what was happening inside her to cause such upset. She did not. I knew she was a young Christian so I suggested we asked Jesus what He had to say about what was going on. We prayed and almost immediately I saw a vivid picture of a suitcase. Just that – nothing else – a suitcase. All I could do was to offer the girl my picture and ask her if it made sense. Long story short, it turned out that everyone in the family lived in fear of the father. They all walked on egg shells around him (he has since become a Christian and is transformed – but that's another story!). This young girl had a slight speech impediment which made her stutter, especially when she was anxious, so the general tenor of the household wasn't conducive to helping her with that! At meal times, if she stuttered her father would become more and yet more angry. It sounded an awful situation. Her mother, in order to 'help', had told the girl she really had to stop stuttering as it produced such anger and disarray in the family and that every time she stuttered she was going to . . . put an item of clothing in a suitcase under her bed and when the case was full, she, the daughter would be sent away.

As the school trip had approached the mother had been putting clothing in the suitcase, as good mothers do at such times, and the next thing was *kapow!* The case was full! It was one of the strangest and most convoluted stories I had ever encountered but we need to know that it is typical of the filth that happens to people in this fallen world. As I have said before, *the enemy we face has no ethics committee.* Praise God we have a Father who sees it all and has the immeasurable power to straighten everything that is bent.

Our loving Father, I give You thanks and praise for Your loving ways that root out our most devastated places so You can pour Your oil upon them. Thank You, Holy Spirit of Jesus, that we can work with You to set the captives free. Where, O Lord, would we be without Your love and Your faithfulness? Amen.

Day 186 – July 4th

It is easy to imagine that Jesus walked under a glorious 'open heaven', (which He did, of course) and that for three years He taught and healed and spoke of the kingdom without anything coming against Him. I do not believe it was so. Jesus was the Son of God and also the Son of Man. He was both, in very real ways. He was not fifty-per cent one and half of the other so that each part of His being existed in a God-walking-the-earth compromise. He was wholly God. He was wholly man. The reason that this matters so much is that we need to understand that Jesus battled through every day amidst vitriolic hatred, loathing, fear and ignorance. Of course, many loved Him also, but even those were apt to let Him down. As we study how Jesus overcame, I pray the Holy Spirit will also enable us. When Jesus went to the house of one of the Pharisees for a Sabbath meal we are told they 'watched Him closely' (or 'insidiously').

'And there in front of Him was a man suffering from dropsy. And Jesus answered and spoke to the lawyers and Pharisees, saying, "Is it lawful to heal on the Sabbath, or not?" But they kept silent. And He took hold of him and healed him, and sent him away. And He said to them, "Which one of you will have a son or an ox fall into a well, and will not immediately pull him out on a Sabbath day?" And they could make no reply to this.' (Luke 14)

It is very difficult to imagine conducting our lives in the midst of such harsh scrutiny and a warped understanding of truth. But Jesus did not back away; He pursued them constantly with truth and wisdom because He loved them and had no intention of letting them slip away lost. It must have been exhausting; this is why it matters to fully appreciate that Jesus really did take on the world as the Son of Man. We cannot know the detail of how He 'operated' but it is an encouragement to us to know that Jesus had daily battles that might potentially have left Him bruised and battered. I do not believe He was immune from hurts; He knew how to deal with them.

Lord Jesus, we see You in our mind, reaching out into every sort of adversity and seeing heaven prevail over sickness and suffering of every sort. Send us out in the power of the Holy Spirit, as lambs into the midst of wolves but equipped with inner wisdom and strength, as You were. I long to see heaven prevail more and more. In Jesus' name. Amen.

Day 187 – July 5th

We looked on a previous occasion at how Jesus was tempted by the 'father of lies' in the wilderness place, when the enemy was desperate to thwart heaven's mission to send God as Man. But going further back we find,

'Then when Herod saw that he had been tricked by the magi, he became very enraged, and sent and slew all the male children who were in Bethlehem and all its vicinity, from two years old and under, according to the timing which he had determined from the magi.' (Matthew 2)

We can hardly imagine the vitriolic hatred and fear that existed in this man's heart. It is filth, in the extreme. That was the extreme opposition that Jesus walked in as He ministered nothing but love and power from His Father in heaven. As we move in the power of Jesus' Spirit we must expect nothing more or less. Remember the grey battleship down in the dock? It is for real. But remember the words of Jesus, those of you who battle against adversity in all its many forms,

'These things I have spoken to you, so that in Me you may have peace. In the world you have tribulation, but take courage; I have

overcome the world.' (John 16)

'The steadfast of mind You will keep in perfect peace, because he trusts in You. Trust in the LORD forever, for in God the LORD, we have an everlasting Rock.' (Isaiah 26)

Jesus has won the battle but it has yet to be worked out in our lives and the lives of those we serve, but we do so from a place of peace in Him who is Lord of all.

Lord Jesus, thank You for these words that declare such a powerful truth. I want to be found in You and in Your peace as I go forth to minister in Your name. In the midst of tribulation, I will take Your stand against the enemy whilst enfolded in Your peace. Amen.

Day 188 – July 6th

There are times in the ministry of Jesus where, I believe, we see the tension between Son of God and Son of Man. In the story of the raising of Lazarus it is the tears of Jesus which tell us so much.

'Therefore, when Mary came where Jesus was, she saw Him, and fell at His feet, saying to Him, "Lord, if You had been here, my brother would not have died." When Jesus therefore saw her weeping, and the Jews who came with her also weeping, He was deeply moved in spirit, and was troubled, and said, "Where have you laid him?" They said to Him, "Lord, come and see." Jesus wept. So the Jews were saying, "See how He loved him."' (John 11)

The indication in the Greek is that Mary's tears were in fact *wailing* and the tears of Jesus *sobbing*. It is clear that this was a scene of raw emotion. And the compassion of Jesus was deeply stirred and He was *troubled*. If we piece together this account we find that Jesus deliberately delayed for four days. He made a point of telling the disciples that Lazarus was not sleeping but dead. He delayed so for the glory of God to be revealed.

I may be wrong but this is one of the moments when Jesus is simultaneously both God and Man, inextricably linked and, possibly, causing Him some 'difficulty'. How difficult it is to walk with people through their very real pain when deep down inside you know it has purpose and direction and that it will lead to our Father being glorified. But, in the meantime, it is dreadful to fully share in that suffering until the light comes. It does not diminish who Jesus was one tiny bit to know that in the midst of the battle, as He pushed back the darkness, He met with torment and very real human struggles. It cost Him dearly to minister the love of God. Hence my thinking that Jesus was not cruising through His mission on earth with nothing but an open heaven over Him. Far from it; and when we struggle, brothers and sisters in Christ, I want you to know that Jesus is right with you. *He understands our struggles.*

Lord Jesus, this is profound but, as I sit with it, I understand more about Your transformed godly Manhood. That You came to earth with a loathing for the domain of darkness and there was real pain for You as You watched those around You struggle with their losses and their hurts; all the results of the fallen world. You hold heaven *and* the wounded reality of our lives in Your hands. You do not compromise on the Father's will. You pressed forward in every way the Father led You, and I praise You for that. Give me, I pray, the same focus and vision for what will be despite whatever might be in front of me. Amen.

Day 189 – July 7th

I struggle to begin to imagine what the heart of God must feel about the desecration of His creation here on earth. If *we* recoil from the horrors around us, what must our Father in heaven feel? And Jesus walked the earth in the midst of all the sad devastation of a fallen world. I also wonder about His times alone up on the mountainside, when He communed with His Father about everything here that was before Him. Profound times, I think.

Inside Jesus, bearing in mind His heaven-sent mission, I feel there must have been, in equal measure, utter love and a rage against everything the enemy had done. Righteous anger is wholesome. It is powerful to bring change. The Holy Spirit fills the bellies of men and women with a fire of the Holy rage of heaven but then He also fills us with His love to venture out in. It is a potent mixture known and understood only in heaven.

'For I will contend with the one who contends with you,' says the Lord in response to the question, *'Can the prey be taken from the mighty man, or the captives of a tyrant be rescued?'* (Isaiah 49). 'Contend' means just what it says in Hebrew; it means to have a 'wrangle'.

When I read of Jesus standing before the tomb of Lazarus, I hear something of the roar of heaven against all that has been corrupted and spoiled.

'When He had said these things, He cried out with a loud voice, "Lazarus, come forth." The man who had died came forth, bound hand and foot with wrappings, and his face was wrapped around with a cloth. Jesus said to them, "Unbind him, and let him go."' (John 11)

It helps me in ministry to understand this holy wrath against the enemy's perversion of perfection. Sometimes He rises in me; I feel it when I pray for people: *'Give the prisoner back! Set him free!'* Hallelujah!

Lord God, our view of You is so small; forgive us. Our understanding of Your passion so limited; forgive us. Come by Your Holy Spirit and fill us with the passion of heaven, with fire and power, we pray. We worship Your holy name, Almighty God, King of heaven and earth. Amen.

Day 190 – July 8th

There are times when we see the angry passion of Jesus manifested, to great effect.

'And Jesus entered the temple and drove out all those who were

buying and selling in the temple, and overturned the tables of the
money changers and the seats of those who were selling doves. And He
said to them, "It is written, 'My house shall be called a house of prayer';
but you are making it a robber's den." And the blind and the lame came
to Him in the temple, and He healed them.' (Matthew 21)

It was clear that this would cause great distress, indignation and
further distance Him from those who deeply resented His ways;
Jesus did not balk at that. It's important to note that nowhere did
Jesus get physical with *anyone*; He turned over tables and chairs and
caused mayhem, and He stopped the temple porters who carried the
merchandise. When He did get physical it was to lay hands on those
who had need. As I pray through this passage I sense again that it was
the same passionate indignation and rebuttal of corruption that Jesus
came against. I don't see Him sitting in a corner and 'calming down'
and then healing the sick; I see it as one and the same. Righteous
anger against the filthy work of the enemy. The Holy Spirit may cause
us to come in the same spirit also.

Lord Jesus, we have so much to learn about Your great heart for
good and for righteousness. Show us what You felt and send us out
crying out the great *'No!'* of heaven, as we come against the works of
the enemy. Amen.

Day 191 – July 9th

Adversity takes many forms but our response should always be the
same: compassion, love and the power of Jesus. Anyone who wishes
to minister to those in adversity really should spend time soaking
in the pages of 'Job'! Not only does it speak of spirit-churning,
unspeakably awful times but it also guides us, those who would be
counsellors and ministry people!

In the midst of all that Job suffered comes the phrase that must
surely be one of the most sublime in all Scripture: *'Though He slay*

me, I will hope in Him' (Job 13). *'Selah'*, as they say in the Psalms, *'Selah . . .'*

We will look at this further but perhaps I may be allowed to point out that those in adversity tend to do one of two things, or possibly both, indicated by the next line:

'Nevertheless I will argue my ways before Him.'

We will either totally trust in God no matter what befalls us, or argue and bargain with Him, or both: *Why me? Have I not served You well? Have I done something to offend You, my God?*

In the next days we will look at what may happen to a man or a woman of God as God leads them through times of extreme adversity. But for today we finish with another verse from Job that would surely be echoed by anyone in a place of adversity.

'Oh that I were as in months gone by, as in the days when God watched over me; when His lamp shone over my head, and by His light I walked through darkness; as I was in the prime of my days, when the friendship of God was over my tent.' (Job 29)

Father, thank You that You sustain us no matter what. You have given us Your word. I am safe in You as my refuge and my salvation. You are my glory and the One who lifts up my head, for ever. Amen.

Day 192 – July 10th

It is important to be positioned properly and soundly in God. There is no other way of saying it or stressing it further; we must know what God has done for us and live in that relationship with Him. Here is St Paul:

'I pray that the eyes of your heart may be enlightened, so that you will know what is the hope of His calling, what are the riches of the glory of His inheritance in the saints, and what is the surpassing greatness of His power towards us who believe. These are in accordance with the working of the strength of His might which He brought about in Christ, when He raised Him from the dead and seated Him at His right hand

in the heavenly places, far above all rule and authority and power and dominion, and every name that is named, not only in this age but also in the one to come.' (Ephesians 1)

And later in the next chapter he tells us that when we were dead in our sinful lives, God *'made us alive together with Christ [by grace you have been saved], and raised us up with Him, and seated us with Him in the heavenly places in Christ Jesus.'* (Ephesians 2)

Beloved, we need to know this in the depths of our spirits. Paul writes it out as he does, knowing that his readers also need to know the blessing and power of *living* in the truth. This is not a matter for academic curiosity; when we speak over others or declare it in faith over our own lives, the enemy has to go. He has no rights to stay any longer. So today we will spend a little while worshipping God for what He has done and praising Him for where He has seated us – with Christ.

Lord God, heavenly King, You have truly overcome everything and we are not simply looking on; You have taken us and seated us in places of honour with Christ. What You have, You have shared freely with Him, and what He has He shares freely with us through Your grace and by Your Spirit, God. I believe it and, Holy Spirit, I ask that You *completely* build this truth into my life. Amen.

Day 193 – 11th

'Store up for yourselves treasure in heaven, where neither moth nor rust destroys, and where thieves do not break in or steal: for where your treasure is, there your heart will be also. The eye is the lamp of the body; so then if your eye is clear, your whole body will be full of light.' (Matthew 6)

The teachings of Jesus are not complicated. He uses words and imagery which speak easily and readily to our hearts, minds and bodies. Jesus might say to us, 'Are you sure what you are striving after is worth the struggle? Are you certain your high-value items in life

266

are really as incorruptible as you think? Are your eyes seeing truth? Do they adore the light, or are they inclined to turn away for fear of being illuminated within?'

Let us partner with Him to get ourselves into the spiritual equivalent of Olympians; gaining stamina from His truth and learning to draw upon Him for our every worthwhile moment. Adversity can come to all but it tends to come and provoke a bigger and more profound battle when we have yet to see Jesus as our only source of life and fulfilment.

Lord, I want to lay before You today anything I value above You. Speak to me, Holy Spirit, of what must be as I walk down to the dock where I see the battleship readying to set sail. Let me take but few things; let my baggage be checked and passed fit for what must come. Lord, I love You and I declare my full devotion to You today. Amen.

Day 194 – July 12th

One afternoon, I had a phone call from a local friend who had slipped and fallen in the shower while trying to round up a particularly hairy spider. His valiant effort to save his daughter's shower-time anguish ended in disaster when his outdoor shoes slipped on the wet surface and he fell and broke his leg. I arrived within a couple of minutes to find he had dragged himself into the living room. His leg was a mess with a compound fracture of his shin bone. We called for an ambulance and immediately began to pray as I wrapped him and made him as comfortable as was possible. When the paramedics arrived, they made to put a line in his arm for painkilling purposes but there was no need as he was by then in no pain.

At the hospital, once the splints were removed, a doctor came to look, ordered x-rays, went 'tch, tch', sucked in his cheeks and shook his head. 'Surgery for you, my friend,' was all he said, and left. We prayed which, as you might imagine in an A&E cubicle with thin curtains, was probably overheard by everyone around. When the x-rays were available we pored over them and the three portions of tibia with two jagged breaks, one of which had made a bid for freedom through his trouser leg. The bones were jumbled and misplaced and the surgeon who came to look explained that it would be alright but would need a reconstruction with considerable metal work and a rod through the tibia, and so on. He let us know he was booking a theatre slot. It still surprised everyone that my friend was still not at all in pain. We prayed some more . . . and then the surgeon who was due to operate came to see for himself. He examined the leg, looked at the x-rays, re-examined the leg, wrinkled his nose and asked, 'Can you raise your leg?' In one swift balletic movement, the leg was duly raised from the trolley. 'I need more x-rays,' he said and left us. 'Pray more,' said my friend, convinced that something was going on, so we prayed more and I spoke healing over this wrecked leg in every way I knew how. When the second set of x-rays returned, to everyone's absolute incredulity and bafflement, the three portions of tibia and two nasty breaks were *perfectly lined up.* I do mean *perfectly,* so much so that to my untrained eye I was no longer sure where the breaks were. The staff, naturally, were all speechless. They put the leg in a cast after a trip to theatre to clean out the wound and the next day he came home on crutches.

'And they brought a blind man to Jesus and implored Him to touch him. Taking the blind man by the hand, He brought him out of the village; and after spitting on his eyes and laying hands on him, He asked him, "Do you see anything?" And he looked up and said, "I see men, for I see them like trees, walking around." Then again, He laid His hands on his eyes; and he looked intently and was restored, and began to see everything clearly. And He sent him to his home, saying, "Do not even enter the village."' (Mark 8)

From which I learn not to stop praying!

Lord Jesus, You are an amazing healer. You astonish us with Your extravagant touch on our bodies. I give You thanks for this special moment when You came and touched this leg with wonderful results. Bless Your holy name, Lord. Amen.

Day 195 – July 13th

When Jesus comes and moves upon us in our times of adversity, we never know what He will do. He *will* hear us and He *will* come. We cannot demand of Jesus what He should do. I wish I could tell you that every time I have prayed for someone they have been healed, changed or set free; I cannot, and if I did, you would not believe me. After many years of praying in all sorts of circumstances I have come to the simple conclusion that sometimes God heals and sometimes He doesn't. As I never know which it may be, I always pray. It's a simple theology of ministry but it suffices for me. I *always* want more, I do see more, and I am always thankful. If someone *in extremis* is filled with God's peace, especially if the person has not experienced His Presence before, I think that is remarkable. Have you noticed how Jesus lays down stepping stones to faith? He begins in one place and takes us on a journey into Him, and those of us who pray should be wise to this and not immediately seek the obvious. I am sure that sometimes Jesus speaks to us of our journey being more important to Him than our destination.

The power of Jesus was 'physically' around Him in a very special way and it seemed as though those with faith could draw on it. It was a very real dynamic event when a godly healing took place. It is important for us to understand this as the Holy Spirit behaves now in precisely the same way as Jesus did then. I have known people be healed in a gathering where Jesus was at work in people's lives, but they weren't prayed for.

'And a woman who had a haemorrhage for twelve years, and could not be healed by anyone, came up behind Him and touched the fringe of His cloak, and immediately her haemorrhage stopped. And Jesus said, "Who is the one who touched Me?"' (Luke 8)

Of course, everyone in the crowd denied it and Peter pointed out that the people around him were all pressing towards Him, but Jesus said, quite definitely, *'Someone did touch Me, for I was aware that power had gone out of Me.'*

This is quite extraordinary; crowds pressed against Him in the jostle, it would seem, and yet one woman pressed in *and touched Him with faith* and was healed!

It is a very touching and beautiful story in many ways. Jesus had huge respect for women and honoured them publicly on many occasions. Here, after the woman has explained all *in public*, Jesus declares her healed. He also set her free of the condemnation and seclusion that a woman with a constant 'issue of blood' would have suffered. He said to her, *'Daughter, your faith has made you well; go in peace.'* He called her 'daughter', did you notice that? He honoured her faith. He told *everyone* she was healed; that was an important part of her restoration.

We need to be aware that the healing touch of Jesus may go far beyond the obvious ailment or problem. We should have our eyes wide open and relish more the beauty of His ways, perhaps.

Father, I love the way You honour people and bring to them restoration that goes beyond broken bodies and ailments. Help me to see as You see, when I am praying. Help me, by the Holy Spirit's nudges in my spirit, to understand what You want to do and to partner You in declaring Your wholeness. Amen.

Day 196 – July 14th

As I have hinted once or twice, I seem to have walked through considerable adversity in the past (and to some extent, still do). It was my late wife who had cancer and died. Running in parallel with her illness, I went through enough problems with my spine and surgery to last anyone a lifetime. There were a few times when we were both in hospital; different ones. But the extraordinary thing, and this is my overarching testimony, is that I came to know God more, to know myself more, and to understand my journey with Him more than I could ever have done if the troubles had not assailed us.

'Many are the afflictions of the righteous; but the LORD *delivers him out of them all.'* (Psalm 34)

I believe it; absolutely. In my experience, however, it goes beyond being 'merely' delivered, as though one juggled an egg in the kitchen and managed somehow to save it from crashing to the floor; it is the journey to deliverance that changes us most. That is what happened to David and it is what happens to many thousands of Jesus' followers. The significance of this, understanding how God may lead us through troubled times, has a massive impact on how we minister to those in need. There are so many beautiful and moving portions of Scripture I could quote but the one that has spoken truth to me so many times is Psalm 84.

'How blessed is the man whose strength is in You, in whose heart are the highways to Zion! Passing through the valley of Baca they make it a spring; the early rain also covers it with blessings. They go from strength to strength, every one of them appears before God in Zion. O LORD *God of hosts, hear my prayer; give ear, O God of Jacob! Selah.'*

You see, beloved of God, we are on a highway. Who travels on a highway? Pilgrims. We are on a journey to God. There are no fast-transit transport systems, not that I have come across, anyway; instead we travel onwards, sometimes together and sometimes solo.

The valley of Baca, or in Hebrew, *Bâcâr,* is a place of *weeping.* The word has an association with balsam trees also. I think it is meant to convey both. When balsam trees are gashed or wounded, they weep. It is the gum from the weeping that is used to create beautiful perfume. Somehow when we weep in this place, it is changed; it becomes a place of springs! Our tears perhaps become the springs; miraculously transformed by God into blessings as we go along and, with every step, we go from strength to strength. How glorious is that truth! I imagine others who look on might not see it; they see perhaps only a band of poor struggling waifs, the 'anawim' of God. Listen: God's ways are not the ways of the world; in His incandescent beauty He is transforming us, from one degree of glory to another. I would go as far as to say, the more glorious we become in His magnificent eyes, so the more ragged and pitiable we may appear in the world's view. Onwards!

My wonderful Father, I give You honour and praise for the magnificence of Your ways; for Your endless holding of my life on my pilgrimage into Your heart; for Your great hands that have not only delivered me but, on the way, You have enabled me to walk on my high places. O my Lord, I worship You today. Amen.

Day 197 – July 15th

There is nothing quite like a serious diagnosis or calamitous news to throw you back on your deepest resources, and God wants you to find *Him* there. Why? Because that is what matters most to Him. Our scaffolding comes crashing down; all those support systems we contrived to hold us up in the day of deep need are shown for what they are when the Lord comes close. These days we speak, post-banks crashing, of institutions that are subjected to 'stress tests' which means, in effect, do they have the resources do cope in the day of financial pressure or even disaster? For our good, God seems to want to 'stress test' His children! It's not a new concept and even the briefest reading of prophets of old reveals God's ways. In the midst of dreadful predictions, here is what Jeremiah speaks.

'Blessed is the man who trusts in the LORD *and whose trust is the* LORD*. For he will be like a tree planted by the water, that extends its roots by a stream and will not fear when the heat comes; but its leaves will be green, and it will not be anxious in a year of drought nor cease to yield fruit.'* (Jeremiah 17)

Such truth.

Father God, may my roots be planted deep in You. May they be found in the day of heat to be deriving nourishment and succour from Your streams of living water. May I, by Your grace and merciful love, be one who produces great fruit even in a year of drought. Amen.

Day 198 – July 16th

I recall one day in the oncology ward, when my wife was on the bed while a sister, by then well-known to us, was attaching the infusion bag on the stand. We both noticed that she winced as she raised her arm. We asked her what the matter was and she related how she had suffered for many months with 'tennis elbow'. She had received treatment and injections but to no avail. Rest, she had been told, might quieten it; not so easy when you are in charge of a busy cancer ward. We asked if we might pray for her, which we then did, and immediately her arm was healed!

There is a strange irony in that the patient is lying on the bed, with cancer, and our prayers brought healing to the nurse! It was one of the first moments when we realised that God could turn situations upside down and, in the midst of our considerable adversity, He would touch lives. I have often told the story of a man who came to me with an inoperable spine condition, extraordinarily similar in medical detail to my own problem and, as I tried to pray, I was in such pain that I could barely lift my hand to his head. As I did so, the considerable power of the Holy Spirit fell on him and when he recovered he realised that he was totally healed!

I did feel a little 'put out' I don't mind admitting, but I learned to rejoice in the blessing of others while our own situation did not apparently change.

One day someone, quite unaware of what was going on in my spirit at this time, brought a word to me; the gist of it was that the Lord said, *You gave your life to Me and I have taken it and I hold it; I have shown you that I am your salvation. I will never let you go. You are Mine and I will do with you as I will because I love you, My son.*

That sorted me out! But it's a word we all need to hear at times; it moves us rapidly from the place of 'me, me, me,' to 'You, Lord; You, Lord; You, Lord.' It should not be strange to us that God chooses to move powerfully in the lives of those around us, using our circumstances to bring healing and salvation to others. It is, my friends, the way of the cross.

'And He said to him, "Truly I say to you, today you shall be with Me in Paradise."' (Luke 23)

Father, I hear the call of Your kingdom on my life. You call to the deep places in me; places that I hardly know but are well known to You. I trust You with my life, in good times and in hard; Your will be done in me. Amen.

Day 199 – July 17th

It became clear to us that Jesus wanted to 'invade' our situation and our home despite or, perhaps, because of our circumstances. There came a particular day, and I cannot remember quite why it was prompted, when we made together a covenant before God. I have written before about the baggage we can sometimes carry and one particular 'brick' in our rucksack is often that we have reacted to the 'offence of God'. God will at times seem to offend us. He is not, of course, but we construct ways of thinking that He does not always share. From our earliest days we learn to cry, 'But it's not fair!' Rest assured, when that little voice rises in you, God is on the move.

Recognising that my then wife was facing a degree of illness that was likely to take her from us, we covenanted with God that we would not in any way take offence at what was happening (or not happening). We simply made an unconditional invitation to Him to come and use us in any way that He chose. I am not sure God needs such an invitation but that is what we did. It was heartfelt and intended to honour God. We knew that He would care for us and that we need not be concerned. It is not an exaggeration to say that neither of us had ever known such peace or such a level of 'sharpness' in the Spirit after that day.

'Seek first His kingdom and His righteousness, and all these things will be added to you,' (Matthew 6) and other such verses speak powerfully at such times. 'Deep calling to deep' perhaps?

We found that, more and more, our diary was full of those who came seeking prayer or healing ministry to body, mind or spirit. Our diary was frequently filled with three appointments six days a week. It was a beautiful and powerful time. My love of Psalm 84, which begins 'How lovely are Your dwelling places, O LORD of hosts . . .' with its emphasis on the Valley of Weeping spoke to us profoundly. We were seeing the springs flow and the 'early rains' as God restored people to a fresh understanding of His love for them.

On some days we found that people were stumbling as they came in and were caused to come low before the King, such was the Holy Spirit's power in our midst. As well as blessing others, we also knew God's remarkable care for us. On one occasion when some children had come, they unfortunately brought with them conjunctivitis which my wife was unable to fight in her weakened state. The next day she woke with fiercely red, burning eyes. Before I phoned for a doctor's appointment I laid hands on her and we prayed. I still have the vivid memory etched in my mind of watching how both eyes, in the course of about thirty seconds, went from red to pink to white. We never did go to the doctor.

'Loving kindness and truth have met together; righteousness and peace have kissed each other. Truth springs from the earth, and righteousness looks down from heaven. Indeed, the LORD will give what is good.' (Psalm 85)

My Father, how indescribably great You are in all You say and all You do. Where else would we go? Who else would we go to? You alone have the words of life. Amen.

Day 200 – July 18th

There were days when what was happening felt like the early account of Jesus in the courtyard of Simon Peter's house.

'While the sun was setting, all those who had any who were sick with various diseases brought them to Him; and laying His hands on each one of them, He was healing them.' (Luke 4)

Many people who came were deeply troubled in mind and spirit but the Lord always seemed to enable us to set them back on their feet. For many, it was a very first experience of the love of God touching their lives. It became commonplace to hardly know how they had arrived at our door; a friend of a friend had usually made a recommendation – in some instances, friends of our university-age children. Unclean spirits took flight in the presence of God, backs were healed, and life-long hurts were lifted from wounded spirits; it was remarkable. On one occasion, I recall we stood praying for the postman in the hall and, as we did so, I was healed of a painful surgical scar. The atmosphere was electric with the light and power of heaven.

We kept the evenings to ourselves. As you might imagine, it was quite miraculous that my wife had energy for all of this but she did and in the evenings we would rest and pray, and read uplifting books. Last thing at night I would take oil and anoint her and pray for healing. The Holy Spirit would be resting on her as we prayed and she would be overwhelmed with His love and peace. We must have done that for at least a year; every night we asked God to bring to us the really big healing we longed to see. He did not.

'Though He slay me, I will hope in Him.' (Job 13)

Father, to know You is to love You. I find words are not easy to come by some days. I have to sit and gaze at Your beauty. I feel Your warm embrace even when the wind screams from without. Do not let me go, God. Amen.

Day 201 – July 19th

It was clear one day that things were not at all well. After a phone call, we were summoned to the hospital urgently. My wife's bloods had taken a great dip and she was fighting an infection. She was neutropenic with a score of less than 0.1. I was told that she was very ill and required 'barrier nursing' to prevent any further infection. Only I was allowed to see her when suitably scrubbed and gowned. The doctor was very serious and spoke kindly and firmly in response to a question about 'when can I go home?' We were told it would take time. My wife was not a good patient in hospital; the proverbial impatient inpatient.

The next day the doctor came to take bloods and again she reiterated the need for four or five days' rest. The lovely doctor was told, 'We are praying,' to which she responded, 'You may be but you are still going to rest!'

I went in a little later and brought with me bread and wine and oil. It was one of the most moving moments I have ever known, sitting on that bed in gloves and gown and mask, as we broke bread, shared the cup and remembered Jesus. I anointed her with oil and prayed. The Holy Spirit was so powerfully present that I had trouble not sliding off the bed!

Later that morning, the doctor put her head round the door. She was ungowned and without a mask. She said quite simply, 'I don't know what you guys are doing, but whatever it is just keep doing it. You are back up to 4.6 and you can go home whenever you want. In all my days in medicine, I have never seen anything like it.'

'I will rejoice greatly in the LORD, *my soul will exult in my God; for He has clothed me with garments of salvation, He has wrapped me with a robe of righteousness, as a bridegroom decks himself with a garland, and as a bride adorns herself with her jewels.'* (Isaiah 61)

Father, we live in days of both sadness and joy. We look around us and all we see weighs heavily upon our hearts, but within we know the joy of the Lord. May we go out with the message of Your Good News on our lips as we declare Your goodness. Emmanuel. You are with us. Amen.

Day 202 – July 20th

'Come, let us return to the LORD. For He has torn us, but He will heal us; He has wounded us, but He will bandage us. He will revive us after two days; He will raise us up on the third day, that we may live before Him. So let us know, let us press on to know the LORD. His going forth is as certain as the dawn; and He will come to us like the rain, like the spring rain watering the earth.' (Hosea 6)

Although the context of that verse is not appropriate, I have always thought of it as restating the infamous words of Job in a different way. Rather as the cornerstone becomes the place we trip and break, or worse, God *allows* adversity to come. He breaks us; He presses us. We have this strange idea that, as fruit, we are to look like shiny full grapes – big clusters. We are no use to God as such; first we must each be pressed. As living stones, we must be broken down before we can be rebuilt.

The days became more difficult but it was as though, in the natural, the summer had moved into autumn and then winter came; in the presence of Jesus, the trees were in blossom and the birds were making nests. I cannot explain that. He had torn us but He had healed us. We wanted for nothing. His peace was upon us and the days were quieter.

Father, there are truths that are beyond us but give us the grace to minister wisely into places of loss. When we do not understand, allow us to bring Your peace. We think of those who are struggling today and pray that they will be enveloped under Your wing and know the great *shalom* of God. Amen.

Day 203 – July 21st

The last chapters of the book of Job are remarkable. As this dear man emerges from his long, dark, ghastly journey, many things become clear to him that he could not see before. His words are few and humble. Does God send adversity? No, I do not believe He does, at least not in our context; but does He allow it? Yes, He does. He does it because we are too precious not to be led through it and out into the Light.

'Then Job answered the Lord *and said, "I know that You can do all things, and that no purpose of Yours can be thwarted. 'Who is this that hides counsel without knowledge?' Therefore I have declared that which I did not understand, things too wonderful for me, which I did not know." Hear, now, and I will speak; I will ask You, and You instruct me. "I have heard of You by the hearing of the ear; but now my eye sees You; therefore I retract, and I repent in dust and ashes."'* (Job 42)

God, Holy God. Your ways are beyond me. I could not plan any days of worth or direction and yet You do that for me. You make me rich; You unfold for me the treasures of darkness. My eyes are clearer now. Let Your Light shine into me; illuminate me, I pray. Amen.

Day 204 – July 22nd

It is not at all surprising that, sung or read, Psalm 23 is the most popular choice for our endings. David wrote it when he was a comparative youth; as a shepherd, he knew well what it was to care for a flock. He saw, in his experience of being frightened and on the run, the immense pastoral instinct of the Lord of Lords. Modern shepherds tend to drive their flocks with dogs or even a quad bike; David went out in front and *led* his flock; the sheep followed him. It is still the way in the Middle East. Here is this glorious psalm with my own slight interpretations of the Hebrew.

'The LORD is my shepherd. I shall lack nothing. He makes me at home in green verdant pastures. He leads me beside a brook that waters and rests me. He restores my soul; He leads me in the paths of righteousness for that is the only way He can be. Even though I walk through the valley of deep darkness, I fear no evil; for You are with me; Your rod and staff bring me comfort. In the midst of my enemies, at the most unlikely moment, You prepare a table before me; You anoint my head as a special, honoured guest; my cup overflows. Surely goodness and loving kindness will pursue me all the days of my life, and I will dwell in Your family home for ever.' Amen.

Day 205 – July 23rd

'No longer will you have the sun for light by day, nor for brightness will the moon give you light; but you will have the LORD for an everlasting light, and your God for your glory.

Your sun will no longer set, nor will your moon wane; for you will have the LORD for an everlasting light, and the days of your mourning will be over.' (Isaiah 60)

We have little idea of what is before us all in heaven but it sounds unimaginably beautiful; the most wonderful place to be. I gather in my mind all the very best days of my life when the Lord has been close, and roll them all into one; I know that represents but a very tiny part of just one minute of what we shall one day see and experience when we are *with Him*! Imagine! Living by the Light of the Risen Lamb! Imagine the worship! O, my Lord!

In the meantime, we are to live as citizens of heaven, seated with Him in that place. It is a truth that can transform our lives right now. As you sit in yet another church wardens' meeting, as you place another bucket under a leak in the roof, on the day when your knee is too painful to walk, when you go into the garden only to see those pesky slugs have destroyed your lettuce seedlings over night, when your best friend has passed away and you watch as the coffin proceeds down the aisle, remember the words of Jesus,

'If I go and prepare a place for you, I will come again and receive you to Myself, that where I am, there you may be also.' (John 14)

Father, we recognise that as Your children here, we are but sojourners. We make our pilgrimage into Your great heart but we have little idea of what it will be like to meet You face to face in our family home; the royal residence of the King. Keep me going, Lord, I pray, faithfully serving You until the day. Amen.

Day 206 – July 24th

The Song of Songs is the most beautiful love poetry, full of barely nuanced erotic meaning but I am sure that the early Christian interpretation, that it represents the longing of Jesus for His Bride, the church, is not far from the truth. For me, on *that day*, it explained all. *'The fig tree has ripened its figs, and the vines in blossom have given forth their fragrance. Arise, my daring, my beautiful one, and come along!'* (Song of Songs 2)

One day the call becomes too strong. 'Come with Me! Come with Me! Come up here and see what must be!' It is a day of excitement and not for mourning. A day to anticipate, as a child, the coming of endless summer days, full of sublime pleasure; it represents the longing and the consummation of all that we are when it is gathered up by the Lord.

'Precious in the sight of the LORD is the death of His godly ones.' (Psalm 116)

And the Lord came and the sunlight of a bright day became as if it was dirty in the light of heaven. These things change you.

My Father, I thank You. I bless You for everything. You are an amazing and beautiful Father to us. Amen.

Day 207 – July 25th

One day Jesus went by boat with His disciples to Dalmanutha. The account in Mark follows the feeding of the four thousand. As soon as they disembarked, Jesus was challenged by the Pharisees who wanted to see an 'attesting miracle'. It was not an innocent request; it was to 'test' Him – there were dubious undertones. The whole thing clearly caused Jesus some distress.

'Sighing deeply in His spirit, He said, "Why does this generation seek for a sign? Truly I say to you, no sign shall be given to this generation."' (Mark 8)

The Greek is difficult; it appears to say, *'If a sign be given it will not be given to this generation.'*

It is quite apparent that all day long people jostled around Jesus for miracles of healing. Quite often Jesus had to retire for that reason, so who is Jesus speaking of when He speaks of 'this generation'? It would seem that, sadly, He is speaking of the religious leaders. The passage continues,

'Leaving them, He again embarked and went away to the other side. And they had forgotten to take bread, and did not have more than one loaf in the boat with them. And He was giving orders to them, saying, "Watch out! Beware of the leaven of the Pharisees and the leaven of Herod." They began to discuss with one another the fact that they had no bread. And Jesus, aware of this, said to them, "Why do you discuss the fact that you have no bread? Do you not yet see or understand? Do you have a hardened heart? Having eyes, do you not see? And having ears, do you not hear? And do you not remember, when I broke the five loaves for the five thousand, how many baskets full of broken pieces you picked up?" They said to Him, "Twelve."'

Jesus continued to quiz them about the feeding of the four thousand and the seven baskets full they collected up.

'Do you not yet understand?'

Pressing ahead into matters of the kingdom is not easy. This is probably the nearest Jesus came to 'losing it'. I make a serious point here. On the one side He has the religious leaders with all their learning and their profound knowledge of the Scriptures; they are still looking for a sign and not understanding that the One they long for has come! On the other side, the ordinary working men he is mentoring and preparing for a supernatural ministry who have no learning but they have masses of first-hand experience. He has just fed first five thousand and then four thousand people. I rather think when He was before the second multitude and His disciples said, *'Where will anyone be able to find enough bread here in this desolate place to satisfy these people?'* Jesus might have been hoping one of them would say, 'Jesus, could I try to multiply the bread and fish myself this time?' Or at least, 'Master, are You going to do it again?'

Instead of which, bless them, all they manage is to sit in the boat thinking Jesus is suggesting someone should have brought the sandwiches! It is quite mind-boggling. How frustrating it must have been for the Lord. Bless Mark for his honesty in recording this!

Father, I am sorry that we don't 'get it'. So much of what You have said passes us by. Forgive us for the days when You show us *so clearly*, and yet we do not go out doing what You have so magnificently equipped us to do in Your mighty name. I commit to trying to learn afresh. Do not give up on us. Keep teaching us the same lessons and may our faith grow by the inspiration of Your Holy Spirit. Amen.

Day 208 – July 26th

In the reading yesterday, we looked at how slow the disciples were to catch on. Jesus asked them several times during His time with them, *'Do you have a hardened heart?'* We are used to the word 'sclerotic' usually applied to some hardened piece of our bodies. That's effectively what Jesus asked them: *'Have you got a sclerotic heart!'*

On the Emmaus Road, two of the disciples met Him but didn't

recognise Him after His resurrection. We cannot know how Jesus appeared so that is quite forgivable. I also think that Jesus had a sense of humour and the conversation He had with them is surely meant to make us smile. I cannot help but think that the reality of the resurrection was such a relief to Him that He might have been glad to have a private chuckle. Don't dismiss the thought out of hand; how would *you* have been feeling on the road that sunny day, fresh out of the tomb having been through the dreadful redemptive experience?

'They were talking with each other about all these things which had taken place. While they were talking and discussing, Jesus Himself approached and began travelling with them. But their eyes were prevented [held, seized] from recognising Him. And He said to them, "What are these words that you are exchanging with one another as you are walking?" And they stood still, looking sad. One of them, named Cleopas, answered and said to Him, "Are You the only one visiting Jerusalem and unaware of the things which have happened here in these days?" And He said to them, "What things?"' (Luke 24)

So the two men brought Jesus up-to-date regarding the seizure of the One they believed was the Messiah, and how the authorities crucified Him . . . and how the women had had an angelic encounter revealing to them that Jesus had risen and that explained why the tomb was empty!

Jesus still didn't reveal Himself but said, *'O foolish men and slow of heart to believe in all that the prophets have spoken!'*

His actual words translate as *'What unintelligent (or "sensory") men and dull of heart (or "not hasty of heart"), to believe . . .'*

The responses of Jesus here on the Emmaus Road and also in the 'no sandwiches' incident tell us a great deal about how we can be. The reason I think that the word 'sensory' is a good one (not 'sensual') in that we are all good at believing in what we can touch, see, smell and so on. Didn't Thomas actually say it? *'Unless I see in His hands the imprint of the nails, and put my finger into the place of the nails,* and put my hand into His side, I will not believe' (John 20). How very sensory!

These stories can be powerful to change us, if we will allow them to do so. I want to ask you a question. (Please don't worry, I often check myself in this respect.) How long do you suppose it takes you to recognise God's presence?

Father, these stories bring a smile to our lips. They are quite funny but also, I know, that they challenge me. My heart can be slow to see You, and my spirit 'sensory'. We long to see more of Your ways and then when You do something unexpected I know I can step back. Thank You that You made a point of blessing those who believe without seeing. Increase my faith, I pray. Amen.

Day 209 – July 27th

Continuing the theme of 'how long does it take us to recognise God' it will only take a moment to realise that many of the times that God has manifested His presence in Scripture, He has been doing unlikely things! It is not only in the post-resurrection accounts that we find Jesus doing the unlikely. Certainly, He hadn't walked through walls to appear inside a locked and barred room before. For Peter it was the opposite! He was getting *out* through locked doors. The account of Peter being set free from prison by a wonderful angelic move of God, whilst under heavy guard, is well known. What makes us smile is that the believers were gathered at John Mark's house praying fervently for Peter's safety (knowing that James, the brother of John, had just been executed by Herod). When he arrives at the door, Peter probably wished they had been a little quicker off the mark!

'When he knocked at the door of the gate, a servant-girl named Rhoda came to answer. When she recognised Peter's voice, because of her joy she did not open the gate, but ran in and announced that Peter was standing in front of the gate. They said to her, "You are out of your mind!" But she kept insisting that it was so. They kept saying, "It is his angel." *But Peter continued knocking; and when they had opened the door they saw him and were amazed.'* (Acts 12)

It does make us smile because . . . just because. Not least, we can see ourselves in these stories.

But when Jesus was taken outside of the city walls and crucified, thereby redeeming the sin of the world, the Passover slaughter to cleanse the sins of tens of thousands of Jerusalem visitors was proceeding within. When the High Priest emerged on the steps and shouted, 'It is finished', as was the custom when the last sacrifice had been made, all but a small handful of devoted followers had missed the greatest moment in history when God also cried out, *'It is finished!'* for the very last time. God has a habit of appearing 'outside of the walls' and, sadly, we have a habit of missing Him.

Lord God, open my eyes, I pray, to the unlikely and Your unexpected moments. Give me clear eyes to see and a heart that leaps with expectant joy at the knocking on the door. I praise You that You are the God of the unlikely. I ask for a child's innocent spirit to believe. Amen.

Day 210 – July 28th

'Permit the children to come to Me; do not hinder them; for the kingdom of God belongs to such as these.' (Mark 10)

When my children were small, we used to have all sorts of conversations at bedtime. It may have been partly down to stretching out the moment but I recall questions such as, 'Did Jesus go to the toilet?' and 'Did He wear socks in bed when He was cold?'

I never minded; indeed, I took delight in them being so natural about the Lord, not least because it demonstrated how they were thinking about Him as a real person and not as a magical man in a book called *The Bible*. I think Jesus would have laughed with twinkling eyes, further extended the lights-out moment, enjoying thoroughly bedtimes in my house! Can you see Jesus like that in your daily contexts? That's how children see Him.

There was a wonderful moment at least thirty years ago when we were staying with my mum and dad and, in the midst of a crazy game of rounders, my mum had twisted her knee. It was painful and swollen. At the children's bedtime they came to say good night and there she was, leg up, resting, with a pack of ice on her knee. One of them said, 'Don't worry, Nana. I shall say a prayer and it will be alright.' The prayer was simple and accompanied by a very small hand resting on her arm. *'Lord Jesus, I know You make people better when we ask You. Make Nana's knee better, please. Amen. Good night, Nana.'*

The next morning my mother was hanging out the washing when the children came down (my mum was an early bird) and I heard the conversation that went, 'Darling, my knee is better today. It's *completely* better.'

'Of course it is, Nana. We asked Jesus, didn't we? Can we play rounders again today when all your jobs are done?'

And the little one skipped away singing, 'Thank you Jesus, Thank you Jesus, Thank You, Lord, for loving me.'

Dear Lord Jesus, thank You. Thank You for loving me. Thank You that You went to the cross and made it possible for Your healing power to make us better. Bless our children and our grandchildren today. Let them keep their childlike faith. Amen.

Day 211 – July 29th

When the seventy-two disciples were sent out, their instructions were remarkably few.

'Whatever city you enter and they receive you, eat what is set before you; and heal those in it who are sick and say to them, "The kingdom of God has come near to you."' (Luke 10)

Jesus also added that if a city did not receive them, they should go into the street and brush the dust from their feet as a protest, saying, *'be sure of this, that the kingdom of God has come near'*. He spelled out the dire consequences for that place in eternity as a result. Wow! Don't mess with God's children when they are out on Father's business!

When they returned, bubbling over with excitement at what had happened, they exclaimed that even the demons had obeyed them as they had ministered. Jesus taught them that their rejoicing should not be about the effects of the authority He had given them, but instead that they were known by Father in heaven. But Jesus *was* excited with them.

'At that very time He rejoiced greatly in the Holy Spirit, and said, "I praise You, O Father, Lord of heaven and earth, that You have hidden these things from the wise and intelligent and have revealed them to infants. Yes, Father, for this way was well-pleasing in Your sight."' (Luke 10)

In the Greek, it says 'He took off the cover'! That's what reveal means! He took the cover off and said, 'Look, little ones!' And Jesus was overjoyed, even dancing, declaring, 'Father, You are giving it away to the kids!' I can imagine Him adding, 'It's what We always wanted to do!' If you are struggling with this concept, you should know that the word used in Greek for 'infants' means 'very little children'; *'nēpios'* indicates children who are really too young to speak. (My word checker has just entirely appropriately suggested that *'nēpios'* might be 'nappies'.)

Father, I love the idea that You really see us as Your kids! I need to get my crusty old heart and mind around this. I thought I had to be wise, sagacious and prudent around You; maybe even a little religious. Set me free, I pray, of all that I might *think* I have to bring to You and immerse me in Your Holy Spirit today. Amen.

Day 212 – July 30th

We do have to be a little wise; not everything that is surprising or very unusual is of God. We can end up with problems if we just assume 'whacky' is automatically the Holy Spirit's work. I also do not want to be at all condemnatory. What I have often seen, though, is the joy that rises in people when they are released from the 'baggage' of being too serious around Jesus or, living in the pre-resurrection solemnity of Good Friday as a way of life. Jesus has risen! He is seated at the right hand of the Father and we are His brothers and sisters and He has chosen to seat us with Him. That makes me smile!

One Easter, many years ago, a baby was born to a delightful couple in our church. She arrived on Maundy Thursday. Sadly, the baby had a massive hole between the two sides of her heart which was life threatening and, in those days, there was little to be done. The parents decided to bring her home, not least because they had another child at home; they knew she might die but they felt they wanted her to be with them.

On Easter Sunday we held our service as was usual at that time in a leaky old community centre, a portable cabin construction that smelt of stale beer from the wedding the night before. I just mention this in case you are picturing this event in a soaring cathedral . . . I was leading the service and, in usual Easter Sunday fashion, we were celebrating the glorious resurrection story. When we came to 'the prayers', the parents quite spontaneously came to the front with the baby and the father, very gently, without a word, put the tightly wrapped newborn in my arms. They just stood there and if any couple have ever pleaded with their eyes, they did so.

Dear man, what was he thinking of? I was lost for words. I held her and stood silently and uselessly, trying to ignore my tears that were splashing onto her tiny shawl. Then something extraordinary happened. One at a time the members of the church gathered round and we began to murmur prayers, holding on to one another as we did so. The murmurings turned to beseeching (remember the 'Oh, now, Lord! Do it now!) and after a considerable amount of prayer, I gave her back to the parents. The service finished and we went our ways.

The story, pieced together, was that on Monday morning this little blue-tinted mite had a pink 'normal' colour. They called the hospital. They were due to return anyway so they were told to come straight in. The staff were amazed as they had expected the worst over the weekend. Far from it, this baby looked incredibly well. Ultrasound was primitive in those days but they did an immediate scan and it was very clear that the hole had gone. They weren't sure, but they felt there might have been a tiny pin hole which, they assured the parents, would close in time.

It was an amazing Easter healing! Praise God! The memory still fills me with a glow and a few tears. It was *wonderful.*

What disturbed me greatly was that a man, indeed a leader, came to me after that service and rebuked me strongly. He had little to say except, 'You shouldn't have done that. When that baby dies, that will not help those parents at all.'

I need to tell you that, not because I hold anything against him, he was forgiven years ago, but because you need to know how tough it can be, even in the midst of God coming down powerfully into our moments. I was devastated, as you might imagine. It is not easy stepping out in faith but I say to you, *'Don't stop! Don't ever stop! Jesus was and always will be overjoyed at your childlike faith.'*

'In Him was life, and the life was the Light of men. The Light shines in the darkness, and the darkness did not comprehend it.' (John 1)

Lord God, no wonder Jesus jumped for joy when His disciples returned. If I have fears and doubts in me, I do ask You, Holy Spirit, to help sort me out. I do not want to be prudent or too intelligent to pray. I want to have the eyes and a heart of faith. Let Your kingdom come! Amen.

Day 213 – July 31st

The end of yesterday's story is in two parts.

The baby grew up into a wonderful girl. Sadly, the effects of oxygen starvation at so critical a stage caused her development to be affected – although such things are in the eye of the beholder! And the One who beheld her loved her more than we can know. She was the most adorable and life-giving child. She beamed from ear to ear and everyone who met her was loved by her and loved her.

It's a mystery, along with all the other mysteries, why God could do an astonishing, out-of-this-world healing like that and let someone not be fully healed. My answer is that God has a different view of 'normal'. She was more 'normal' than all of us and had love beyond any capacity that I have. We have to be aware that we can fail to 'get it' because we do not understand what God is doing.

As far as my 'denting', again, a strange moment happened ten or even fifteen years later when I was involved in a ministry training weekend. To cut a long story short, to facilitate what we were doing, I offered to take the place of the one to receive prayer. The person who was demonstrating had a very accurate word of knowledge about this event that had happened so long ago that it was completely out of my mind. With a little probing it emerged from my 'basement'. I had no idea how much hurt I had carried from this wounding. I had forgiven the man concerned but somewhere, deep down, I was still really wounded.

'Though a host encamp against me, my heart will not fear; though war arise against me, in spite of this I shall be confident. One thing I have asked from the LORD, that I shall seek: that I may dwell in the house of the LORD all the days of my life, to behold the beauty of the LORD, and to meditate in His temple. For in the day of trouble He will conceal me in His tabernacle; in the secret place of His tent He will hide me; He will lift me up on a rock.' (Psalm 27)

God, You are a magnificent Father to me. I am lost for words. You look after every detail of my life. You care passionately that I am a whole man; that I function well and that my spirit remains open to You and all that You have for me. Thank You for saving me, loving me, and healing me. Amen.

AUGUST

Day 214 – August 1st

I am watching the seagulls flying in a stiff coastal wind. It is a bright evening and the surf is starting to crash on the beach and a few brave youngsters are pressing into the water, surf boards under their arms. The gulls are simply riding the wind. They are maintaining a fine balance between remaining quite still and being blown fiercely backwards. Every now and then they wheel around and glide at very high speed, making the most of the breeze until they turn once again and ride the air currents. It seems a little pointless but I imagine what they are doing is watching and waiting all the time for a feeding opportunity.

I feel there is something about these birds that speaks to me of how we are to be with God in the Spirit. None of us see action in ministry all the time. I am not sure we could cope if we did! Jesus took time out, climbing the hills and mountains to spend time alone communing with Father. We need to do the same otherwise we will soon find ourselves 'running on empty'. There are times when we can run well during impossibly demanding circumstances and when we need to do that we find God energises us for the duration.

David speaks of *'For by You I can run upon a troop; and by my God I can leap over a wall'* (Psalm 18). In some translations, it speaks of running upon 'a furrow'; I am sure it is intended to be 'a furrow'. If you have ever tried running across a ploughed field, you will understand what David is saying. It's incredibly difficult; all normal poise and balance is lost. Running on a furrowed field is a recipe for a broken ankle! But, says David, when I need to, God enables my feet. More than that, if I need to leap over a wall, with God, I can do it. But he is not suggesting that he spends his life doing these things!

To come back to the gulls, they are in their natural environment; they are designed to remain airborne riding the wind. It is not an effort for them. All they need to do is to slightly trim their wing angle and they stay there; perfect repose! We also need to develop this gift in our lives; to remain poised, completely ready for action, scanning the landscape for the next word, the next moment, but at rest with our Father.

Father, I see Jesus covering the ground at a rate that astonishes me, but I also see Him resting with You. Teach me to find balance in my days, to find a place of repose in You and to soar when the winds of the Holy Spirit blow. Amen.

Day 215 – August 2nd

One of the reasons we can fail 'to get it' is that we are far from 'at rest'. There is a young blackbird in our garden that dashes back and forth, lunging at the ground, missing the worm, dashing again, and so forth. I think he must have expended the equivalent of a worm's worth of nourishment by the time he finds one! The older blackbird is there, head cocked to one side, watching intently. They say that the blackbirds and thrushes can *hear* the worms coming up, encouraged by their feet tapping. How restful is that? It's amazing!

Sometimes the disciples behave rather like the young blackbird. The intention is vaguely in the right direction but it is misplaced zeal!

'When the days were approaching for His ascension, He was determined to go to Jerusalem; and He sent messengers on ahead of Him, and they went and entered a village of the Samaritans to make arrangements for Him. But they did not receive Him, because He was travelling towards Jerusalem. When His disciples James and John saw this, they said, "Lord, do You want us to command fire to come down from heaven and consume them?" But He turned and rebuked them, and said, "You do not know what kind of spirit you are of; for the Son of Man did not come to destroy men's lives, but to save them." And they went on to another village.' (Luke 9)

This is an astonishing story but let us not condemn these men. It demonstrates the messes we can get in when we make *assumptions* concerning what God is doing! It also might be a reminder that because God appears to have done something *once* He may not have set a precedent which gives us licence to do the same! In some versions, it tells us that the disciples added 'as *Elijah did'*. (Elijah under very different circumstances had called down fire.)

The story is self-explanatory in many respects; the Samaritans had not done the disciples any harm but merely reacted out of their cultural and religious differences. The disciples also seem to have not yet fully understood that the ministry of Jesus was to be marked by miracles of mercy and compassion! Jesus thus rebuked them for their misplaced zeal but it was a strong rebuke: *you are coming in the wrong spirit!*

How wise we need to be. How easy to set up a Ministry of Spitting in Eyes, or some such! After all, it does *say* in the Scriptures that Jesus did that. We do not have licence to take offence when people disagree with us, or to be thoughtlessly whacky in our ministry. In my experience, when the Holy Spirit asks us to do something unusual, there is a huge 'knowing' about it. It is often a spontaneous rising in us that seems wholly right in that moment and, for me, that is out of character. If I feel peace about acting out of character, usually it is God!

I emphasise this because many people have come to our door over the years who are casualties of less than thoughtful ministry in churches. The damage done to an individual's faith can be immense. Indeed, I recall watching someone who believed that Jesus had given him a ministry of very loudly shouting healing commands right in people's faces! He went down a line of people who had all put their trust in God and come forward for prayer. All it did was to knock people backwards with shock (and head for the door as soon as decency allowed). It would be mildly funny in *Evan Almighty,* but it is not; these are real lives.

Father, thank You for this precious lesson that the apostles, very courageously, included in their accounts. It is so good for us to have it, to learn by it and to take on board the profound lessons. Holy Spirit, I ask that all I do will have the stamp of Your authenticity on it; that it will reflect Your heart and that those who come will be blessed by You. Amen.

Day 216 – August 3rd

1 Corinthians 13 speaks to us of acting in love and not out of desires for self-aggrandisement or selfish aims. It is a well-known reading at weddings but the intended readers were those in the church; its aim is to teach us how to behave in Christian life, in ministry and in our worship together. When we absorb this into our lives, all will be well. I can have the most astonishing ministry, be laden with gifting from God and see miracles at every turn *but,* writes Paul, without love *I am nothing.*

Did you hear that? *Nothing!*

'Love is patient, love is kind and is not jealous; love does not brag and is not arrogant, does not act unbecomingly; it does not seek its own, is not provoked, does not take into account a wrong suffered, does not rejoice in unrighteousness, but rejoices with the truth; bears all things, believes all things, hopes all things, endures all things. Love never fails. (1 Corinthians 13)

Wow.

Lord, I need to sit with that once more. I ask Your forgiveness for failing so often to behave as heaven would have me do in my life. Amen.

Day 217 – August 4th

We are going to move our focus now from the emphasis being on failing to 'get it' to some intricate examples of Jesus' ministry that take us 'up a notch'; to stretch us in the Lord and His goodness! There are many beautiful examples of Jesus modelling treating people well. Many of these occasions focused on women; He had a very great heart-desire to treat women well, contrary to the norms of Middle Eastern life.

Before we do, I would like to offer you three scriptures from the Old Testament.

'O LORD, the hope of Israel, all who forsake You will be put to shame. Those who turn away on earth will be written down, because they have forsaken the fountain of living water, even the LORD.' (Jeremiah 17)

'I will not punish your daughters when they play the harlot or your brides when they commit adultery, for the men themselves go apart with harlots and offer sacrifices with temple prostitutes; so the people without understanding are ruined.' (Hosea 4)

'He has told you, O man, what is good; and what does the LORD require of you but to do justice, to love kindness, and to walk humbly with your God.' (Micah 6)

There is something shockingly understanding about the ways of God. We find Him, in Scripture, focusing on those who are genuinely to blame for a given state of affairs and not condemning those who are in the wrong against whom it would be barely just to level accusation. Justice is His way. It is not to give us licence to behave badly; it seems to be to do with the Old Testament equivalent of 1 Corinthians 13; the Micah 6 passage above.

So, before we plunge into another series of adventures let us spend a while reflecting on how we act towards others and before God.

Holy Spirit, I ask you now to reveal to me any of my ways that fall short of Your call to loving kindness, humility, justice and mercy. I will spend time quietly in Your presence and I trust You to speak if there is anything I should attend to. Amen.

Day 218 – August 5th

Jesus has spent the night on the Mount of Olives and in the early morning He went to the temple where all the people came to Him and He sat teaching. The following happens in front of an audience.

'*The scribes and the Pharisees brought a woman caught in adultery and, having set her in the centre of the court, they said to Him, "Teacher, this woman has been caught in adultery, in the very act. Now in the Law Moses commanded us to stone such women; what then do You say?" They were saying this, testing Him, so that they might have grounds for accusing Him. But Jesus stooped down and with His finger wrote on the ground.*' (John 8)

This was an unpleasant situation for everyone, particularly for the woman who potentially might suffer ridicule and shaming at the hands of a mob. It is unlikely that this was a 'court' in any sense; the leaders who brought her did so to ensnare Jesus, not to find her guilty. It is appalling what men will do from fear; she was used for 'target practice' for their cowardly venom. It must have been uncomfortable for those who happened to be sitting there listening; perhaps it wasn't. Perhaps this was a bit of 'sport'. We cannot tell. But, make no mistake, the whole foul force behind this was the malevolence of the learned ones for Jesus. Their intention was to so jam Him in a corner that whichever way He moved they would bring a conviction against *Him* – not her.

Jesus says nothing but bends to write in the earth; as it was in the temple it is reasonable to assume he wrote in the sand and dust on the floor. I have heard so many explanations for this and suggestions as to what He was writing, but I believe His actions have their origins in the verse we read yesterday from Jeremiah.

'*Those who turn away on earth will be written down, because they have forsaken the fountain of living water, even the LORD.*' (Jeremiah 17)

It was customary that the names of those who were found guilty of serious offences against the Law would have their names written in the earth, usually by the gate, as a sign that they had turned away from God having forsaken the Lord. One assumes this was because *the earth* and heaven were witnesses.

Without a word, Jesus signals to the crowd who have brought the woman in, that something is very wrong. Is He writing *her* name? No, He is writing too much. Could the Teacher be writing *their names* in the earth? Could He be? Is He saying that they have forsaken the fountain of living water by their behaviour? After all, they have not been straightforward; *where was the man who was with her when she was caught?* The Law was clear: both man and woman were to be stoned if found guilty of adultery (Deuteronomy 22).

Jesus is telling them, I believe, that they are *seriously out of order* and that they have wilfully and corruptly used Scripture inappropriately for their own ends. So, what of the *'walk justly, love mercy'* of Micah 6?

These men had a great deal to think about. It had suddenly become very serious indeed. *Jesus reveals the hearts of men.* They were learning once more that it is wise not to mess with the Lord.

Lord Jesus, I know I am too fond of making judgements about people in my heart, usually because it makes me feel better about myself. I know it offends You and I do not want that. Forgive me, Father, and speak to me sharply when I fall into this trap. Teach me to love mercy and loving kindness. Amen.

Day 219 – August 6th

We see in this story, where Jesus is confronted by the scribes and Pharisees, the fullness of justice and mercy as it is in heaven. Jesus wrote in the dirt and I am guessing that some of the gathering were probably getting the message but they persisted, we are told, until Jesus straightened up and said to them, *"'He who is without the sin among you, let him be the first to throw a stone at her." Again He stooped down, and wrote on the ground'* (John 8).

This is not a silly battle; Jesus pitting His wits and knowledge of Scripture against the hypocrites: *it is God at work.* This is how He is. He *is* love and mercy. He is justice. Jesus does not condemn people; He comes to make them well. But if they persist in 'forsaking the fountain of life, even the Lord' He will use their own folly against them. This is not only history; we see it happening every day as contemporary fact. But He still does it to turn men's hearts, if at all possible.

'When they heard it, they began to go out one by one, beginning with the older ones, and He was left alone, and the woman where she was, in the centre of the court.'

This tells us a great deal. 'In the centre . . .' indicating the original listeners are still there; this is being played out like some ghastly drama in the round. It also tells us that the oldest decided first that it was politic to call it a day. It's easy in a cosy cabal to dream up plotting plans. No doubt they drew strength and encouragement for their cowardly act when they envisaged how it would be, before the event; no doubt it was all planned. No one anticipated this outcome. The wise ones, the ones with a few grey hairs, realised. Then, the younger ones, deflated, their sense of self-righteousness shown up for what it was, follow. It is not a pretty scene and I doubt there was any sense of having won the round in the heart of Jesus; just immense sadness and maybe anger also.

Father, what silly games we play. How we lose the way. Thank You that in Your mercy and love and great forbearance, You put up with us and You will not let us go. Amen.

Day 220 – August 7th

We see in this remarkable account so much of the true character, loving creativity and immense patience of the Lord. We can only imagine what this poor woman felt, used as a pawn in a grim religious game of chess by those who should have been leaders and pastors and experts in how to live godly lives. What was she wondering before Jesus spoke?

'Straightening up, Jesus said to her, "Woman, where are they? Did no one condemn you?" She said, "No one, Lord." And Jesus said, "I do not condemn you, either. Go. From now on sin no more."' (John 8)

Jesus' behaviour reflects the aspects of grace that should be apparent in our own relationships and actions; we also should be highly relational, creative and redemptive. Some have suggested that this woman might have been Mary; we cannot tell. If it was Mary we can understand why she lavished such worship on Jesus. If it wasn't Mary this time, she also had her moment in another time and place, when she was lovingly cleansed and set free also.

Jesus has navigated right down the middle, taking the course between upholding the Law and licence; 'the mountains and the swamps', someone once said.

Lord Jesus, Your love and Your immense wisdom and warmth towards us, Your lost children, are so very great. Teach us to see how to be. It is not about learning Your words; it is about heart surgery. We need You. Amen.

Day 221 – August 8th

A few days ago, I used the phrase 'Jesus reveals the hearts of men'.

Luke records that Simeon spoke to Mary and Joseph of that in the temple when Jesus was but a baby.

'Simeon blessed them, and said to Mary, His mother, "Behold, this Child is appointed for the fall and rise of many in Israel, and for a sign to be opposed – and a sword will pierce even your own soul – to the end that thoughts from many hearts may be revealed."' (Luke 2)

The briefest glance at the Gospels will show us that Jesus does indeed reveal what is in men's hearts. He speaks of many things which act as deep provocations to us; to what we *assume* is the way of God. We need to be very wise and, further, to be leaning in on the

Holy Spirit's understanding and guidance as we speak or act in His name. God doesn't always act as we think He should. Because Jesus is deeply concerned with our hearts, with truth and our eternal destiny, He may decide to challenge us concerning His Lordship, rather than heal, and speak words that do not bring peace when we would rather preach 'nice' words. I have a thought process which helps me to embrace many of the ways of Jesus. It is the *'Surely, You wouldn't do that, would You?'* moments that should concern us and, as we go deeper with God, we will be exploring this and the consequences for our lives as we journey with Him. We think that as believers and disciples we will always understand Him; that we will have insider-revelation, but we do not always have such privilege.

"'For My thoughts are not your thoughts, nor are your ways My ways," declares the LORD. *"For as the heavens are higher than the earth, so are My ways higher than your ways, and My thoughts than your thoughts."'* (Isaiah 55)

Are we really ready for this?

Father, You are a God of surprises and they are not always what we want to hear and see. Give me a heart that is genuinely open to what You are doing; to think the unthinkable of You. Shake up my preconceptions of You and bring me into the light of the kingdom, I pray. Amen.

Day 222 – August 9th

As we consider some *'Surely, You wouldn't do that, would You?'* moments of God, we will see that it is true! God has done so many things in that way. Think for a second of the most basic tenets of our faith; that Jesus was sent from heaven by God, to be a King, and destined to be nailed to a cross where He would die to redeem the world! Who would have thought that? *Surely, You wouldn't do that, would You?* That the birth of the King would be in a filthy cattle shed, amidst the animals, in a tiny place called Bethlehem, a town renowned for raising sheep for slaughter in the Temple . . . *Surely, You wouldn't do that, would You?*

Even the most basic choice God made, to choose a people to call His own, who were essentially unknown and indistinguishable from so many other tribes and races . . . *Surely, You wouldn't do that, would You?*

In our own lives, we might reflect on this question for there are sure to be historic events in our lives, and moments yet to come when, under our breath, we mutter, *Surely, You wouldn't do that, would You?*

'I heard and my inward parts trembled, at the sound my lips quivered. Decay enters my bones, and in my place, I tremble.' (Habakkuk 3)

It often provokes a time of revelation when we sit with this and reflect honestly before God on the times that have not really made sense, and we may have been very unwilling partners with Him, and yet God has done something really remarkable.

I recall a time when I was in and out of the spine rehab unit over very many months. I dreaded having a relapse and going back in for treatment or surgery. One time this happened was just after New Year in 2000. I called the hospital and received the response I did not want: *you had better come in; bring your things* . . . On this occasion I was not at all happy about it, not least because my wife was far from well and I wanted to be at home. I fumed my way onto the ward and all through the epidural infusion that followed. But, in the middle of the night, when my infusion was being checked, the nurse struck up a conversation about her own personal problems and how she saw no way out. There, perched on the side of my bed in tears, at three in the morning, she gave her life to the Lord.

I almost heard Father say, *'Now do you see why you had to be here, My son?'*

I went home the next day.

Surely, You wouldn't do that, would You?

My Father, I love Your ways, even when I cannot understand them. I want to be a flexible and willing lover in Your kingdom and, having given my life to You, I really do want You to be able to do *anything You wish* with me. Forgive me for the times when I have fumed and railed against You through nothing more or less than ignorance. Amen.

Day 223 – August 10th

There are one or two occasions when Jesus 'acted out a parable' for real and some of these moments verge on the *'Surely, You wouldn't do that, would You?'* principle.

'Now in the morning, when He was returning to the city, He became hungry. Seeing a lone fig tree by the road, He came to it and found nothing on it except leaves only; and He said to it, "No longer shall there ever be any fruit from you." And at once the fig tree withered.' (Matthew 21)

Mark gives a slightly different account. There they hear Jesus speak to the tree but Mark adds *'for it was not the season for figs'* (Mark 11). Mark always adds the detail. Later, in the evening, the disciples pass the tree and see that it has withered from the roots up. Why make that point? It is because it showed them this was a supernatural event; trees do not wither from the roots. It is the succulent, fragile greenery at the top which withers first. The tree had been cursed!

When the disciples asked Jesus how the fig tree withered so quickly He responded by encouraging them in their faith, telling them if they command the mountain to up and be cast into the sea it will happen if they have faith.

'All things you ask in prayer, believing, you will receive.' (Matthew 21)

Being with Jesus while He demonstrated faith in action must have been a huge stimulus to them, but a scary one at times. Can you imagine *seeing* that happen? There is an element of this story which might strike fear into our hearts. This is the Lord of Lords who could strike us dead at His feet. That He does not is because for us who believe in Him as Lord and Saviour, His grace was poured out on us from the cross and we are no longer the people under His wrath. It is not just about a fig tree that is long dead and shrivelled.

There was a deeper message in the fig tree borne out by other teachings; time was limited for those who didn't receive Him, and worse for those who continued to deny who He was. The coming of the kingdom was revealing the hearts of many, revealing those entrenched religious ways for what they were: empty and powerless traditions that were, at the very least, preventing people coming to God.

Even John the Baptist spoke so, as a prophetic declaration of the coming mission of the Christ.

'Therefore bear fruits in keeping with repentance, and do not begin to say to yourselves, "We have Abraham for our father," for I say to you that from these stones God is able to raise up children to Abraham. Indeed the axe is already laid at the root of the trees; so every tree that does not bear good fruit is cut down and thrown into the fire.' (Luke 3)

These were times of profound challenge and change amid heavenly scrutiny and demands for authentic spirituality.

Lord God, we should never take anything for granted. We exist by Your grace and in Your faithfulness. May we always be a people who respond with integrity before You. Amen.

Day 224 – August 11th

The account of Jesus' parable of the fig tree in the vineyard slices even closer to the reality of an impending end to the worthless and corrupted religious traditions, which were set against the mission of Jesus and all He stood for. In terms of the *'Surely, You wouldn't do that, would You?'* it gives us food for humble thoughts.

'And He began telling this parable: "A man had a fig tree which had been planted in his vineyard; and he came looking for fruit on it and

did not find any. And he said to the vineyard keeper, 'Behold, for three years I have come looking for fruit on this fig tree without finding any. Cut it down! Why does it even use up the ground?' And he answered and said to him, 'Let it alone, sir, for this year too, until I dig around it and put in fertiliser; and if it bears fruit next year, fine; but if not, cut it down.'" (Luke 13)

Three of the four years are passed before what? We can view the occasions when Jesus spoke angrily against the religious leaders, with a superior air: *we are the ones who are getting it right; we understand Who the Messiah was . . .* but beware! I feel the need to come low before the Lord at these times: we are not yet at the end of history; there are many injunctions of the Lord that I cannot say I have always fulfilled. There will always be opportunities for self-righteousness and if they aren't there, we can usually create them. Jesus speaks to us still with the same sense of gravity about our churches, fellowships and relationships. Peter and Paul speak many wise words in their epistles which we would be wise to take very seriously and we ignore at our peril. These are words for now!

'The end of all things is near; therefore, be of sound judgement and sober spirit for the purpose of prayer. Above all, keep fervent in your love for one another, because love covers a multitude of sins. Be hospitable to one another without complaint. As each one has received a special gift, employ it in serving one another as good stewards of the manifold grace of God. Whoever speaks, is to do so as one who is speaking the utterances of God; whoever serves is to do so as one who is serving by the strength which God supplies; so that in all things God may be glorified through Jesus Christ, to whom belongs the glory and dominion forever and ever. Amen.' (1 Peter 4)

What a yard-stick for the contemporary church.

Father, You speak to Your people throughout the generations. Your message is always the same and very clear. Let us not rest easy in our salvation but work it out with fear and trembling. Let us not be conceited but instead live in reverence for You and Your ways. Holy God, I worship You today. Amen.

Day 225 – August 12th

When I reflect on the seriousness of the days of the early church, there are many times when we find the apostles and followers speaking out despite the immense risk to their lives and well-being. It is still so today in many parts of the world. Being a Christian is a life-calling and a calling to life.

'Now about that time Herod the king laid hands on some who belonged to the church in order to mistreat them. And he had James the brother of John put to death with a sword. When he saw that it pleased the Jews, he proceeded to arrest Peter also.' (Acts 12)

He did it on not much more than a whim; it pleased people and won him loyalty. *'Surely, You wouldn't do that, would You?'*

And some of the greatest changes in the history of the world came through the Apostle Paul.

'As [Saul] was travelling, it happened that he was approaching Damascus, and suddenly a light from heaven flashed around him; and he fell to the ground and heard a voice saying to him, "Saul, Saul, why are you persecuting Me?" And he said, "Who are You, Lord?" And He said, "I am Jesus whom you are persecuting, but get up and enter the city, and it shall be told you what you must do."' (Acts 9)

And don't forget also,

'But a man named Ananias, with his wife Sapphira, sold a piece of property, and kept back some of the price for himself, with his wife's full knowledge, and bringing a portion of it, he laid it at the apostles' feet. But Peter said, "Ananias, why has Satan filled your heart to lie to the Holy Spirit and to keep back some of the price of the land? While it remained unsold, did it not remain your own? And after it was sold, was it not under your control? Why is it that you have conceived this deed in your heart? You have not lied to men but to God."' (Acts 5)

Ananias died there at Peter's feet and three hours later his wife also.

Maybe the God we have made for ourselves is too nice. *Surely, You wouldn't do that, would You?* But He did. And no doubt the shockwaves reverberated around the new church and everyone lived in deep awe of the Lord and reverenced Him profoundly.

'And great fear came upon the whole church, and over all who heard of these things.'

My Lord, by Your grace I stand. It is Your grace and majesty that has taught my heart to fear. Sometimes it feels as though the question I want to ask is not *'Why do You do these things?'* but instead, *'Why do you not do them?'* I stand in Your grace, aware that my every breath comes by Your loving kindness and mercy. Amen.

Day 226 – August 13th

For those wondering if your author has lost it and is going to dwell for the remainder of the summer in gloomy thoughts about all the fearful things God has done, I want to say, no, I will not be, but it would be a serious mistake for me to write a book the pages of which did not truly reflect the character of the God we love and serve.

I have had one or two profound experiences in God's presence when His love has been so great that, when in them, I have been very seriously fearful for my life. If you thought you read that incorrectly, you didn't. Love that is so completely full of passion, grace and mercy is utterly painful to experience. It is the out-of-this-world Person of God that one becomes aware of in those moments; that we are simultaneously exposed to *all* the facets of God's being at once. We do not experience *only* the Father's heart, or *only* His *love*, or *only* His judgement or His forgiveness; it is the fact that He is One. When He comes at you in a rolling tidal wave of His majesty, power and love, believe me, you will not be having a cosy chat on the settee. That is not to say God cannot love you in that way; He can, and will, but suffice it to say, I cannot see film of a massive roller coming in from the ocean without remembering with reverence the night when *I saw* the waves of His goodness crash onto me. He is an *awesome* God!

I also feel quite strongly that when I speak or write or in any other way represent the Lord, I am pleased if you like what I say and, if it helps you as you journey with Him, that is splendid; I am genuinely delighted but I do not worry about what you think of me. I write and speak as I believe the Lord would have me do. The only glory I seek is from Him, not from you; sorry.

'I have come in My father's name, and you do not receive Me; if another comes in his own name, you will receive him. How can you believe, when you receive glory from one another and you do not seek the glory that is from the one and only God?' (John 5)

So said the Lord when He was criticised for healing on the Sabbath. Jesus saw and came against the religious folk who were all trying to outdo one another for the wrong reasons and in the wrong way. They longed for the approval of men. They sought glory among men. Jesus effectively said, 'You cannot function like that if you want to be My disciple.' It is only God's opinion that will count if you are His.

Father, Your love and majesty defy words on a page or even as the spoken word. You are beyond description and beyond anything we know. Forgive us, Lord, for we have made You too small. We have created You in our likeness and You are not. I live to please You, Your Majesty; only You. Amen.

Day 227 – August 14th

One of the best known 'live parables' was at the wedding in Cana, where Jesus performed a highly prophetic and challenging miracle that goes beyond the obvious 'wow' factor of the astonishing supernatural.

'On the third day there was a wedding in Cana of Galilee, and the

mother of Jesus was there; and both Jesus and His disciples were invited to the wedding. When the wine ran out, the mother of Jesus said to Him, "They have no wine." And Jesus said to her, "Woman, what does that have to do with us? My hour has not yet come." His mother said to the servants, "Whatever He says to you, do it." Now there were six stone water pots set there for the Jewish custom of purification, containing twenty or thirty gallons each. Jesus said to them, "Fill the water pots with water." So they filled them up to the brim. And He said to them, "Draw some out now and take it to the headwaiter." So they took it to him.' (John 2)

As we look at this, we note it was the 'third day'. What might that mean? If we look back to the beginning of the gospel, we find John declaring, *'In the beginning was the Word'* and later, *'And the Word became flesh.'*

It is as though John is re-declaring the original creation story. His references to Jesus' mother as *'Woman'* remind us of Eve as the 'woman' as she was referred to in the Garden of Eden story. Although Jesus' language sounds a little harsh towards her it is surely not so but much more to do with the slow unravelling of this 'live parable'. Perhaps she is the 'new Eve' speaking to the 'new Adam'; who knows. There may be nothing in this but I believe it is there to see. Was the Holy Spirit speaking clearly to Mary, prompting her to participate, led by the Conductor of the holy symphony?

The most challenging aspect of this is the question, *is it possible to change Jesus' mind?* It appears that His mother did so persuade Him; not to do something that was out of the Father's will, but to bring it forward.

It was not His time, He said, and then it *was* His time. Let the intercessors of the world take note! The original word from Eve took everything off track with her Adam but perhaps this 'new Eve' triggers Him to usher in the restoration of all things; the reversal of the original tragic story.

And then there is the miracle itself performed with 'purification jars' in which He creates the new wine. Gallons of it! It must have been a very good wedding party given that they had already drunk the bar dry; a very serious and socially awkward moment for a bridegroom implying that his resources are depleted. Despite being 'new wine' this is the best wine that they have drunk; it is the new wine of the kingdom! The 'old wine' has been drunk to the dregs.

Seen at one level it is a remarkably 'earthy' miracle; creating wine for a party which would almost certainly have led to a good degree of merriment. Where is the point of that? But it speaks profoundly of the mission of Jesus, that it is a decisive moment; it is provided extravagantly and provides an abundance for all who wish to partake. The Word of God is amazing, my friends!

Lord God, we stand breathless as we begin to glimpse the intricacies of all You have prophesied, planned and revealed throughout history! It is like a glorious symphony gradually gaining momentum but which cannot be prevented from bursting out for all to hear. Lord, in the light of such magnificent ways how can we not trust You? Thank you for John who brings us such profound insights into the Master's ways. May this story also speak to me of the Father's detailed plans for each one of us. Amen.

Day 228 – August 15th

It would be remiss not to look at this passage in the light of yesterday's reading.

'But no one puts a patch of unshrunk cloth on an old garment; for the patch pulls away from the garment, and a worse tear results. Nor do people put new wine into old wineskins; otherwise the wineskins burst, and the wine pours out and the wineskins are ruined; but they put new wine into fresh wineskins, and both are preserved.' (Matthew 9)

This is a key explanation as to why the ministry of God, as revealed in the mission of Jesus, could not be contained in old structures. God was doing a completely 'new thing' in so many ways that we cannot find space to describe the extent to which God was bringing change. It was spoken of by the prophets many hundreds of years previously, and yet it was not understood.

'But for you who fear My name, the sun of righteousness will rise with healing in its wings; and you will go forth and skip like calves from the stall.' (Malachi 4)

And after saying these things, Jesus went and brought Jairus' daughter back to life and, on the way, the woman with the issue touched Him and was released from her torment. It was the new wine of the kingdom flowing for those who had eyes to see it, and it provokes me to wonder if I am truly ready with fresh wineskin at the ready for what God may be pouring out in these days. I pray that I am poised and attentive along with His church.

Father, I find myself caught up in the excitement of those days. My heart skips at the fresh winds that were blowing; yet it is more than just an exciting account, for the Holy Spirit continues to speak to us now of the new wine. Show us how to build wineskins that will truly meet the needs of the new wine of the kingdom in our day. May we be wise in what we preserve and what we discard. Amen.

Day 229 – August 16th

'Oh, give thanks to the LORD, call upon His name; make known His deeds among the peoples. Sing to Him, sing praises to Him; speak of all His wonders. Glory in His holy name; let the heart of those who seek the LORD be glad. Seek the LORD and His strength; seek His face continually.' (Psalm 105)

Sometimes we have to stop and come before our God with praise; 'Oh give thanks,' the psalmist declares, using the word *'yâdâh'* which means 'to throw the hands in the air in worship'! It is a very active word used to describe the hurling of a stone or, in times of distress, to wring the hands. To join with him in this psalm we need to step out of our refrained worship style and be demonstrative. It's not always easy and we tend to be self-conscious in a gathering but I think of myself at such times as worshipping before an audience of One: the Lord Himself! When I do that everyone else fades away. To call upon His name is just that: to call Him by name! 'O Holy God', we cry as we extend our arms and hands into the air, and we tell of His wonders. 'Do you know what He has done for me!' No wonder those who seek the Lord thus have glad hearts! It is quite impossible to be anything but glad.

O my Lord! I worship You today for the great King that You are. I think of all the things You have accomplished and my heart swells with praise and thanksgiving. You make me smile; You make my heart glad! Amen.

Day 230 – August 17th

'Vindicate the weak and fatherless; do justice to the afflicted and destitute. Rescue the weak and needy; deliver them out of the hand of the wicked. They do not know nor do they understand; they walk about in darkness.' (Psalm 82)

When I read this psalm I often think what a wonderful explanation of all that is in the Father's heart! If you want to know what the Father, the Son and the Holy Spirit are about in these days, look no further! The Father wants to become a father to those who are lost and have none; He wants to bring the justice of the kingdom to those who are locked in affliction; He wants to free those who are gripped in the wicked hand of the enemy. And we are to be those who shine like lights in their darkness and beckon them into the brilliance of the Son. That's so wonderful!

Father, send me out on Your business, I pray. Open my eyes that I may see those who are trapped, afflicted and longing for rescue. Often, they have the appearance of those who are OK; the world has camouflage-power to dress up that which is not as though it is. May we be those who see as You see, and shine with kingdom brilliance, crying out with the call of the Father's heart! Amen.

Day 231 – August 18th

I was a shepherd once. I had fifty or so ewes so I know what it is to care for the flock, particularly in summer when we frequently had towards two hundred; each of them had four feet and I understand fully what it is to trim all those feet and groan with a very sore back at the end of the day! My children used to think it was amazing that they all knew my voice. When I stood at the gate and did my call, 'Hoa, hoa, hoa!' they would all charge down from the hill looking expectantly . . . Jesus knew that when He spoke of sheep and shepherds *everyone* would understand.

'To him the doorkeeper opens, and the sheep hear his voice, and he calls his own sheep by name and leads them out. When he puts forth all his own, he goes ahead of them, and the sheep follow him because they know his voice.' (John 10)

The strange thing is we are told that they could not see the relevance; they all understood about the sheep but not why the Teacher was speaking so. He explained further that He is the door by which the sheep come and go.

'If anyone enters through Me, he will be saved.'

And finally, *'I am the good shepherd; the good shepherd lays down His life for the sheep.'*

They would have understood all of this. Good shepherds would sometimes have to stand their ground against wild beasts; men such as King David who learned skills with his sling in his shepherd days. I don't for one second say that I had to put my life on the line for my sheep although I did go to great ends sometimes. In the middle of the night, I would wake immediately if one of the flock was in trouble. I could usually even tell what the problem was by the level of pleading in their 'baaaaing'! As often as not, one of them would be pressing forward to crop tender shoots and get caught in the brambles in a hedge. Why they did it at 3am I never discovered, but I would get up, pull on wellies and a boiler suit over my pyjamas and go out with a bright torch and a pair of secateurs to set them free. They are such silly creatures; all of them go astray!

The shepherd hears your voice. Believe it! And Jesus says that you will recognise His also.

Jesus, this is such a simple parallel but it speaks so much of the profound simplicity of the Father's heart for His people. We are known to You and so are You to us. You care and are attentive to us and ultimately, in obedience to the Father's will, You did lay down Your life. What a Shepherd You are. Amid our folly and stupidity, You did all You could to get us back to the safe place. Bless You, Lord. Amen.

Day 232 – August 19th

The trouble really came in earnest when Jesus took the Shepherd theme to its ultimate conclusion and confronted those who did not accept He was the Messiah. They wanted to be told plainly, without further suspense; they said, 'Are You the Christ?'

Jesus answered them, "I told you, and you do not believe; the works that I do in My Father's name, these testify of Me. But you do not believe because you are not of My sheep. My sheep hear My voice, and I know them, and they follow Me."' (John 10)

The idea of there being 'sheep', and separately 'My sheep', comes from the custom of penning all the sheep together in a communal safe place at night, in a corral of thorn bushes and walls and a watchman who was not actually an owner-shepherd was left in charge until morning. Often the watchman would maintain the pen at his expense and effort and offer his services to the shepherds. In the morning, the shepherds would return and the gatekeeper would open the corral and the owner would call; the sheep who knew the shepherd's voice would come to him and follow them. Everyone would have understood this so Jesus was making quite a point! He continued:

'I give eternal life to them, and they will never perish; and no one will snatch them out of My hand. My Father, who has given them to Me, is greater than all; and no one is able to snatch them out of the Father's hand. I and the Father are one.'

At that point, His listeners picked up stones to kill Him. It was the unique Father-Son relationship He spoke of that was so difficult to hear and to bear. It is strange as the very thing which attracts us – to be known, to be saved, to be entirely safe in the enormous arms of the Great Shepherd – is the *very thing* which attracts us! Or is it? Once we know the truth it certainly is but the story is as relevant now as before. Men long to be found but they have a problem with being found. Someone once described the spiritual predicament of man as 'wanting to hide, longing to be sought but very confused about being found'.

I once took a friend to a meeting because he said that if he witnessed a miracle first hand he would believe. We went and, knowing that healing prayer would be offered, I took him to the front to watch. A man was prayed for who had a very sizeable tumour protruding from his neck. As he was prayed for the tumour diminished until there was nothing visible. I said nothing to my friend but later he declared, 'There must be some other explanation.' This has happened twice to me.

I find it immensely encouraging that Jesus spoke of belief in the miracles as being so close to belief in God. There is a fine line; *seeing* a miracle is not the same as acknowledging the God who performed it but it makes me feel that we should never be afraid to pray for people and ideally do it in front of others. Unlike my friend, many are changed by seeing the supernatural God at work. No wonder they are called 'signs and wonders'; signs to make us wonder.

Lord God, Your goodness and willingness to bring healing is a wonder to us and yet we know people's eyes can be veiled from the truth. Give us strength on the days when people do not believe just as happened to You, and give us deep wisdom to recognise that it is Your power and Your responsibility, not ours. Amen.

Day 233 – August 20th

It is a mystery why men and women do not believe when confronted by the manifestations of a living God. Just to gaze on the many-coloured beauty of a sunset, the flourish of the Creator's hand on the canvas of the sky, is enough to bring some men to their knees and yet at other times it is so hard to bring people to faith.

The Old Testament prophets were severely challenged by the same phenomena throughout their lives as they sought to provoke whole nations, especially Israel, to come to their senses. The enemy blinds eyes and sets up bastions of unfaith in people's lives. But our God is in pursuit, never fear!

'Therefore, the LORD longs to be gracious to you, and therefore He waits on high to have compassion on you. For the LORD is a God of justice; how blessed are all those who long for Him.' (Isaiah 30)

It is a mystery that has frustrated every one of us, no doubt, but we must believe as we venture out with the Good News that God can call even those with stubborn mindsets. Change can happen quite suddenly; often we cannot even explain how God does it, but He does!

While I worked among the elderly, I met a man who we will call Reg. He was a proud man, a wiry nonagenarian who was self-made and had become reasonably wealthy through his business acumen. He was quite sharp in a rather quick-to-judge way but beneath his exterior he was generous and warm-hearted (-ish). We learned to respect one another although it was clear that he had no time for my faith. Gradually, through what I used to refer to as the hum-drum

317

foot-washing kindnesses, he was moved. When he was too unwell to shop, I often went for him. When he felt frail, I would offer him a wet shave, knowing that he liked to be well-turned-out, and so gradually we grew fond of one another. He first began to express an interest in my faith through no spoken word from me, and it began with silly questions and comments such as 'Heaven must be a very big place if He can fit us all in up there.' Eventually, he cornered himself with his questions and answers to his own questions, so that I asked him if he would like me to explain properly. He agreed so I shared with him the Good News of Jesus, our Saviour. He was not overly impressed but I left him with the excellent Alpha publication *Why Jesus?* He had been very critical of people who 'ram their faith down your throat' so I was always cautious.

I deliberately never mentioned it or asked him if he had read it but one day he told me that he had read 'my booklet'. I said I was pleased and that I hoped it helped him. Later he said again, 'I have read that booklet, you know,' and then added, 'I read it every night but I still struggle.' At about that time he became very seriously ill as his cancer advanced and further conversation became impossible. I visited him every day and did all I could for him to keep him comfortable. We were by then quite openly fond of one another. One morning I went to see him and realised he was fading. He reached up from his bed as if to embrace me. I went close so that he could hug me which he did for a long time. He kissed my cheek and then said, very clearly, in my ear, *'I think my Lord is calling me.'* Through tears I prayed for him. That night he passed away. At his funeral, I told the story of his journey to faith but there were many there with apparently deaf ears to the Shepherd's call. It's a mystery but listen, *it is the Holy Spirit's work* and He calls, not us.

Lord God, I praise You for the many men and women who heard Your call. I look forward to meeting them all in Your kingdom. I have a feeling there may be a few surprises too. People who I thought were deaf but who turned out to be listening. Show us who to go to with Your love and with the Good News, Lord Jesus, and may we learn to trust You to call Your sheep at the right time. Amen.

Day 234 – August 21st

The depiction of God's people in the first chapter of Isaiah is a chilling description of what can be if, as a people, we wander away from the Lord.

'*They have abandoned the* LORD, *they have despised the Holy One of Israel, they have turned away from Him. Where will you be stricken again, as you continue in your rebellion? The whole head is sick and the whole heart is faint. From the sole of the foot even to the head there is nothing sound in it, only bruises, welts and raw wounds, not pressed out or bandaged, not softened with oil. Your land is desolate, your cities are burned with fire, your fields – strangers are devouring them in your presence; it is desolation, as overthrown by strangers.*' (Isaiah 1)

It is a desperate picture. Imagine going to the doctor and having even half of that told you in his diagnosis of your condition! But this is their *God* who speaks; their Father, the One who has led them through calamity after calamity. Throughout there is a deep longing on the part of God:

'*Sons I have reared and brought up, but they have revolted against Me. An ox knows its owner and a donkey its master's manger, but Israel does not know; My people do not understand.*'

They have literally forgotten where their home is, their family roots. No wonder Jesus was so fierce towards those who led people astray.

Isaiah tells them that God is weary of bearing them up, tired of their limp rituals; their sin-laden spirits and their hypocrisies being paraded before Him.

It is staggering to read Isaiah (or any of the other prophets); as

New Testament believers, we might believe that God has changed, or at least Jesus has come and He is the nice guy, unlike God who is the grumpy baddie of old times (sorry, Lord). If you believe that, even a fraction of it, I have news for you: God does not change. Yes, His grace is now more readily available to us through Jesus Christ but God does not change. I have a witty sticky on my wall; it says, '*Someone around here has to change, and I do not change, says the Lord.*' It's true; Scripture tells us so.

In the same chapter of Isaiah, we find God saying:

'"*Come now, and let us reason together,*" says the LORD. "*Though your sins are as scarlet, they will be white as snow; though they are red like crimson, they will be like wool. If you consent and obey, you will eat the best of the land; but if you refuse and rebel, you will be devoured by the sword.*" *Truly, the mouth of the LORD has spoken.*'

Do you hear the call of our Father? *Just come back! Come back to Me before it is too late.*

As I look around me, I do find myself exhaling and thinking, 'There but for God's grace . . .'. The state of our land, our democratically achieved appalling decisions, our ignorance of the plight of the have-nots, the orphan and the widow, whilst the rich pile up their riches . . . We think *God won't notice!* Or maybe, in this 'post-truth age', *There is no God now so who will admonish us? We can do whatever we want and can get away with . . .*

What was it David wrote in his psalm? '*The LORD is in His holy temple; the LORD's throne is in heaven; His eyes behold; His eyelids test the sons of men.*' (Psalm 11)

My Father, sometimes we need to come before You in humble repentance for the way we are in these times. We know Your judgement can be swift but we beseech You to bring men and women to their senses. Raise up men and women of God in these days to speak out; prophets who will beckon people and point them to You; to break them out of their drunken stupor and their fake world views and assumptions that they receive as truth. O Jesus, we honour You as Saviour of the world, and cry out to You, *Hope of our Hearts* come into our midst, send revival, we pray. Come to save! Amen.

Day 235 – August 22nd

When I watch Jesus, I learn that I am to be loving, and to express through my words and deeds His passion for the afflicted and the lost. But I also realise that I should be speaking out without fear or favour and challenging wrong and causing upsets, disturbing those whose comfort zones are established to cushion them in their blissful ignorance! God is raising up shakers in the land! He has an interest in our nation that goes way beyond saving souls. He takes a very keen interest in governments and bankers and the ethics of trading, from the top of society to the bottom. God *is justice*, just as *He is mercy*; they are at the very heart of His person.

In the books of Kings, we can read again and again,

'He did right in the sight of the Lord . . . only the high places were not taken away . . .

But he walked in the way of the kings of Israel, and even made his sons pass through the fire, according to the abominations of the nations whom the Lord *had driven out from before the sons of Israel . . . He sacrificed and burned incense on the high places . . . The sons of Israel did evil things secretly which were not right against the* Lord *their God . . . They set for themselves sacred pillars and Asherim on every high hill . . . They served idols . . .'*

It is into this desperate story of man's failure to wholly love God that Jesus came to break it open and destroy evil. He knows what is to come.

"Be on guard, so that your hearts will not be weighted down with dissipation and drunkenness and the worries of life, and that day will not come on you suddenly like a trap; for it will come upon all those who dwell on the face of all the earth. But keep on the alert at all times,

praying that you may have strength to escape all these things that are about to take place, and to stand before the Son of Man." Now during the day He was teaching in the temple, but at evening He would go out and spend the night on the mount that is called Olivet. And all the people would get up early in the morning to come to Him in the temple to listen to Him.' (Luke 21)

Lord, we come to You to seek Your strength and Your inspiration for these days in which we live. May we model our comings and goings on Yours; spending time with God as a high priority for our lives, to receive nourishment, refreshment and purification. Make us ready to stand in Your presence, Jesus. Amen.

Day 236 – August 23rd

It is difficult to know how much and how often Jesus spoke out against the religious leaders of His day. From the Bible records it would appear that they repeatedly and frequently tried to come against Him, sometimes very deviously, and He responded accordingly. He seemed to speak most often about hypocrisy: heart attitudes versus outward shows, legalism and their lack of spiritual life and genuine leadership.

Are there lessons we can learn? Paul and the other apostle writers clearly also expended time and energy coming against corruptions of the faith, carefully guiding those in leadership.

'Shepherd the flock of God among you, exercising oversight not under compulsion, but voluntarily, according to the will of God; and not for sordid gain, but with eagerness; nor yet as lording it over those allotted to your charge, but proving to be examples to the flock. And when the Chief Shepherd appears, you will receive the unfading crown of glory.' (1 Peter 5)

Probably one of the most useful pieces of advice was written by Paul in his letter to the Christians in Colossae. As was the case in many trading centres, religions and cultures mixed and brought about all sorts of infiltrating corruptions. It is not very different to our situation today, if I may say so. In Colossae, there were threads of spiritualism, Judaism, philosophical influences and taboos that had to do with food, sexuality and dress. So, Paul writes,

'If you have been raised up with Christ, keep seeking the things above, where Christ is seated at the right hand of God. Set your mind on the things above, not on the things that are on earth. For you have died and your life is hidden with Christ in God. When Christ, who is our life, is revealed, then you also will be revealed with Him in glory. Therefore consider the members of your earthly body as dead to immorality, impurity, passion, evil desire, and greed, which amounts to idolatry. For it is because of these things that the wrath of God will come upon the sons of disobedience, and in them you also once walked, when you were living in them.' (Colossians 3)

He continues to speak about lies and slander and anger and the renewal of the self to the new self in the image of the Creator.

As a rule, we don't enjoy being told from the pulpit how to behave but I don't think it happens often! Not as often as Paul would doubtless have us teach the fundamentals! But we need this sound teaching in our days, in the same way as a pilot boards a ship with charts and knowledge and can then steer a great ship safely to its berth in a harbour. It would be considered facile if we heard of a ship's captain who either delegated command to an inexperienced hand or alternatively threw a wobbly when the pilot stepped on board, claiming he knew how to sail a ship, without any help, thank you very much! It would be folly of the highest order.

And so, let us willingly immerse ourselves in the instruction of the church fathers and ask the Holy Spirit to guide us all our days. Let us keep humility as the norm, and accountability to one another as good wisdom. We know most of the time when we are out of order but men do ignore the Holy Spirit's 'checks' and plough on regardless. I thoroughly recommend opening ourselves up daily to

His guidance and never using the excuse of a heavy work load or a pressured diary to skip it. Bless you all.

Lord Jesus, You are so wise and have seen so many go off the rails of faith. I want to say today, I do not want to be another casualty. I submit to Your gaze today and if there be any corrupted way in me please shine the light of heaven on it and make me pure, that on the day, I will be found standing. Amen.

Day 237 – August 24th

I find it immensely beneficial to use my computer. I am using it right now! It is certainly one up on my pen and longhand! May I tell you that in my study (we call it 'The Shack' and it is outside in the garden) I have no internet connection. I do enjoy looking things up on the internet indoors and I have found much fine preaching and teaching there. But there is also a lot of rubbish which can fill our minds and hearts and on occasions attack our spiritual lives also. I have made a conscious decision not to boost my signal or add a cable to my study. I am not a Luddite; I am just being wise! I know, for example, that I can become obsessed with reading the political news in all the different formats it appears in; it can make me fretful and pensive, far from the attitude of mind I really want to have as my stance of 'repose'. We forget that 'the news' is 'views' and is an industry persuading you to follow them; but is it good for you? David was very clear about who he would allow to minister to him and how he would be at home.

'I will walk within my house in the integrity of my heart. I will set no worthless thing before my eyes . . . My eyes shall be upon the faithful of the land that they may dwell with me; He who walks in a blameless way is the one who will minister to me.' (Psalm 101)

Surfing the internet is a popular pastime but it is generally quite fruitless and runs the risk that you will succumb to the massive and ingenious pressures of a vast selling machine! Or alternatively, you may find that you cannot bear being out of touch with family and friends, and the draw of the internet contact 'with the world' will erode your sense of peace and stillness. Tell me if I am wrong... No, I thought so! Let us be very wise about what influences our souls.

Jesus models something very precious. He takes Himself away from the clamour of exhausting ministry days and goes to quiet places. After the news that John had been beheaded He tried to get away but the crowds followed and He fed the 5000. After that he finally succeeded in finding quiet, restorative time. I have always thought He needed time alone to 'process' the death of cousin John, a faithful servant who had served Him well. He needed to grieve, perhaps.

'Now when Jesus heard about John, He withdrew from there in a boat to a secluded place by Himself; and when the people heard of this, they followed Him on foot from the cities . . . After He had sent the crowds away, He went up on the mountain by Himself to pray; and when it was evening, He was there alone.' (Matthew 14)

I do know that I am no use to God or man if I have not knelt and drunk from the River.

Lord, I know that my head has a limited capacity to take in information so I want to set my heart upon what You have to say to me! Because Your love has given me life, I will fix my eyes on Your face, my ears on Your words and my heart on the revelation You give to me. Help me to be wise about all I read, all I watch and those I allow to form my opinions. Amen.

Day 238 – August 25th

In three of the Gospels I read that Joseph of Arimathea, who was a prominent member of the council, and someone who was waiting for the kingdom of God, went to Pilate to ask for Jesus' body. John adds another piece of information.

'After these things Joseph of Arimathea, being a disciple of Jesus, but a secret one for fear of the Jews, asked Pilate that he might take away *the body of Jesus; and Pilate granted permission. So he came and took away His body. Nicodemus, who had first come to Him by night, also came, bringing a mixture of myrrh and aloes, about a hundred pounds in weight.'* (John 19)

We know that Nicodemus came to see Jesus and there is a lengthy report of the conversation in John 3, but it also tells us that *Nicodemus was a man of the Pharisees, a ruler of the Jews.* He was just as a good Pharisee should be: a seeker of the truth. He bravely stood up for Jesus in council and was rounded on for doing so.

"'Our law does not judge a man unless it first hears from him and knows what he is doing, does it?" They answered him, "You are not also from Galilee, are you? Search, and see that no prophet arises out of Galilee.'" (John 7)

So, what we know is that the disciples did not ask permission to take the body of Jesus away for burial (there is no account of where they were that night – we assume they were fearful for their well-being) but a Pharisee came. Hmm. Joseph of Arimathea was almost certainly also a Pharisee and a member of the council with Nicodemus.

Jesus was shown hospitality by members of the sect, was warned that there was a threat against His life by Pharisees, and Gamaliel, although not necessarily a believer, argued for open-mindedness.

When I read casually about the Pharisees, or perhaps listen to what people say and preach about them, I end up making the very generalised and judgemental assumption that they were all very bad news! We can do that in our day about people in church; leaders who have funny hats, or dog collars, or those who espouse a view that it's OK to wear shorts and a sweat shirt to preach, or worship bands, or organs, or speaking in tongues, or just about anything and anyone! We need to say, 'Whoa! Does this attitude honour God?'

We will think some more about what the Pharisees *did* get wrong but I wonder if we might use this as an opportunity to bring before

God all those with whom we don't see eye-to-eye within the church? Is it possible that we might be making judgements in much the same way as I make judgements in error about the Pharisees? It is a serious thing to make a judgement before God. When we withhold forgiveness or judge another, we are risking being judged in that area, as though we forego our forgiveness, so we need to be very careful. Such thoughts make me scurry to humble prayer!

Lord God, I do come before You and confess my willingness to make assumptions about people and to pass judgement on them. If I do this in the family of the church, I am judging someone who You have chosen to forgive! Who do I think I am? I am sorry, Lord, and I ask for You to challenge me in my spirit when I get this wrong. Unity is so important and I can be the one to damage it. Forgive me. Amen.

Day 239 – August 26th

David wrote: *'How good and how pleasant it is for brothers to dwell together in unity! It is like the precious oil upon the head, coming down upon the beard, even Aaron's beard, coming down upon the edge of his robes. It is like the dew of Hermon coming down upon the mountains of Zion; for there the LORD commanded the blessing – life forever.'* (Psalm 133)

May I point out that sisters are not neglected! The word is 'âch', it means 'kindred' that is of a family . . . *when kindred dwell together in unity.*

Abraham and Lot were kindred but they had to agree to separate and live apart in different regions. In the psalm, David is quite specific; it is about *dwelling together.* How he must have yearned for that, coming from a family that was not very together. This is a psalm that was sung on the way up to Jerusalem when everyone was of one heart. No doubt they had differences, likes and dislikes, but they were bound in unity as the kindred of the Lord and they were on the way to worship Him!

When Moses anointed Aaron to the priesthood, he used oil and the picture here is of extravagant use of it, so much so that it runs down his beard and to the edge of his robes! The oil indicated blessing and prospering under the Lord's hand, and holiness too. What a lovely picture! Only liquids flow down and here two liquids are mentioned; the other is the dew, and, in particular, the dew of Mount Hermon. Hermon is to the north of Jerusalem and the melt water flows down the mountain and feeds into the Jordan and is very much a river of life in a place that might otherwise be dry.

And here, in the place of unity, God commands blessing! But take note: it does not say that brothers are to dwell together in *uniformity* or *conformity*. The word is *unity*: '*How good and pleasant it is for brothers to dwell together in unity! It is like the precious oil upon the head, coming down upon the beard, even Aaron's.*' We can be different but still find unity. Really!

Father, thank You that You have made us a kindred people! That is wonderful and I really do not want to behave as anything other than a child of Your grace. How it must wound You when we do not recognise this in our spirits. Thank You also for difference and variety and that together we form Your body, the church. May You see fit to let Your blessing flow in our midst! Amen.

Day 240 – August 27th

Having had a brief interlude to dwell on unity, we return to the Pharisees, a learned tradition, steeped in the Talmud, the Law (Torah) and so on. Not surprisingly, the Talmudic literature and teachings condemn some of the things that Jesus also found fault with. It is very clear: hypocrisy, pretence, and pride are all written about and do not receive any approval. The writers and the fathers of the traditions were not corrupt; not at all. It is, in short, not very different from the New Testament. It sets us the highest standards and then, guess what happens? *We* are the problem. We do not take sufficient notice!

The Talmud even specifies the types of hypocritical traps the followers of the tradition might fall into and, guess what? So does the Bible in the New Testament.

Let us be clear that Jesus, in His scathing denunciations of the Pharisees, was sometimes speaking of their misuse of their position, their hypocrisy (that they did not do what they taught), and the habit of circling the Law with impossible demands. The latter had its origins in attempts to prevent people from getting anywhere near breaking the Law but it became pedantic and burdensome and, in the end, became nothing but a hindrance. But, you know, when I gather together some of the things Jesus spoke about to the Pharisees, I sometimes wonder if He might say just the same or very similar things about us! Do we ever polish the outside to look thoroughly wholesome when inside we might well be found to be lacking? Are our church services ever 'shutting up the kingdom of heaven against men'? Dear friends, to come back to my original point three days ago, about being critical concerning difference and variety among those of faith, how careful we need to be! Which is probably why Jesus saw the need to give that talk about planks in eyes . . .

'Do not judge so that you will not be judged. For in the way you judge, you will be judged; and by your standard of measure, it will be measured to you. Why do you look at the speck that is in your brother's eye, but do not notice the log that is in your own eye?' (Matthew 7)

Day 241 – August 28th

Believing the impossible! That was the opposing Pharisees' main problem. Whatever you may think of *Alice in Wonderland*, there is a very amusing exchange with the Queen who exhorts Alice to *try* to believe impossible things. Alice tells her that it is no use *trying* to believe impossible things. The Queen retorts that Alice probably hasn't had enough practice and explains that when she was young she practised for half an hour a day and that sometimes she believed as many as six impossible things before breakfast!

We can only guess what the Pharisees thought when Jesus declared,

'I am the light of the world; he who follows Me shall not walk in the darkness, but will have the Light of life.' (John 8)

They accused Jesus of being His own witness, so Jesus replied,

'Even if I testify about Myself, My testimony is true, for I know where I came from and where I am going; but you do not know where I come from or where I am going. You judge according to the flesh; I am not judging anyone. But even if I do judge, My judgement is true; for I am not alone in it, but I and the Father who sent Me. Even in your law it has been written that the testimony of two men is true.'

Whatever they may have felt about the miracles they saw and heard of, Jesus seemed to be speaking of things that were mind-bendingly difficult to fathom. He still does that; He speaks to every one of us seemingly impossible things. The great disappointment of Jesus was that these men who had been brought up on the great teachings of the Prophets who mainly pointed to the coming of the Christ and yet, when He was in their midst, they judged according to the flesh; in other words, by what was in front of them. They did not have faith that could stretch beyond their traditional beliefs. Some did; some decided to explore the unlikely to see if it measured up to what they had been told to expect. Nicodemus had a conversation with Jesus that accelerated from 0-78 mph at a rate which he could not cope with. But he came with an honest and enquiring heart and Jesus met him right there.

'Rabbi, we know that You have come from God as a teacher; for no one can do these signs that You do unless God is with him.' (John 3)

Which is a polite and deferential way to start a chat. Jesus answered and said to him, *'Truly, truly, I say to you, unless one is born again, he cannot see the kingdom of God.'*

God has a way of doing that. You think you are having one

conversation but quite suddenly you are having another. It happens in a blink. I once had a long conversation (it was one-sided) with God about why baptism in the Holy Spirit just couldn't be right. I wasn't a cessationist; it just seemed *impossible*! So, God was patient with my polite preamble over quite a few weeks and through several sermons (sorry folks) until, finally, I dried up. My problem was not that I was *resisting*, I just had no expectation of my faith life being anything other than 'passion in my tradition'. In the end, God said something along the lines of, 'Well, My son, I don't want to force anything on you that you don't want, but why don't you ask *Me* if it's real?' I had to agree. I had run out of road.

I was wall-papering at that moment on a Sunday afternoon, dressed in . . . wall-papering clothes. There was a knock on the door and a friend from another church was standing there talking nonsense. 'God told me to come and get you and to take you to our meeting and I won't take no for an answer,' he garbled. He was actually a very shy man! Which explains how I came to be filled with the Holy Spirit and declaring the praises of God in a pair of paint-splattered trousers with paper snips and a plumb bob in my back pocket.

The point of this story is to say, eventually, if you want to be a follower of Jesus, you will have to get used to the idea that God is the God of the 'impossible' and He does all sorts of things that our natural minds cannot fathom! That was why many of the Pharisees struggled so. They had their God safe in a dusty old box full of precious parchments. Fortunately, in that sense, God is *never* 'safe'!

'If anyone is thirsty, let him come to Me and drink. He who believes in Me, as the Scripture said, "From his innermost being will flow rivers of living water."' (John 7)

Father, thank You that Your promise has always been to pour out Your Spirit on mankind, and when He comes He brings with Him the surprises of the Father. May I trust You and yearn for You more and more. On the days when it seems that Your way is 'impossible', may I respond simply with a child-like cry of, 'Yes!' from my inner most place. Amen.

Day 242 – August 29th

One of the most extraordinary 'discoveries' I made about God is that He heals people. I had no idea. No idea at all. When I became a Christian in an unexpected sovereign move of God in the early '70s I had, like most people, heard the Bible stories of Jesus healing men and women. I don't remember hearing them but I am sure I did, at Sunday school and then probably also later in the Boys' Brigade. But my head and heart never made the connection. Even when the Lord turned me upside down (and shook my pockets out) and I was awash with His mercy and generosity towards me, I still had no idea.

As a seven-year-old, I recall my mother taking me to the doctor with terrible pains in both of my knees. It was dismissed as 'growing pains'. I never bothered a doctor again until my late teens when I was suffering so much that I could hardly walk at times, and sitting still was agony. I couldn't decide whether to sit or stand and would frequently have to stand at the back in tutorials as an undergraduate as I was in such pain. When I did go to the doctor it was diagnosed as a juvenile inflammatory condition. Not much was done to help as I recall.

About a week after God took hold of my life, I realised that I did not need to exercise on the side of my bed before I could stand. I still didn't make the connection! But after a few weeks I was completely healed. Years later, although I do suffer in many parts of my body, my knees remain very strong.

'And He entered again into a synagogue; and a man was there whose hand was withered. They were watching Him to see if He would heal him on the Sabbath, so that they might accuse Him. He said to the man with the withered hand, "Get up and come forward!" And He said to them, "Is it lawful to good or to do harm on the Sabbath, to save a

life or to kill?" But they kept silent. After looking around at them with anger, grieved at their hardness of heart, He said to the man, "Stretch out your hand." And he stretched it out, and his hand was restored.' (Mark 3)

My Lord and my King, how did I not recognise the Great Physician? Thank You that You are the healing God; the God who heals broken bodies, minds and spirits by the power of Your wonderful love. Amen.

Day 243 – August 30th

Whatever ministry we are engaged in, I do believe that we should always, in faith, create an environment for God to do *more* of whatever He seems to be doing! Just after healing the man in the synagogue we are told,

'Jesus withdrew to the sea with His disciples; and a great multitude from Galilee followed; and also from Judea, and from Jerusalem, and from Idumea, and beyond the Jordan, and the vicinity of Tyre and Sidon, a great number of people heard of all that He was doing and came to Him. And He told His disciples that a boat should stand ready for Him because of the crowd, so that they would not crowd Him; for He had healed many, with the result that all those who had afflictions pressed around Him in order to touch Him. Whenever the unclean spirits saw Him, they would fall down before Him and shout, "You are the Son of God!" And He earnestly warned them not to tell who He was.' (Mark 3)

I think it is safe to say that revival accompanies Jesus! These people were clearly making very considerable journeys to see and hear this man. In our present age, we have no concept of what it must have meant to have a healing touch from the Lord and to be released from a lifetime of disability. This sort of response still occurs in some parts of the world where faith seems to rise strongly. But what interests me most is that the boat is clearly prepared for Jesus to continue His ministry from the water's edge. It isn't for Him to escape! When the auditorium is too crowded, make it bigger!

I sometimes sit and imagine what these Galilean scenes must have been like, often wondering whether Jesus managed the difficult balance of delivering His message *and* the signs that accompanied Him wherever He went.

Whatever He did then, I do long for Him to do the same now. Imagine your local church under siege because so many people want to come in. That is the result of revival, and even in our own times there have been great moves of the Holy Spirit in Great Britain and elsewhere in the Western world. I long for more!

Lord, we can hardly begin to imagine what it was like to be in such a vibrant environment; vibrant with the glory and power of God. Send Your Holy Spirit on us I pray and, I beseech You, do it soon! If we aren't ready, please prepare us for that day. Amen.

Day 244 – August 31st

The pursuit of 'vain things' is a problem that still confronts our spirituality today, just as it did thousands of years ago. The Hebrew words for idols give us a clue: 'âtsâb' which means 'image' or 'idol', and 'ĕlîyl' which means 'good for nothing' or 'a vanity'.

'The idols of the nations are but silver and gold, the work of man's hands. They have mouths, but they do not speak; they have eyes, but they do not see; they have ears, but they do not hear, nor is there any breath at all in their mouths. Those who make them will be like them, yes, everyone who trusts in them.' (Psalm 135)

Most of us do not have physical idols in our houses, by which I mean carved figures, although I must say I am always astonished how often one sees fat, eyes-shut Buddha statues in homes and gardens. They are supposed to convey an atmosphere of serenity and calm. I wonder what else they may convey.

In Psalm 106 we are told that *'They made a calf in Hore, and worshipped a molten image. Thus they exchanged their glory for the image of an ox that eats grass. They forgot God their Saviour, who had done great things in Egypt, wonders in the land of Ham and awesome things by the Red Sea.'* The word used for 'image' in that verse is a third word, *'tselem'*, meaning 'an illusion' or 'a phantom'. Put like that it is laughable; an ox that eats grass as a god!

Some of the language used to indicate the activity of pursuing idols and vain things is described as 'puffing and blowing' and 'panting after', again providing an insight into these insidious influences.

We are unlikely to have such things as subjects of worship but, in ministry to people at various times, I have been acutely aware of how crystals, lucky charms, and superstitions and behaviours which border on spiritualism have come to play a role in lives. We need to understand that it is not 'the thing' that is necessarily harmful to our spiritual progress but how it draws us away from God and the rightful place He holds in our lives. I wonder if it would be a healthy exercise to look at the things which demand priority of our time, our energy and possibly even our 'worship'. Ask the Holy Spirit if we have any 'vain things' in our lives.

Lord God, heavenly King, You make it clear that we are to have no other gods or idols in our lives, and that our worship is to be to You alone; that our consulting will be only of You. Forgive us, Father, for the times when other influences can become obsessive, seemingly promising us health or prosperity or long life. Father, speak to me now by the Holy Spirit if there are issues I should address and grant me Your great wisdom today, I pray. Amen.

SEPTEMBER

Day 245 – September 1st

There are often interesting items in the news concerning the very great lengths we will go to in order to prolong life, or somehow defeat the processes of ageing. Sometimes, also, cases concern 'ending life' rather than prolonging it. In short, we want to 'have control' over all our circumstances. We want to be able to buy a cream for our faces that will defy the ageing process, develop diets and exercise regimes that will somehow keep us in prime condition, and we spend countless billions on surgery to undo every fat or thin quirk of nature. I have no problem with looking after ourselves well so that we might avoid illness or debilitating conditions but, in the extreme, all of the above seem to represent 'huffing and puffing after vain things', and the industries concerned are very willing to take your money and offer you multitudes of dubious cures!

Psalm 139 speaks of God forming our innermost parts; weaving us in our mother's wombs; of being fearfully and wonderfully made . . . and yet somewhere along the line we seem to be ready to abandon that belief and see ourselves in some other less than acceptable way. I appreciate that I am running the risk of losing a good number of readers, many of them female, but I want to put it to you all, *men and women alike,* can you imagine how wonderful life would be if we *didn't* set such great store by these things? Is it possible we might be considerably *freer* than we are at present?

'Your adornment must not be merely external – braiding the hair, and wearing gold jewellery, or putting on dresses; but let it be the hidden person of the heart, with the imperishable quality of a gentle and quiet spirit, which is precious in the sight of God.' (1 Peter 3)

The reason I include that is to point out that Peter is inferring that 'adornment' is not just external. Is there, therefore, an *inner adornment* and is it 'visible' and does it count? I believe the answers are 'Yes', 'Yes', and, 'Yes'! I think this wise advice might apply to men and women given that we are all, in these days, prone to fashions, trends and vanities!

I like to have a haircut and be well-groomed and clean. I try to dress appropriately, certainly in public, and in that way never cause offence. (I will wear what I want in the garden!) My idea of causing offence would be to preach and find that listeners miss what God might be saying because they are overly concerned with how I appear. It's not vanity; more a question of honouring people appropriately. When I worked among the elderly I found this really mattered. We will say more of this later, but let's pray.

Father, I really want my 'inner adornment and beauty' to count before You. If I have aspects of my life out of balance please show me. It affects my spiritual life and matters greatly that I don't exhaust myself chasing after vanities. Amen.

Day 246 – September 2nd

There are many good men and women for whom the pursuit of outward perfection and good looks has become a major distraction and, sometimes, an immense burden. It feels sad to me when I come across it; it is difficult to define so I may well get myself into deep water here! One of the problems created by the 'perfection industry' is, straightforwardly, that of various regrets that follow. Treatments go wrong; fortunes are invested and there is often sadness when, after everything is accomplished, it actually doesn't necessarily make one feel better concerning the things which originally troubled us. The Bible has remarkable stories of a different sort of beauty being portrayed even by the most unlikely people.

'Mary then took a pound of very costly perfume of pure nard, and anointed the feet of Jesus, and wiped His feet with her hair; and the house was filled with the fragrance of the perfume.' (John 12)

Lord, teach us what beauty really is and what You treasure in us. In this story of a restored life being poured out for You in worship, we glimpse what matters in heaven. Amen.

Day 247 – September 3rd

One of the other difficulties we have created as we pursue the perfect face, the perfect body, the perfect eyebrows, or the perfect physique, leaves me wondering about those who cannot ever achieve this so-called 'perfection', and are left feeling utterly sidelined by it all. It is a small jump from self-obsession with such things to actively making some people feel ostracised by their natural appearance, or by their age, or just by their inability to finance these pursuits! It can be a crushing experience for some. We *know* what counts but somehow it doesn't always reach our 'knower'.

A good few years ago, some friends in my church had their firstborn child, a son. His name was Gavin. His mother went through a very difficult childbirth and it later transpired that Gavin had suffered during this time. It became apparent after a short while that the little chap was blind. A little later it became clear that he was also deaf. He didn't have the normal range of controlled movements or reflexes that children should have at the prescribed ages. Quite simply, he did not develop; his little brain had been damaged. His parents loved him dearly but their disappointment and anxiety for him were huge. The burden of watching this little one was incredibly painful for them; he could not respond to external stimuli and, each day was spent sitting all day long in a large bouncy chair and, as far as we could tell, Gavin was in dark silence. Unless one approached him carefully, the shock of being touched would frighten him terribly. He began to have seizures which, despite the many drugs he was given, became worse and worse and seriously threatened his well-being. By the time he was six, his life at times hung on by a thread. The amazing thing was that this wee mite was such a beautiful little man! He radiated an inner beauty which is beyond me to explain. Everyone wanted to come and help or just to spend time in his company. How do you explain that? We prayed and prayed for him and then, one night, a group of us gathered with his parents to pray for him because he was so ill. We all independently felt the Lord say very distinctly, *'Let him come to Me.'*

Gavin died peacefully not long after that. At his funeral, which was packed with friends and family, testimony after testimony was given concerning Gavin's amazing gift of bringing people to life. Over and over, different friends said, 'Gavin taught me more about life than anyone else has done.'

Can anyone explain that? He was immobile, very ill, blind and deaf. In the course of his short life, he never spoke one word.

Outwardly, this little man had nothing to offer; inwardly, his spirit was bursting with life.

'You have taken hold of my right hand. With Your counsel You will guide me, and afterwards receive me to glory.' (Psalm 73)

Father, such mysteries bring me to my knees in hushed awe. I need to learn afresh that it is the spirit of a man you cherish. You recreate beautiful spirits in bodies that remain broken. Help me to see as You see, and to lead people in the pure way of life eternal. Amen.

Day 248 – September 4th

'Now Jonathan, Saul's son, had a son crippled in his feet. He was five years old when the report of Saul and Jonathan came from Jezreel [that his father and grandfather had died], and his nurse took him up and fled. And it happened that in her hurry to flee, he fell and became lame. And his name was Mephibosheth.' (2 Samuel 4)

We don't know what happened to the child; he may have been dropped on his spine and partially paralysed. Many years later when Mephibosheth was a middle-aged man with family of his own, David became king over all Israel. Despite all that Saul had done to make David's life a misery, in a touching story David seeks to find any remaining family members in order to honour the memory of Saul and Jonathan. Mephibosheth probably thinks David is to deal severely with him when word comes that the king has sent for him. He is convinced David will be seeking to finish the family off for good; in those days, it might well have been so. He prostrates himself before David and asks, *'What is your servant, that you should regard a dead dog like me?'* (2 Samuel 9).

Far from harming him, David makes total provision for him, settling on him all that he would have inherited from his grandfather's estate, his continuing sustenance from the lands, and David also insists he dine with him at his table; the king's table. A remarkable display of great kindness, an inner beauty we might say, to a man who was, superficially, nothing but a disabled fugitive. I can only imagine that this kindness restored the spirit of Mephibosheth and maybe even went as far as to heal his wounded family story. The story speaks very much of the restoration of broken mankind by the selfless gift of Jesus on the cross. Not many of us were beautiful but the Father saw something else in each one of us and wants us restored and seated at His table also.

O Lord our God, how foolish we can be. We *know* the truth and yet we chase vain idols for not much benefit. I want to cultivate a heart of beauty and generosity. Forgive me for pursuing things that do not matter and neglecting the things that do. Give me wisdom, I pray, and eyes to see the beauty in those around me that You see. Amen.

Day 249 – September 5th

Without going into volumes about my own life and the adversity I have encountered along the way, or detailing all that has happened to my body, I would say that it is not much fun being ill or suffering from disease! I have a condition that has greatly changed my physical abilities and my general mobility, and it has required endless treatments and medication. By comparison with many I meet I have a good quality of life. I am not a complainer, but, like many others, I find the process of being repeatedly 'stripped away' very difficult.

To begin with it felt transitory: I knew I would make a recovery; all I needed to do was *wait* and try to become fit again. But, as time went on and reoccurrences of the same sort of problem happened, I found my 'fit-man identity' dashed and I had to reinvent myself in a different role and 'find myself again'. Then it happened all over again and, this time, with less expectation of recovery than before, I reinvented myself yet again and emerged in a different guise. Deep down I gradually understood what we all know: that my true identity is not in *what I can do*. Do I wish it were all otherwise? I am not sure. I will always remember my late wife saying, as her days drew to a close, *'I would not have had it any other way.'* A remarkable 'healed-person' statement that was honestly spoken and heartfelt. Her justification for saying such a thing was quite simply that the discovery of what is beautiful and really matters in life cannot always be found in the fullness of life with good health and few constraints. It is very much the story of Job. That, my friends, is *healing*.

So, at each stage of life I try to find God's purposes for me in *that* season. The extraordinary thing is that when I think I have less, God has shown me that in His grace I can have *more*! This is not a neat mental-flip to kid myself about my present or my future; it is the reality of our lives in God.

'How blessed is the man whose strength is in You, in whose heart are the highways to Zion!' (Psalm 84)

May I say that it has not been a smooth highway. I did not slip into the successive seasons accompanied by the quiet 'snick' of a synchronised gear box changing up a gear for a steep hill; at times, it felt as though I had a rucksack of boulders on my back and sharp grit in my shoes.

I do recall being greatly comforted by the Psalms; circumstances drove me into them and as I travelled in them I found new riches.

'You have held my eyelids open; I am so troubled that I cannot speak.'

Then the psalmist recalls how good circumstances were once before (not always entirely helpful) and asks, *'Will the Lord reject forever? And will He never be favourable again? Has His loving kindness ceased forever? Has His promise come to an end forever? Has God forgotten to be gracious? Or has He in anger withdrawn His compassion?'*

How real this man is able to be with God! But then he says something quite remarkable:

'It is my grief that the right hand of the Most High has changed. I shall remember the deeds of the LORD*; surely I will remember Your wonders of old.'* (Psalm 77)

It appears that God did not necessarily change the specific circumstances that constituted the problem, instead He changed the psalmist's heart attitude towards them, and then he found he *could* be blessed by meditating on the Lord's history of His goodness.

And so God strips us away and, each time He does so, we discover we know Him a little better. But rarely is there not involved an 'Ouch', if not a silent scream!

'Christ of the mysteries, I trust You to be stronger than each storm within me. I will trust in the darkness and know that my times, even now, are in Your hand.' Amen.

Day 250 – September 6th

The great predicament for those of us who pray for physical healing is that we know that sometimes God heals and sometimes He does not heal. I have written about this before and explained that I always pray on the basis that Jesus tells us to do so and after that we leave it to Him. A friend once told me God had spoken to him the memorable words, *'Mea forca; Mea culpa,'* when he was ministering in South America. *'My power; My responsibility.'* A revealing lesson for us all to take on board and rest in! Following that simple maxim would save much of the striving which can inflict itself on recipients of healing ministry.

Sometimes the 'big miracles' happen without any particular warning or insight. I recall arriving at a week-long conference that we were leading and, as often happens, I feel God draw my attention to this person or that. A woman sat in the midst of the delegates and for no apparent reason I felt that God said, 'I want you to pray with her this week.' I didn't rush to do so, not least because I wanted the atmosphere and direction of the week to be established and for us to build a relationship with the conference members.

During the middle of the week we began making appointments for prayer and this lady came to one. She had breast cancer and was very seriously ill with lung tumours; it had spread to her other organs. She had received her last chemotherapy and had been told that it had achieved only minimal effects. The doctors did not envisage further treatments beyond palliative care. We listened carefully and respectfully to all she had to say. It was clear that she was more concerned with her young family and her husband and how they would cope without her rather than being desperate for healing. I must admit I did think that healing would take care of most of her worries! We laid hands on her and prayed for her and I remember that it wasn't a particularly remarkable time; at least no change occurred as one might have observed outwardly. She was blessed and we felt deeply empathetic with the pain of her journey.

A week or two after the conference we had an email saying that she was very pleased because her blood tests had shown a remarkable and inexplicable change for the better. At home, we rejoiced with her and prayed more. A week or so after that we received another email to say that everyone at the hospital was flabbergasted by the extent of her recovery; it appeared her condition had gone into 'reverse'. The emails kept coming and her cancer was eventually declared to not be present in her body any longer. Praise God for all the people who faithfully prayed for this lady, for the medics who treated her, and praise God for His immense goodness to us! The last I heard was that she had gone back to part-time work, had been to Africa and started a charity, and her life was in full swing!

'But He was pierced through for our transgressions, He was crushed for our iniquities; the chastening for our well-being fell upon Him, and by His scourging we are healed.' (Isaiah 53)

God, I bless You! You are an amazing, loving and merciful God. When You release Your power into our midst, anything can happen and I long to see more. Thank You so much for all You do through our prayers. Amen.

Day 251 – September 7th

Inner beauty seems to be apparent when the deep *shalom* of God invades us and overpowers our un-peaceful places. It seems to come to people almost irrespective of physical wholeness; indeed, as I suggested before, it does often appear that the people who have less 'physical body wholeness' do genuinely have more of the peace and the power of God about them. There are many remarkable stories written by people who experienced this extraordinary blessing. I rather imagine that it has to do with the 'little children inherit the kingdom' principle of Jesus. When we are physically impaired, we do have to trust more; not just for daily needs to be met but for God to *make sense* of our circumstances. Our faith grows as we lean in on God in our distinct lack of self-sufficiency!

Paul suffered what he referred to as a 'thorn in the flesh'. We don't know what it was, although there have been various suggestions including a stammer. I doubt that is so. The most likely problem He suffered from was a problem of poor eyesight. Some say that he may have suffered from shingles resulting in damaged vision. We cannot know until we meet him one day. What an amazing time that will be talking with Moses and Paul and many others, if we can be persuaded away from worshipping the Lamb!

'Because of the surpassing greatness of the revelations, for this reason, to keep me from exalting myself, there was given me a thorn in the flesh, a messenger of Satan to torment me – to keep me from exalting myself! Concerning this I implored the Lord three times that it might leave me. And He has said to me, "My grace is sufficient for you, for power is perfected in weakness."' (2 Corinthians 12)

It appears that Paul believes that God knows how he might be potentially in character so has allowed something to keep him in a place of relying totally on God. The idea that power is perfected in weakness is a sound one. 'Perfected' in Greek, implies a 'filled up' state in the literal sense of full-filled. It's not that God could not have used Paul at all; the implication is that He could do all He desired, with Paul's infirmity in place.

If you are in that place of asking repeatedly to be relieved of such a burden, I want to encourage you. If I have a testimony, it is that in the Baca Valley places of life, God moves most powerfully. I have challenged those who claim that the healing of Jesus is always available to us; that if we don't receive it there is a lack of faith somewhere, either in us or those who faithfully pray. I say emphatically, 'No,' that is not right. More, it can be a very wounding theology of ministry. One day we will all know total healing, new bodies, no tears and so on, but the kingdom of God is 'now amongst us' but 'not yet fulfilled'. Apart from anything else, when should we cease praying for the elderly, for example, if we declare that prayers for healing should always be prayed and we should always be in expectation for complete restoration? There is a flaw in the notion, I suspect.

For me, yes, I do pray for healing for my own body, as do many others, and sometimes I have experienced it very powerfully, but I will rest in the goodness of the Lord to me *apart* from having a sublimely beautiful body! That is to me a place of peace to know and love God from that place of complete repose – and then occasionally

He delights me with a surprise!

Dear Lord Jesus, our eyes can often focus on the wrong things. It is our journey with You, and our *knowing of You* that seems to matter most in Your kingdom. May we find rest in this and not be offended on the days when You faithfully partner us in days of difficulty. Amen.

Day 252 – September 8th

'Joshua did as Moses told him, and fought against Amalek; and Moses, Aaron, and Hur went to the top of the hill. So it came about when Moses held his hand up, that Israel prevailed, and when he let his hand down, Amalek prevailed. But Moses' hands were heavy. Then they took a stone and put it under him, and he sat on it; and Aaron and Hur supported his hands, one on one side and one on the other. Thus his hands were steady until the sun set. So Joshua overwhelmed Amalek and his people with the edge of the sword.' (Exodus 17)

In the realm of men being called to partner with the Spirit of God, there are many deep mysteries. I have alluded to occasions when one man has been touched by the power of God and the one next to him is not. If the presence of Moses was not enough to enable his people to prevail in battle, but his raised hands influenced the outcome before God, we must, surely, wonder why it was so. Was it that Moses' hands were powerful before God? Or was there, perhaps, a great significance attached to the support they gave to one another? Those who have tried to hold their own hands up high for a few hours will appreciate why Moses needed help to do so; the question is, *why did God only work in battle when his hands were held high?* The answer could be that it was a visible sign to the people. The answer could be, quite simply, *that it was so.*

Sometimes we need to find peace in the response *'because it is so'.* God does not always explain Himself to us. He is surrounded in clouds and great mystery. I have several 'unexplained mysteries' in my life. I was married to a wife who died of cancer. I remarried, very joyously, to a woman who had also had cancer; very serious cancer from which she was not really expected to survive. She survived and lives a normal life! The two events, one dying and one being healed, ran quite separately but in parallel time. It was a great joy to be with Hannah, my wife, when she was finally discharged from the oncologists' care after her long and demanding treatment. Can anyone explain such a mystery? No. The answer is, 'Because . . .'

'My grace is sufficient for you.' (2 Corinthians 12)

My Lord and King, there are many things I long to understand; answers I seek You for, but I pray that You will grant to my heart Your great peace and trust. I ask You, Holy Spirit, to give me a faithful heart, one that unswervingly trusts the Father in all things. Amen.

Day 253 – September 9th

Jesus said to His disciples not many days before His death,

'I have many more things to say to you, but you cannot bear them now.' (John 16)

Continuing this theme of the 'mysteries of God'; we can all come across them in our journeying with the Lord. Sometimes we glimpse an answer, usually fleetingly; something that makes sense for just a millionth of a second and then it is gone.

One day, not long after my wife had died, I was in a service along with other members of a ministry team. After, the congregation were invited to ask for prayer. I saw a lady who I had never seen before; she looked at me, hesitated, and then gathered herself and walked towards me. Her eyes brimmed with tears as she took a deep breath and said, 'I have just been diagnosed with breast cancer.'

To be completely honest with you, I felt like screaming. I felt as if to shout out to the Lord, *'Why do You do this to me?'* I didn't of course; I listened carefully and I prayed. I followed the Holy Spirit's guiding as best I could as I prayed. It was a long prayer. There were a few tears from each of us. When we finished praying, I could see my prayer-team partner giving me a wide-eyed look, not disapprovingly. She told me afterwards, 'I just thought *where did that come from?*'

The lady wiped her eyes and looked at me steadily and said, very quietly, 'How on earth did you pray for me like that?'

Naturally I didn't want to say as I felt the answer would be a distinct discouragement so I shrugged my shoulders and probably smiled awkwardly. She repeated the question so, I took a breath and told her: 'My wife died recently from breast cancer.' At that moment, the only explanation I can offer is that the Holy Spirit came upon her very powerfully. She met with the power of God. I have not seen her since that day and have no idea how our Father touched her life.

Why did that happen? 'Because . . .'

And in that we rest until we have attained such a spiritual condition that we can truly bear the full knowledge of His ways.

'Deep calls to deep at the sound of Your waterfalls; all Your breakers and Your waves have rolled over me.' (Psalm 42)

Lord Jesus, I am content to sit at Your feet. I know You are wondrous in all Your ways and I do trust You. I absolutely trust You. Give me peace in the areas of my life, particularly in the places of disappointment and loss, that I may rest in You. Amen.

Day 254 – September 10th

Sometimes the mysterious and extravagant ways of God amaze us. Here is a deeply moving story of God meeting the need of a widow *in extremis.* Her late husband had been a 'son of the prophets', presumably one of a band of men who raised young prophets and assistants in a 'school'. Elisha came by and she cried out to him explaining that the debt collector was about to take her two children as slaves, in payment. This is truly a story of redemption in more ways than one.

'Elisha said to her, "What shall I do for you? Tell me, what do you have in the house?" And she said, "Your maidservant has nothing in

the house except a jar of oil." Then he said, "Go, borrow vessels at large for yourself from all your neighbours, even empty vessels; do not get a few. And you shall go in and shut the door behind you and your sons, and pour into all these vessels, and you shall set aside what is full." (2 Kings 4)

The woman did as she had been told and the sons passed her the jars and she poured until they ran out of jars and then the oil stopped.

Elisha told her to sell the oil to pay her debts and to live from the remainder. I think we are to assume that these were *big jars,* not jam jars that we might use for bottling plum jam; flagons we might say. Wow. She suddenly had the sort of quantity of oil an olive grove farmer might expect from an annual crop!

It reminds us of the five loaves and two fish in the multiplying hands of Jesus but it speaks beyond that; the oil of the kingdom continues to pour as long as there is need. It is copious and extravagant! It also speaks of God's abundant care for widows and orphans who, throughout Scripture, are shown to be close to His heart.

It speaks to me personally as a reminder to always look around at what *is* available to work with in days of apparent depletion; of empty oil vessels waiting to be filled that there might be plenty and more. We will look at this story again.

Lord God, this is a wonderful story of Your abundant provision for a lady You respected and honoured who was in need. Let our hearts feed on this story by faith and read the many layers of truth in it. Amen.

Day 255 – September 11th

In the days of Elisha many of the people were pursuing worship of evil, idolatrous gods. Baal worship was common, led by no less than the king. The schools of prophets are mentioned elsewhere; they were keeping the flame going for God in the land. The schools were like

Bible training schools. Elisha as the key prophet in the land would have had a professorial roving ministry in the school. The widow in the story would have known this and she looked to Elisha as a leader.

'Now a certain woman of the wives of the sons of the prophets cried out to Elisha . . .' (2 Kings 4)

I wonder what she is really crying out? I think she is really crying out to God and, as far as she is concerned, Elisha is His representative. We can be like that for people too. People have sometimes said, 'Do something!'

'Your servant my husband is dead . . .' The man of God was dead and so there was a godly responsibility for her in the Law of Moses. It might not be entirely Elisha's personal responsibility but he represents 'justice'. She makes a point of saying, *'Your servant feared the* LORD.' The notion of her two children being taken into slavery was serious. People could be taken as hired men in lieu of debt but not as slaves. Further, such hired men and women would be released after seven years at Jubilee. This sounds like it was for good. Her sons who would provide for her when she was older were being taken away.

Elisha asks her an important question, *'What shall I do for you?'*

If you have ever been in dire straits you will know that it is possible to go around in circles shouting, 'It's not fair! Why has this happened to me?' So when he asks her what she wants him to do it is important. What do you want God to do for *you* today?

'What do you have in the house?' he asks her. This is an important question. If you are going to ask for God's help, start by making an offering of what you *do* have. She has a small amount of an important commodity: oil. Everyone needed oil. If you had oil you were rich. It's all she has so asking her to work with the only item she has left is a major point of surrender.

Elisha then does an important thing: he sends her out on a faith trip; she has to be involved in procuring this supernatural provision. She had to go around asking and maybe explaining why she needed jars. Oil jars were precious so the community were to step up also. *The Law said they had a responsibility towards her as well as family.* When she returns, presumably with her sons, they are all laden with vats and flagons and the scene is set. The oil flows until there is exactly the right amount.

God has a regular saying He whispers to me. It first happened after He provided in some particular circumstances years ago, and when I gave thanks He said very clearly, *'There will always be enough, My son.'*

Sometimes I would be doing a DIY job and just finish with the last drop of paint, or the last nail, or find the wood I had was just perfect for the job. I became so used to it that Father and I would chorus together, 'There will always be enough!' It may sound a trivial thing but it has grown my faith! In my view, prosperity is always having just enough to meet genuine needs.

This dear woman was profoundly blessed by this miracle of provision to her but it goes beyond having enough oil. Her sons were safe, family life was no longer threatened and, most importantly of all, I think she must have grown through it all.

Lord, Your stories are amazing as we peel off the layers with You. Thank You for all this teaches me. Let me learn to look around and see what I have that I might offer to You. I surrender all I have to You, Lord God. Amen.

Day 256 – September 12th

Over many years there has been much spoken and written about the so-called 'prosperity gospel'. The fundamental notion is that God is generous and if you give, usually to one of his intermediaries, such as a preacher or a healer, He will bless you in return. I call that a slot machine. I put my money in, select my choice of coffee, and out come the goods. As always, such things are corruptions of the truth. God is generous, very generous beyond belief, and He will prosper the faithful but in Scripture the prospering of God is not only about money. It is about being blessed.

Jesus had a famous prosperity gospel.

'Now when Jesus saw a crowd around Him, He gave orders to depart to the other side of the sea. Then a scribe came and said to Him, "Teacher, I will follow You wherever You go." Jesus said to him, "The foxes have holes and the birds of the air have nests, but the Son of Man has nowhere to lay His head."' (Matthew 8)

That's it; the prosperity gospel of Jesus! He also had an equally direct way to gather followers:

'Another of the disciples said to Him, "Lord, permit me first to go and bury my father." But Jesus said to him, "Follow Me, and allow the dead to bury their own dead."' (Matthew 8)

There was no apology, no explanation. Jesus comes first and if you want to be His disciple the in-work benefits are few, aside from eternal life. I often wonder if Jesus speaks this way because He was calling people to a life of *faith*, which is dramatically different from a life of common sense and normal 'decorum'. Whatever prompted it, it is a far cry from our calls to faith . . . while the worship band plays softly, come up if you want to . . .

Lord Jesus, I admit that the directness of Your calling challenges me very deeply. I put so many things ahead of You, if I am honest; I know I do. But the prosperity of God follows those who are totally devoted to You. Teach me to see my circumstances through Your eyes and may I always hold material things very lightly indeed. Amen.

Day 257 – September 13th

In a similar vein to yesterday's thought about the hard road of following Jesus, we find prophets being called of God to do extraordinarily tough things as declarations of God's heart.

Ezekiel was called to prophesy the siege and desolation of Jerusalem. As so often happened, he acted out something which had a significance way beyond the action. He took a brick and carved the city's name on it, 'Jerusalem', and then he had to build a model siege ramp and all the accoutrements representing the coming invasion. He then had to position himself with an iron plate between him and the model. Then God spoke.

'This is a sign to the house of Israel. As for you, lie down on your left side and lay the iniquity of the house of Israel on it; you shall bear their iniquity for the number of days that you lie on it. For I have assigned you a number of days corresponding to the years of their iniquity, three hundred and ninety days; thus, you shall bear the iniquity of the house of Israel.' (Ezekiel 4)

Later, Ezekiel was to repeat the process on his right side for forty days for the iniquity of Judah. Then he was to bare his arm and prophesy against Jerusalem. God added that he would restrain Ezekiel so that he could not turn over. In the whole process, Ezekiel's only grumble was that when he was told to bake his bread over a fire of human dung, he declared he could not so defile himself. God relented and allowed him to bake bread over a cow dung fire instead but the bread ration was tightly controlled and very meagre to indicate the consequences of the siege for the inhabitants.

So, who wants to be a prophet? Presumably he was allowed to have a reprieve from lying on his side so that he could cook his bread. Perhaps not. Perhaps his assistant did that. What a way to treat your servants!

There is something mysterious and powerful about the symbolism of prophetic acts. In every case I can think of, words might have sufficed to communicate the warning but they do not satisfy God's heart nor speak to men's spirits.

I recall once when some friends had a particularly difficult personal 'bridge to cross' and I had been praying about the timing of the event in question and asking that God would let them know when it should be so that all would go well for them.

Quite suddenly, God told me to go and buy a hibiscus plant! I did so and faithfully gave it to them with the words, 'It will be when the hibiscus flowers.' It seemed crazy but the flowering time was exactly the right time and all went incredibly well and everyone was very blessed! I am not complaining about God's ways, merely pointing out that we do need to take note of the still small voice; it is often Him and of great significance. But why the Lord didn't just tell me the date, I do not know! Maybe I do . . . Wouldn't I sound arrogant in those circumstances, and, further, where would be the involvement in the mystery of waiting!

Majestic Father, may I be responsive always to the promptings of the Holy Spirit; to be a faithful and sensitive messenger. Thank You for Your mysterious ways and the way that, through prophetic acts, You convey so much more and always in deeply memorable ways. The Spirit of Jesus *is* the Spirit of Prophecy and all that You speak will resonate with the truth of heaven. Amen.

Day 258 – September 14th

Several years ago I was speaking at a conference and, after one of the sessions, a dear man came to me with a bruising tale of something that had happened in his life. He very much wanted to be free from the effects of it so we prayed together and asked the Lord if He would heal this man's broken story. I felt God say to tell him to cross the bridge and He would meet him when he took the first steps and reached the middle. Rather like the widow's oil that Elisha was to multiply so abundantly, this man had to make a move; so often God does this. He is saying, 'Step out in faith and I will meet you.'

It happened that there was a bridge in the grounds and I suggested that we went there to literally 'cross the bridge'. I felt that God wanted him *to do it* rather than just talk about it. He waited by the bridge while I crossed over and then I called him: 'In the name of Jesus, I call you now to cross the bridge and to leave your broken story behind.' As he reached the exact mid-point, the Holy Spirit came upon him very powerfully and healed him of his troubled past amid much laughter and tears.

'As we were staying there for some days, a prophet named Agabus came down from Judea. And coming to us, he took Paul's belt and bound his own feet and hands, and said, "This is what the Holy Spirit says: 'In this way the Jews at Jerusalem will bind the man who owns this belt and deliver him into the hands of the Gentiles.'" When we had heard this, we as well as the local residents began begging him not to go up to Jerusalem. Then Paul answered, "What are you doing, weeping and breaking my heart? For I am ready not only to be bound, but even to die at Jerusalem for the name of the Lord Jesus."' (Acts 21)

God wasn't revealing a surprise for Paul; he already knew! God had laid the outcome on Paul's heart. In the previous chapter of Acts, Paul spoke as he left Ephesus:

'And now, behold, I know that all of you, among whom I went about preaching the kingdom, will no longer see my face.' (Acts 20)

So often God speaks to us in prophecy *that which we already know*; it is a confirmation of something and, in this case, for others also to see and hear, spoken by a man who presumably had no natural knowledge of Paul's thoughts. It pleased God to say, 'I want you to know, Paul is in My hands'! This is why it is so important to be ready with a word of prophecy. It may not make any sense to you but it may bring untold blessing to the recipient!

Lord God, You make provision for us and care for us at so many levels. You speak to us through Your word, making inked words on the page come alive with holy fluorescence and You speak profoundly to our spirits. You have done it for many hundreds of years, so guiding men and women in Your service. You are the Spirit of Prophecy. Cause us to seek You more and more for the riches of Your word to us, in Jesus' name. Amen.

Day 259 – September 15th

It seems from Scripture that sometimes God wants to check if a person can hear Him accurately before he is sent out. God spoke to Jeremiah.

'The word of the LORD came to me saying, "What do you see, Jeremiah?" And I said, "I see a rod of an almond tree." Then the LORD said to me, "You have seen well, for I am watching over My word to perform it."' (Jeremiah 1)

God then gradually adds His explanations to what Jeremiah sees and sends him out with His word.

'Thus He showed me, and behold the Lord was standing by a vertical wall with a plumb line in His hand. The LORD said to me, "What do you see, Amos?" And I said, "A plumb line." Then the Lord said, "Behold I am about to put a plumb line in the midst of My people Israel."' (Amos 7)

The question *'what do you see?'* is a question God often asks. He may draw our attention to something that is happening and ask us *'what do you see?'* You can *see* in the natural but also *feel* something is being associated with it. Ask God; say, 'Lord, are You showing me something? Should I take note?' I encourage people to do 'people-watching'; godly people-watching! Look at people and try to read them in partnership with the Holy Spirit. I love sitting somewhere and just observing people and asking the Lord, 'What is going on in that person's life?' Remember how Jesus said to Simon the Pharisee, *'Do you see this woman?'* (Luke 7).

Sometimes the Father will tell you what to say to them. There is no need to be afraid; when God speaks, all we need to say is, 'Is that really You?'

Check with Him. I always have a deeper feeling than just curiosity or the whim of a passing thought.

I recall once watching people coming in to a Sunday meeting and I saw a lady and had an immediate thought about her but I wasn't sure. If it was true, it would have been quite serious. I turned away and then looked again and the word I had been thinking was 'written' on her forehead just like those labels we write for party games when people guess who we are! It was God's way of saying, 'Yes, you were absolutely right. You heard me.' Later in the evening I prayed with her. Having politely introduced myself, I said, 'I had a feeling that . . . and I might be wrong . . . but is God saying that you . . .' I have never known anyone take offence at that as it sounds immensely caring!

Lord, being with You is an exciting adventure! I love hearing You speak about Your children and it is wonderful when You use us to bring the love of the Father to them. Send Your Holy Spirit on me to develop and tune my ear and my heart to Your words and encourage me to trust You and speak out. I trust You to stop me if I am not right and if You don't give me a check in my spirit, I will go in Your name! Amen.

Day 260 – September 16th

'And He called the twelve together, and gave them power and authority over all the demons, and to heal diseases. And He sent them out to proclaim the kingdom of God, and to perform healing.' (Luke 9)

Have you ever wondered what it means when it tells us, *'He gave them power and authority'*? I wonder how that was different from the experience after Pentecost when the Holy Spirit came upon them and was *within them* and worked *through them*. I may be wrong but one seems to confer a status – *You have my permission and authority to do this* – and the other, the Holy Spirit, who is the life of Jesus *in them*. I am not splitting hairs here. I have been with people with profound ministries and, when on team with them, I found I was experiencing things that were not normal for *me*! I felt that I was 'under the person's authority' or their anointing. It was not just a case of being 'inspired' by their faith; it was as if their mantle embraced me.

When Jesus met the centurion, he requested of Jesus concerning his servant boy who was gravely ill. Jesus said that He would go and heal him. There followed an extraordinary story whereby the centurion, feeling he was not worthy to have Jesus come under his roof, said,

"'But just say the word, and my servant will be healed. For I also am a man under authority, with soldiers under me; and I say to this one, 'Go!' and he goes, and to another, 'Come!' and he comes, and to my slave, 'Do this!' and he does it." Now when Jesus heard this, He marvelled and said to those who were following, "Truly I say to you, I have not found such great faith with anyone in Israel."' (Matthew 8)

What the centurion described was having authority to command in certain situations, which Jesus remarks upon as having great *faith*. Is this a conundrum? We need to look at Jesus' words to His disciples when He spoke the so-called Great Commission.

'All authority has been given to Me in heaven and on earth. Go therefore and make disciples of all the nations, baptising them in the name of the Father and the Son and the Holy Spirit, teaching them to observe all that I commanded you; and lo, I am with you always, even to the end of the age.' (Matthew 28)

Jesus spoke of 'all authority' being His; not 'My great faith'. He was sending them out in the awareness that it was *His word* that empowered them. The centurion knew that his own word, as such, held little sway but, any command he gave was backed up by the entire power and force of the vast Roman Empire and Caesar himself. To argue with the soldier was to have the audacity to question the Grand Emperor. Jesus saw that the man understood being *under* authority. The centurion had taken a vow to Caesar and, in return, the Roman Empire had reciprocated by honouring him. He was vested with power just as certainly as if Caesar himself drew up in his chariot! And so it is with us. Christ is *in us* in the person of His Spirit, and our faith is that it is so! Understanding authority and having faith go together. When we speak to this or that situation it obeys us *as long as we are in tune with the Spirit of God and His will.*

Holy God, thank You for giving us Your Spirit. Thank You for positioning us in the spiritual realms so that we speak with the authority of our Father. May our faith grow and grow to see the reality of this partnership being worked out more and more every day. Amen.

Day 261 – September 17th

Paul writes famously to the church in Ephesus, the paragraph which begins,

'I pray that the eyes of your heart may be enlightened, so that you will know what is the hope of His calling, what are the riches of the glory of His inheritance in the saints, and what is the surpassing greatness of His power towards us who believe.' (Ephesians 1)

If you have doubts about the power God vests you with, I do suggest reading this chapter and the following one at least once every day for at least six weeks! It will change you as the truth of heaven invades your spirit! Pray, *'God, illuminate the eyes of my heart!'*

The same power that God exerted in Christ when He was raised from the dead and then seated Him in heaven, ruling over *all things* as the Head of the church, His body, is *the same power* God graces to us; His inheritance in us (not our inheritance, note). Later we read,

'But God, being rich in mercy, because of His great love with which He loved us, even when we were dead in our transgressions, made us alive together with Christ (by grace you have been saved), and raised us up with Him, and seated us with Him in the heavenly places in Christ Jesus.' (Ephesians 2)

These scriptures will do more to inform and grow your faith than anything else! You can read about the miraculous moves of Jesus and that will certainly stimulate your faith, but the very first thing to have welded into our spirits like a massive anchor on a sea-going ship is this statement of *where you are now seated* as a believing follower of the Lord Jesus. You may have your feet firmly on the earth for a season or two but spiritually you are where? Seated with Christ and in Christ in the heavenly places. What an amazing life-changing truth!

Glory to You, God in the highest, that by Your unfathomable mercy and love, when I believed, You gave me a new life. You have raised me up and seated me with Your beloved Son in the highest places, sharing all that He has. It was by Your grace. I did nothing to achieve this. Bring me fully alive to these immense truths, I pray. Amen.

Day 262 – September 18th

A similarly famous paragraph begins one chapter further on in Ephesians which has the same power to transform us.

'For this reason I bow my knees before the Father, from whom every family in heaven and on earth derives its name, that He would grant you, according to the riches of His glory, to be strengthened with power through His Spirit in the inner man, so that Christ may dwell in your hearts through faith; and that you, being rooted and grounded in love, may be able to comprehend with all the saints what is the breadth and length and height and depth, and to know the love of Christ which surpasses knowledge, that you may be filled up to all the fullness of God.' (Ephesians 3)

It's that great anchor again or, in Paul's words, 'rooted and grounded'. What are we to be rooted and grounded in? The love of God or, to be more precise, the *agape* goodness and benevolence of God; the love that gives all and asks for nothing as Christ comes to dwell in our hearts. This is Paul writing brilliantly, encouraging us to become inextricably bound up in the character and the ensuing outpouring of God. When Christ is made welcome to abide in our hearts will not His love and His power flow out of us in uncorrupted, beautiful streams of life? Cry out with me, 'My Lord, come and abide in my heart and let Your power flow from my inner person. May I be *possessed* by Your love.'

Lord, it appears these scriptures beckon me to go deeper into You and to long more for Your living dynamic presence within me. I pray that You will give me as much as I can hold and increase the scope of my heart to receive more. O Lord, be glorified in me! Amen.

Day 263 – September 19th

As we journey so we learn, and as we learn so we yearn. Paul entreats God to open the eyes of our hearts that we may fully understand what He has done, and that we may be able to *comprehend* the overpowering majesty of the love of Christ. As they say, *what is there not to like?* But Jesus made it very clear what was involved in being full of His life.

'*Abide in Me, and I in you. As the branch cannot bear fruit of itself unless it abides in the vine, so neither can you unless you abide in Me.*' (John 15)

The idea of 'abiding' is fully brought home by the image of the vine and the branches. All of Jesus' listeners would have grasped the simple notion that an unconnected branch cannot live. It cannot be in the vine for some of the time; abiding means *living* there and finding a permanent abode. Later, in the New Testament Paul speaks about Gentile believers being grafted into the vine where each will find life.

Many years ago I taught grafting as part of a horticulture course. Mostly we grafted apple branches onto root stocks. The cuts are made carefully and deliberately and each is notched to receive the other part. I used to recommend liberally licking the cut surfaces before pressing them together and bandaging them in place; such is the need for an intimate join which will encourage the life of the parent plant to flow to the new branch. It's a miracle of nature that the cut surfaces do join, as remarkable as the self-healing properties of broken bone. The point to note is that once they are joined, whether branch or bone, it is quite impossible to part them; the two truly become as one. Praise God that the life of Jesus flows into us and does the same. We become one with Him and where He is, we are, and where we are, He is. If He is seated in the heavenly realms with His Father, we are there also.

Jesus, the images You used to explain the intimate relationship You intended Your followers to share with You is breathtaking. You call us close, to know You intimately ... ... inst ... ... You. Holy Spirit, would You draw me close and make this revelation a reality in every aspect of my life. Amen.

Day 264 – September 20th

When Jesus was twelve His parents took Him to the temple, as was the custom. His parents trusted that He was safe with friends, we presume, because after a day's journey back home they discovered He was missing from their travelling band. When they returned to Jerusalem He was found with the teachers engaged in earnest discussions. His parents quite naturally chastised Him for causing worry and Jesus' reply was,

'Why is it that you were looking for Me? Did you now know that I had to be in My Father's house?' (Luke 2)

His reply did not make much sense to them but it should to us. The communion between Father and Son was a fact of who He was. It was quite impossible not be about His Father's business and when we are filled with the Spirit of the Lord we also will find it the most natural thing to be attending to the Father's house affairs and, conversely, if we are apart from Him, I put it to you that the pangs of homesickness should beckon us back to His side. Is that how it feels for you? Or are you used to having long periods of your life lived apart from Him as though you might be a commuter returning only in the evenings or for your 'quiet times'? I believe it is a high priority for us to be so engaged with the life of the Almighty; so much so that we will feel unbearably cut off if we drift away. I practise this by taking a verse from a psalm or a scripture and try to repeat it frequently and pray from that place during the day. It is amazing that, very often, the circumstances of the day will line up with the word of God I am focusing on for that day. To be quite honest with you, that is the origin of this book; most days I scribble a note and carry it with me.

Father, I never want to be away from my Father's house. I want You, Jesus, to be living in the Father's house in me! What a picture that is! Holy Spirit, please show me what Family Life should be like. Amen.

Day 265 – September 21st

One of the 'spin-offs' of living in the Father's presence is that it becomes extraordinarily difficult to sin! Have you noticed that? The vital relationship with God leaves no space for behaving in any manner not worthy of Him. I liken it to a water barrel with leaves, silt and mud in it, but when a flowing hose jet of water is plunged into the water butt and left there, you will find, if you return later, the water is crystal clear. The water purges the impurities which float to the top and are eventually carried away. It may not happen immediately but it will if the cleansing stream constantly flows through it!

'Then I will sprinkle clean water on you, and you will be clean; I will cleanse you from all your filthiness and from all your idols. Moreover, I will give you a new heart and put a new spirit within you; and I will remove the heart of stone from your flesh and give you a heart of flesh. I will put My Spirit within you and cause you to walk in My statutes, and you will be careful to observe My ordinances.' (Ezekiel 36)

What a wonderful picture of cleansing and then coming fully alive to God and all His ways!

Lord God, I hear what You are saying to me. I welcome Your cleansing stream of life and the heart surgery that will follow according to Your promises. I long to be clean! Not just passably clean but crystal clear reflecting your beautiful face in Your deep, clean waters within me. May my new heart beat only to the sound of heaven. Amen.

Day 266 – September 22nd

We can sometimes fail to understand what God is not the same as saying we do not work hard enough to believe it. The renewing of our minds after our new births in God takes time to come to full effect. Often the course of the Living Water comes up against things from our life stories so that we don't *feel* can be true and the enemy will try to persuade us that we are not made anew. Beware of your feelings, I say! Feelings come and go as the tides on the beach. It is the truth that counts; God's healing whole truth.

'And although you were formerly alienated and hostile in mind, engaged in evil deeds, yet He has now reconciled you in His fleshly body through death, in order to present you before Him holy and blameless and beyond reproach – if indeed you continue in the faith firmly established and steadfast . . .' (Colossians 1)

Jesus *has* now reconciled you in His fleshly body through death! He doesn't have to do it again and again and neither has He missed anything. His atonement paid the price. You *are* redeemed. 'It is finished,' Jesus cried from the cross. The more we welcome the Holy Spirit's streams of life, the more we will find we are cleansed and aligned with the truth of God's ways. I meet many people who are 'stuck'. No amount of sympathising will help (indeed it may hinder). No, it is the out-working of atonement that brings change. When I come up against flaws and deficiencies in my own life, I speak to my soul and say, 'You had better catch up with reality and see what Jesus has done!' I then read edifying scripture to my own soul.

Lord Jesus, thank You that through Your grace and great mercy I am a new person. My sanctification sometimes takes a while to be worked out and worked in, but I will partner with You to work out my salvation as I reverence You and am changed. My soul, listen to the words of the Father! May I be filled with Your glory! Amen.

Day 267 – September 23rd

As we 'practise the Presence of God' not only do we find it difficult to grieve the Holy Spirit within us, we also find that we flow with His desires for us and those around us. Have you ever sat in a church business meeting when it has seemed difficult to discern the way ahead? I have an expression that I repeat to myself and occasionally express to others: *'The Holy Spirit is not divided. Let's see what He has to say.'*

The council at Jerusalem wrote a letter for Paul and others to be sent with as they journeyed to Antioch; it included the wonderful phrase, *'It seemed good to the Holy Spirit and to us . . .'* (Acts 15).

Whether today brings you to a moment of great decision-making or you are just going through the normal 'small' things of life, it is a wonderful habit constantly to enquire, 'What do You think, Holy Spirit?'

I have lost count of the times in ministry that I have asked that question, or maybe enquired during my work, 'Where should I go next, Holy Spirit?' only to find that the next place I am persuaded to go to is the one where the presence of the pastor is needed. So many times the elderly folk I served would say, 'How did you know to come right now?' and I sometimes replied, quite honestly and naturally, 'It seemed good to the Holy Spirit and me . . .'

Holy Spirit, we are told that You would lead us into all truth so I ask that I may learn to enquire of You more and more until it becomes quite natural to turn to You. As our Father, I know You are interested in every moment of my day. Speak to me freely and naturally, I pray. Amen.

Day 268 – September 24th

One of the joys of hearing the Holy Spirit speak about every-day matters, as He prompts and draws your attention to things and to the people around you, is that you will become naturally prophetic. Confidence will grow in your capacity to hear God! David writes,

'He leads the humble in justice, and He teaches the humble His way.' (Psalm 25)

I see this as simple as a child who recognises the mother's or father's voice and that recognition of the familiar brings trust and confidence to then act in a certain way. The known parental spoken word brings comfort in frightening situations. We say to frightened children, 'It's alright; I am here.' I cannot count the times God has spoken to me, 'David, don't worry; I am in control and I see the way ahead.' Or maybe in a time of perplexity we might say, 'Don't worry; we will work this out together . . .' It is a small step to hearing the voice of the Father and being able to speak out with His words: 'I feel God is saying this to you . . .'

It is astonishing to fully realise that Jesus leaned entirely on His Father in the most wonderful partnership.

'Truly, truly, I say to you, the Son can do nothing of Himself unless it is something He sees the Father doing; for whatever the Father does, these things the Son also does.' (John 5)

God will speak to us and guide us in detailed ways as much as we need to hear; through Scripture and through speaking to us. He does not always show us the whole blueprint, I find, but He does always show us the next step. It can be a mistake to expect a huge spotlight to illuminate the entire road ahead. It is where to put one's foot next that matters most!

'Your word is a lamp to my feet and a light to my path.' (Psalm 119)

'The mind of man plans his way, but the LORD directs his steps.' (Proverbs 16)

Father God, I thank You for Your guiding ways. As one of Your sheep I learn to recognise Your voice. Teach me to lean in on You at all times and to learn the good habits so that in difficult moments I have the confidence to trust in my understanding of Your voice and Your leading. Amen.

Day 269 – September 25th

I am often amused by the ways that Father speaks; He seems to delight in teaching us to undo riddles rather than just speak a direct word. He makes me smile! It causes us to engage with Him.

One such time happened a few years ago when I went to see a lady, a close friend of my late wife. I cannot tell this tale in its fullness as it might seem in questionable taste but you will gather the gist of it. As we neared her house I began to feel what I can only describe as a heavy feeling in my nether regions (that is all the detail I intend to provide). Knowing that Father often speaks to me through strange feelings in my own body, I began to think that there might be something wrong with this friend but, as we sat around with tea and cakes, I could not quite bring myself to ask her the direct question! In the end, I broached it by way of asking after her general health. She assured me she was fine. The heavy feeling low down continued perhaps even more acutely. I asked again, whereupon my wife, who knew, burst out laughing and came out with it directly. Fortunately, we all had a good laugh but she assured us she was well and I put it down to not hearing God clearly. As we rose to go the feeling nearly overwhelmed me and I staggered, such was the discomfort. I said, 'Look, something is wrong somewhere – somewhere low down – what is going on? And then on some impulse said, 'Have you got a cellar?'

The whole story then came out that she and her husband had spent a lot of energy, time and money converting the cellar into a den for their teenage children. As soon as they had finished this immaculate conversion, their neighbour started doing some very heavy work in his house and the new plaster started to fall from their own basement walls and ceilings. 'I am furious with him,' our friend declared, 'absolutely livid. I am so cross that it is ruining our family life. When I spoke to him he was so rude and off-hand . . .'

It was clear that the feelings she was harbouring for her neighbour were doing her no good at all and we sat down to talk and pray it through, and eventually the man was forgiven. It all turned out well in the ensuing weeks.

Why can God not say, quite simply, 'You are going to your friend's house and she is really angry with her neighbour who is spoiling their basement and she needs to forgive him.' I do not know the answer to that. Most likely is my lack of capacity to hear! In my 'defence', I would offer that what I was feeling in my body paralleled what our friend was feeling in her spirit – perhaps.

'So Pharaoh spoke to Joseph, "In my dream, behold, I was standing on the bank of the Nile; and behold, seven cows, fat and sleek came up out of the Nile, and they grazed in the marsh grass. Lo, seven other cows came up after them, poor and very ugly and gaunt, such as I had never seen for ugliness in all the land of Egypt; and the lean and ugly cows ate up the first seven fat cows. Yet when they had devoured them, it could not be detected that they had devoured them, for they were just as ugly as before. Then I awoke."' (Genesis 41)

Lord God, You are a God of mysteries and we do not always understand Your ways but we come humbly before You and ask that You will open our ears and our hearts to receive Your leading. Teach us to ponder Your words and pictures and receive Your revelation through them. Amen.

Day 270 – September 26th

Sometimes, God will speak to us in dreams. I am sure that most of my dreams are not worthy of further thought but there are times when I feel strongly on waking that I am to take note and I usually try to write it down as soon as possible. When a dream is from God, I know it; it stays with me in every detail and is quite apart from normal 'nocturnal ramblings'. Sometimes what I write seems very unlikely but I record it faithfully.

'Now the birth of Jesus Christ was as follows: when His mother Mary had been betrothed to Joseph, before they came together she was found to be with child by the Holy Spirit. And Joseph her husband, being a righteous man and not wanting to disgrace her, planned to send her away secretly. But when he had considered this, behold, an angel of the Lord appeared to him in a dream, saying, "Joseph, son of David, do not be afraid to take Mary as your wife; for the Child who has been conceived in her is of the Holy Spirit. She will bear a Son; and you shall call His name Jesus, for He will save His people from their sins." . . . And Joseph awoke from his sleep and did as the angel of the Lord commanded him, and took Mary as his wife, but kept her a virgin until she gave birth to a Son; and he called His name Jesus.' (Matthew 1)

What an amazing story! The nature of this very remarkable news would need some considerable explaining in human terms, but the impact of the dream on Joseph was sufficient and had massive consequences for God's plans, and for the history of the world.

Joseph had a similar experience in advance of the terrible 'slaughter of the innocents'. He was told to take the mother and her child and flee to Egypt and safety before Herod began his murderous pursuit of Him. The account records very straightforwardly that,

'Joseph got up and took the Child and His mother while it was still night, and left for Egypt. He remained there until the death of Herod.' (Matthew 2)

A warning dream indeed! Let us ask the Lord to speak to us in our dreams as we seek Him as the Shepherd of our lives.

Lord God, I ask that my sleep might be sanctified before You. As I rest each night, I entrust my mind to You so that not only may I sleep well and be refreshed but that You would also send Your Holy Spirit to touch my spirit and bring me revelation about Your path for me and those I serve. Amen.

Day 271 – September 27th

God is not averse to putting dreams in other people's minds to achieve His ends. Gideon was about to go out to battle against the Midianites and Amalekites. He had 32,000 men and the story tells us that God wished him to go out to war with many fewer warriors lest they might think they had found victory in their own strength. God reduced the number to 300 men, which probably seemed woefully inadequate to Gideon given that the enemy were as numerous as locusts, and their camels without number. As if responding to his unease, God told him to go down with his servant to hear what the enemy had to say. They crept down to the enemy camp and overheard one of them telling his dream to a friend.

'And he said, "Behold, I had a dream; a loaf of barley bread was tumbling into the camp of Midian, and it came to the tent and struck it so that it fell, and turned it upside down so that the tent lay flat." His friend replied, "This is nothing less than the sword of Gideon the son of Joash, a man of Israel; God has given Midian and all the camp into his hand."' (Judges 7)

It is clear that Gideon also received this as the word of God as he bowed down to worship when he overheard these words. And just as God had promised, his hand was strengthened when he heard and the enemy was defeated. The word of God had instilled such fear of Gideon's God and His chosen men that the enemy fled, fighting one another on the way. This is an astonishing account of the prophetic word at work, this time to the enemy who also received the revelation of the dream's interpretation!

Perhaps we should be very wise in ministry when dreams are given to people we may consider to be 'unlikely material' for godly dreams! I have only come across this once: someone came reporting a troubling and repetitive dream; it was a vivid warning dream from the Holy Spirit about how they needed to repent and turn to Christ and little interpretation was needed from me! The point about it was that the very real sense of danger of being 'lost' apart from Christ had been brought home by the clarity of the dream, in ways that my words would never have achieved. Rarely have I experienced someone coming to see me declaring, *'Tell me how I can be saved . . .'*

Lord God, You have promised to speak to us through dreams and visions and I offer myself to You, in faith, and ask You to speak to me more and more in this way. Thank You for the times You have guided me with dreams that have spoken powerfully of Your thoughts and Your plans and given to me clarity and conviction. Wonderful Holy Spirit, I praise You today for all Your special ways. Amen.

Day 272 –September 28th

When the spiritual atmosphere surrounding an important situation 'heats up' God can speak in many ways. I recall quite recently sitting in a traffic jam and becoming acutely aware of three things being spoken to me in rapid succession. It wasn't at all clear what it all meant but when I later looked up the verses I could understand what God was speaking about: a change of circumstances for me was on the way! Occasionally, I have brought what I felt to be a word from the Lord to individuals; it has made no sense to me and, sometimes, it makes no sense to them either, but God has a way of preparing us for events that might shake us but for the fact that God has shown He is in them by speaking before they came to pass. We have a very loving, caring Father!

I met a lady in our Christian bookshop and I greeted her in a friendly manner. She surprised me by saying, 'Oh, David, hello!' (I didn't recognise her.) She explained that at a meeting where I had spoken, I had given her a word that I felt was from the Lord about something that was to happen and the gist of it was, *'When* it happens, do not fear. I am in it with you.' Several days afterwards, her husband was involved in a very serious car crash and she spent months nursing him back to health. Her heart, throughout the whole time, she told me, was full of that assurance that God was with her in a remarkable way, every step of the way.

We will look later at how the atmosphere changed around the time of the birth of Jesus but how many of us have forgotten that small verse inserted by Matthew into the account of the trial of Jesus.

'While he [Pilate] was sitting on the judgement seat, his wife sent him a message, saying, "Have nothing to do with that righteous Man; for last night I suffered greatly in a dream because of Him."' (Matthew 27)

We know nothing further of the significance of that dream and that message but I always imagine it played a part in how carefully Pilate listened to and appeared to be moved by the words and behaviour of Jesus.

Dear Father, how easy it is to underestimate Your power to intervene supernaturally, to prepare and to influence our life moments. I pray that as I go through life, my antennae will be tuned to every whisper from You. Thank You that You care so much that You often do speak of things that are to come simply to let us know that we are never without a Good Shepherd. Amen.

Day 273 – September 29th

I often think that one single moment in the life of one of the early church believers radically changed the history of the world.

'Now there was a disciple at Damascus named Ananias; and the Lord said to him in a vision, "Ananias." And he said, "Here I am, Lord." And the Lord said to him, "Get up and go to the street called Straight, and inquire at the house of Judas for a man from Tarsus named Saul, for he is praying, and he has seen in a vision a man named Ananias come in and lay his hands on him, so that he might regain his sight."' (Acts 9)

Not surprisingly, Ananias queried the instruction saying that Saul was a much-feared man on account of his treatment of the believers who called on the name of the Lord, but God responded, *'Go, for he is a chosen instrument of Mine, to bear My name before the Gentiles and kings and the sons of Israel; for I will show him how much he must suffer for My name's sake.'*

Ananias is hardly mentioned again in Scripture other than in Paul's testimony; his was a very small 'walk on' part but what an unfathomably great part that was! He went to Saul as bid by the Lord and Saul was released from his blindness and filled with the Holy Spirit that he might go out and serve the Lord. It is easy to gloss over the immense faithfulness of this servant, Ananias, and his simple acceptance that the Lord does speak thus. We might all need to take heed; our Father can speak to us and send us on what might seem to be a relatively minor errand. Ananias had no hindsight to understand the story that was to unfold as a result. He was, quite simply, a faithful and courageous servant who trusted God to speak into his life.

Father God, *'Tune my spirit to the music of heaven, and, somehow, make my obedience count for You'*. Amen.

Day 274 – September 30th

As we seek to increase our readiness and availability to hear God speak to us, there is one other story to think about. We are familiar with the centurion who met Jesus but less well-known is the centurion called Cornelius. We are told that, despite being a Roman, he was a devout believer, in that great metropolis of life, Caesarea, where he gave generously to the Jews.

In the afternoon, he had a clear vision of an angel of God who came to speak with him. He was afraid as most people are when an angelic visitation occurs.

'[Cornelius] said, "What is it, Lord?" And he said to him, "Your prayers and alms have ascended as a memorial before God. Now dispatch some men to Joppa and send for a man named Simon, who is also called Peter; he is staying with a tanner named Simon, whose house is by the sea." When the angel who was speaking to him had left, he summoned two of his servants and a devout soldier . . . and after he had explained everything to them, he sent them to Joppa.' (Acts 10)

It was a day's journey but in the amazing timing of God, the next day Peter was praying on the housetop and he received from the Lord the next piece of the unfolding supernatural jigsaw.

He was on the roof of the house, hungry for lunch when he found himself in a trance; a state of ecstatic closeness to God. Three times he received the same vision: a great sheet with all sorts of creatures was lowered before him.

'A voice came to him, "Get up, Peter, kill and eat!" But Peter said, "By no means, Lord, for I have never eaten anything unholy and unclean." Again a voice came to him a second time, "What God has cleansed, no longer consider unholy." This happened three times.'

In the extraordinary timing of God, Peter was being prepared to share the Good News with the Gentiles and at that very moment they are knocking at Peter's door! The Holy Spirit simultaneously spoke to Peter that three men were at the door and that he was to accompany them without doubt or misgiving.

When Peter arrived at Caesarea the next day, Cornelius had assembled his family and close friends so Peter began to share with them all the story of Jesus' redemptive life and death. As he did so, before he had finished speaking, the Holy Spirit fell, as if by confirmation, on all present!

Dare we ever doubt the capacity of God to arrange circumstances so that the glorious story of His great love for mankind can be told? I suggest not! We must accompany our prayers for those who have not yet encountered Jesus, with a passionate faith and expectation that God will do extraordinary things to make it possible. This is our Lord and God!

Father, Son and Holy Spirit, we see in this glorious account how You all participate to bring glory to Almighty God. Increase our faith to see wonders performed as we go with the gospel. May I learn to walk on my high places with You, O Lord. Amen.

OCTOBER

Day 275 – October 1st

Psalm 73, a Psalm of Asaph, one of the worship leaders, is extraordinary for its honesty. Most of us will read it and identify with it in some respect. He begins with a simple assertion of the truth.

'Surely God [Elohiym] is good to Israel, to those who are pure in heart!' (Psalm 73)

Quite suddenly and early on he recounts with candour how he got into trouble and sets the theme for the entire psalm.

'But as for me, my feet came close to stumbling; my steps had almost, for I was envious of the arrogant as I saw the prosperity of the wicked.'

In the normal course of life, we tend not to be envious of the *obviously* wicked and their prospering but this is subtler, for it reads more literally, *'I was envious of the boastful as I saw the* 'shalom' *of the morally wrong.'*

Have you ever thought, why do I bother to try to live a righteous life when all around me are those who seem to be doing pretty well and they don't spend all their time going after God and His ways? Many of us have. It's all to do with perspective. We can see the here and now (it looks fine) but we don't see the eternal (these people are lost and so far from the truth of God). It's so important for us to be responsive to the nudges of the Holy Spirit who seeks to sanctify us and protect us from going astray. The shepherd's voice might be saying, 'I know the grass is much greener over there but what *you* can't see is the cliff; please keep well away from the edge!'

The psalmist analyses why the way of the wrongdoers appear to be wrapped in *'shalom'* – peace, well-being, prosperity and so on.

'There are no pains in their death and their body is fat' (they have plenty). *'They are not in trouble as other men nor are they plagued like mankind . . .'*

But he does see it for what it really is:

'Therefore pride is their necklace; the garment of violence covers

them. Their eye bulges from fatness; the imaginations of their heart run riot...'

He explains the means of how they get away with it and are apparently in a place of peace, through self-deception,

'They say, "How does God know? And is there knowledge with the Most High?"'

He analyses his own near-miss crash further so that you may also understand your own potential folly:

'Surely in vain I have kept my heart pure and washed my hands in innocence; for I have been stricken all day long and chastened every morning.'

It is not easy being a Christian. There is a very real cost and every single day there are choices to be made by each one of us: the wide gate, or the narrow one? At times you may find yourself on the receiving end of the enemy's taunts – *Is it all worth it?*

Asaph continues by explaining the consequences of getting it wrong:

'If I had said, "I will speak thus," behold, I would have betrayed the generation of Your children.'

The psalmist is under no illusions about the consequences of crashing his faith; it would all go way beyond himself and the damaging ripples would spread far and wide. He was deeply troubled by such a potential outcome, and then comes a very important line:

'Until I came into the sanctuary of God; then I perceived their end.'

When we stay close to God and fellowship with Him we see all things from *His* perspective not along our own blinkered sight-lines. In the place of knowing and being known, God will guide us. This psalm is such phenomenal advice and every discipleship group should study it to bring into the open our reactions and struggles with temptations. Being tempted is not a sin. I will say it again: being tempted is not a sin. Let us encourage one another with truth and keep one another from *pursuing* temptation and the consequences of departing 'the sanctuary of God'.

My Lord and King, I want to ever be found near to You, sitting at Your feet, imbibing Your wisdom and truth. Help me to see my struggles for what they really are: my sanctification in the face of the enemy's taunts. *'Lead me not into temptation and deliver me from the evil one'*. Amen.

Day 276 – October 2nd

The psalmist in Psalm 73, which we read yesterday, did presumably write the entire psalm *after* what he perceived as his own narrow escape. He wasn't scribing the psalm as it all happened; rather, he gives us the benefit of his hindsight and wisdom. He sees the consequences of going away from God so very clearly and also God's tendency to leave men to discover the folly of their ways in order to bring them to the place where they might see their arrogance for what it is and then come humbly before Him. God has time to wait although, surely, it must pain Him to watch us.

'Surely you set them in slippery places; you cast them down to destruction. How they are destroyed in a moment! They are utterly swept away by sudden terrors! Like a dream when one awakes, O Lord, when aroused, You will despise their form.'

He reflects on how he was reacting from a wounded place, his heart was not in good shape; he was bitter – like an animal before God, he states; totally without any sensitivities, but still God held onto him throughout.

Those of us who have made mistakes, prompted by bitterness or unforgiveness, will recognise how true this all is. When we harbour such thoughts, they may do untold damage to our hearts, bodies and minds; the psalm is so vivid!

The warming news is that he is able to reflect on the goodness of God.

'You have taken hold of my right hand. With Your counsel You will

guide me, and afterward receive me to glory. Whom have I in heaven but You? And besides You, I desire nothing on earth. My flesh and my heart may fail, but God is the strength of my heart and my portion forever . . . but as for me, the nearness of God is my good; I have made the Lord GOD *my refuge.'* (Psalm 73)

What a wonderful expression to take forward into the coming day: *the nearness of God is my good.* It is a confession that will ward off many temptations. Speak that in the face of the enemy's taunts: *the nearness of God is my good.* It speaks of truth and our heart's desire.

Father, Your nearness is my good. I declare that today. When a small part of me might go astray from You, it is to be my declaration: *the nearness of my Lord is my good.* Hallelujah! Thank you, Jesus! Amen.

Day 277 – October 3rd

I am often caused to reflect on the character of God, by which I mean, what will impact us when we meet Him? His glory and beauty, yes; the unimaginably, bright light that emanates from Him, surely. But *His character?*

'*But the fruit of the Holy Spirit is love, joy, peace, patience, kindness, goodness, faithfulness, gentleness, self-control.'* (Galatians 5)

If this is the fruit of the Spirit of God it means that this is His character and this is what heaven is like. Imagine that: being met by wave after wave of all those wonderful attributes being rolled over us. It would feel like nothing we have ever met on earth! We only glimpse these in part; in God's presence, we will doubtless see them in their glorious fullness. How can we ever not want to be filled to over-flowing with these godly characteristics? Come, Holy Spirit!

Yes, Father, send Your Spirit on me today, I pray, that I may become recognisably like You: full of Your fruit in my life! May the life sap that streams from Your heart fill me so that my natural growth is towards producing Your fruit in my life. May I look like Jesus, think like Jesus, react like Jesus. Amen.

Day 278 – October 4th

Sometimes we glimpse other aspects of God's character. I am always caused to pause when I read,

'With the kind You show Yourself kind; with the blameless You show Yourself blameless; with the pure You show Yourself pure, and with the crooked You show Yourself astute.' (Psalm 18)

The Hebrew word for 'astute' is *'pâthal'*; it also means 'to struggle' or 'wrestle'. Can you imagine God as a wrestler? But remember Jacob who wrestled with God until break of day. It also can mean 'morally tortuous'. Can a holy God be 'morally tortuous'? I believe so. Far from being immoral, Jesus was certainly very cunning in the manner that He dealt with many people who crossed His path. They came with complex motives but the 'wrestler' in Jesus was for no other end than to lead them into the truth.

'Then they sent some of the Pharisees and Herodians to Him in order to trap Him in a statement. They came and said to Him, "Teacher, we know that You are truthful and defer to no one; for You are not partial to any, but teach the way of God in truth. Is it lawful to pay a poll-tax to Caesar, or not? Shall we pay or shall we not pay?" But He, knowing their hypocrisy, said to them, "Why are you testing Me? Bring Me a denarius to look at." They brought one. And He said to them, "Whose likeness and inscription is this?" And they said to Him, "Caesar's." And Jesus said to them, "Render to Caesar the things that are Caesar's, and to God the things that are God's." And they were amazed at Him.' (Mark 12)

If that isn't wrestling, I don't know what is! I think the constant message to those who sought to be devious with Him was, 'Don't mess with the Son of Man.'

Lord Jesus, I praise You that in the pursuit of truth in me You are a wrestler and You never allow me to distort reality; You do it not to win but to bring me into life. Thank You that You have persevered and been immensely patient and kind with me. Amen.

Day 279 – October 5th

The intricacy of the parables of Jesus came from the most astonishing and profound mind ever. The story of the poor man Lazarus who lay at the gate of the rich man who had five brothers, is a parable about how easy it is to miss perfection if you do not have a heart like God's heart and instead remain lifeless and un-giving towards those that God cherishes in this world. This is the only parable story where Jesus named anyone. The poor man's name is Lazarus or Eleazar which means 'God is helping'.

If you read the account, you will notice that Jesus begins,

'And a poor man named Lazarus was laid at [the rich man's] gate, covered with sores and longing to be fed with the crumbs which were falling from the rich man's table; besides, even the dogs were coming and licking his sores.' (Luke 16)

The phrase in Greek *'even the dogs'* could be translated *'but in stark contrast the dogs were coming and licking his sores'*. Jesus does seem to be saying, Listen, *if you don't have mercy, rest assured, yes, even the dogs will.* The dogs were caring for the man in the absence of the rich man's care. That was how bad this was.

The big punch in this story slips by almost unnoticed towards the end when the rich man begs from the fiery heat of Hades to send word to his father's house where he has *five* brothers to warn them of the impending doom that awaits them if they carry on as they are. They would repent, says the rich man, if someone went to them from the dead. Abraham, upon whom Lazarus rests, refuses, telling them that they have all the instruction they need from Moses and the Prophets. Finally, Abraham retorts,

'If they do not listen to Moses and the Prophets, they will not be persuaded even if someone rises from the dead.'

And so, Jesus tells the Pharisees that they, above all, have all they need to recognise the Messiah when He comes – but they do not see

Him. The real sting comes in adding up how many brothers there were: five at home and one in Hades as a result of his unbelievable selfishness. That's six. If they had indeed invited the poor man, Lazarus, they would have had the perfect number at their table: seven. In Hebrew culture, seven is the number of perfection and fulfilment. They had missed it. What a warning from the lips of the Master!

'With the crooked You show Yourself astute.' (Psalm 18)

Lord God, Your wisdom and brilliance pierces hearts and leaves no place to hide from Your unblinking stare. Have mercy on me. May I learn to act justly, love as You do, be moved with kindness and walk humbly with You, my Lord and King. Amen.

Day 280 – October 6th

In the next studies, we will be continuing with the notion that Jesus is both remarkably astute but also demands a great deal of those who might follow Him. In Luke chapter 9 we find what I often refer to as 'The chewy sayings of Jesus' or *'The path to radical discipleship'*.

Jesus set the disciples on a remarkable journey which must have been as exciting as it was daunting for anyone who chose to follow Him.

'And He called the twelve together, and gave them power and authority over all the demons and to heal diseases. And He sent them out to proclaim the kingdom of God and to perform healing.' (Luke 9)

Whenever I read this I find myself picturing the moment this happened. I have no particular reason for suggesting this but I picture the Lord taking infinite care of each man, praying and prophesying over them in turn. I don't see Him just issuing a generalised command. I don't know about you but I would have needed great encouragement at that moment! Perhaps they didn't; perhaps they were so excited that they couldn't wait to 'get up and at it'. But here comes the 'chewy' bit,

'And He said to them, "Take nothing for your journey, neither a

staff, nor a bag, nor bread, nor money; and do not even have two tunics apiece.'"

If they did feel vaguely confident surely this news that they were to travel 'light' must have shaken them. Go with nothing. All the normal accoutrements of a journey you are to leave behind.

'But, Master, what if we meet a band of robbers or even a wild animal? No bag? Nothing at all to eat, and no means even to buy bread? And no spare tunics either?' I think we can all imagine how that might have felt; but what was Jesus doing? Is this the gospel of prosperity that we spoke of before?

Many years ago, I went on 'survival training', the intention being that you mastered the skills of surviving on the Brecon Beacons with nothing; but even then, I recall having a backpack, spare socks and pants, some string, a knife, a snare, and a few tins of what were affectionately called 'Compo Rations'. If you remember these, you will recall tins of delights such as ham and egg pie, biscuits, steak and kidney and so on. This happened in the 1970s and the tins were all labelled with the Ministry of Defence symbol and, most disconcertingly, a date: 1944! In other words, if you got into a very tight squeeze you had *something* to fall back on. But here Jesus sends His followers out with *nothing*. He is expecting them to meet with God-given hospitality along the way. This is to be a journey of *grace*. They are to discover the great gift of faith and peace for their own needs. This was not an outreach where they were pre-booked in a local hotel for the duration of the trip. They were *entirely* dependent on God.

Lord Jesus, I will be honest; I recognise a call here that I would be deeply concerned to receive. If my children were being sent out thus, I would probably be smuggling a few items of essential food into their pockets. I still have to learn at the deepest level of my being that Your provision for my life is complete. I will want for nothing as I serve You and go out in Your name. Amen.

Day 281 – October 7th

The disciples were sent out with nothing; no back-up systems were in place for them. They had no real idea of where they were going or what they might meet on the way. Jesus was intent on them each being thrown back on the Father alone, as indeed He, Himself, was. We never know what God is going to do; in truth, we only know what He is doing right now. Our Father's capacity to provide when we have no time to prepare, or inkling of quite what to prepare for, keeps us in a state of wonder at God. Hence, for them, no bag, no spare tunic, no bread.

When Abraham was sent out we are told,

'By faith Abraham, when he was called, obeyed by going out to a place which he was to receive as an inheritance; and he went out, not knowing where he was going. By faith he lived as an alien in the land of promise, as in a foreign land, dwelling in tents.' (Hebrews 11)

As we reflect on the 'chewy sayings' we will find that so much of what we do is not really in like-spirit. How we like to plan the details of our ventures. We hesitate to go out without 'shape' being in place. There is a mentality that to fail to plan is somehow 'irresponsible'. How many times I have spoken at services where a very detailed plan (with anticipated timings) is passed to all the participants: Welcome; Song 1; Notices; Children go out to Sunday school; Song 2, 3 and 4 . . . It's not that God cannot move within a plan but why would He where there is no true reliance on Him through the Holy Spirit's leading?

Each day should be a 'sent out day'; go out today trusting that God will order your moments and probably surprise you too!

Lord God, we are reluctant to let go and leave our securities behind. May today, and indeed my life, be a 'sent out' life where I have no thought for what I shall wear or what I shall eat, that I shall draw close to You, knowing You as my Provider; the One who holds the blueprint for my life in His hand. Amen.

Day 282 – October 8th

When dusk began to fall one day, after Jesus had been teaching a multitude of people, the disciples, expressing genuine care for the people, said to Jesus, *'Send the crowd away, that they may go into the surrounding villages and countryside and find lodging and get something to eat; for here we are in a desolate place'* (Luke 9).

Send them away . . . a completely understandable expression but how at odds with the core teaching that Jesus seems determined to impart. Jesus does not 'send people away' to find provision elsewhere. I have often thought that in counselling or ministry – *maybe I should send them elsewhere* – and then God sends a check in my spirit: *'you meet their need. In Me you have all they need.'*

'But He said to them, "You give them something to eat!"'

It's very difficult to imagine what that might have felt like; looking out upon countless rows of faces each gazing intently on the One who had been teaching them that full reliance on their heavenly Father was the only true way. If I might make a suggestion at this point, if you have a situation that seems beyond you at this present time, imagine looking out on it, as the disciples did in the failing light, while you hear the words of Jesus, *You give them something . . . You can solve this . . . You can bring change . . .*

The first time the disciples saw Jesus feed a multitude, imagine what they thought as Jesus commanded them, *'Have them sit down to eat in groups of about fifty each.'* What would it be like to walk among the crowds indicating, *'The master says . . .'* If we understand this we will find that it relates to many of our own doubts about our capacity to minister.

And then Jesus asks them for the five loaves and two fish and I lay them in a basket, feeling woefully inadequate . . .

It's not possible, is it?

Lord Jesus, I realise that I need to see through *Your* eyes not mine.

I see difficulties and challenges and You seem to see opportunities for *glory*, so I ask, Holy Spirit, to fill me with the courage of heaven. Amen.

Day 283 – October 9th

The meal is over. Hundreds upon hundreds of happy laughing faces; people who have had more to eat perhaps than they can remember. Your mind spins; your imagination and understanding are stretched. Who is this who breaks the bread and the fish so many times, who fills the baskets to take out to the crowds while we all stand amazed? We hear His blessing and watch His hands and His eyes as they look up to heaven.

'Now take the baskets and gather up the leftover food . . .'

There were twelve baskets *full*! There was such plenty that as we moved among the crowds and they gathered their scraps and held them up to be placed in the baskets, we found ourselves wondering why Jesus sent us to gather the remains of the meal.

Twelve baskets!

There will always be enough for the twelve of you. I can even feed you with what is left over.

'Do not fear, from now on you will be catching men.' (Luke 5)

Father, I see it now. You are the Provider. I bring to You my small offerings in faith, my inadequate prayers, my feeble preparation for preaching, and my wobbly discipleship, my hopeless inadequacy. You are the Multiplier and the One who takes what isn't anywhere near sufficient and makes it plentiful. Amen.

Day 284 – October 10th

There is a vast difference in the quiet belief and trust that *knows* God can always look after us and will do because He is our Father, and the disastrous times in the desert.

388

'And in their heart they put God to the test by asking for food according to their desire. Then they spoke against God; they said, "Can God prepare a table in the wilderness? Behold, He struck the rock so that waters gushed out, and the streams were overflowing; can He give bread also? Will He provide meat for His people?"' (Psalm 78)

It's interesting, that word 'desire'; its root is in 'body' or 'life'. When all we see and feel is the cravings of our body and that becomes our prayer, we somehow become like querulous children; there is no trust, instead we whine, 'but I'm hungry and I am lost and I think I will probably die . . .'

How different it is to keep one's focus on the face of the Great Giver, to constantly be full of affection for Him and His amazing, loving ways, and not, instead, fretfully watching His hand.

We will never 'test' God if we are full of worship and love for Him. Everything flows from that place of adoration.

Father, I love You. As Habakkuk said, 'even if the fields are empty' I will still worship You and love You because You are my Father. On the days when my healing doesn't come through, I will gaze in Your face and see Your eyes full of love for me. I always want You to be the focus of my desires. Amen.

Day 285 – October 11th

We are told that after the feeding of the five-thousand, Jesus was alone praying, except that He wasn't alone as His disciples were with Him. We know this because He questioned them, *'Who do the people say that I am?'* (Luke 9). The disciples replied with the current theories they heard every day: John the Baptist, Elijah, a prophet of old . . . So Jesus asked, *'But who do you say that I am?'*

In your radical discipleship of the Lord Jesus there will always come a moment when He will turn to you and say, *'Who do you say that I am?'* It often happens in the quiet moments, not in front of crowds when you are preaching and it is easy to be bold, wild and extravagant, but in the still times when you are least expecting it. I include this in the 'chewy sayings' because the question is perhaps more complex than it seems at first glance. To reply with merely the words, 'You are Jesus, the Messiah, my Lord,' can unmask the poverty of relationship in our hearts or our lifestyle. Maybe Jesus is really asking, *Who does your heart, life and soul declare that I am?*' That's why He takes you away to a quiet place to ask you. His question is the beginning of an intense conversation. It's not an interview for a job; there's no need to stretch the A level grades or the 'previous experience' to impress Him. He asks simply, 'Who do you say that I am?' It's a question that can stretch me spiritually to my most profound and honest limits. *'I say that You are . . .'*

Lord, You challenge me with this question. How can I fully look You in the face when there are unresolved issues in my heart? I want to come, to run to You with an undivided heart and embrace You in fullness of joy, but there are things that hold me back. But You have asked me; now I will answer You with truth and integrity . . .

Day 286 – October 12th

Not long after the 'mountain top' experience of the multitude being fed and the encounter when Peter, inspired by the Holy Spirit, has answered Jesus, *'The Christ of God'*, it appears that Jesus immediately plunged the disciples into the valley where the hard things must be said. In response to Peter's prophetic declaration they were all warned to tell no one of His true identity, saying,

'The Son of Man must suffer many things and be rejected by the elders and the chief priests and scribes, and be killed, and be raised up on the third day.' (Luke 9)

It is beyond me to imagine how that must have felt in the light of their recent experiences demonstrating beyond doubt that *this was the One.* The disappointments and shocked moments of my life seem to pale into comparison with what the disciples must have felt.

The incredulity that what had started so remarkably and changed all their lives was to *end*. And what does He mean, *'be raised up'*?

The disciples were in that moment, I imagine, catapulted into a different perception of what was happening. It was finite; it would not continue forever. I can only think that one of my next questions might have been, *'. . . and what about us?'*

Jesus replied to the unspoken question with a piece of riveting and, I imagine, perplexing explanation of what might be entailed for those who wanted to continue to follow Him.

'If anyone wishes to come after Me, he must deny himself, and take up his cross daily and follow Me. For whoever wishes to save his life will lose it, but whoever loses his life for My sake, he is the one who will save it.' (Luke 9)

Suddenly we are not merely spectators of the supernatural wonders we have been attending. Suddenly, it is very personal.

Lord Jesus, these words are some of the most challenging words You spoke: I must disown my own self to be Your follower; I must come to know self-denial to the point of my own death. We are not playing at this any longer, are we? I did all sorts of things to become Your disciple but now I understand; this journey may cost me everything upon which I base my life. Amen.

Day 287 – October 13th

'Chewy sayings' are never easy.

'For what is a man profited if he gains the whole world, and loses or forfeits himself? For whoever is ashamed of me and My words, the Son of Man will be ashamed of him when He comes in His glory, and the glory of His Father and of the holy angels.' (Luke 9)

Jesus often spoke using hyperbole. None of us can possibly 'gain the whole world' but we might well forfeit our life in the pursuit of impossible and pointless dreams that have no meaning in reality. In the materialistic, consumerist society in which we live it is easy to be sucked into the endless pursuit of more and more possessions and also into the vortex of disappointment as each successive acquisition is shown to be what it is. The phrase 'everything you never wanted and more' sums it up eloquently.

But Jesus is saying more than that here. He is referring to those not only who find it difficult to pursue and invest in kingdom values but who also find it a step too far to declare publicly their allegiance to the King of kings. Perhaps that is why the restoration of Peter was so important that morning on the beach beside the Sea of Galilee. Jesus was intent on him being released from the crushing knowledge and shame of his own betrayal of the Master. We all find it difficult to speak about our faith outside of church but we are all set apart and then sent out to be heralds of the Good News of Jesus Christ. Let us not forget that, but instead join with countless disciples through the generations who have trembled at the thought but have then discovered the blessing of being obedient.

'When the apostles returned, they gave an account to Him of all that they had done. Taking them with Him, He withdrew by Himself to a city called Bethsaida.' (Luke 9)

Lord, I am tired of pursuing things that do not satisfy my hunger or slake my thirst. I know that You alone are the One to pursue with all my heart and all my soul and, as such, I realise it is time to go out as a herald and declare Your worth to those I meet. May I become a loyal messenger who speaks the truth without fear of the disapproval of men. Amen.

Day 288 – October 14th

We have thought before about the transfiguration of Jesus on the mountain, when He went up accompanied by Peter, John and James.

In that place of witnessing the glory of God on Jesus, it is clear that Peter found himself being uncomfortable if not feeling lost at the rare and most wonderful experience. Jesus is speaking with Moses (the Law) and Elijah (the Prophets) about His own 'exodus'. Plans are being made for a journey to another hill, the one outside Jerusalem where the glory of the Son will be revealed in a way that only Moses and Elijah can, as yet, understand.

And Peter is quite lost. Shall I build shelters for each of you? This is wonderful. Will we be staying here? He doesn't see the journey ahead.

Then God speaks; not exactly a chewy saying but one that startles the men into holy silence.

'While he was saying this, a cloud formed and began to overshadow them; and they were afraid as they entered the cloud. Then a voice came out of the cloud, saying, "This is My Son, My Chosen One; listen to Him!"' (Luke 9)

If you are privileged to have close encounters with God you will probably find that at some point much is expected of you. The profound moments are given that we might be silent and hear the Almighty God who we worship, speak. Listen to Him. Listen to Him.

My Lord and my God, I am in hushed awe before You. I will stop scurrying around with my nervous, futile plans and my hopeless, knee-jerk reactions to Your glory. Let me listen to You. Amen.

Day 289 – October 15th

Jesus returns with the men who have been told to remain silent concerning the mountain-top encounter. Never doubt the immense effect it had had on them. I recall a holy night with the Lord and, after, I could not even *think* of Him without my heart trembling inside me and my body buzzing. But they descend into the valley where the demons are shrieking and men implore for the healing of their dreadfully afflicted sons.

"'I begged Your disciples to cast it out and they could not." And Jesus answered and said, "You unbelieving and perverted generation, how long shall I be with you and put up with you? Bring your son here."' (Luke 9)

Chewy words indeed. Harsh words? Perhaps. True words? Yes. As the crowds murmured in awe at the deliverance, Jesus speaks to His disciples. The preparations with Moses and Elijah now a clear reality in the heart and mind of the Master.

'Let these words sink into your ears; for the Son of Man is going to be delivered into the hands of men.'

Jesus is seeking to transform these men that they might be imbued with the vision, power and reality of heaven. If Jesus ever speaks to you in that way, take my advice: it is best to listen.

Father, I know that I cannot hope to understand all that You have for me to do and to live through, but I pray that I will be open to Your profound preparation of me for Your purposes. May Your kingdom come in me. Amen.

Day 290 – October 16th

There are some moments when, as we read Scripture, our eyebrows are raised. But let us not be too quick to judge.

'An argument started among them as to which of them might be the greatest.' (Luke 9)

We can only assume that they were debating their failure to deal with the demon, as men are inclined to do after the event. Have you ever heard children after a serious admonishment? *'I told you we should have done that! I said, didn't I?'*

Jesus, fully aware of what was really going on, ever patient and seeking to bring the truth home to them, took a little child and stood him beside Him. Imagine that. Jesus is sitting perhaps, and draws the child close, holding with His hand or maybe with His arm around him.

'Whoever receives this child in My name receives Me, and whoever receives Me receives Him who sent Me; for the one who is least among all of you, this is the one who is great.'

As we venture forth, let us be aware that even if we don't *say* it, we can think proud thoughts and sit in judgement over others in our heads. Our ambitions can at any moment trip us up. These words of Jesus echo to us in every situation. 'Come low before Me. Come low, and I will raise you up.'

Jesus, I am sorry for the times when I have sought to demolish brothers and sisters to elevate myself, not trusting that You hold every individual journey in Your capable hands. Let me be like that little child beside Jesus, full of simple faith and a heart capable of great love and trust. Amen.

Day 291 – October 17th

We have given thought already to that moment when two of the disciples, outraged that anyone might not receive Jesus, thought to call down fire and have them consumed. Jesus had sent messengers ahead to Samaritan villages as He journeyed to Jerusalem. There is a parallel here in the Old Testament and we are reminded of the words of Malachi who, 400 years previously, foresaw how messengers would be sent ahead to prepare hearts and minds. This is a strange 'exodus' journey that Jesus is engaged in. Moses and Elijah had each had their journeys and prepared the way for the King of kings. We can find reflections of this final journey throughout Scripture but it is not the time to destroy the resistance; it is only the enemy seeking to throw havoc in the way of the Lord.

'But He turned and rebuked them and said, "You do not know what kind of spirit you are of; for the Son of Man did not come to destroy men's lives but to save them." And they went on to another village.' (Luke 9)

One wonders if it was anxiety that prompted such a suggestion or perhaps a desire to please, but it illustrates how easily we can fall into wrong-thinking at times. A chewy moment? Yes, certainly. It demonstrates that it is possible for you and me to 'come in the wrong spirit'. We may not be wanting to call down fire but have you ever thought it would be so much easier to do a certain thing if someone else wasn't around, slowing the progress and being contentious at every turn? I know I have.

God, give me patience as I journey but, more than that, I ask the Holy Spirit to give me the visionary insights of heaven to understand why men react as they do to the advancing kingdom, and may I be quick to bless and encourage, and not to curse. Amen.

Day 292 – October 18th

We have previously looked at what I referred to as the 'prosperity gospel of Jesus', expounded to the man who vowed to follow the Master wherever He might go.

'And Jesus said to him, "The foxes have holes and the birds of the air have nests, but the Son of Man has no place to lay His head."' (Luke 9)

The truth is that Jesus did have places to lay His head. We know the gospel writers referred to 'the house' in Capernaum; Jesus did at times have lodging. The important point that Jesus is making to this would-be follower is that if you choose to be a disciple you cannot expect to make assumptions about permanence or a settled and comfortable state. Maybe Jesus had specific insight into this man's expectations but it should be said that, if the Holy Spirit blows where He chooses, how can we ever make long-term plans about homes or future plans? How much time do we spend on our 'nests'? I often look at the walls in my house or the paintwork and think, 'I really should re-do that soon.' We can all give inordinate amounts of time, energy and resources to projects that, if we were true pilgrims, might be ranked of a much lower order. I am not suggesting that we all live in temporary canvas shelters in the woods where we freeze each winter because to have heat available is to be unspiritual! But we can hold such things lightly and in proportion. Be ready to let go of anything the Lord might call you to put down. Strangely, or perhaps not so strangely, He seems to ask us frequently to lay down the things that matter most to us! This is a holy highway we are travelling and God knows when we are too settled in our hearts' desires to be effective. Change is here to stay!

God, I thank You for every provision You have made in my life. I am so grateful but I am acutely aware that I have so much when others have so little. I gladly renew my wallpaper while others have no roof. I eat out at great cost while others have no bread. Help me to hold all things lightly and thankfully and be ready to move when You call. Amen.

Day 293 – October 19th

I don't know if this is a common thing with drivers but I found that if I tried to drive in a straight line and then gave my close attention to something else, even a protracted stare in the wing mirror, I found I veered off course! It wasn't a lot but it was problem that I tried to sort out during advanced driving. It's not easy to overcome.

Jesus said to him, "No one, after putting his hand to the plough and looking back, is fit for the kingdom of God." (Luke 9)

The 'him' in this verse was the man who had indicated he wanted to follow Jesus but sought permission to first say 'goodbye' at home. Not an unreasonable request, you may say (and frankly it sounds a little harsh). I imagine Jesus knew that when it comes to a life following Him, it is the first flash of faith to follow that counts. The alternative, at a moment of greatest weakness and vulnerability, would be to accept the impossibility of going home and saying, 'I have met this amazing man; I believe he may be the long-awaited Messiah and I really need to go to follow Him.' The resulting conversation can be well imagined!

But it is more than that. Anyone who has ever steered a plough (not with a modern tractor with GPS and auto-steer functions) will know that to keep on course you can only do one thing: *look forwards!* I have only ploughed with a shire horse once but turning around was guaranteed not only to produce a major wobble in the furrow but there was a good chance of falling over your own feet as you tried to furrow-hop. It just doesn't work. Jesus knew everyone would understand the analogy; everyone understood the rigours of ploughing especially on stony soils. So is it a little harsh? Not really. Is it demanding? Certainly it is. But Jesus knew the rigours of the life this man wished to be joined to. Think about what was ahead!

For us living in the twenty-first century, we are inclined to say, 'I am sure it will be alright,' to all manner of things that might loom large upon someone's confession of faith but we need to be *exceedingly careful* when it comes to establishing God's terms and conditions. We sin, and God hates sin. To become fit for the kingdom we must get cleaned up. We hesitate to be as firm as Jesus was for fear of offending people! Jesus regularly offended people and never sought to explain Himself, as is clearly the case with this man and the other who wished to first bury his father. Jesus establishes His Lordship from the very first. It was a very high responsibility for a son to bury his father. Jesus said in effect, 'If you follow Me, I come above *all other calls* on your life.'

How does that sit with you? It is a very serious question, isn't it? So here is a very serious prayer, one that we shouldn't embark upon unless we are willing to risk hearing the Lord rebuke us.

Lord God, I know that Your call on my life comes first and because the manner in which I run my life is so important to You, I come before You now and ask You to speak with me concerning anything in my lifestyle that is not of You or not fit for Your kingdom. I ask You to bring healing and resolution to these things. Amen.

Day 294 – October 20th

As we leave the 'chewy sayings' of Jesus, I hope you will agree with me that when we take time to engage with the demanding sayings of Jesus, we can find ourselves challenged at a level we were not necessarily anticipating. Jesus always takes us deeper through His word and through various situations in our lives, particularly times of adversity. I am aware that I emphasise this latter point repeatedly. The cross of our Lord Jesus *is* the believer's core-teaching on adversity. It is the nature of Almighty God to deliver impartation to us, His children, when all else is stripped away and we then reach the end of our own resources. Our own resources, gifting, talents and so on will never be sufficient.

Shortly before the death of Moses, he spoke to the people of Israel that he would not cross the Jordan with them but he said,

'It is the LORD *your God who will cross ahead of you; He will destroy these nations before you, and you shall dispossess them. Joshua is the one who will cross ahead of you, just as the* LORD *has spoken.'* (Deuteronomy 31)

Later, Moses spoke to Joshua in the sight of all the people,

'And the LORD *is the One who goes ahead of you; He will be with you. He will not fail you or forsake you. Do not fear or be dismayed.'*

Throughout time, God has spoken to His people in all circumstances, 'Do not fear. I am with you.' The words echo throughout eternity. Let Him speak to you as you release to Him areas where your life needs healing, whether it be in your body, mind or spirit. Whatever else you may do in these days, listen to Him and go forward through whatever apparent obstacles might *seem* to be in your path. The only destination to the rearward is Egypt and slavery.

'He will cover you with His pinions [feathers], and under His wings you may seek refuge.' (Psalm 91)

Lord God, I really do know that You are my provider, my shelter and very good Father. At times I realise that this knowing hasn't yet worked its way into every warp and weft of my being; I am so thankful for the many times You have cared for me and provided in impossible situations. I choose to rest under Your mighty wings today and humbly bring before You my anxieties. I leave them with You. Amen.

Day 295 – October 21st

The end of Moses' life seems to have been one of the most natural endings ever recorded. He knew he was near his end, he made preparation and blessed everyone. He climbed to a high vantage point where he glimpsed the lands that God had promised through the generations. Moses had played his part. He died, we are told, in good health.

'*Although Moses was one hundred and twenty years old when he died, his eye was not dim, not his vigour abated. So the sons of Israel wept for Moses in the plains of Moab thirty days; then the days of weeping and mourning for Moses came to an end. Now Joshua the son of Nun was filled with the spirit of wisdom, for Moses had laid his hands on him; and the sons of Israel listened to him and did as the* LORD *had commanded Moses. Since that time no prophet has risen in Israel like Moses, whom the* LORD *knew face to face.*' (Deuteronomy 34)

Several years ago, my wife and I knew a wonderful bubbly Christian lady who was in her early nineties; she effervesced with the life of the Holy Spirit and shared her love of the Lord with all she encountered. She was remarkably well for her age. One day, she went upstairs for a little 'quiet time' with the Lord and went to be with Him; just like that, lying on the bed. It's a very 'natural' thing to pass on in that way although it is often a shock for those left behind, but there is something very wholesome about it, especially when the body is still fit. It is as though the spirit has to go back to heaven, despite the body being capable of continuing life as we know it. The Lord calls 'time'.

I also notice that the Israelites mourned for thirty days. It seems rather cool and cut and dried and I don't think I really believed it could be so until I experienced *exactly* that for myself. I asked the Lord how I should grieve when my late wife died. I asked Him because it has always seemed to me that being released from mourning is a spiritual healing of the body, mind and spirit and it happens in many different ways. I had barely thought about that small detail in this passage before but the Lord drew my attention to it and said, quite clearly, *'Give Me thirty days and I will heal you.'*

I can tell you it was not an easy or comfortable time but every day, all day, I made worship and prayer my rhythm. The Lord came close and prepared me for moving forwards in very remarkable ways which I cannot tell here. It's an arresting thought that we were made for eternal life and, as such, we are not equipped for grieving, hence the need to healed and released from the pain of loss.

Lord, why do we fear our endings when You are there waiting for us? Thank You for the never-ending life You have given us through Jesus which we receive as a grace gift from You. Nothing will separate us from Your love. When our work is done here please take us peacefully and quietly to be with You forever and heal those who are left behind. Amen.

Day 296 – October 22nd

Someone once said that they wished the epitaph on their grave to read, *'He served the Lord in his generation.'* It is a wonderful but simple aspiration which honours God.

Have you ever thought what God might say to you, or speak over you? Have you asked Him what He would like to say about you? We often ask the Lord to speak His word for other people but why not ask Him for yourself? It is extraordinarily edifying and highly affirming to hear God speak. We need to hear it!

'Now when all the people were baptised, Jesus was also baptised, and while He was praying, heaven was opened, and the Holy Spirit descended on Him in bodily form like a dove, and a voice came out of heaven, "You are My beloved Son, in You I am well-pleased."' (Luke 3)

We see in this short description that the Holy Spirit came to Jesus as something which could be seen! There is nothing left to the imagination here. He was like a dove!

And then the words which speak of Jesus' identity, *My beloved*

Son, and words of approval, *In You I am well-pleased.* Jesus was God's 'pride'; God delighted in Him. He had the imprint of God on His great heart.

Sometimes, hearing God speak in this way can radically change your life. We all need to know that we belong to Father (our identity as a son or daughter) and to be affirmed, *'How much I love you . . .'* It is very clear that it is so in Scripture but to hear it, or have the truth spoken over us is mighty powerful. I recall when someone prophesied over me, *'I call you, son';* three times the word came. I was on the floor! I know that that is true from Scripture but God knows when we most need to hear it directly and He often does speak such things and it is glorious. Never be afraid to ask Him, 'Lord what do You want to say to me, Your child?'

Lord God, it is glorious the way You speak to Your children. Speak to me now, I pray. I am sitting here quietly to hear Your words of life and love. Amen.

Day 297 – October 23rd

There are wonderful moments in the lives of Joshua and Gideon and many others when God speaks to affirm and call and reassure – even to these men with the hearts of giants! Over and over God speaks, 'Do not fear! Have courage!' God has to do that because it *is* frightening to be called by the living God. I notice that Gideon has something in his heart that God has seen. He was called for a purpose; it was not a good time for Israel and Gideon was to be a redeemer leader-figure in their midst. Israel had done precisely what God had forbidden them to do.

'Now it came about when the sons of Israel cried to the LORD on account of Midian [the Midianites were devastating the land of Israel] *that the LORD sent a prophet to the sons of Israel and he said to them, "Thus says the LORD, the God of Israel, 'It was I who brought you up from Egypt and brought you out from the house of slavery. I*

delivered you from the hands of the Egyptians and from the hands of all your oppressors, and dispossessed them before you and gave you their land, and I said to you, "I am the LORD your God; you shall not fear the gods of the Amorites in whose land you live. But you have not obeyed Me.""' (Judges 6)

That was how they got into the place of fear! 'Trust Me, do as I say and you shall not fear,' is a central message of God to his people throughout generations!

The threat was very real but *the lack of faithful stance in God* meant they were vulnerable. If you aren't hidden in God as the eternal refuge, you *are* vulnerable. How we would all do well to learn this!

Gideon is caught up in the threat and his heart is longing for the times past when God was so present to them, working His miracles and wonders. He is looking for revival in the land but we find him threshing in secret in a winepress to prevent the Midianites seeing him and robbing him. You do not thresh in a winepress! You thresh where the wind is blowing! It had all got very muddled.

But listen, and take heart: God breaks in; an angelic presence declares, *'The LORD is with you, O valiant warrior.'*

We can imagine Gideon looking up and saying, 'Who? Me? Valiant?' Trust God; His word to us won't always be a neat fit with our obvious circumstances. Crucially, God sees something in his heart.

'Then Gideon said to him, "O my lord, if the LORD is with us, why then has all this happened to us? And where are all His miracles which our fathers told us about, saying, 'Did not the LORD bring us up from Egypt?' But now the LORD has abandoned us and given us into the hand of Midian."'

Like many of us, Gideon *longs* for the Lord, but the problem is deep-seated; it is the disobedience and the lack of trust that has caused the crash!

The angel replies,

"'Go in this your strength and deliver Israel from the hand of Midian. Have I not sent you?" [Gideon] said to him, "O Lord, how shall I deliver Israel? Behold, my family is the least in Manasseh, and I am the youngest in my father's house." But the LORD said to him, "Surely I will be with you, and you shall defeat Midian as one man."'*

God has spoken! Next time you are in a fix but your heart is longing for better days, take courage and expect the Lord to surprise you with beautiful words of encouragement: 'You go in My strength!'

Lord God, it's so wonderful that You know our true heart desires and even when we are caught in problems and don't see the cause let alone the solution, You breathe on the flickering flame in our breast. Send me out, Lord, in the power of Your name! Amen.

Day 298 – October 24th

It's not very surprising that, even after Gideon's encounter with the Lord, who spoke encouraging words over him, he still needs further evidence of the authenticity of the call. So often, although we long for a change in circumstances, maybe healing of some sort, we get a mindset about how difficult change would be. It can be a real problem for our faith. We need to *see* it! God didn't seem to mind.

'So Gideon said to Him, "If now I have found favour in Your sight, then show me a sign that it is You who speak with me. Please do not depart from here, until I come back to You, and bring out my offering and lay it before You." And He said, "I will remain until you return."' (Judges 6)

When Gideon had set the bread and the young goat before the Lord, the angel touched the bread and meat with his staff and fire sprung up from the rock and consumed them. Then the angel departed leaving Gideon declaring,

"'Alas, O LORD GOD! For now I have seen the angel of the LORD face to face." The LORD said to him, "Peace to you, do not fear; you shall not die."'

Later, Gideon had to be reassured again when he twice set the fleece before the Lord. The second time he did it he must have been aware that he was 'skating on thin ice' as he sought the Lord asking Him not to be angry with him for doubting. Gideon wanted 'belt and braces' reassurance! But the wonderful news is that God did not mind and twice showed Gideon that He would be faithful to His promise. We can conclude from this that it is our God's nature to reassure His children and, being the generous Father He is, when we aren't certain of our next step or wonder if it is of the Lord's leading, we should not be afraid to say, 'Sorry, Lord, but could you just . . .'

Thank You, Father, for the countless times I have needed Your reassurance and the times that You have patiently led me into truth. Increase my faith through those moments that I will learn to hear Your voice and know I can respond in simple faith and obedience. Amen.

Day 299 – October 25th

I find so often in my own life and in the life journeys of others, that our doubts can arise because we have failed to either be obedient to God's ways and ended up in trouble, or we have not deeply imbibed the truth and hence the power of His teaching.

One of the great verses of Scripture which we have mentioned before is Paul's letter to the Ephesians.

'But God, being rich in mercy, because of His great love with which He loved us, even when we were dead in our transgressions, made us alive together with Christ (by grace you have been saved), and raised us up with Him, and seated us with Him in the heavenly places in Christ Jesus.' (Ephesians 2)

No wonder that before this, Paul wrote a prayer for you and me and countless others throughout the ages:

'I pray that the eyes of your heart may be illuminated, so that you will know what is the hope of His calling, what are the riches of the glory

of His inheritance in the saints, and what is the surpassing greatness of His power towards us who believe.' (Ephesians 1)

When we are at rest, when we know that we are seated in the heavenly realms with Christ, not surprisingly, our world changes. The seating of God's children with Jesus is not down to meritorious personal confessions of faith which continually happens through time; it is part of God's covenant of restoration because God intends to share fellowship with us as He did in Eden. *It has happened.* Paul's letters use the aorist tense: it *has* happened. Jesus perfected the covenant on the cross when He cried, *'It is finished.'* Until that time, the Father and Son were still working but now is the day of rest. We are to find a place of 'repose' with Jesus and that is the position we go out from. If God speaks to you and says, '*O valiant one, go out and claim the territory back in My name,*' we don't need to ask Him to substantiate His injunction with a fleece! Imbibe the truth, my friends, and be greatly encouraged! It is finished. It cannot be added to or detracted from. You have His word. Go! Those who believe *are seated* in heavenly places in Christ!

Lord Jesus, all praise and glory to You that You have finished the Father's work and by His mighty power You were raised up to take Your royal place at His right hand. Grow my spirit, I pray, to absorb this truth; that I am with You in the heavenly realms. Your word is truth to me and I will believe You. Thank You. Amen.

Day 300 – October 26th

The verse that follows this great assertion regarding where the children of God sit, is reflected in so much of the teachings of Jesus. The Parable of the Wedding Feast indicates that the Father will hold a banquet for the Son. He spoke at the Last Supper of drinking wine again in His Father's kingdom.

'And when He had taken a cup and given thanks, He gave it to them, saying, "Drink from it, all of you; for this is My blood of the covenant,

which is poured out for many for the forgiveness of sins. But I say to you, I will not drink of this fruit of the vine from now on until that day when I drink it new with you in My Father's kingdom.'" (Matthew 26)

The Lord may have been speaking metaphorically regarding the wine of the coming kingdom but I rather think not. It will be so at the Banquet!

While in prayer once, I had a brief vision of a banqueting hall which defied my earthly senses. It was beautiful beyond any compare. There were so many rows to my right and left that I could not possibly have counted them. The perfectly set gleaming tables stretched away over the horizon. It was literally breathtaking.

One day the fruit of His labours will take their places to honour the Bridegroom. 'All is ready,' we will be told. 'Come.'

Who can resist such love and faithful determination to bring us home?

When Jesus spoke saying, 'I will come again,' it was the word of a betrothed to His beloved. That was what young men did. They offered the cup to the betrothed before the gathered family and then, when it was accepted and drunk, went away to prepare a place for her. The bridegroom came back when all was made ready, to take her to the new home.

'In My Father's house there are many dwelling places; if it were not so, I would have told you; for I go to prepare a place for you. If I go and prepare a place for you, I will come again and receive you to Myself, that where I am, there you may be also.' (John 14)

Lord, there is so much we see only dimly but one day we will see clearly the most beautiful detail of all that You have worked for and prepared for us who love You. We praise You today and ask again that You will send us out in Your power with news of the kingdom of God which is at hand. Amen.

Day 301 – October 27th

One of the saddest notions ever is expressed in the parable Jesus told which is often called the Parable of the Dinner or the Banquet. When all was ready, the man offering hospitality at his table sent his bond-servant to tell all who had been invited that they should now come.

'At the dinner hour he sent his slave to say to those who had been invited, "Come; for everything is ready now." But they all alike began to make excuses.' (Luke 14)

The word for 'excuse' is not quite what it might seem. It can confer just that, an excuse, but it also has notions of *spurning, shunning* or *deprecating*. The thrust of their refusals was that the Banquet wasn't sufficiently significant for them to attend. One can only assume that the parable was directed at those who found such fault with the authenticity of Jesus as the Messiah. The excuses that were offered were distinctly lame; none of them – the newly acquired land, the new five pairs of oxen or the new marriage – really constituted a reason to decline the invitation. It is a parable that has just as much significance today as it did then. People create excuses for themselves to avoid the call of Jesus. In my experience the *Person of Jesus* always speaks to people but how often do we truly reflect Jesus in that way? So often we offer religion, disguised in one form or another, making it possible to find any number of excuses not to respond. In this story, it is the people who might never have expected to receive an invite, who possibly had a genuine excuse not to attend, who filled the banquet places.

The man who sent the invites in this parable is determined to fill every place and sends his servant out further and further to find those who will respond to the call 'to come'. The 'have-nots' of life are called, and those whose priorities are at fault, those who afford such worth to their status and their 'acquisitions', remain outside the banqueting hall door. We have no excuse for not responding.

'*The heavens declare His righteousness, and all the peoples have seen His glory.*' (Psalm 97)

Lord Jesus, Your call is so very simple: '*Come to Me.*' You set no standards for being with You, except that we *come* to You, the Living Lord. Lord, I come. Amen.

Day 302 – October 28th

As we draw this group of readings to a conclusion and leave our focus on how God speaks and encourages us with His words, it is good to reflect on how life-changing it can be for us as we engage with God in deep reflection and meditation on His Word. I cannot tell you how, over the years, patient study of the Word, not in a slavish, bookish way but with a heart that delights to learn at greater depth, has resulted in meeting with the Holy Spirit and being profoundly inspired. My walk with the Lord has become 'easier' as a result, by which I mean I strive less when I realise just how much God has finished! I only need to walk in His ways!

I love Psalm 91 in which God speaks to one of His children and expresses a truth that is there for every one of us.

'*Because he has loved Me, therefore I will deliver him; I will set him securely on high, because he has known My name. He will call upon Me, and I will answer him; I will be with him in trouble; I will rescue him, and honour him. With a length of days I will satisfy him and let him see My salvation.*' (Psalm 91)

Lord God, it is a wonderful thing that You desire nothing more for us than to *know You*. For in Your wisdom You have planned it that to know You is to love You and be willing to do all that You call us to do. I do love You, my Lord and Master and Friend. Amen.

Day 303 – October 29th

Ethan expressed so simply the fundamental truth about God. Having extolled the virtues of God's mighty arm and all that He had done through David, the psalmist writes this (and if you want to know why God has done all that He has done and why His children get so excited about Him as Father this may well explain all):

'Righteousness and justice are the foundation of Your throne; loving kindness and truth go before You. How blessed are the people who know the joyful sound!' (Psalm 89)

The joyful shout, or even a trumpet blast, may have referred to the declaration of the seventh month of rest.

*'Again the L*ORD* spoke to Moses, saying, "Speak to the sons of Israel, saying, 'In the seventh month on the first of the month you shall have a rest, a reminder by blowing of trumpets, a holy convocation. You shall not do any laborious work, but you shall present an offering by fire to the L*ORD*."'* (Leviticus 23)

It was the end of the harvest, when all was well and the festal shout ascended to the Lord accompanied by sacrifice. It was a time of rest and profound reconciliation.

It reminds me that, in the context of all the Lord has accomplished within His own remit of righteousness and justice, kindness and faithfulness, that we may now be seated with Him in heavenly places, there really should be a great shout of worship from the people of the Lord and a great laying down of lives in sacrifice to our Father, the Living God. The substance of revival perhaps?

Lord, You call us to partner with You from the place of rest; to send up a great cry from the holy gathering here and then to go out in Your name. We are blessed. We hear the joyful sound of heaven! Amen.

Day 304 – October 30th

How desperately sad it is when a people who have so much to live for, squander their spiritual inheritance on ungodly living.

It was not long after Gideon's remarkable call that he was sent out by the Lord to destroy the altar of Baal and to tear down the Asherah pole beside it. Profound signs of the extent to which the people of God had gone astray to worship vain corruptions of their own making. *It was his own father's altar!* Gideon was fearful of displeasing his father so he went at night with his own servants and destroyed it by stealth. No wonder Gideon needed to know for certain it was the Lord who had called him to do this. He built an altar to the Lord and burned the carved statue to sacrifice the bull he had been told to take along with him. It was a courageous move indeed. In the morning when the people saw the wreck of the idol, they called for Joash, Gideon's father, to bring out his son that he might be punished by death. But listen to this.

'But Joash said to all who stood against him, "Will you contend for Baal, or will you deliver him? Whoever will plead for him shall be put to death by morning. If he is a god, let him contend for himself, because someone has torn down his altar."'

Wisdom! When we go out in God's name to secure the territory that He has sent us to, God has a way of defeating those who we *imagine* might be firmly in our way. It seems that somewhere, deep in this father's conscience, he was able to recognise that this was God and it was not wise to go against Him. Perhaps deep down in his person he knew how far they had gone away from the Lord's precious ways. Who knows? Never be surprised when people who you cannot see as anything but immoveable blockages suddenly 'change sides' and become your fiercest advocates! It was a blockage indeed that was removed that night! Not long after we read,

'So the Spirit of the LORD came upon Gideon; and he blew a trumpet, and the Abiezrites were called together to follow him.' (Judges 6)

'Thus let all Your enemies perish, O LORD; but let those who love Him be like the rising of the sun in its might.' (Judges 5)

Lord, thank You for the men of God who show us how we can

be before You; going out in response to Your word, full of faith, or even quaking in our boots. Your power to arrange circumstances and people's hearts is quite amazing and we ask that as we contend at Your bidding, You will show us how to operate as a people of deep trust in our Father's faithfulness and righteousness. You have broken the power of darkness over the land. Hallelujah. Amen.

Day 305 – October 31st

Today we reflect on the One who is the Light of the world. He has such zeal to accomplish all things. Speak it over your neighbourhood and over your nation today. The Holy One, the Lord reigns!

'The LORD will go forth like a warrior, He will arouse His zeal like a man of war. He will utter a shout, yes, He will raise a war cry. He will prevail against His enemies. "I have kept silent for a long time, I have kept still and restrained Myself. Now like a woman in labour I will groan, I will both gasp and pant. I will lay waste the mountains and hills and wither all their vegetation; I will make the rivers into coastlands and dry up the ponds. I will lead the blind by a way they do not know, in paths they do not know I will guide them. I will make darkness into light before them and rugged places into plains. These are the things I will do, and I will not leave them undone."' (Isaiah 42)

Praise God for Your single-mindedness, Jesus! I pray for You to presence Yourself in our midst. Lead the blind into Light. Make the way smooth beneath their feet so they may walk forward and entrust themselves to You. How small is our vision of how You are! You are light and power unimaginable! Forgive us. Tune my spirit to the music of heaven and somehow make my obedience count for You this day. Amen.

NOVEMBER

Day 306 – November 1st

As we study Scripture, we observe that God speaks many times to solitary figures and at other times it seems as though the impact of the God who speaks to His people gains great momentum, as if to build crescendo; a heavenly symphony with many instrumentalists. The build-up to the coming of Christ is one such time and another is the restoration of the Temple after God's people had been taken captive in Babylon; the temple was in total ruins.

The books of Ezra and Nehemiah are both highly relevant to this period but so, too, are Haggai, Esther, Zechariah and Malachi, all contemporaries of that period. We have looked at Habakkuk, who speaks powerfully into the origins of the Babylonian overthrow and their earlier rise to power which was complete by about 650 BC. The tides of who God allows to wield power come and go in history. The Babylon (Chaldean) civilisation that had taken the people of God into captivity fell to the Medes and Persians in 539 BC.

It is so easy to slip into the spiritual mindset that only our present times really matter; the truth is that we learn so much about the heart, power and intentions of God by meditating on and studying major Old Testament events. We also learn to not make wild assumptions about what God is doing (or not doing) in current times!

'Look among the nations! Observe! Be astonished! Wonder! Because I am doing something in your days – you would not believe if you were told.' (Habakkuk 1)

So God spoke to Habakkuk before the Chaldeans swept through the land and carried Israel into captivity. The God of justice undertook to hold the Babylonians guilty for what they were to do, but it was all part of God's unimaginable plan to bring His people back to faithfulness and the pure worship of their loving God.

Some of the greatest nations in the world have slowly left behind their Christian heritage and deserted truth, and now, with great pride, they hoist the sickening symbols of vain pride and idolatry. Such is man's arrogance that he does not even disguise his actions. Reading the OT Prophets, the men and women who God raised to speak out 'now words' to the people of God, serves to remind us that God will not be mocked or His great heart intentions thwarted. Are we ready? God is righteous, loving, faithful and just, but as we considered before, we must remember what a friend of mine says: 'God is not always "nice".' God, You wouldn't do *that*, would You?

'The LORD reigns, let the peoples tremble; He is enthroned above the cherubim, let the earth shake!' (Psalm 99)

So let us devote ourselves with open hearts, to understand what God may be saying to us in our days.

'I will stand on my guard post and station myself on the rampart; and I will keep watch to see what He will speak to me.' (Habakkuk 2)

'Take pains with these things; be absorbed in them, so that your progress will be evident to all,' wrote Paul to Timothy concerning his walk with the Lord (1 Timothy 4).

Father, I choose to open my heart to Your wisdom in our days that You might speak to me about the times we live in. I come humbly before You. Make my eyes clear eyes, and the hearing of my heart sharp, that I may not be swept along by the thousands of voices that clamour with so much news and views. I want to be a watchman on the ramparts for You. May I have the humility to be free from assumptions about our future but instead be inextricably bound to the desires of the King of kings. Amen.

Day 307 – November 2nd

'But do not let this one fact escape your notice, beloved, that with the LORD one day is like a thousand years, and a thousand years like one day.' (2 Peter 3)

Peter is describing here the last days, speaking of how there will be many who will mock and say, 'It's always been like this . . . you are not saying anything different . . . so where is God?' Peter stands his ground remarking that, as his own days draw to a close, he wishes to stir up those of transparent, clear, deep-thinking, reminding us that we should not forget the words of the holy prophets or Jesus. *He will come back!* And what is more, it has slipped their thinking, he adds, referring to those who mock, *everything is being preserved only until the day of destruction when all men will be judged.* Peter speaks, I always think, with the quiet authority of one who was there on the Mount of Transfiguration. He *knows* the glory which is to come and is outspoken against anyone who might scornfully speak otherwise.

We need to be a people who are not only very seriously caught up in what the Lord is doing in our day but also have a context both in time and in 'His-Story'. We must pray with all urgency for a profound move of the Lord to wake up men and women from their blind slumbers. We are blessed beyond all measure to be living in the days we inhabit and to be involved and so aware of the Lord in our generation. Many have been less fortunate and, as we read the holy prophets of history, it is good to remember that the countless lives of which we read were real men and women, and real families caught up in earth-shaking events. These are not quaint old stories for 'Sunday school' retelling, but accounts of unbelievably awful times for the people of God. No doubt among the many who wandered from their faith and were lost, there were also many godly people. Jesus spoke to His disciples and, if possible, His words are now truer than ever.

'Blessed are the eyes which see the things you see, for I say to you, that many prophets and kings wished to see the things which you see, and did not see them, and to hear the things which you hear, and did not hear them.' (Luke 10)

There is something deeply sobering about that. Rejoice before God that we have what we have in these days but do not neglect to reflect that many accomplished much more then than we do, with considerably less revelation, and often at a very great personal cost. Everything is in place for us to be deeply moved of God as we have never been before as He continues to impact the nations. We must be His faithful and holy people.

Holy God, we come low before You, Father, aware that we live in the last days when Your revelation is so full and, yet, we also have such a capacity to be quietly emasculated regarding the truth. Father, I pray that You will not allow me 'to sleep at the wheel'. May every day count for Your glory. Amen.

Day 308 – November 3rd

Sometimes when we watch world events shaping, it appears almost inconceivable that A could become B, let alone X, Y or Z! Our hearts strain to see God in circumstances that may appear very bleak, spiritually speaking. But wait; changing A into Z is exactly what God has done throughout Scripture and we should be wise and faithful in our thinking!

'Now in the first year of Cyrus king of Persia, in order to fulfil the word of the Lord by the mouth of Jeremiah, the Lord stirred up the spirit of Cyrus king of Persia, so that he sent a proclamation throughout all his kingdom, and also put it in writing.' (Ezra 1)

When I read that I notice that Ezra records twice *'Cyrus the king of Persia'*. It almost reads as though he wishes the reader to realise the enormity of this; *it really was this mighty king, yes, that's right, Cyrus,* who ruled the most enormous empire! God was going to stir this foreigner's heart! We are also told very clearly why God did this; it was to *fulfil a word* He had spoken to his prophet.

When God had first inspired Jeremiah, as a young man, it was with major words against God's people who were way off-course. At one point, he was told to speak a word at the city gate.

"'Hear the word of the Lord, all you of Judah, who enter by these gates to worship the Lord!" Thus says the Lord of hosts, the God of

Israel, "Amend your ways and your deeds, and I will let you dwell in this place."' (Jeremiah 7)

He was a brave man to speak so, but the point was, it was *God's* word. The people were in a spiritual mess; idolatry in Jerusalem, even in the temple, hideous acts of demon worship prevailed and many of today's woes were prevalent then. A little later God spoke to him, as to his own journey as a great man of God who was to lead a painful life under God's hand.

'As for you, do not pray for this people, and do not lift up cry or prayer for them, and do not intercede with Me; for I do not hear you. Do you not see what they are doing in the cities of Judah and in the streets of Jerusalem?'

Imagine how Jeremiah must have felt, if you can. God is not 'nice' and neither is He a tame God who does our bidding and tolerates us, however much we might think it is alright to behave appallingly. God called 'time' and will call 'time'. People do not like to hear that and unsurprisingly there were attempts to silence Jeremiah; he was beaten and put in the stocks but the moment he was out he prophesied vividly against his tormentor, Pashur the priest. Everywhere Jeremiah went, even amongst his friends, he was mocked, reproached and treated as a laughing-stock. The book of Jeremiah is not cheery, bedtime reading but I urge you to study it. With reading, I promise the Holy Spirit will enable you to understand an aspect of God's holy being, and that He may be still speaking to us in these days.

What was the word that Ezra referred to? After many harrowing personal experiences and dreadful times for the people, Jeremiah spoke thus,

'For thus says the LORD, "When seventy years have been completed for Babylon, I will visit you and fulfil My good word to you, to bring you back to this place. For I know the plans that I have for you," declares the LORD, "plans for welfare and not for calamity to give you a future and a hope. Then you will call upon Me and come and pray to Me, and

I will listen to you. You will seek Me and find Me when you search for Me with all your heart." (Jeremiah 29)

Well-known words, often spoken as comfort and reassurance, but usually out of context. God had spoken and His word was not going to fall to the ground! Experiences which would purify the people of God were on the way.

Lord God, what can I say? I bow low before Your majestic all-seeing Presence. Have mercy on us in these days, I pray, and enable us to become again a prophetic people who can hear the authentic word of the Lord. May my ears not be stroked with words I want to hear but instead, will You speak of Your wondrous ways. Amen.

Day 309 – November 4th

In the midst of all that befell them it is worth noting that God wished Jeremiah to know that He continued to value hearts that were running after Him; those who would not be corrupted. He spoke, after key people had been taken into captivity from Jerusalem.

'The LORD showed me: behold, two baskets of figs set before the temple of the LORD! One basket had very good figs, like first-ripe figs, and the other basket had very bad figs which could not be eaten due to rottenness.' (Jeremiah 24)

The Lord asked Jeremiah to tell Him what he saw, which he did. Then God spoke again.

'Thus says the LORD God of Israel, "Like these good figs, so I will regard as good the captives of Judah, whom I have sent out of this place into the land of the Chaldeans. For I will set My eyes on them for good, and I will bring them again to this land; and I will build them up and not overthrow them, and I will plant them and not pluck them up."'

God is a God of infinite justice, goodness and righteousness and His love is unquenchable, but to those who constituted the rotten figs, whose hearts God knew, an awful future awaited them, Jeremiah was told to prophesy.

As we read these ancient scriptures we can know once again the God of faithfulness who we can utterly trust, but also, they refresh and deepen our understanding that God is a God of *covenant*. He longs for our faithful hearts and our profound devotion.

'If I shut up the heavens so that there is no rain, or I command the locust to devour the land, or if I send pestilence among My people, and My people who are called by My name humble themselves and pray and seek My face and turn from their wicked ways, then I will hear from heaven, will forgive their sin and will heal their land.' (2 Chronicles 7)

Lord God, my Father. It is so easy in these days to conclude that personal faith is an individual's choice, and so it is, but I know that my own prophetic part is to declare the fullness of Your name to all who will hear. Where I place my heart matters profoundly to You, and You are not indifferent to men and women who are lost. Send me out, I pray, to bring home the lost sheep. Amen.

Day 310 – November 5th

I defrosted the freezer today! The weather has been so cold that there was not a chance of anything defrosting, safely wrapped up in bags outside on the floor! It was the right moment. The job was overdue and thick ice covered all the shelves and jammed the doors. I have a very relaxed way of doing the job; I cover the floor and the bottom with piles of newspaper and a tray to catch the bits, and then I set a fan heater on top speed, point it in the freezer and come back later. (I am sure you have done the same!) Within a short while this wonderful household aid is clean, wiped dry and unrecognisable!

Have you ever seen God breathe on a hard-hearted, locked up, frozen person? It is miraculous to watch and we must always hold in our hearts the image of God doing this as we pray for our friends, our nation and the world powers. God is in the business of making His Light shine into the darkest places, and He unlocks the water in ice and even rocks! Yes, this is our mighty God! Hallelujah!

And so, at the right time God breathed on Cyrus. I am sure there were probably moments in Cyrus' life when God had been warming him and preparing him, but now He moved on him to stir his spirit to God-centred action.

'I have also called you by your name; I have given you a title of honour though you have not known Me. I am the LORD, and there is no other; besides Me there is no God. I will gird you, though you have not known Me; that men may know from the rising to the setting of the sun that there is no one besides Me. I am the LORD, and there is no other, the One forming light and creating darkness, causing well-being and creating calamity; I am the LORD who does all these.' (Isaiah 45)

Bless You, O mighty God. I stand in awe of Your ways. I thank You and praise You that through Jesus You called me to life after I had been dead in my sins. You wiped me clean through His blood and You made me fit for Your purposes. Amen.

Day 311 – November 6th

The stirring of the spirit in God's chosen instrument, Cyrus, caused this king to issue a decree.

'Thus says Cyrus king of Persia, "The LORD, the God of heaven, has given me all the kingdoms of the earth and He has appointed me to build Him a house in Jerusalem, which is in Judah. Whoever there is among you of all His people, may his God be with him! Let him go up to Jerusalem which is in Judah and rebuild the house of the LORD, the God of Israel; He is the God who is in Jerusalem. Every survivor, at whatever place he may live, let the men of that place support him with silver and gold, with goods and cattle, together with a freewill offering for the house of God which is in Jerusalem."' (Ezra 1)

Wow! That is, to use that much over-used word, truly 'awesome'. Cyrus wrote the edict down and it was appropriately archived, which became very significant to the people of Israel years after

Cyrus' influence ended. All the articles of silver and gold which Nebuchadnezzar had stolen and placed in the temples of his gods, were retrieved and returned. They totalled over 5000 pieces. Twenty-four thousand one hundred and forty-four people left with their leaders and the Levites. They left to go to their homes in Judah and to Jerusalem. This is an extraordinary story of God's supreme sovereignty over all men and every circumstance. We cannot know what Cyrus perceived in his heart but, clearly, he was mightily convicted of the right way forward. We know God can change men and women's hearts as the Holy Spirit comes upon them so we shouldn't be surprised, but let this moment of ancient history when God changed the direction of an entire nation be a stimulus to us as we pray for those in high government across the world.

'First of all, then, I urge that entreaties and prayers, petitions and thanksgivings, be made on behalf of all men, for kings and all who are in authority, so that we may lead a tranquil and quiet life in all godliness and dignity. This is good and acceptable in the sight of God our Saviour, who desires all men to be saved and to come to the knowledge of the truth.' (1 Timothy 2)

Lord God, heavenly King. I worship You today, joining with countless children to lift before You those who hold positions of authority in our land. We pray for our Queen and give thanks for her witness to the world, and we pray for her parliament and councils, at all levels, throughout the country. We pray for peace, for wisdom and for godly rule. Amen.

Day 312 – November 7th

'The LORD reigns, let the peoples tremble; He is enthroned above the cherubim, let the earth shake! The LORD is great in Zion, and He is exalted above all the peoples. Let them praise Your great and awesome name; Holy is He.' (Psalm 99)

I think about the 'OMG' expression which trips off people's lips so readily and think, *if only they knew . . .* I pray for a time when those same words are spoken in hushed awe all over the land, as they have been in times of revival. I know it can happen because my own 'God if you are there' prayer provoked such a move in heaven that I was totally changed, forever. My heart was melted in fear and utter humility before the love and mercy of the One who sits enthroned. *The LORD is great in Zion. Holy is He.* You probably have your own story of God's amazing grace coming upon you. Rejoice in that story today and let it spur you on in prayer for those you long to hear cry, '*O my God!*'

Father, You listened to my every word, through my entire life, I believe that, and when I uttered those words You sent Your Holy Spirit to say, *I am here!* I can hardly believe the enormity of Your grace and Your intense desire to bring us back to Yourself. I bless You, God, today, and I would like to pray now in faith for . . .

Day 313 – November 8th

It was clear early on that a call to *purity* was one of the hallmarks of this move of God as the people went back to Judah. Priests who lacked authenticated 'pedigree' were excluded. The mixed marriages between Israelites were a cause for much heartache, for many had taken wives and husbands who were from foreign races and were not followers of the living God. Integrity before God was everything. In the seventh month (remember 'seven'?) the entire nation gathered in Jerusalem '*to a man*' we are told. Imagine that. The leaders set up an altar to the Lord amid the foundations of the temple. We cannot tell for sure but it appears they cleared enough of the ruins to ascertain exactly where it should be and they sacrificed morning and evening, day after day. When the foundations for the new temple were built, they celebrated before the Holy God again.

'*The priests stood in their apparel with trumpets, and the Levites, the sons of Asaph, with cymbals, to praise the LORD according to the directions of King David of Israel. And they sang, praising and giving thanks to the* LORD, *saying, "For He is good, for His loving kindness is upon Israel forever." And all the people shouted with a great shout when they praised the* LORD *because the foundation of the house of the* LORD *was laid.'* (Ezra 3)

Some who gathered there were men of a good age and could recall the earlier temple, and they wept. Others shouted for joy and it is said it was impossible to distinguish the shouts from the weeping, but the sound was heard from far away. God's people were coming back. Such inexpressible joy was, for some, doubtless tinged with memories of the dreadful day when Nebuchadnezzar's armies swept into the city.

There is a powerful parallel that I see here, not to do with buildings and physical ruins but the state of many affairs in our land. They are in ruins and God's people are called to rebuild the church in all its glory so that once again, instead of being a peripheral and irksome thing, it will beckon people to the glory of the Head, who is in all and over all, and before whom every knee shall bow.

Lord God, I long to see Your church excited; not about the promise of restoring sacred buildings but about the reality of Your presence in our midst. Sound the trumpets and may the shout for Your glory be heard far and near. Amen.

Day 314 – November 9th

It wasn't long before the opposition tried to disrupt things in Jerusalem. Ezra records that the enemies of Judah and Benjamin heard of the temple building and came along offering to assist! Whether this was a subtle ploy or a genuine offer, albeit a mistaken one, it was not a good idea. The 'volunteers' claimed that they, too, had been worshipping the same God. Actually, it wasn't so, as they spoke of the days of making sacrifice to Nisroch, a demon god. I am sure that the Israelites could have done with some extra pairs of hands but, wisely, they perceived that God was calling His people alone to work with holy hands and hearts. Purity means more to God than we will ever know.

The resistance soon became clear for what is was and the agitation increased until finally a letter was written by the opposition to the king, who was no longer the benevolent Cyrus but Artaxerxes. How about this for a scurrilous attack? *'Let it be known to the king that the Jews who came up from you have come to us at Jerusalem; they are rebuilding the rebellious and evil city and are finishing the walls and repairing the foundations . . .'* and so it carried on in a sneaky, spiteful and untrue way (Ezra 4).

As my friend in ministry was sometimes heard to say, 'Folks, it's clear which side they are batting for.' The enemy detests the worship of the One true God in heaven.

Work stopped according to a decree issued by the king, seemingly a fictitious one, but one that carried the threat of force if it was disobeyed. When the prophets Haggai and Zechariah became involved they spoke out with great courage in the name of the God of Israel, that work should continue and so the God-fearing leaders did just that, ignoring the protests. Eventually the original decree from Cyrus was uncovered in the Persian archives and everyone backed down and work progressed. The edicts of a Persian king were forever and could not be revoked. The power of the prophetic word from the throne room of God carries more weight than any other in the entire world. Moreover, from that moment the favour to the Israelites increased!

As a result, the king issued another decree, more generous than the original.

'Leave this work on the house of God alone; let the governor of the Jews and the elders of the Jews rebuild this house of God on its site. Moreover, I issue a decree concerning what you are to do for these elders of Judah in the rebuilding of this house of God: the full cost of it is to be paid to these people from the royal treasury out of the taxes of

the provinces beyond the River, and that without delay.' (Ezra 6)

The decree continued, instructing that everything they needed in order to offer sacrifices should be supplied also! Any man who was found violating the edict was to be put to death in a very unpleasant manner.

Isn't that amazing? What a turnaround! How wonderful God is; how beautiful His sovereign hand. It helps my faith when I study these stories and it should encourage us all when we are involved in projects that God has ordained. Opposition will come; don't be discouraged! God will double His efforts on behalf of His children.

'Let the favour of the LORD our God be upon us; and confirm for us the work of our hands; yes, confirm the work of our hands.' (Psalm 90)

Father, I praise You for your faithfulness in Your amazing dealings with Your children. It teaches me to trust You for everything even when the work is slow to bear fruit and I feel discouraged. Your word goes out and it does not fall to the ground without accomplishing what You intend. Amen.

Day 315 – November 10th

There is neither time nor is this the place to fully sketch out the history of this period. It is complex, as twice the Israelites and various tribes were released to return from captivity to go back to Jerusalem.

The book of Esther (another must-read) is the most beautiful and intriguing story of God's faithfulness although, strangely, His name is not once mentioned. His blessing and prospering are with us at all times, in every thread of our lives. As Psalm 139 declares, we cannot escape His kindness or His care! Just as before, His purposes and sequencing of events are often obscure but what God is doing among the people of the earth today is just as far-reaching as it was in Esther's day.

Esther, by the most extraordinary twists and turns and Daniel-like acts of bravery in the face of threats against her own life, and the potential vicious treatment of her own people, demonstrates the goodness of God and the mystery of the journey He sometimes leads us on. When Esther's position is elevated beyond her imagination to be the wife of the *massively* powerful king of Persia, Xerxes, her 'uncle', Mordecai, utters this famous and deeply significant phrase.

'And who knows whether you have not attained royalty for such a time as this?' (Esther 4)

This is a verse that speaks to me powerfully and maybe to you also. Who knows why you have attained *royalty* for such a time as this? A King whose power and majesty makes Xerxes look like a minor clerk, has called you from a place of being totally lost; He has placed a ring on your finger and a royal robe around your shoulders and called you to be a co-inheritor with His precious Son. He has bathed you and cleansed you and washed away your filthy stains, and then anointed you and called you into His presence. Beloved, think on this; let the knowledge of this pervade your deepest parts.

'And who knows whether you have not attained royalty for such a time as this?'

What is God calling you to that is yours alone, prepared for you to enact with courage and faith in Your Father? In Esther's case, it was to radically change the circumstances of the Jews; not just to save them but to elevate them once again to a place of honour and favour! Know this: the King you serve never changes; this is the One we read of in stories such as Esther, and the woman caught in adultery and the demonised man at Decapolis. Our God reigns and He calls us to partner with Him.

O Sovereign Lord, as I meditate on who You are I see that most of my time I live in a fog. I know I am Yours but I do not live in the reality of *all You are* and all You have made me to be. Fill me afresh with Your Holy Spirit's truth. Thank You that by Your grace I have attained royalty for such a time as this. Open my days to me, I pray. Amen.

Day 316 – November 11th

There is a wonderful moment in the story of Esther when the king had a restless night and the whole story supernaturally pivots around this point. It tells us that goodness and service of God will never be forgotten. The 'uncle', Mordecai, had once preserved the king's life by bringing to his awareness a plot against him and this had been recorded in the chronicles of the times. Kings kept detailed journals of all they did, a great blessing to us also as many such records form detailed parts of Scripture. As his servants read to him, he was told again the story of Mordecai's goodness! Realising that this loyal Jew had never been rewarded or honoured for his deed, the story suddenly turns against Haman the vindictive, manipulative, cruel man who had plotted against Mordecai and intended to wipe out the Jews in the kingdom.

Rather as Joseph was elevated by the Pharaoh, so is Mordecai; he is instructed to write a charter for his own people's well-being and to seal it with the king's signet. The edict went out through all the land!

'*Then Mordecai went out from the presence of the king in royal robes of blue and white, with a large crown of gold and a garment of fine linen and purple; and the city of Susa shouted and rejoiced. For the Jews there was light and gladness and joy and honour.*' (Esther 8)

Again, we see how God can cause any man to change the course of history with one touch from the King. Let us be encouraged and have our faith stretched; let us have our minds renewed by the Holy Spirit bringing these truths to us again that our eyes may be open wide, *for such a time as this.*

Holy, holy God. Your ways are hidden from us but I thank You that You have called us to go out from Your throne room dressed in royal attire to bring life; to bring light and gladness and joy and honour. God, I bow before You and bless Your holy name. Amen.

Day 317 – November 12th

The fore-knowledge of God, if I may call it that, has played out in so many contemporary stories in our own age. In Scripture, we find the simplest of untutored working men and women being transformed by the hand of God upon them, into the people that God *sees*.

The twelve apostles who went out from that room early on the day of Pentecost were, at heart, fishermen. They probably had gnarled hands, weather-beaten faces and down-to-earth, rough ways but it was their hearts that God saw and nurtured. If we met them, I am sure we would not immediately recognise them as 'religious' leaders! They were, however, men deeply transformed by the Holy Spirit within them. When Peter stood to declare his first sermon he was not a 'spiritual medium' with a message for the people; when the Holy Spirit comes, we *become* the spiritual messengers – the message is a part of ourselves – we are sacramental messengers in the hands of God. God doesn't bolt on a little revelation here and there, some sort of annexe to our real selves; we are *transformed*. The disciples didn't *learn* anything from Pentecost; it made them the incarnation of what they preached. They were witnesses! And so for us; we are to be witnesses.

'*Men of Israel, listen to these words: Jesus the Nazarene, a man attested to you by God with miracles and wonders and signs which God performed through Him in your midst, just as you yourselves know – this Man, delivered over by the pre-determined plan and foreknowledge of God, you nailed to a cross by the hands of godless men and put Him to death. But God raised Him up again putting an end to the agony of death, since it was impossible for Him to be held in its power.*' (Acts 2)

Witnesses! We also carry the message of the resurrection *in us*. We are the message. We are prophetic weapons in the hands of God, ready to demolish every contentious argument against Him. We do not have it in our minds; we carry the message in our whole beings. This is one of the things we can learn from these saints of old. They were not automatons! They *were* the message.

Lord God, I pray that You will so invade every part of my being that I will truly become the message. Come, Holy Spirit, and wake me up to all that You have ordained for my life. Amen.

Day 318 – November 13th

Jeremiah flowed with many powerful prophecies. Here is one.

"'Therefore behold, days are coming," declares the LORD, *"when it will no longer be said, 'As the LORD lives, who brought up the sons of Israel out of the land of Egypt,' but, 'As the LORD lives, who brought up the sons of Israel from the land of the north and from all the countries where He had banished them.' For I will restore them to their own land which I gave to their fathers. Behold, I am going to send for many fishermen,"* declares the LORD, *"and they will fish for them; and afterwards I will send for many hunters, and they will hunt them from every mountain and every hill and from the clefts of the rocks."'* (Jeremiah 16)

This is an extraordinary message of both condemnation but also, note, hope. It is being spoken long before the event. God knows the hearts and lives of everyone, He declares; they are not hidden from His face.

'For My eyes are on all their ways; they are not hidden from My face, nor is their iniquity concealed from My eyes.'

Before the people are even banished, God speaks of restoration.

'I will first doubly repay their iniquity and their sin, because they have polluted My land; they have filled My inheritance with the carcasses of their detestable idols and with their abominations . . . Therefore behold, I am going to make them know . . . My power and My might; and they shall know that My name is the LORD.'

There is much within this to reflect on. Our God is very serious about being known. That word in Hebrew means so much more than we might mean when we say, 'I know my address' or 'I know my friend, John'. Being 'known' implies a great intimacy, a sharing of beings; hearts and minds and souls entwined. It is sometimes used to indicate the most intimate joining together of a man with a woman in love and passion.

Our amazing Father God wants us to *know Him* and in knowing Him, to know His identity: *'I am the Lord.'*

My Father, I thank You that I know You. I know Your name, Father, Son and Holy Spirit. It is by Your grace alone that I can come into this most intimate place with You. It is a *miracle* of Your grace that I, who was once so far off, have been welcomed in. You opened the gates of glory to me, through Jesus the beloved Son, who went and paid many times over the cost of my sin that I need not be banished to captivity and isolation. Thank You. Amen.

Day 319 – November 14th

Many prophesy. Paul speaks about the prophetic gift in a passage that is frequently muddled in interpretation; it speaks of the use of tongues in public. His emphasis is simply that it is both a courtesy and effective to have people understand what is being said. But here is Paul speaking of the power of prophecy.

'But if all prophesy, and an unbeliever or an ungifted man enters, he is convicted by all, he is called to account by all; the secrets of his heart are disclosed; and so he will fall on his face and worship God, declaring that God is certainly among you.' (1 Corinthians 14)

Later, Paul encourages us all:

'Therefore, my brethren, desire earnestly to prophesy, and do not forbid to speak in tongues. But all things must be done properly and in an orderly manner.'

We can learn so much about the way God uses humble men and

women to speak His words. Prophesying should not be done lightly, but with love and a genuine desire to build up the people of God. Yes, it is true, God sometimes admonishes but there is always *hope* within it. Jesus has the last word on prophecy, not least because *He is the Spirit of Prophecy*. Jesus said, '*Yet wisdom is vindicated by her deeds*' (Matthew 11).

This is a reference to Jeremiah 29.

'*For thus says the LORD of hosts, the God of Israel, "Do not let your prophets who are in your midst and your diviners deceive you, and do not listen to the dreams which they dream. For they prophesy falsely to you in My name; I have not sent them," declares the LORD. For thus says the LORD, "When seventy years have been completed for Babylon . . ."*'

In other words, Jesus is saying, *prophecy will be known as authentic by whether it comes true!*

There is much we could reflect on here about prophecy but mostly we can learn by knowing God and being known by Him. Jesus was humble and always pointed towards hope. He still speaks in the same way.

Dear Father, thank You for the gift of men and women who hear and speak Your words whether through preaching or by a particular prophetic word. Your church needs edifying by sound wisdom and deep insight so we pray, raise up the prophetic gift in our midst and guide us into truth and humility. Amen.

Day 320 – November 15th

God speaks through Jeremiah repeatedly of the hope that is before the people and it is good to remember that as we journey in life. We do have very difficult times, individually and together, but God always speaks hope over us; a way through. God is not a God of dead-ends.

I recall a word once amid a church in some degree of turmoil;

it was simple, loving and really stopped everyone and called them to humility. In humility was the answer to their difficulties and dissention. *'Come low before Me and I will raise you up.'* It wasn't complicated but those few words speak to us profoundly of our muddles and times when we can be at odds with one another and full of 'our own voice'. Fulfil a primary, humble act of the spirit before God to honour Him and He will do the rest.

'Thus says the LORD, *"Behold, I will restore the fortunes of the tents of Jacob and have compassion on his dwelling places; and the city will be rebuilt on its ruin, and the palace will stand on its rightful place. From them will proceed thanksgiving and the voice of those who celebrate; and I will multiply them and they will not be diminished; I will also honour them and they will not be insignificant. Their children also will be as formerly, and their congregation shall be established before Me."'* (Jeremiah 30)

And,

'Hear the word of the LORD, *O nations, and declare in the coastlands afar off, and say, "He who scattered Israel will gather him, and keep him as a shepherd keeps his flock." For the LORD has ransomed Jacob and redeemed him from the hand of him who was stronger than he. They will come and shout for joy on the height of Zion, and they will be radiant over the bounty of the LORD.'* (Jeremiah 31)

That is our God! Hallelujah! He speaks with hope.

My God and my Lord, I praise You that Your name is always *hope*. You are the hope of our hearts. You are the great Shepherd and You delight when Your flocks return to You. Amen.

Day 321 – November 16th

It will be a joyful reading (if you have set out to study Jeremiah) to read that something highly significant changes just over half-way through the book, and it begins, *"'Behold, days are coming," declares the LORD . . .'*

"As I have watched over them to pluck up, to break down, to overthrow, to destroy and to bring to disaster, so I will watch over them to build and to plant," declares the LORD . . . *"Behold, days are coming," declares the* LORD, *"when I will make a new covenant with the house of Israel and with the house of Judah, not like the covenant which I made with their fathers in the day I took them by the hand to bring them out of the land of Egypt, My covenant which they broke, although I was a husband to them," declares the* LORD. *"But this is the covenant which I will make with the house of Israel after those days," declares the* LORD, *"I will put My law within them and on their heart I will write it; and I will be their God, and they shall be My people."'* (Jeremiah 31)

Although these words were spoken, you will see if you are reading the book that it was a promise of a distant day of hope. It was not yet the time and indeed worse things were yet to come first. Many times, the prophets spoke of times to come; surely a reflection of the hope that God gives to those who are close to Him but also because God *always* shows us a better way. Some prophesied 'peace' in Jeremiah's day but it was not a word from the Lord. God was not saying 'Everything is fine; do not worry . . .' The *timing* of the fulfilment of prophecy is everything.

Father, thank You that You are the God of hope. When things seem dark You speak of light; when things are oppressive, You speak of lifting up and breaking free. Holy Spirit, would You seed in my heart the message of hope that I may be through and through a messenger of good news and, as such, to be seen and heard to be singing a different song. Amen.

Day 322 – November 17th

What was the message that was *so different*? We take the message of the new covenant almost 'for granted'; it is our essential personality and our identity in God, but imagine how startling this must have seemed.

"'But this is the covenant which I will make with the house of Israel after those days," declares the LORD, "I will put My law within them and on their heart I will write it; and I will be their God, and they shall be My people.'" (Jeremiah 31)

To be inwardly led by God, as opposed to outwardly through the Law and through mediators, was an experience that had only been known by exceptional people who tended to be among the prophets and anointed leaders. This was to be for *every man*. Jeremiah's prophecy continues:

'"They will not teach again, each man his neighbour and each man his brother, saying, 'Know the LORD,' for they will all know Me, from the least of them to the greatest of them," declares the LORD, "for I will forgive their iniquity, and their sin I will remember no more.'" (Jeremiah 31)

We might wonder about *'they will not teach again'* in the context of what we believe and do in the raising of disciples but the Hebrew word used there is *'lâmad'*, a word which does mean 'to teach' but might be better understood as 'goad'; it has associations with learning by application of the rod, something that wasn't unknown in those times (and wasn't unknown here not so very long ago!).

The meaning is clear: God is going to change the fundamental *relationship* of man with God. His ways will be written deep in our hearts and our longing for Him will be a spiritual yearning and learning process. Sadly, many of us still have elements of *lâmad* expectation in us; that God will get us to do what He wants with threat of punishment and by pain and huge effort of will. It reminds me of my Latin teacher at school. I would like to say to you today, God is not like a Latin teacher armed with a heavy ruler which is used more for knuckles than to draw straight lines.

John wrote: *'We have come to know and have believed the love which God has for us. God is love, and the one who abides in love abides in God, and God abides in him. By this, love is perfected within us, so that we may have confidence in the day of judgement; because as He is, so are we in this world. There is no fear in love; but perfect love casts out fear, because fear involves punishment, and the one who fears is not perfected in love. We love because He first loved us.'* (1 John 4)

I pray you can really see the difference and be filled with joy that our loving God ushered in His covenant of love through the redemption won by Jesus on the cross of Calvary. *Jesus* has taken the punishment which should be ours; *we* were under judgement, not Jesus.

Father, thank You for Your love for us; that You give Your Spirit to change us and teach us about Yourself and to bring us into intimate relationship with You. I surrender to You today all thoughts that I must live and learn in fear of You. May my soul be cleansed of anything that lingers from my story which speaks to me of punishment and less-than-perfect love. I want to live in holy fear; in awe of the love of my Saviour God. Thank You that Jesus took my punishment. Show me the difference, I pray. Amen.

Day 323 – November 18th

The story of Jeremiah's life is extraordinary and very sad. Most of all that even his name has passed into usage indicating a gloomy, wet-blanket of a person. Jeremiah was far from this but instead, from his earliest days, was called to speak for God. He was punished for his faithful obedience, ostracised to the extent that even his family wished him harm. He lived under the reign of five or more kings, some of whom were appalling leaders, cruel and demonised. One of them, the king at the time of his birth, Manasseh, sacrificed his own children in demon worship and was responsible for Isaiah being sawn in two. No wonder God ear-marked this man to 'build up' and 'throw down', which is the meaning of his name. How did the people of God err so far and to such great extremes as this? It is a question just as much for our own days, I suspect. Are there sound voices in our day calling people back to God and, more, will people hear? The capacity of man to fly in the face of God is beyond comprehension but that is what they did, and still do.

When the people decided to head for Egypt and what they perceived to be safety from the Chaldeans, they sought Jeremiah for the Lord's word. He said, 'Do not go,' but they went regardless. God was trying to establish a remnant in Judah, a remnant He would protect and nurture, instead they fled. At one moment Jeremiah was actually told to prophesy the enthronement of Nebuchadnezzar in Egypt, an event God told would happen after he and his armies had over-run the Pharaoh, which in due time they did. Jeremiah, it seems, died in Egypt.

The Babylonians in Judah were surprisingly kind to Jeremiah, and during the long exile of the rest of the people, life settled to some extent. They were benevolent considering they were an occupying force. Then a hot-headed and ungodly young king in Jerusalem, Zedekiah, decided to rebel against Babylon. It was a pointless and futile gesture that cost him his life. Nebuchadnezzar swept in and Jerusalem was raised to the ground, its palaces and the temple torn down and burned. A tiny remnant remained who were subsistence farmers.

If you have read Jeremiah, you may have noticed that not all the events are recorded in a seemingly chronological order. It is a complex book but the parts we have looked at help to show the heart of God for His people and how the hearts of the people were far from God. It is an immensely sad story that still has the power to move me to tears.

We end where we started, when Cyrus' heart was stirred by God. It was a time that Jeremiah had prophesied seemingly many, many years before; before all the needless tragedy and suffering. It is worth reading in its entirety as it conveys all that we have been thinking about and more:

'For thus says the LORD, "I have heard a sound of terror, of dread, *and there is no peace . . . Alas! for that day is great, there is none like it; and it is the time of Jacob's distress, but he will be saved from it. It shall come about on that day," declares the* LORD *of hosts, "that I will break his yoke from off their neck, and will tear off their bonds; and strangers will no longer make them their slaves. But they shall serve the* LORD *their God and David their king, whom I will raise up for them. Fear not, O Jacob My servant," declares the* LORD, *"and do not be dismayed, O Israel; for behold, I will save you from afar, and your offspring from the land of their captivity. And Jacob will return and will be quiet and at ease, and no one will make him afraid. For I am with you," declares the* LORD, *"to save you; for I will destroy completely all the nations where I have scattered you, only I will not destroy you completely. But I will chasten you justly and will by no means leave you unpunished."'* (Jeremiah 30)

How wonderful that God in His infinite mercy did find a way to release us from our 'incurable wounds'; that 'healing for the sores' did come, that One did pay the price for our 'great iniquity' and our 'numerous sins'.

'Simon Peter answered Him, "Lord, to whom shall we go? You have words of eternal life. We have believed and have come to know that You are the Holy One of God."' (John 6)

God of mercy and love, my heart is saddened by the ceaseless rebellion of Your creation. May these ancient stories which are but yesterday to You, spur me on into the place of thanksgiving, prayer and longing, that the *knowledge* of Your glory shall fill the earth. Amen.

Day 324 – November 19th

'Hope deferred makes the heart sick, but desire fulfilled is a tree of life.' (Proverbs 13)

In the light of all we have been reading, there comes, perhaps, a fresh understanding of what it is to be 'heart sick' and the profound consequences of what may occur when it extends to the heart-sickness of society. I have met, many times, individuals who are, without doubt, 'sick of heart'. I often wondered if it is 'homesickness', spiritually-speaking, given that it is only God who can heal our condition and, somewhere deep inside, we have in our beings a deep grieving from the Garden of Eden and a profound longing for what was lost – intimate fellowship with the Father.

This is not the place for an in-depth study of addictions but let it be recognised that in all the Old Testament stories we have read, the people are searching for *something* to bring about their fulfilment. I believe that God wants our only addiction to be Jesus; He knows that when that longing is satisfied, or there is at least the promise of fulfilment, the heart's sickness will be engaged on its journey of redemption and healing. Unfortunately, the enemy comes along and has a ready supply of sources of false-spirit-assuaging ideas which always appear attractive and beguiling; they can never satisfy and always lead to deeper and deeper errant pursuits of wholeness in body, mind and soul.

That, in summary, is the basis of the constant failure of God's people to come to Him. In one shape or form every failure is a reflection of Eden's tragedy.

'But evil men and impostors will proceed from bad to worse, deceiving and being deceived. You, however, continue in the things you have learned and become convinced of, knowing from whom you have learned them, and that from childhood you have known the sacred writings which are able to give you the wisdom that leads to salvation through faith which is in Christ Jesus.' (2 Timothy 3)

Father, I thank You that You alone satisfy my deepest longings and I give You praise for the grace You poured into my being to heal my heart-sickness and restore me to You. The only true tree of life is found in Your garden and You are the Gardener. Thank You. May I go out with Your great heart filling my spirit causing me to beckon people home. Protect those I love from being led astray by false and vain things, I pray. Amen.

Day 325 – November 20th

It is an extraordinary thing when a prophet not only speaks but is called to physically model what God is saying to His people. We spoke of Ezekiel being called to act out the siege of Jerusalem; Jeremiah was told to buy land when everyone was leaving, as a statement concerning the future for Israel, and Hosea, in what is one of the most dramatic lives lived as a message, was told by God,

'Go, take to yourself a wife of harlotry and have children of harlotry; for the land commits flagrant harlotry, forsaking the LORD.' (Hosea 1)

Hosea was a prophet from an earlier time than we have been considering before but it makes little difference as we seek to hear God speak to us. The first chapters deal with their stormy marriage and the three children who were born, only one of whom seems to have been Hosea's. It is the story of a faithful husband who longs for fidelity in his marriage with a loving, committed wife, but she continues to go astray becoming a prostitute and a slave. Eventually she returns having 'crashed' and Hosea loves her and forgives her and takes her back. Hosea's entire life was born of a desire to serve the Lord in His quest to reach the people's hearts. It is quite extraordinary. At the end of the book, the last chapter concerns the blessing that awaits Israel when the nation changes its ways, ceases to look to foreign nations and gods and returns from chasing vain idols.

'Nor will we say again, "Our God," to the work of our hands. For in You the orphan finds mercy. I will heal their apostasy, I will love them freely, for my anger has turned away from them. I will be like the dew to Israel; he will blossom like the lily, and he will take root like the cedars of Lebanon. His shoots will sprout, and his beauty will be like the olive tree and his fragrance like the Cedars of Lebanon. Those who live in his shadow will again raise grain, and they will blossom like the vine. His renown will be like the wine of Lebanon.' (Hosea 14)

At the very end, God describes Himself as a luxurious cypress tree and He says that their fruit will come from Him. Whoever is wise let him understand these things . . . for the ways of the Lord are right.

Thank You, Lord, for Your faithfulness to us even when we go far away from You. You never give up on us but always keep the door open that we might return to You. You are truly like a beautifully luxuriant and aromatic tree, spreading Your branches to shade and protect those who will come to You. The generous fruit of Your kingdom satisfies all needs. You are the all-satisfying One. I can never repay You for all You have extended to me. Bless You, God. Bless Your holy name. Amen.

Day 326 – November 21st

God gives graphic illustrations to His prophets that they may understand the intentions of His great heart. They are wonderfully positive and really begin to speak to a future. Ezekiel was once shown in a vision how the city of God and the temple would be, in extraordinary detail. It was the most beautiful building. As a prophecy, it was intended to spur on the people to leave behind 'their harlotry and the corpses of their kings when they die' (i.e. their monuments which had become a part of their idolatry) and their high places.

'As for you, son of man, declare the temple to the house of Israel, that they may be ashamed of their iniquities; and let them measure the plan.' (Ezekiel 43)

It seems as though God is saying, 'You have been striving for beauty and something to stir your spirits and made a hopeless mess. See what I have planned!'

Ezekiel saw the glory of God flowing from the east and it filled the temple. His glory was such that it reminded the prophet of previous visions of destruction when the glory of God had left, and he was greatly afraid.

'And behold, the glory of the God of Israel was coming from the way of the east. And His voice was like the sound of many waters; and the earth shone with His glory . . . I fell on my face . . . and the Spirit lifted me up and brought me into the inner court; and behold, the glory of the LORD *filled the house. Then I heard one speaking to me from the house, while a man was standing beside me. He said to me, "Son of man, this is the place of My throne and the place of the soles of My feet, where I will dwell among the sons of Israel forever. And the house of Israel will not again defile My holy name."'* (Ezekiel 43)

Ezekiel was told to declare the beauty of the temple and if the people were appropriately ashamed of their iniquity, to make the details known.

Lord, we know that Your glory no longer resides in a temple but as we read this it brings home how real and how wonderful it is *to see Your glory.* May we who live Your risen life, be fully glorious in the presence of Your Holy Spirit in us. All of this, Lord God, makes me realise afresh how easy it is to bring offence against You, the Holy God. May I know what it is to live a holy life, to live for Your glory. Amen.

Day 327 – November 22nd

In the same vision of the temple, Ezekiel saw the Rivers of Life flowing from the temple which was filled with God's glory. Water was flowing from under the threshold of the door to the east. Then he saw the water trickling from the south side also. The man took him a considerable way down stream and led him into the waters first to his ankles, then to his knees and then to his waist. Eventually . . .

'Again he measured a thousand [cubits]; and it was a river that I could not ford, for the water had risen, enough water to swim in, a river that could not be forded. And he said to me, "Son of man, have you seen this?" Then he brought me back to the bank of the river. Now

when I had returned, behold, on the bank of the river there were very many trees on the one side and on the other.' (Ezekiel 47)

The man explained to Ezekiel where the river would flow and how it would support life and then he told him,

'By the river on its bank, on one side and on the other, will grow all kinds of trees for food. Their leaves will not wither and their fruit will not fail. They will bear every month because the water flows from the sanctuary, and their fruit will be for food and their leaves will be for healing.'

As I reflect on this, I feel I am profoundly connected to a sense of the things Jesus spoke of so often. His sayings sometimes seem strange to our ears but it is important to recall that Jesus speaks and acts from a full knowledge of His Father's glory and the rivers of life which flow from the throne. It is truly awe-inspiring to picture it and my faith grows and strengthens as I stand and gaze with Ezekiel.

Bless You, my glorious Father. The glories of Your person and the glory that flows from Your throne room are beyond my words so I will be hushed and ask You to touch me with fresh revelation. May I walk out into those ever-deepening Life-giving waters. Amen.

Day 328 – November 23rd

Ezekiel's life was phenomenally difficult. When you read the entire book, you will find that there is little there to cheer. People dip into their Bibles for quotes and verses but they do not often open the chapters of Ezekiel in that way! It certainly holds no incentive to seek to become a prophet! This man of God was not an automaton who simply churned out the words of God as they came to him. *He lived it.* God's thoughts became his very being. God's distaste for the behaviour of His peoples and His revulsion for their idolatry must have filled Ezekiel's entire person. Imagine living your life like that. Remember, at the beginning of his prophetic ministry, he had to eat the scroll that God fed him.

'Son of man, eat what you find; eat this scroll, and go, speak to the house of Israel . . . Son of man, feed your stomach, and fill your body with this scroll which I am giving you.' (Ezekiel 3)

Strangely, or perhaps not strangely, it felt sweet as honey in his mouth. He was told to speak to them although they would not listen to him; God knew that, because they weren't listening to *Him*. But He made Ezekiel's face as hard as their faces; his forehead like flint so he would not be afraid or dismayed before them when he spoke.

'Moreover, He said to me, "Son of man, take into your heart all My words which I will speak to you and listen closely."'

He was no automaton. Try not to pass over this as history. Sit with it; I think it can speak to every one of us about how we handle the word of God. *Fill your entire body with these words . . .* What does that speak to you, today?

Father, Your words are life and truth. You do not call me to ingest the Scriptures I read day by day but You do call me to take them into my whole being that they may become the very substance of all that I am. I open myself up to You, that Your words and Your desires would be so much a part of my spirit that what You say is what I will be, what I will speak, and what I will do; that it will be natural for me to be Your supernatural child. God, I praise You today and sit before You in full expectation that You will speak to me. Amen.

Day 329 – November 24th

God once took Ezekiel in the Spirit, not long after his early commission, and lifted him up to a heavenly place.

'The Spirit lifted me up and took me away; and I went embittered in the rage of my spirit, and the hand of the LORD was strong on me.' (Ezekiel 3)

It's not completely clear why his spirit was raging (Hebrew *'chemâh'* means 'heat'). I assume it was because God had shown him how the people were in God's eyes and they were not listening to a word He said. But what was the next thing that happened? It tells us a great deal.

'Then I came to the exiles who lived beside the river Chebar at Te-labib, and I sat there seven days where they were living, causing consternation among them. At the end of seven days the word of the LORD *came to me . . .'*

One of the things about this passage is that *Ezekiel really was there!* He was causing them consternation; they could see him sitting by the river; a very still figure looking on and worrying the exiled people who lived nearby. What is clear is that it did not happen 'in the Spirit', so to speak. He had been *relocated.* Amazing! And what was he to do after this incredible positioning under the hand of God? *Sit still for a week and watch.* I am guessing that in that week God's hand was still on him strongly but he was learning to find peace in that place of anointing.

God then delivers Ezekiel a word which is for him alone. It shows how our awesome God requires our faithfulness and absolute obedience in ministry. It could be quite fear-provoking. God told him that he a) was appointed a watchman over Israel and b) that when God spoke a word, however tough on the recipient, however unpalatable, Ezekiel was to deliver it. They might not listen and that would not be held against him but if he didn't deliver it *'his blood I will require at your hand'.* In other words, it wasn't up to Ezekiel to weigh up whether the word was 'nice' or 'appropriate'. Having told Ezekiel the ground rules for working together God told him to go onto the plains where He would speak again.

Lord God, these stories from past days bring me to a place where I inevitably am caused to see how my life measures up against this man of God that You had chosen to sanctify for Your purposes. I stand in awe of You and Your calling. Let my heart be open to Your plans for me and may I always be found in a place of obedience and willing servanthood, and my personal thoughts and my indignation be silent. Amen.

Day 330 – November 25th

When Ezekiel travelled out to the plain he met there with the glory of the Lord.

'So I got up and went out to the plain; and behold, the glory of the LORD was standing there, like the glory which I saw by the river Chebar, and I fell on my face. The Spirit then entered me and made me stand on my feet, and He spoke with me and said to me, "Go shut yourself up in your house. As for you, son of man, they will put ropes on you and bind you with them so that you cannot go out among them. Moreover, I will make your tongue stick to the roof of your mouth so that you will be mute and cannot be a man who rebukes them, for they are a rebellious house. But when I speak to you, I will open your mouth and you will say to them, 'Thus says the Lord GOD.'"' (Ezekiel 3)

He saw the glory of God *standing there*. His reference to the Chebar is not from his quiet seven days but from the time of his first calling which we find in the opening chapter of the book. When he sees the glory of the Lord again, he immediately falls on his face once more. He knew afresh what it was to be in the overwhelming presence of the glorious Lord of Lords.

And in that place God explains that whatever he sees and whatever it might provoke in him, to plead with the people, to argue or to intervene, his tongue will stick to his palate until such time as God frees him and then he shall speak the words of the Lord. I cannot add anything to that by way of explanation. It demonstrates what it is to be a servant of the Lord. It shows us how careful we must be; however tempting it may be to speak, to keep silence unless the Lord speaks.

Oh, my Lord, I know I need to learn this truth in ministry. I have so much in me that is of no use to You: my wounded story, my sympathies, my natural desire to 'help'. May I only speak when You give me the words. Amen.

Day 331 – November 26th

As we focus on these stories we do so not to become great students of the prophet's life or to compete on *Mastermind* – 'And what is your chosen subject? The life of Ezekiel' – but to become disciples of the great King we serve. These are His ways and it is deeply challenging to break out of some of the more normal characterisations of God that we are brought up on. It will do us no harm! If God wants any part of it to 'stick' as we pray, He will do it. We seek Him every day for fresh revelation of *who He is*. What was right for Ezekiel may not be right for us but, the Author of these days does not change and we need to know Him. Our faith will grow, I promise.

The most 'unnerving' moment in Ezekiel's life, for me, is that moment when the love of his life, his wife, dies and God speaks to him.

'Son of man, behold, I am about to take from you the desire of your eyes with a blow; but you shall not mourn, and you shall not weep, and your tears shall not come. Groan silently; make no mourning for the dead. Bind on your turban, and put shoes on your feet, and do not cover your moustache and do not eat the bread of men.' (Ezekiel 24)

That evening his wife died and the following day he did as instructed. Ezekiel was to *be a sign to the people.* When the people asked him what he was doing (or perhaps *not* doing) he was to speak.

'Thus says the Lord God, "Behold, I am about to profane My sanctuary, the pride of your power, the desire of your eyes and the delight of your soul; and your sons and your daughters whom you have left behind will fall by the sword."'

He continued by saying that they were to do as he was doing when God allowed the temple to be destroyed; not showing any manifest signs of mourning but instead they would groan inwardly and rot in their iniquity. Messengers would come to him with the news that they had escaped the destruction to bring word of the tragedy and then Ezekiel would be able to speak and effectively say, 'Now you know; the Lord told you through me being a sign to you. Now you know that He is the Lord.'

This is an extraordinary prophetic move of God that must surely have taken Ezekiel to the very edge of what any man can cope with. That it was *true* and it *did* happen the way the Lord said it would, might have helped the prophet to understand, but this event verges on the incomprehensible. But this is our God. His ways are not our ways, He tells us. God give me faith to follow You wherever You may lead. I know You will; it is my own testimony. Where You have called me, You have equipped me; where You have led me You have caused my heart to be softened and to bow before You in 'impossible' times.

God, holy God, sometimes I shudder in my Spirit when I understand the times and life events You bring men and women to walk through. By Your grace each one of us has the life we have, and the days we enjoy. May I always hold onto *everything* in my life with a light touch, thoroughly surrendered to You, my King. Amen.

Day 332 – November 27th

It is wonderful to read a piece of prophetic writing from so long ago, and feel caught up in the timeless 'now' of it. As Ezekiel engaged with the Spirit of God and explored the glory and the power and beauty emanating from the throne, so may we also.

Earlier, Ezekiel was caught up in another vision, which had a specific meaning in the story of God's people, but it can also speak to us powerfully now as we understand how God works to bring restoration. The so called 'Valley of Dry Bones' vision, made famous by song, is one of my favourite readings that fills me with faith! It is not just the words that fill me with hope but also Ezekiel's own story. He had not been able to prophesy for a long time.

'*The hand of the* LORD *was upon me, and He brought me out by the*

Spirit of the Lord *and set me down in the middle of the valley; and it was full of bones.'* (Ezekiel 37)

The moment I visualise this, I see a scene that might well be out of a TV Western, set in the desert. In the desert 'dry' takes on a new meaning! Dry means parched, arid, desiccated, lifeless. We have all seen films in which the hero or heroine trudges through such places in search of life. The human body, not being designed to resist such onslaught, inexorably tends toward death. The bones in this scene are so dry that they 'clink'. Tinder dry thorn bushes bowl past in the blasts of heat.

That is how God sees His people, but He speaks to Ezekiel those incredible words, *'Son of man, can these bones live?'*

The answer Ezekiel gave is, *'O Lord* God, *You know.'*

What a wise answer. In the face of extreme challenge, how many of us develop our own thoughts: *If I just do that . . . then that . . . maybe . . .*

No! Be still! *O Sovereign Lord, You know how to do this. I don't.*

In my own life I say, 'David, unless God has clearly spoken, don't look for your own thoughts, or even for God to come in a certain way. Make space for Him and look *for Him.'* There's a great deal of difference between expecting and seeking God for an A–Z map plan, and simply being His child and waiting for Him to come in *any way He chooses*! Ezekiel's journey with God into humanly-speaking impossible territory, into the land of *total* surrender to the person of God, meant that his response was perfect. *You know, Lord.*

Father, my Father, You alone know. I am aware that so many times I either think I know (after all, I am so wise) or I base my solution for 'now' on what I have seen You do in the past. May I have the profound humility to acknowledge before You, *only You know, Lord.* I will wait for the breath of Your Spirit to stir my spirit and to give me sight and words and understanding. Amen.

Day 333 – November 28th

It is very helpful to read Paul's words on how God called him. What it was not, perhaps surprisingly, was the delivery of *a message*. He was not given a download of theological treatise to share with whoever would listen. Before King Agrippa, Paul related how he was converted by a startling sovereign move of God. Jesus spoke to him while Paul was devastated and blinded on the ground.

'Get up and stand on your feet; for this purpose I have appeared to you, to appoint you a minister and a witness not only to the things which you have seen, but also to the things in which I will appear to you; rescuing you from the Jewish people and from the Gentiles, to whom I am sending you, to open their eyes so that they may turn from darkness to light and from the dominion of Satan to God, that they may receive forgiveness of sins and an inheritance among those who have been sanctified by faith in Me.' (Acts 26)

A minister and a witness . . . no message there, note. 'Minister' is sometimes translated 'servant' but it more-or-less means 'under oarsman'. He wasn't appointed to be the coxswain or the harbour pilot but a lowly oarsman. That was his calling as far as we can define it. He was to work and toil on a journey that he would not even be able to see, while the Skipper called, *'Pull, pull, pull . . . right oars only . . . pull, pull.'* He had no say. He just toiled as God directed.

Ezekiel knew that. He was a servant. Few of us develop such servant hearts. When we do, we become a pure reflection of Jesus who had the greatest servant heart ever.

God, I understand what it is to be Yours, and I want to know what it is to be totally *given to You*. I will come with no pre-conceived ideas of what my life might look like in God. Let me be filled with a desire for You alone and give me, I pray, a servant heart; attentive to You and no one else. Amen.

Day 334 – November 29th

Ezekiel's response to the Lord, 'You know, Lord', provoked the response we know so well. Ezekiel was to declare that the dry bones would hear the word of the Lord. He continued by speaking out the words God gave him.

'Behold, I will cause breath to enter you that you may come to life. I will put sinews on you, make flesh grow back on you, cover you with skin and put breath in you that you may come alive; and you will know that I am the LORD.' (Ezekiel 37)

Ezekiel heard it first: the precursor to life; bones rattling. The sinews and flesh and skin grew on the bodies and the impossible seemed to be happening, but there was no breath in them.

'Prophesy to the breath . . . "Come from the four winds, O breath, and breathe on these slain, that they come to life."'

Before him the great mass of people came to life and stood up; an 'exceedingly great army.'

There are many ways of interpreting this scripture; it was highly symbolic of what God was going to do in His people. The breath, of course, is the Spirit of God; the word 'breath' and 'Spirit' are as one. It was an awesome and inspiring moment of hope. He began to see that out of utter desolation, God could and would restore His beloved child, Israel. God brings Life! For me, I also see that after enduring the life of service, Ezekiel has been utterly faithful even though he once declared that he had had enough. He is now in a position of being trusted with *great authority*; he can now speak the dead into life at God's command.

Lord, now I know that You hold all things in Your hand. You are holy and righteous and Your power extends across all places and all times. Everything is dependent on You, the Giver of Life, and I worship You today. Amen.

Day 335 – November 30th

We cannot leave Ezekiel without going back to the beginning, to meditate a while on the vision that first put fire and fear and awe-struck love of God into his heart, soul and mind. He was by the River Chebar when a vision of heaven began. He saw things indescribable that are difficult to fully understand although our spirits rise with his as we hear of the beauty of the angelic forces and the servant beings. But there comes a point when even those visions pale into almost insignificance.

'Now above the expanse that was over their heads there was something resembling a throne, like lapis lazuli in appearance; and on that which resembled a throne, high up, was a figure with the appearance of a man. Then I noticed from the appearance of His loins and upward something like glowing metal that looked like fire all around within it, and from the appearance of His loins and downward I saw something like fire; and there was a radiance around Him. As the appearance of the rainbow in the clouds on a rainy day, so was the appearance of the surrounding radiance. Such was the appearance of the likeness of the glory of the LORD. And when I saw it, I fell on my face and heard a voice speaking.' (Ezekiel 1)

Perhaps we might finish with the words of Psalm 102:

'For He looked down from His holy height; from heaven the LORD gazed upon the earth, to hear the groaning of the prisoner, to set free those who were doomed to death; that men might tell of the name of the LORD in Zion and His praise in Jerusalem, when the peoples are gathered together, and the kingdoms, to serve the LORD . . . But You are the same and Your years will not come to an end . . .' Amen.

DECEMBER

Day 336 – December 1st

We have been journeying through some difficult passages that have doubtless stretched us, and caused us to ponder the very nature of God, but I make no apology for that. It is so important that we understand 'His-Story'. To fully comprehend the coming of Christ the Messiah as a baby to earth, is to fully understand the accounts of the people of God as they have journeyed with their Creator. As we come to the season of Advent, I appreciate that the timing of Christmas, calendar-wise, is not accurate, but things are what they are; late December is when much of the world celebrates God breaking into the endless cycle of sin and failure to usher in One who would break the death-spiral for all time. Let us agree that Jesus was almost certainly born in the autumn, probably at the Feast of Tabernacles, and leave it to rest there. We should not be overly concerned with the technical details but instead understand what our heavenly Father is doing through history and, in our day.

'Then the LORD God called to the man, and said to him, "Where are you?"' (Genesis 3)

We start December going back to the beginning both of this book, the Bible, and to that saddest of all questions: *Man, where have you got to?* What has happened to you? What have you done? One hesitates to put words into the mouth of the Lord but there is a sense in which we can hear Him saying, *'Everything was so perfect; why did you make that choice? Look at what your decision has brought on you . . . Do you begin to understand what you have lost, My child?'*

Father, I see and understand now how, in the fullness of Scripture, You have committed to restoring all things. I welcome You in this Advent season and I pray that I will continue to receive Your revelation, day by day, and be filled with Your Spirit, holy God. Thank you for Jesus who came to do the Father's will and restore all of creation to Your plan. I thank You and praise You for Your unswerving faithfulness to us. Amen.

Day 337 – December 2nd

I was privileged to have a father who was practical, from whom I observed that, with energy, application and careful planning, it was possible to *make things happen.* I learned as I watched him (although I never achieved his skill with the milling machine and lathe). It was the principle that I learned. I, in my turn as a father to my children, taught them. My sons had a little bench at the end of my bench and there they learned to saw, drill and hammer wood. They had a bin of off-cuts of wood; a little boy's delight!

When one of them began to achieve rudimentary success, he nailed together 'a plane'. In reality it was clumsy and comprised a few chunks of hefty joist ends but I praised his efforts and encouraged him to finish it by painting it. We found a tin of light blue paint and after a few hours it was painted, as was the bench, the floor, his clothes and hands. I am sure you can imagine the scene. I praised him further: 'That's a beautiful plane, well done!' Whereupon he looked me straight in the eye, holding up his cumbersome sticky offering, and said, 'Daddy, make plane fly.'

I struggled with that. I had no way to explain to a four-year-old the laws of aerodynamics, or that I had no capacity to make an engine suitably powered for *that* plane, but I heard something in that moment that has stayed with me and it still warms and stirs my heart. *The son trusted the father.* That is faith!

The analogy will, I am sure, break down at some point, but in 'His-Story' we see the Father gazing at the mess and the Son looks to Him who can do all things and, unlike this human dad, He says, 'Father, we can make this plane fly. Together we can make it soar again and loop the loop and it will gleam in the Light of the Son and be wonderful; just as we imagined it would be . . .'

'For as high as the heavens are above the earth, so great is His loving kindness toward those who fear Him. As far as the east is from the

west, so far has He removed our transgressions from us. Just as a father has compassion on his children, so the LORD *has compassion on those who fear Him. For He Himself knows our frame; He is mindful that we are but dust. As for man, His days are like grass; as a flower of the field, so he flourishes. When the wind has passed over it, it is no more, and its place acknowledges it no longer. But the loving kindness of the* LORD *is from everlasting to everlasting on those who fear Him.'* (Psalm 103)

It is when we are caught up in that loving kindness that our days will not only be holy days but they will be forever holy days. What a plan!

My Father, thank You for Your plan and Your unchanging love and determination to ensure that we can be caught up in Your great love for all eternity. Thank You for Your great grace poured on my life that, through Jesus, I might be made to fly. I want to soar with You. Amen.

Day 338 – December 3rd

And so it was, that in the heart of the Father there was a plan. *Hundreds of years* before the most amazing moment in 'His-Story', when the Son of God was born into the world, Isaiah was encouraging Ahaz to trust in the Lord and not in foreign kings when the following anxious conversation came about.

'Then the LORD *spoke again to Ahaz, saying, "Ask a sign for yourself from the* LORD *your God; make it deep as Sheol or high as heaven." But Ahaz said, "I will not ask, nor will I test the* LORD*!" The he said, "Listen now, O house of David! Is it too slight a thing for you to try the patience of men, that you will try the patience of God as well? Therefore, the Lord himself will give you a sign: Behold, a virgin will be with child and bear a son, and she will call His name Immanuel."'* (Isaiah 7)

Wow! Imagine that at a PCC meeting! 'Excuse me, how does that help us?'

The name Immanuel or Emmanuel means 'God is with us'. Not

up there, way above the heavens, inaccessible and distant but *with us*. I doubt that it would even be clear what *God 'with us'* might have meant exactly; how could it have been clear? With the benefit of 'His-Story' we can know this but, at the time, it might not have been so evident. The promise was made to the two small kingdoms of Judah and Benjamin, for the Northern Tribes were allying themselves with Syria at that time. This mention of the coming Messiah is as strange as David slipping into profound prophecy concerning the death of Christ in Psalm 22. It is as though for brief moments these two men of God glimpsed what was to be; they were ahead of their time in terms of understanding the secrets of God's heart.

God be with us; the cry of many hearts since the beginning of time as if it might be the call of *homesick* hearts. It remains the cry of many hearts today, expressed in many ways; the cry of the heart for fulfilment. Fulfilment comes by no other way than Jesus.

Lord, You are amazing! You thrill my heart. Show me the areas where my heart seeks fulfilment apart from You that I may give to You an undivided heart. Thank You, that in Your grace You brought me home. God with me. Amen.

Day 339 – December 4th

Matthew, the Gospel writer, knew that it was important for his readers, predominantly those of Jewish backgrounds, to see that the birth of Jesus was thoroughly grounded in Scripture. As he relates the story of the angel speaking to Joseph concerning Mary and the baby, Matthew is at pains to connect these events with prophecy.

'But when he had considered this [releasing Mary from the betrothal], behold, an angel of the Lord appeared to him in a dream, saying, "Joseph, son of David, do not be afraid to take Mary as your wife; for the Child who has been conceived in her is of the Holy Spirit" . . . *Now all this took place to fulfil what was spoken by the Lord through the prophet: "Behold, the virgin shall be with child and shall*

bear a Son, and they shall call His name Immanuel," which translated means, "God with us."' (Matthew 1)

Whether it was the power of the angelic encounter or Joseph's grounding in Scripture and his reverence for the Lord, but he obeyed and took Mary as his wife and she remained a virgin until after she gave birth to Jesus. It is a remarkable call for any man; many men must have dwelt upon this moment in the Christmas story, thinking, *how would I have coped with that?* It is a wonderful truth that throughout time there have been many men called upon to fulfil their small but crucial part in the unfolding of the Messiah's birth. Praise God for them all.

Lord God, thank You for the Josephs, the Davids, the Isaiahs and countless others who are with You in glory now gathered around the Lamb, each one receiving honour as a faithful servant of the High King. May I also be aware of my part in Your Story and serve You willingly and gladly with all my heart as I journey onwards, never fully knowing where Your influence will flow out through me. Amen.

Day 340 – December 5th

If you are familiar with the Festival of Nine Lessons, you may know Isaiah's other prophecies concerning the Messiah. They are scattered throughout and appear like shining lights amidst quite a lot of gloomy prophecies pointing to the terrible things that God's people would suffer as they journeyed further and further from the Lord and His faithfulness.

'The people who walk in darkness will see a great light; those who live in a dark land, the light will shine on them.' (Isaiah 9)

The 'dark land' is 'tsalmâveth', literally, the shade of death, the grave. It is to those who have no hope that the light of the Living Lord will come and, as we reflect on this today, perhaps we may see that *He continues to do so.* I recommend that as you walk around the places you frequent, you take with you in your heart these great scriptures and declare them . . . *'the people who walk in darkness will see a great light'.* The words of Isaiah still hold true, with the promise of healing in our land. And as we pray for other lands, whether it be North Korea or Saudi Arabia, India or Nigeria, let us declare it: *'The people who walk in great darkness will see a great light.'* Come, Lord Jesus!

Jesus, I thank You and praise You for the many times that I have seen Your light shine into the darkness and break the grave-power over prisoners who lived in doom; shackled to destitute places of no hope. May these words speak life over the places where we set our feet. Amen.

Day 341 – December 6th

'For a child will be born to us, a son will be given to us; and the government shall rest on His shoulders; and His name will be called Wonderful Counsellor, Mighty God, Eternal Father, Prince of Peace. There will be no end to the increase of His government or of peace.' (Isaiah 9)

A 'son' will be born; a *'bên'*, a builder of the family line. The Son will be like the Father and He will have no limitations; everything that is in the Father's heart will be achieved. This is the most beautiful prophetic word and deserves no amplification from me.

Amen and amen.

Day 342 – December 7th

Just as the angels reinforced the authenticity of their message with Joseph, so they did the same with Zacharias, the father of John the Baptist. The prophet Malachi (*My Messenger*) spoke in a time of discouragement when the Jews had returned to Jerusalem but there was strong despondency; things did not seem to be going well. But he was a voice both of direction and hope. He challenged the people to respond appropriately and conscientiously to God. Malachi has a way of prophesying with a question that he then answers.

"'From the days of your fathers you have turned aside from My statutes and have not kept them. Return to Me, and I will return to you," says the LORD *of hosts. "But you say, 'How shall we return?' Will a man rob God? Yet you are robbing Me! But you say, 'How have we robbed You?' In tithes and offerings. You are cursed with a curse, for you are robbing Me, the whole nation of you! Bring the whole tithe into the storehouse, so that there may be food in My house, and test Me now in this," says the* LORD *of Hosts, "if I will not open for you the windows of heaven and pour out for you a blessing until if overflows."'* (Malachi 3)

This is not really speaking about crops, although it did make sense to them at the time as they had suffered droughts and crop failures, but it was about *how the people of God should live.* Jesus spoke once saying, *'Give to Caesar what is Caesar's and give to God what is His'*, and it was a way of life that they were near to achieving but the disappointments kept coming. How that can resonate in our own days also. We think sufficient is enough; we consider that giving God a nod in what we do is enough. No! God says bring into My kingdom *everything* that is Mine, and you will see. I promise you, you will see! My abundance will be upon you so greatly that it will overflow!

At the end of Malachi, we have the promise.

'Behold, I am going to send you Elijah the prophet before the coming of the great and terrible day of the LORD. *He will restore the hearts of the fathers to their children, and the hearts of the children to their fathers, so that I will not come and smite the land with a curse.'* (Malachi 4)

My Lord, how we tend to 'short-change' You. We cannot trust; we fail to put ourselves *entirely* in Your hands. We ask You to come but our embrace is cool, our longing half-hearted and our ways are man-made and far from holy. Holy God, we come to You in our day and pray that You will awaken hearts to the Lover's Call. May we see the fulfilment of Your plans in our nation, through days of revival as we wholeheartedly turn back to You, the Living God. Amen.

Day 343 – December 8th

It is doubtless the Gospels of Mathew and Luke that best describe the 'Christmas Story'. Luke tells the remarkable story of Elizabeth and Zacharias, two elderly people who loved God and were righteous and really walked the walk with the Lord. They had once longed and prayed for a child but presumably those days of hope were over as they were 'both advanced in years'.

It was a rare thing to be chosen by lot to perform the 'burning of incense' in the temple Holy of Holies. Many priests never had this very special opportunity. When the day came, he was there all alone while the multitudes were outside praying.

'And an angel of the Lord appeared to him, standing to the right of the altar of incense. Zacharias was troubled when he saw the angel, and fear gripped him. But the angel said to him, "Do not be afraid, Zacharias, for your petition has been heard, and your wife Elizabeth will bear you a son, and you will give him the name John. You will have joy and gladness, and many will rejoice at his birth . . . And he will turn many of the sons of Israel back to the Lord their God. It is he who will go as a forerunner before Him in the spirit and power of Elijah, to turn the hearts of the fathers back to the children, and the disobedient to the attitude of the righteous, so as to make ready a people prepared for the Lord."' (Luke 1)

In this truly staggering moment Zacharias finds himself having the words of Malachi spoken to him straight from heaven! The time is now! Your son is the One! Long after you gave up praying for a son, the Lord remembers your prayers! God has spoken and is moving His mighty hand. I wonder which was the greatest challenge to this godly man's faith: the promise of a son, or the promise that this boy would come in the spirit of Elijah? Amazing days; ones in which we see the symphony building; the music is becoming more overwhelming by the week.

My Lord, what an amazing God You are. Your glorious plan is being revealed in the hearts and lives of godly men who long for You. I shouldn't be surprised, I know, but I am in awe of Your works. May this humble man's story also be mine; the right heart, in the right place, at the right time. Glory to God. Amen.

Day 344 – December 9th

There is a moment in the interaction between the angel and Zacharias which, if I am honest, make the hairs on the back of my neck prickle; it always does. Zacharias is wondering if he is day-dreaming, perhaps; can this really be true? It is too amazing to take in. He asks the most human question ever.

Zacharias said to the angel, "How will I know this for certain? For I am an old man and my wife is advanced in years." The angel answered and said to him, "I am Gabriel, who stands in the presence of God, and I have been sent to speak to you, and to bring you this good news."" (Luke 1)

Somehow this question sums up the doubts that many of us have in our hearts on days: *how can I be certain of this?* We want to believe but circumstances just make the possibility of the promise a stretch too far! We want to simply reply, 'Yes, Lord!' And then comes the answer of all times, and it is this that makes me tremble.

'I am Gabriel, who stands in the presence of God . . .'

I wonder if that profoundly affects you also. Words fail me.

Father in heaven seated upon the throne of glory, You send Your messengers with authority and with power, to speak to Your faithful children. This is so wonderful and yet, by Your grace, we have the Holy Spirit given to us, not Your messenger. It is You who comes to us! I am awe-struck before You as I seek to comprehend this truth. Emmanuel, *God with us!* Glory to You, Jesus! Amen.

Day 345 – December 10th

"'But as for you, Bethlehem Ephrathah, too little to be among the clans of Judah, from you One will go forth for Me to be ruler in Israel. His goings forth are from long ago, from the days of eternity" . . . *And He will arise and shepherd His flock in the strength of the* LORD, *in the majesty of the name of the* LORD *His God.'* (Micah 5)

There you have it. The promise spoken from long ago, but more than that, from the heart of God in eternity. This is the One who will come to do what no other has done. He is the One who will declare,

'I am the good shepherd; the good shepherd lays down His life for the sheep. He who is a hired hand, and not a shepherd, who is not the owner of the sheep, sees the wolf coming, and leaves the sheep and flees, and the wolf snatches them and scatters them.' (John 10)

The crescendo builds. It is as if heaven is putting the key pieces into Father's eternal jigsaw puzzle. For all time the picture has not been clear; it is all there, somehow, but not formed. Now is the time for the eternal plan to begin to take shape!

I was a shepherd of a flock once and I did care deeply about my sheep, as I have indicated before, to the extent of going out in the dark to rescue them. I once asked a man who was not a shepherd to look after my flock while I went away on holiday. I stressed the importance of bringing them all in once a day to count them and check their well-being. It was summer and the high season of fly-strike; I will spare you the gruesome details but flies lay eggs in the sheep's moist fleece and the maggots burrow downwards into . . . it is a horrid thing and a foul way to allow an animal to suffer although, as spiritual parallels go, it speaks volumes.

When I returned, I immediately went to the hill where they were grazing and I called. The sheep came quickly to my call. I counted: two missing. One was dead, hidden in a hedge having been eaten alive and the other was in desperate need of treatment. What a picture of the people of God. The Good Shepherd came to finally take on the one who has no ethics committee and no scruples. Believe it, beloved, *He is the One! Jesus.*

God, in Your love and in Your wisdom, You alone knew what was needed. The other shepherds had failed. The flock was scattered and without hope. You sent the One who would lay down His life for people like me. I am eternally grateful for Your grace and Your love to me. All I can do is worship You with all my being. Amen.

Day 346 – December 11th

Not surprisingly, when one of the angelic host of heaven visits, coming down into the domestic circumstances of everyday lives, the result is fear or a profound troubling, and so it was with Mary, six months after Gabriel's visit to Zacharias.

'And coming in, he said to her, "Greetings, favoured one! The Lord is with you." But she was very perplexed at this statement, and kept pondering what kind of salutation this was. The angel said to her, "Do not be afraid, Mary; for you have found favour with God. And behold, you will conceive in your womb and bear a son, and you shall name Him Jesus. He will be great and will be called the Son of the Most High; and the Lord God will give Him the throne of his father David; and He will reign over the house of Jacob forever; and His kingdom will have no end."' (Luke 1)

It is quite impossible to even begin to guess how one would react to such news, even allowing for the possibility that as a God-fearing woman she might have some idea of the Scriptures which pointed to the coming of Messiah. It is *the vision.* Later, comes the 'how'. I also find myself visualising when Luke sat with her years later, they might be together discussing the day that changed the world. *'Can you recall exactly what he said to you?'* asks Dr Luke.

I imagine that those moments were remembered in every tiny detail; burned into her spirit in vivid clarity. When God comes, we just do remember. This promise, amid all the wonder of the prophetic words uttered, still posed one problem. Like Zacharias, earthy problems remain.

'Mary said to the angel, "How can this be, since I am a virgin?"'

And then comes 'the how'.

'The Holy Spirit will come upon you, and the power of the Most High will overshadow you; and for that reason, the holy Child shall be called the Son of God.'

Over many years this simple promise (not the vision but the 'how') has caused people immense difficulties; as though in some strange way God, our High King, could not overcome biology. I would say to those who are struggling so, if from my own personal experience, I have known the God of heaven give a boy a new eye when he was born with only one eye, if He has with one touch straightened spines that were very bent, if He has joined bones and devastated cancerous growths, why might you worry about *biology*? God caused an ovum to form a complete zygote, a fertilised egg, by inserting supernatural chromosomes. I say, 'Come on, is your God too small?'

The whole issue of *'your God is too small'* plagues many committed Christians and has the potential to rob you of swathes of your faith. It *does* matter that we believe these things not least because there are millions of other moments when God has overshadowed His children and miraculous and unthinkable things have happened! These events happen *every day*. We need to grow our faith, as Jesus repeatedly admonished and then encouraged His disciples. *'O you of little faith. What am I to do with you?'* The only answer is to come to the Father with your doubts, and to ask Him for more of His Holy Spirit and His revelation. When you doubt, ask to believe, but don't tell Him why you shouldn't believe, or ask Him to solve your riddles.

'Do not be afraid, little flock, for your Father has chosen gladly to give you the kingdom.' (Luke 12)

Really, He has. He didn't have to do that but the glorious truth is

He did. To you. He is the most generous giver you will ever know.

Father, thank You for these wondrous stories of that first Christmas. Let me see them in the context of Your longing, throughout all time, that You might have a people of faithfulness and truth. Overshadow me, I pray, and fix in me a fresh understanding of the things of heaven, born of Your great heart for us Your flock, Your children and Your church. Amen.

Day 347 – December 12th

It is a wonderful moment when Elizabeth meets her cousin Mary, and there is a moment when the Holy Spirit comes close to them both. Zacharias and his wife had, after his term of office was over, returned home to a city in Judah where Mary went to join them for three months.

'Now at this time Mary arose and went in a hurry to the hill country, to a city of Judah, and entered the house of Zacharias and greeted Elizabeth. When Elizabeth heard Mary's greeting, the baby leaped in her womb; and Elizabeth was filled with the Holy Spirit. And she cried out with a loud voice and said, "Blessed are you among women, and blessed is the fruit of your womb! And how has it happened to me that the mother of my Lord would come to me? For behold, when the sound of your greeting reached my ears, the baby leaped in my womb for joy. And blessed is she who believed that there would be a fulfilment of what had been spoken to her by the Lord."' (Luke 1)

As a father of several children, I know well the delight of expectant mothers, particularly first-time mums, when they gather and compare notes; and this is full of domestic charm but the detail here of them both knowing that all of this was the Lord's doing is wonderful. Luke records this carefully for a reason. It is unlikely, we must assume, that Elizabeth had been told, at least not by Mary. Without social media and a postal service, it seems that Elizabeth might not have known of Mary's state. It makes little difference whether she did or not but given the miraculous baby that Elizabeth was carrying in her womb, she probably thought *she* was the one with the startling news! It is a moment of deep encouragement to Mary; it is as though God is speaking to her, reassuring her, saying, 'You see, my child! My promise is true!' Luke records it not for its domestic beauty but because it is a *supernatural moment*, surely? And Mary, overwhelmed with the Holy Spirit, prophesies powerfully, way beyond her natural ability. That is what God does!

'And Mary said: *"My soul exalts the Lord, and my spirit has rejoiced in God my Saviour. For He has had regard for the humble state of His bondslave; for behold, from this time on, all generations will count me blessed."'* (Luke 1)

She continues wonderfully with the prophecy now known as the 'Magnificat'. It is beautiful and remarkable and joins up many pieces of the 'jigsaw'. The fragment which catches my eye is the use of the word '*agalliaō*' translated 'rejoiced'. It means properly to *'jump for joy'*. It is the same word that is used to describe the happiness of Jesus when the seventy-two returned and recounted all they had seen God doing. Can we join her in that joy?

Father God, you are so powerful in all that Your mighty hand achieves as You fulfil Your plans, but I see also that You are so caring and encouraging as You enfold this woman in Your Spirit to tell her that 'all is well'. Amen.

Day 348 – December 13th

These days in December have always been very special to me. It was during this time of year that I sat in a hospice day after day and read the Luke and Matthew accounts to a wonderful woman who would have jumped for joy also, had she been physically able to do so. It is the enfolding in His great arms that makes such a state of spirit possible. Heaven is coming close and in these days of expectation that we are reading about, we see another powerful move of the Holy

Spirit as John is born to Elizabeth and Zacharias. Everyone expected that he would be named after his father, such was the custom, but Zacharias and his wife knew otherwise.

'And he asked for a tablet, and wrote as follows, "His name is John." And they were all astonished. And at once his mouth was opened and his tongue loosed, and he began to speak in praise of God. Fear came on all those living around them; and all these matters were being talked about in all the hill country of Judea. All who heard them kept them in mind, saying, "What then will this child turn out to be?" For the hand of the Lord was certainly with him.' (Luke 1)

If the Advent period is a symphony, it is as though the percussion has just come in! Something is afoot and the manner of Zacharias losing his ability to speak in the temple and its restoration as he declared John's name, sealed it for the onlookers and those who heard. I doubt that anyone was surprised when John became something of a desert recluse, following the Nazarene way of life, and abstaining from any alcohol which was unusual in those days. One imagines him being an unusual child; remember, we are told he was *'filled with the Holy Spirit even from his mother's womb'*. It is interesting to ponder what Zacharias and Elizabeth, John's elderly parents, made of it all; it must at times have seemed like a dream.

Lord, Your ways sometimes startle us but You are careful to draw attention to the things of Your heart that should really matter to us; we take note. Thank You for the sign-posts that You place on our paths; the days when we know that Your finger prints are on the moments of our days as You direct and encourage us. You are a faithful, loving Father. Amen.

Day 349 – December 14th

I wonder how, as a priest, Zacharias viewed his days. What had he achieved in his life? Was it more or less over? Was it time to settle down and enjoy the time he and Elizabeth had left to them . . . We cannot know but if you had asked them as they went into late middle age, still childless, *nothing* could have prepared them for what was to come! For Elizabeth, we know a little of what she felt. She is recorded as speaking out relief that her childless days were over.

'This is the way the Lord has dealt with me in the days when He looked with favour upon me, to take away my disgrace among men.' (Luke 1)

For Zacharias, the birth of John heralded the coming of the Holy Spirit to him. He prophesied powerfully as God came upon him.

'Blessed be the Lord God of Israel, for He has visited us and accomplished redemption for His people, and has raised up a horn of salvation for us in the house of David His servant – as He spoke by the mouth of His holy prophets from of old . . .'

And of his son, John,

'And you, child, will be called the prophet of the Most High; for you will go on before the Lord to prepare His ways; to give to His people the knowledge of salvation by the forgiveness of their sins, because of the tender mercy of our God, with which the Sunrise from on high will visit us, to shine upon those who sit in darkness and the shadow of death, to guide our feet into the way of peace.'

I see in my mind this elderly man, tenderly cradling his newborn child and, as the Holy Spirit enabled him, speaking over baby John these powerful words from heaven; declaring over him his destiny in God! It is truly wonderful, and as though those jigsaw pieces were falling rapidly into place in those exceptional days.

Bless You, Lord, for Your consistent loving message of hope throughout the generations, in the face of a rebellious people, and Your tender mercy that has brought through to the unimaginable – God made man – the manifestation of Your love in the world. No longer do we question 'When?' or 'How?' for all is being revealed. Thank You for Your revelation to us, Your beloved children. Thank You for Jesus. Amen.

Day 350 – December 15th

'He is the LORD *our God; His judgements are in all the earth. He has remembered His covenant forever, the word which he commanded to a thousand generations, the covenant which He made with Abraham.'* (Psalm 105)

Although we are told that 'with the Lord, one day is as a thousand years and a thousand years as one day' there is something quite remarkable as I reflect on Abraham, sitting outside the tent door, shading from the heat of the sun, when three men joined him. Abraham and Sarah also were advanced in years. Amidst incredulous doubts, perhaps, the angelic being declares that great truth, paraphrased here in my own words:

'Is any word spoken by the Lord too wonderful for the Lord?' (Genesis 18)

The word 'wonderful' means 'difficult' and is often used in praise of God; He does 'difficult things'; His way is to do 'wonder-full' things. The word that was spoken that day to Abraham and Sarah was in a sense the beginning; the very first 'difficult' step in the creation of a people who would one day be ransomed and forgiven, who would love and serve the Lord and worship Him as Majestic King. When God has spoken of the 'wonderful', He will do as He says; the wonderful will come. In that phrase uttered by the angel we see the point: *is anything that the Lord has spoken too difficult for the Lord?* It is interesting that in Isaiah, we read that 'His name shall be called, *Wonderful* Counsellor'. Are we ready for the accomplishments of the Wonderful One who does *difficult* things?

Lord God, You are the *Wonderful One* who does everything beyond our imaginings. You are the Accomplisher, the Author and the Finisher. God, the Alpha and the Omega, I worship You today as I see You holding *everything* in Your great hands. Amen.

Day 351 – December 16th

As we journey through the generations there are indeed many signposts of what will be, even amidst appalling unfaithfulness, God has always held out hope for mankind; He still does. Long after Abraham, we read,

'Then a shoot will spring from the stem of Jesse, and a branch from his roots will bear fruit. The Spirit of the LORD will rest on Him, the spirit of wisdom and understanding, the spirit of counsel and strength, the spirit of knowledge and the fear of the LORD. And He will delight in the fear of the LORD and He will not judge by what His eyes see, nor make a decision by what His ears hear; but with righteousness He will judge the poor, and decide with fairness for the afflicted of the earth.' (Isaiah 11)

And,

'In that day the Branch of the LORD will be beautiful and glorious, and the fruit of the earth will be the pride and the adornment of the survivors of Israel. It will come about that he who is left in Zion and remains in Jerusalem will be called holy – everyone who is recorded for life in Jerusalem.' (Isaiah 4)

I will sum up with the words of the writer to the Hebrews,

'God, after He spoke long ago to the fathers in the prophets in many portions and in many ways, in these last days has spoken to us in His Son, whom He appointed heir of all things, through whom also He made the world. And He is the radiance of His glory and the exact representation of His nature, and upholds all things by the word of His power. When He had made purification of sins, He sat down at the right hand of the Majesty on high.' (Hebrews 1)

Emanuel! God is with us! Join with me in praising Him today.

Lord Jesus, we praise You that You are with us. You left Your Father's side and abandoned Your glory to come to us as a small child in these wondrous ways. You accomplished everything Your

Father had called You to, then You returned to Him, to take Your place, the place of high honour. We worship You today, our High King of Glory. Amen.

Day 352 – December 17th

There is some considerable degree of variance with the Christmassy story told in carols and traditional versions, and the real events around Christ's humble birth. The record of Mary and Joseph travelling to Bethlehem, with the mother heavy with child, to comply with the Roman census was probably less romantic than you might guess from Christmas cards and folksy songs! The Caesar (Augustus) had decreed that all over the Empire, men and their dependents were to register in their birth towns and cities. In these days of online registration and polling it is easy to assume that was a speedy affair but there is not much doubt that it was anything but and may well have involved copious paperwork.

The couple probably set off in plenty of time and then spent a good while there in the city. It was likely that the census also recorded possessions and land entitlements and other information. It would have been a long haul with all available accommodation full for weeks at a time; not a pleasant experience for families with children let alone a mother with child.

'And everyone was on his way to register for the census, each to his own city. Joseph also went up from Galilee, from the city of Nazareth, to Judea, to the city of David, which is called Bethlehem, because he was of the house and family of David, in order to register along with Mary, who was engaged to him, and was with child.' (Luke 2)

I often find myself thinking, *could God not have made things a little easier for them?* Have you ever been involved in a project that you *know* the Lord is calling you to but, at every important point, hurdles materialise from nowhere, knotty problems arise and everyone involved becomes exhausted? If you do, reflect for a moment on

Joseph's predicament: his wife struggling with early labour pains while he searched, desperate for some accommodation. How would he have felt when nothing materialised? One can only imagine that he wanted to arrange something better for his betrothed than an animal shelter or, perhaps, a cave. But that was where they were staying. The one who was blessed, literally, *indwelt by God,* found a resting place amid the straw and bedding. But we must trust God's provision. It was right; God does not make mistakes.

'But as for you, Bethlehem Ephratah, too little to be among the clans of Judah, from you One will go forth for Me to be ruler in Israel. His goings forth are from long ago, from the days of eternity.' (Micah 5)

I appreciate we looked at that verse a few days ago but it strikes me as so wonderful that these days, as Joseph wandered the streets, are *from the days of eternity.* This is no accident, and I am sure it is no coincidence that it is also the place where David spent the days of his youth. God draws together thousands of threads from history: Ephratah is the ancient name for Bethlehem and the surrounding areas; it is where Rachel died giving birth to Benjamin; it is the place where King David caught the vision for building a place for God to dwell. The jigsaw is taking shape under God's hand.

Lord God, sometimes I wonder if there is any pattern to my life; sometimes it looks like a huge muddle. I reflect on why this event occurred, or that moment happened as it did. But now as I sit with these wonderful accounts of the birth of Your Son, I realise that all things are in Your great hands. No detail and no circumstance slips by You without it having purpose and resonance in The Story. Bless You God. Thank You for the pages of my life story, even when I didn't like it. I honour You today. Amen.

Day 353 – December 18th

'And she gave birth to her firstborn son; and she wrapped Him in cloths, and laid Him in a manger, because there was no room for them at the inn.' (Luke 2)

So, there it is. The Son of God, the Saviour of the world, the Christ, the long-awaited Messiah is born to bring salvation to the world. His name means exactly that: '*Saviour*'. He is born in poverty and lowly circumstances; more or less as a refugee under a government of occupation. It is said that when Jews travelled, their tradition required them to carry a very long roll of cloth for wrapping a body. It could be that the strips of cloth that Mary wrapped her baby in were in fact grave clothes; maybe He was born as He was to leave thirty-three years later, still possessing no earthly home, relying on loaned premises where He could rest. Who knows? In truth, the Greek does not support that idea (although we might agree that God might do just that). Instead the 'swaddling cloths' is a reference that goes back in prophetic history. Ezekiel speaks of God's unfathomable grace to rebellious Jerusalem, saying,

'*As for your birth, on the day you were born, your navel cord was not cut, nor were you washed with water for cleansing; you were not rubbed with salt or even wrapped in cloths. No eye looked with pity on you to do any of these things for you, to have compassion on you. Rather you were thrown out into the open field, for you were abhorred on the day you were born. When I passed by you and saw you squirming in your blood, I said to you while you were in your blood, "Live!"*' (Ezekiel 16)

The passage continues with God showing how he cared for Israel but how, tragically, they went terribly astray. The point being, it is likely that God would have shown Jesus to be cared for and wrapped in those cloths. Possibly *both* are true but, as we will see, the babe wrapped in swaddling cloths was to be *a sign*.

God, we have a sense as we meditate on this that the birth of Jesus was to be a sign to all generations afterwards, that You chose for Your Son to be born as a *sign* to all of us; not born in royal palaces nor with the appearance of the Prince of Peace. You challenge our pre-conceived notions about who You are to this day. Your ways are wonderful. Wake us up to the revolution that was ushered in that day; to news of great joy that shall be for all men. Amen.

Day 354 – December 19th

The account of the angels visiting the shepherds on the hills of Judea near Bethlehem is quite remarkable. Sadly, it tends to be swallowed up in the 'sanitisation' of the Christmas story, whereby art and song has painted for us a very different picture.

'In the same region there were some shepherds staying out in the fields and keeping watch over their flock by night. And an angel of the Lord suddenly stood before them, and the glory of the Lord shone around them; and they were terribly frightened. But the angel said to them, "Do not be afraid; for behold, I bring you good news of great joy which will be for all the people; for today in the city of David there has been born for you a Saviour, who is Christ the Lord. This will be a sign for you: you will find a baby wrapped in cloths, and lying in a manger."' (Luke 2)

One struggles to imagine this moment. The men were mega-frightened (Greek *'megas'*) at the shining, glorious figure before them in the dark. The symphony of the coming of the Son is now swelling in fullness; the whole orchestra plays in great unison; the heavenly music of rejoicing is now made known to lowly working men.

'And suddenly there appeared with the angel a multitude of the heavenly host praising God and saying, "Glory to God in the highest, and on earth peace among men with whom He is pleased."'

Those who were present at the Dales Bible week will remember the most beautiful angelic singing that was heard in Harrogate, at night, that week in 1977. It was not only for those in the showground but anyone in the vicinity heard it also. I only mention that because it is quite possible that many heard the angelic chorus praising God that night in Bethlehem; the glorious news was out! In the context of our long journey through Old Testament prophecies, I pray you will be caught up in the heavenly excitement of this moment that changed history. 'His-Story' was coming to fulfilment! I also find it immensely moving that these men on the hills were ordinary working people, most likely hired men, watchmen engaged to oversee and keep safe during the night the various shepherds' flocks. How appropriate that the News is granted to the watchmen!

My wonderful God, I do not want to miss the thrill of this moment; enthuse me to overflowing with the glorious detail and, by Your Holy Spirit within me, reveal to me the truth. Let me see the glory and wonder of this moment when, out of Your immense love and merciful heart, You gave us Your Son. You loved the world so much that You gave us Your only Son, Jesus. That's how You loved us! Glory to God. Amen.

Day 355 – December 20th

So much of the Christmas story is wondrous. Imagine Mary, who for many months has guarded the secret of the revelation that has been given to her. She has been at risk of social scorn and disapproval. Despite her knowing, I find it difficult to believe that there were not days when doubts assailed her. But now, here in the stable among the signs of animal husbandry, the noise of a crowded city and the comings and goings, some visitors arrive. They are rough working men.

'When the angels had gone away from them into heaven, the shepherds began saying to one another, "Let us go straight to Bethlehem then, and see this thing that has happened which the Lord has made known to us." So they came in a hurry and found their way to Mary and Joseph, and the baby as He lay in the manger. When they had seen this, they made known the statement which had been told them about this Child. And all who heard it wondered at the things which were told them by the shepherds. But Mary treasured all these things, pondering them in her heart.' (Luke 2)

Can you imagine? The men come in declaring, 'We saw angels! Myriads of them. They were singing the praises of heaven! Did *you hear? It was such beautiful music. I tell you, we were terrified. Absolutely scared out of our wits but the angel said that we were not to be afraid for the Messiah had been born in Bethlehem and it was wonderful news for everyone ... And here we are. This is the little One! It's been the most amazing day of my life! There we were; it was just another night ...'*

Dear Lord. 'There we were; just another night.' God, I praise You that Your ways of breaking in and turning our world upside down for good, just thrills me and fills me with hope. In the light of this, I know You will accomplish all things. Your promises are good ones. You offer to us all the gift of life. In this little One are wrapped up all the promises from eternity. Bless You, God! Amen.

Day 356 – December 21st

There are so many layers in this story and the more you peel away, the more profound their impact. Bethlehem, literally 'House of Bread', or in some Arabic tongues 'House of Meat', is the location for the birth of the One who is to declare, 'I am the Bread of Life'; who is to speak of never thirsting and never going hungry in His presence and, most of all, who will one day break the bread and declare, *'This, My body is given for you'* and *'this cup which is poured out for you is the new covenant in My blood ...'*

It surely is no coincidence that the presence of so many sheep and their shepherds around Bethlehem and in the Judean hills was because it was the place where the lambs were raised for the sacrifices in the temple. This is our God. For all eternity, He has willed that His Son, the Redeemer of God, will be born in the place where the sacrificial lambs are husbanded; countless tens of thousands of them for the Passover. Few knew that the Lamb had been born of God who was to take away the sin for all eternity.

'Every priest stands daily ministering and offering time after time the same sacrifices, which can never take away sins; but He, having

offered one sacrifice for sins for all time, sat down at the right hand of God, waiting from that time onward until His enemies be made a footstool for His feet. For by one offering He has perfected for all time those who are sanctified.' (Hebrews 10)

As Zacharias spoke in his prophecy, *'He has raised up a horn of salvation for us in the house of David His servant.'*

My Lord, as I see the pieces of Your astonishing jigsaw fall into place I am in awe of how You have accomplished salvation. We struggle with Your-Story sometimes but realise that in Your great love You have prepared perfectly for us. Nothing is left undone. You are a wondrous God and Your love for me leaves me standing before You in worship. Amen.

Day 357 – December 22nd

We need to move between the Matthew and Luke accounts to piece together all the account of the birth and early days of Jesus. His parents went to the temple for the rituals of purification, and dedication of the firstborn male child, and there they met Simeon who prophesied over Jesus. I wrote about Simeon's prophecy (August 12th) but for our purposes now, seeing how the pieces of the glory jigsaw fit together, let us have another look. He was a remarkable elderly man.

'And there was a man in Jerusalem whose name was Simeon; and this man was righteous and devout, looking for the consolation of Israel; and the Holy Spirit was upon him. And it had been revealed to him by the Holy Spirit that he would not see death before he had seen the Lord's Christ.' (Luke 2)

He was in the Spirit when the family came to the temple and Simeon knew! Imagine that! *'Selah'* as they say. What a man of God. He was a watchman; he was standing on the walls, so to speak, looking for that which was promised. His life honoured God and God responded to His faithful servant to reveal to him His Salvation. We take such scriptures in our stride, as we read, but pause and ponder the full significance of that. Think of the thousands of worshippers he must have watched coming and going in the temple. On that day, the Spirit led him to be in at just the right time, looking the right way and to 'see' them. There is something very wonderful about 'knowing' something so surely in the Spirit.

And for Mary and Joseph yet more wonder; a further piece of the jigsaw in place. The symphony is now picking up earlier melodies and repeating them in many variations. How wonderfully confirming for them. They were '*amazed at the things which were being said about Him*'.

Father, this passage tells me so much about being a faithful servant; standing on the walls waiting for a glimmer in the night sky. Show me, I pray, the paths to being and seeing in the Spirit as this dear man was. May I similarly *see* in my lifetime the light of Your salvation being worked out in the lives of those around me. Amen.

Day 358 – December 23rd

'*Incline Your ear, O Lord, and answer me; for I am afflicted and needy. Preserve my soul, for I am a godly man. O You my God, save Your servant who trusts in You. Be gracious to me, O Lord, for to You I cry all day long. Make glad the soul of Your servant, for to You, O Lord, I lift up my soul.*' (Psalm 86)

This is such a wonderful psalm of King David. One of the later lines is '*Unite my heart to fear Your name.*' I rather think Simeon would have prayed that psalm. The entire psalm speaks of David's passion for his faithful and loving God, who is there for him in all circumstances. His plea for an undivided heart, a whole heart, one which has no distractions, is indeed a wonderful thing to behold. 'Hedge my life around,' David asks, 'save me . . .' How beautiful. It reminds me profoundly of a special day when an undivided heart, made whole by God's abundant goodness, could no longer be apart from Him.

God, I bless You for the many ways You have guarded and guided my life. You truly 'hedge me around' and keep me safe. In the day of my trouble I called to You and You answered me. Glory to You, Lord God. Amen.

Day 359 – December 24th

The story of the wise men, who came seeking to pay homage to King Jesus, is an extraordinary and very wonderful one. There are all sorts of diversions we could make here, but we won't. Suffice it to say that when God wants to write something across the heavens, He will. We shouldn't be surprised, and one day we also may see 'signs in the heavens'. Every day is a sign in the heavens for all to see if they have sight to see but the magi came in pursuit of someone very special. It happened some time after the birth of Jesus. Matthew is precise that the magi came to 'the house' – the domestic residence. The family were back at home.

The magi's journey to the home of Jesus could well have happened when Jesus was a toddler. It was almost certainly not, as often depicted, that the wise men came to His birthplace. They fell down before Him and worshipped and gave Him gifts of gold, frankincense and myrrh, typical of the gifts that would be given to royalty. They were almost certainly not Jews but the Lord can guide whoever He wishes and their gifts, most agree, were deeply prophetic, speaking of His Royalty, His High Priestly role and His death.

And so, as we contemplate the birth of the King of kings, birthed into this world as a miracle gift to us, let us set aside romantic notions and appreciate afresh the sorrow of the Garden of Eden; the grief of the loss of a place to dwell with God. God has placed a standard on the earth, a sign to gather around: *'This is My beloved Son, in whom I am well-pleased.'*

'Then in that day the nations will resort to the root of Jesse, who will

stand as a signal for the peoples; and His resting place will be glorious.' (Isaiah 11)

My Lord, my God and my King. What joy bursts in my heart. You have raised a sign to all the people of earth! 'This is My Son!' Lord, we make our homage to You today, bowing humbly before You and worshipping You as our Lord and King. Bless God for His goodness to us. Amen.

Day 360 – December 25th

Bless you, reader, on Christmas Day!

"'Behold, My servant, whom I uphold; My chosen One in whom My soul delights. I have put My spirit upon Him; He will bring forth justice to the nations. He will not cry out or raise His voice, nor make His voice heard in the street. A bruised reed He will not break and a dimly burning wick He will not extinguish; He will faithfully bring forth justice. He will not be disheartened or crushed until He has established justice in the earth; and the coastlands will wait expectantly for His law." Thus says God the LORD, who created the heavens and stretched them out, who spread out the earth and its offspring, who gives breath to the people on it and spirit to those who walk in it, "I am the LORD, I have called You in righteousness, I will also hold You by the hand and watch over You, and I will appoint You as a covenant to the people, as a light to the nations, to open blind eyes, to bring out prisoners from the dungeon and those who dwell in darkness from the prison. I am the LORD; that is My name; I will not give My glory to another, nor My praise to graven images. Behold, the former things have come to pass, now I declare new things; before they spring forth I proclaim them to you." Sing to the LORD a new song, sing His praise from the end of the earth!' (Isaiah 42)

And so today we join with the heavenly host in declaring His praises.

Thank You, Father, for Jesus the Son.

Lord God, today I stand before You in profound appreciation for all You have done to restore all things; to break the power of that sad day when we all went away from You. Give me a heart to run after You, I pray, a messenger's heart with a herald's cry, *'The King is here!'* Amen.

Day 361 – December 26th

I like Boxing Day; I always have, even as a child. I liked the relaxed way of it, the cold meats and creamy mashed potatoes and pickles for lunch, and sneaking into the fridge for a nibble of stuffing from the turkey! On Christmas Day, everything seemed so pressured and so distracted, with so much effort put into trying to create 'perfection' for a day, an ambition we all know is doomed to fail; a far cry from the heart of it all. It is rather like the Martha and Mary moment when Jesus, on the road, was invited to their home. Perhaps Lazarus their beloved brother was there also but he isn't mentioned yet.

'She [Martha] had a sister called Mary, who was seated at the Lord's feet, listening to His word. But Martha was distracted with all her preparations; and she came up to Him and said, "Lord, do You not care that my sister has left me to do all the serving alone? Then tell her to help me." But the Lord answered and said to her, "Martha, Martha, you are worried and troubled about so many things; but only one thing is necessary, for Mary has chosen the good part, which shall not be taken away from her."' (Luke 10)

One gets a sneaking feeling that when Jesus responded to Martha and spoke of her being 'troubled about so many things', He may have been speaking about her general mental and spiritual attitude rather than specifically preparing the meal that day. I rather think that it must have been so as it is quite extreme, even when you are with someone you love and know well, to say, 'Hang on. I'm flogging myself over a hot stove; don't you care?'

Be honest, have you ever felt like saying that? *Of course you have!* Just like me. The reply of Jesus goes to the heart of our predicament. The description of Martha being 'distracted' (Greek *perispaō*), means 'distracted' but can be translated '*to be dragged around everywhere*'! It is a certain sort of distraction and not of the fleeting variety. The expression is a graphic one that may well describe many of us. Being dragged around is usually, though not always, of our own making. We have to *allow* ourselves to be treated so. Spiritually it seems to indicate a lack of 'peace'. John records that Jesus twice spoke the word over the disciples when He came into their midst after the resurrection. The Greek word *eirēnē* means, by implication at least, 'still', 'quiet', 'rest' and 'at one'. For me, I know, I can readily be caught up in the 'I oughts . . .' of life. I see things that need doing and I feel I must do them! It's my choice whether I do such things or not; no one is pushing me! The 'ought' often comes from our deep desire to please, or a fear of not being pleasing. As recipients of God's profound grace, it is so important to rein in these temptations to be 'dragged everywhere'. God loves you *exactly* as you are and no amount of rushing around will affect His love for you.

There is really only 'one thing' that matters, said Jesus.

Lord, today I will sit at Your feet. I will take a little time out with my Lord. I want to hear You speak; I want to catch Your words to me. Forgive me for giving space in my head to the voices that urge me on in ways that I should put down. I am so grateful for Your love for me; that You love me just as I am. Amen.

Day 362 – December 27th

As you may have gathered, my late wife died immediately before Christmas. People say, 'Oh, what a terrible time to lose someone,' and whilst I understand what they mean, it wasn't so for me; far from it. The notion that it might be a constant annual reminder is daft! No one who loses a spouse will skim by the anniversary because it happens to be October 3rd or May 7th! I think what they mean is *it is likely to affect you at this special time of year.* Let me share a few thoughts with you that are closely related to the Martha and Mary story we looked at yesterday.

When that happened to me, we had enough warning that it was likely to be so and as a result we made no plans for Christmas. My choice was for the 'children' (all young adults) to make plans to do whatever they wished, as normal, and, if they needed the distraction of friends or other occupations, they knew they were welcome to pursue them. We agreed to get together soon after the festive season. And so it was that I was on my own that first Christmas. I was pleased for them and I was pleased for me; I had no energy or inclination to 'be festive'. I slept the sleep of the exhausted, took my faithful hound for a long walk on the beach and then came back to a cheese sandwich and a mug of soup. Imagine that! Christmas dinner!

I recall vividly and, indeed, I made a thorough journal note (although it is too personal to share here), so I do have a record of what it felt like. One of the things I noted was walking along roads and seeing in many houses, Christmas lights and candle-lit tables, festivities and general frolicking, and thinking, 'just this once, I have the better part'. The feeling of God being sufficient for me, and the longing in my spirit to be thoroughly enmeshed with Him was so overwhelming that it would have been *very difficult* to be with anyone else. God can do this, He really can. He can wrap you in His wings; there is no better place to be. It is *'the one thing'* . . .

'The Lord is my shepherd, I shall not want. He makes me lie down in green pastures; He leads me beside quiet waters. He restores my soul; He guides me in the paths of righteousness for His name's sake. Even though I walk through the valley of the shadow of death, I fear no evil, for You are with me; Your rod and Your staff, they comfort me. You prepare a table before me in the presence of my enemies; You have anointed my head with oil; my cup overflows. Surely goodness and

loving kindness will follow me all the days of my life, and I dwell in the house of the LORD *forever.'* (Psalm 23)

Lord, I know that there will be many today who are experiencing grief and loss. Christmas as we have made it can be a tough time. I pray for them that the reality of Your presence will be right there for them, right in the midst of the toughest part. Would You bless them and hold them today, grip them firmly in Your mighty hands. I know You will never let them go. Amen.

Day 363 –December 28th

We return to the Christmas story . . . the wise men came via Herod the king, and their questions provoked quite a response for we are told, 'Herod was troubled and all Jerusalem with him,' by which we assume Matthew means the religious leaders. Word was spreading and causing consternation all around.

'Gathering together all the chief priests and scribes of the people, he [Herod] inquired of them where the Messiah was to be born. They said to him, "In Bethlehem of Judea; for this is what has been written by the prophet" . . . Then Herod secretly called the magi and determined from them the exact time the star appeared.' (Matthew 2)

The visit of the magi triggered a very dark time in the land and, as we discussed before, despite the magi being warned not to return to Herod, and Joseph being also told in a dream that the king had malevolent intentions towards the Son of God, the repercussions were extremely cruel and evil. Joseph obediently took the family to Egypt while terrible destruction was carried out on behalf of Herod: the so-called 'Slaughter of the Innocents'. All boys two or younger were murdered. Jeremiah had written hundreds of years before,

'Thus, says the LORD, *"A voice is heard in Ramah [a southern part of Judah], lamentation and bitter weeping. Rachel is weeping for her children; she refuses to be comforted for her children, because they are no more."'* (Jeremiah 31)

It is Matthew who makes that connection for his Jewish readers. It was a horrendously dark time for Bethlehem and thereabouts, and anyone who doubts the malevolence of the enemy for anything that is beautiful of God, should take note. He is a nauseating, ugly character. Such is the power of jealousy. Herod was a terrible character, caught in a power struggle in his own mind. He was crowned 'King of the Jews' by the Roman senate but he was a king without a kingdom; no wonder he descended into paranoia when the wise men came asking where the 'King of the Jews' might be found. In the ensuing slaughter, he murdered his own son. In his cruel life, he killed members of his wider family, and purged many who he thought spoke words against him, even from among the Pharisees. I mention that because his own traits were remarkably aligned with Satan's; evil jealousy is a phenomenon we see in our own day. Beware: that is a powerful combination. But it seems the slaughter was the last cruel act that this disturbed man accomplished before he died.

Father, we know that there are many who suffer appalling cruelty and persecution because of their unswerving faith in the Son of God. The battle is won but, in these days, we ask for Your protection for those who are establishing the beach head for the Son of Glory. We wait for Him to move upon the earth when all will be revealed as the earth is filled with the *knowledge* of His glory. Thank You for Jesus, our Lord and King, who is seated with You in glory. All praise to You, Father, Son and Holy Spirit. Amen.

Day 364 – December 29th

Archelaus took over a portion of the land of his father Herod's rule, including Judea, and he did not inspire in Joseph confidence for the well-being of his family.

'But when Herod died, behold, an angel of the Lord appeared in a dream to Joseph in Egypt, and said, "'Get up, take the Child and His mother, and go into the land of Israel; for those who sought the*

Child's life are dead." So Joseph got up, took the Child and His mother, and came into the land of Israel. But when he heard that Archelaus was reigning over Judea in place of his father Herod, he was afraid to go there. Then after being warned by God in a dream, he left for the regions of Galilee, and came and lived in a city called Nazareth, this was to fulfil what was spoken through the prophets: "He shall be called a Nazarene."' (Matthew 2)

And so, the scene was set for Jesus to enter His ministry on earth. Through so many twists and turns of history, the Messiah is present in the land of God's people as had been repeatedly prophesied hundreds of years before. It is extraordinary to see prophecies fulfilled; most have been but a few remain. They also will be fulfilled in God's perfect timing.

'Then you will say on that day, "I will give thanks to You, O LORD; for although You were angry with me, Your anger is turned away, and You comfort me. Behold, God is my salvation, I will trust and not be afraid; for the LORD GOD is my strength and song, and He has become my salvation." Therefore you will joyously draw water from the springs of salvation. And in that day you will say, "Give thanks to the LORD, call on His name. Make known His deeds among the peoples; make them remember that His name is exalted." Praise the LORD in song, for He has done excellent things; let this be known throughout the earth. Cry aloud and shout for joy, O inhabitant of Zion, for great in your midst is the Holy One of Israel.' (Isaiah 12)

Lord God, heavenly King, I bring You my honour and praise today that You alone are mighty to achieve and fulfil all your promises. Your will be done. I sing a new song of the Lord's might and His beauty. My heart shouts out, 'The Lord is great!' Amen.

Day 365 – December 30th

'To Him who loves us and released us from our sins by His blood – and He has made us to be a kingdom, priests to His God and Father – to

Him be the glory and the dominion forever and ever. Amen. Behold, He is coming with the clouds, and every eye will see Him, even those who pierced Him; and all the tribes of the earth will mourn over Him. So it is to be! Amen. "I am the Alpha and the Omega," says the Lord God, "who is and who was and who is to come, the Almighty."
(Revelation 1)

Dear Reader, I wish to say something heartfelt to you today. So often in Scripture we see that clouds are to do with God. We are told He is surrounded by cloud. As we journey to Him those clouds do, in some strange way, become our suffering, our losses and the adversity that we and others encounter; even the glorious positives so often are quite inexplicable apart from His clouds. My testimony is that when we cease seeing those clouds as the substance of things coming to *defeat* us, to *perplex* us and to *cast us down,* and understand instead that it is *in those clouds* that the Spirit of God reveals Himself to us, nurtures us and beckons us onwards, then our faith in our great Father in heaven will grow. Do you know that God cannot come to you but in clouds? Think of Peter, James and John on the Mount of Transfiguration! They were fearful as the cloud enveloped them. God doesn't *teach us* new things in the clouds. My experience is that in those clouds, *He breaks the power of what we have learned*; instead we know Him more, and trust Him as he reveals Himself to us.

May God bless you as you journey. When the blackest days come, days full of dark clouds (and they will come), stare at them and do not be downcast; do not let the darkness in any way detract from what you know of Your Father in heaven. As you gaze, I promise you the clouds will fade and the glory of the Lord will be revealed to you on that day when you faithfully stand and wait for Him.

'In whirlwind and storm is His way, and clouds are the dust beneath His feet.' (Nahum 1)

Did you catch that, my friends? The clouds are but the dust beneath our Father's feet.

God, I thank You that in all my life You have been faithful. You have never let me down; far from it, You have lifted me up. I have walked on my high places by Your grace even in the days when everything was seemingly stripped away. I praise You that in those clouds I met You. I love You and my heart sings for joy at Your holy name. Amen.

Day 366 – December 31st

'Therefore, the LORD longs to be gracious to you, and therefore He waits on high to have compassion on you. For the LORD is a God of justice; how blessed are all those who long for Him.' (Isaiah 30)

At the end of the year and the final thought in this book, as we venture into another year, let us put down a marker; a word that sums everything up, if that were possible!

In this verse from Isaiah we see and understand something very fundamental for you and for everyone you care for and pray for; that God is waiting for you. He, who is on high, waits for you. He waits for individuals, He waits for your village and your town, and He waits for entire nations. What does He wait for? He waits on high to . . .

God, I thank You and praise You for Your great heart and Your desire to be a gracious, loving Father, and the Great Giver to Your children. In the light of Your ways, I understand why You say, *'Do not fear . . . Trust in Me . . . I am . . .'*

So, with all my heart, I come. Amen.

26. Matthew 9
27. John 6
28. Luke 4
29. Luke 5
30. Luke 5 and 1 Peter 1
31. Luke 5

April
1. Matthew 17
2. 1 Kings 18
3. Psalm 8
4. Peter 4
5. James 2
6. James 5
7.James 5
8.James 5
9.James 5
10. Psalm 32
11. Isaiah 61
12. John 15
13. John 17
14. John 16
15. Psalm 90
16. Matthew 11
17. Matthew 11
18. Matthew 11
19. James 3; Psalm 57
20. Luke 12
21. Luke 19
22. Matthew 26
23. Psalm 139; 1 Thessalonians 5
24. Colossians 1
25. John 4
26. Luke 13
27. Luke 22
28. Luke 22
29. Luke 24
30. John 19

May
1. John 21
2. John 21
3. John 2 ; John 18
4. John 21
5. Acts 1

6.1 Corinthians 15; Acts 1
7.Joel 2; John 16
8. 1 Peter 1
9. James 2
10. James 5
11. James 5
12. James 5
13.James 5
14. Psalm 32
15. Psalm 32; Isaiah 61
16. Romans 8
17. Romans 8; 1 John 4; Luke 4
18. Luke 15
19. Romans 7; Luke 15
20. Luke 15; Ephesians 1
21. Luke 15
22. Luke 15
23. Psalm 146; 1 John 2
24. Luke 9; Matthew 17; Mark 9; 2Chronicles 7; 2 Peter 1
25. Mark 9
26. Luke 9
27. Psalm 42
28. Mark 9; Matthew 19; James 3
29. Numbers 16
30. Isaiah 50
31. Isaiah 42

June
1. Psalm 1
2. Psalm 1
3. Proverbs 25
4. Revelation 21
5. Jeremiah 18
6. Philippians 2
7. Philippians 2
8. Psalm 119
9. Psalm 49
10. John 7
11. Psalm 65
12. Mark 10
13. John 15
14. Luke 8
15. Romans 5
16. Psalm 139

17. Luke 1
18. Genesis 32
19. Isaiah 7; Luke 1
20. Mark 10
21. Mark 5
22. Mark 5
23. Mark 7; Mark 5
24. Mark 7
25. Psalm 25
26. John 14
27. Luke 3
28. Mark 1; Genesis 3; John 16
29. Psalm 15
30. Matthew 21; Psalm 118; Job 13 and 42

July
1. Mark 18
2. 2 Kings 13
3. John 16
4. Luke 14
5. Matthew 2; John 16; Isaiah 26
6. John 11
7. Isaiah 49; John 11
8. Matthew 21
9. Job 13 and 29
10. Ephesians 1 and 2
11. Matthew 6
12. Mark 8
13. Luke 9
14. Psalms 34 and 84
15. Jeremiah 17
16. Luke 23
17. Matthew 6; Psalms 84 and 85
18. Luke 4; Job 13
19. Isaiah 62
20. Hosea 6
21. Job 42
22. Psalm 23
23. Isaiah 60; John 16
24. Song of Songs 2; Psalm 116
25. Mark 8
26. Luke 24; John 20
27. Acts 12
28. Luke 10

29. Luke 10
30. John 1
31. Psalm 27

August
1. Psalm 18
2. Luke 9
3. 1 Corinthians 13
4. Jeremiah 17; Hosea 4; Micah 6
5. John 8; Jeremiah 17
6. John 8
7. John 8
8. Luke 2; Isaiah 55
9. Habakkuk 3
10. Matthew 21; Luke 3
11. Luke 13; 1 Peter 4
12. Acts 12, 9 and 5
13. John 5
14. John 2
15. Matthew 9
16. Psalm 105
17. Psalm 82
18. John 10
19. John 10
20. Isaiah 30
21. Isaiah 1; Psalm 11
22. Luke 21
23. 1 Peter 5; Colossians 3
24. Psalm 101; Matthew 14
25. John 19 and 7
26. Psalm 133
27. Matthew 7
28. John 7,8 and 3
29. Mark 3
30. Mark 3
31. Psalm 135

September
1. Psalm 139; 1 Peter 3
2. John 12
3. Psalm 73
4. 2 Samuel 4 and 9
5. Psalms 84 and 77
6. Isaiah 53
7. 2 Corinthians 12

8. Exodus 17
9. John 16; Psalm 42
10. 2 Kings 4
11. 2 Kings 4
12. Matthew 8
13. Ezekiel 4
14. Acts 20 and 21
15. Jeremiah 1; Amos 7; Luke 7
16. Luke 9; Matthew 8 and 28
17. Ephesians 1 and 2
18. Ephesians 3
19. John 15
20. Luke 2
21. Ezekiel 36
22. Colossians 1
23. Acts 15
24. Psalm 25 and 119; John 5; Proverbs 16
25. Genesis 41
26. Matthew 1 and 2
27. Judges 7
28. Matthew 27
29. Acts 9
30. Acts 10

October
1. Psalm 73
2. Psalm 73
3. Galatians 5
4. Psalm 18; Mark 12
5. Luke 16; Psalm 18
6. Luke 9
7. Hebrews 11
8. Luke 9
9. Luke 5
10. Psalm 78
11. Luke 9
12. Luke 9
13. Luke 9
14. Luke 9
15. Luke 9
16. Luke 9
17. Luke 9
18. Luke 9
19. Luke 9

20. Deuteronomy 31; Psalm 91
21. Deuteronomy 34
22. Luke 3
23. Judges 6
24. Judges 6
25. Ephesians 1 and 2
26. Matthew 26; John 14
27. Luke 14; Psalm 97
28. Psalm 91
29. Leviticus 23
30. Judges 5
31. Isaiah 42

November
1. Psalm 99; Habakkuk 2; 1 Timothy 4
2. 2 Peter 3; Luke 10
3. Ezra 1; Jeremiah 7 and 29
4. Jeremiah 24; 2 Chronicles 7
5. Isaiah 45
6. Ezra 1; 1 Timothy 2
7. Psalm 99
8. Ezra 3
9. Ezra 4; Psalm 90
10. Esther 4
11. Esther 8
12. Acts 2
13. Jeremiah 16
14. 1 Corinthians 14; Matthew 11
15. Jeremiah 30 and 31
16. Jeremiah 31
17. Jeremiah 31; 1 John 4
18. Jeremiah 30; John 6
19. Proverbs 13; 2 Timothy 3
20. Hosea 1 and 14
21. Ezekiel 43
22. Ezekiel 47
23. Ezekiel 3
24. Ezekiel 3
25. Ezekiel 3
26. Ezekiel 24
27. Ezekiel 37
28. Acts 26
29. Ezekiel 37
30. Psalm 102
December

1. Genesis 3
2. Psalm 103
3. Isaiah 7
4. Matthew 1
5. Isaiah 9
6. Isaiah 9
7. Malachi 3
8. Luke 1
9. Luke 1
10. Micah 5 John 10
11. Luke 1 and 12
12. Luke 1
13. Luke 1
14. Luke 1
15. Psalm 105; Genesis 18
16. Isaiah 11; Hebrews 1
17. Luke 2; Micah 5
18. Luke 2; Ezekiel 16
19. Luke 2
20. Luke 2
21. Hebrew 10
22. Luke 2
23. Psalm 86
24. Isaiah 11
25. Isaiah 42
26. Luke 10
27. Psalm 23
28. Matthew 2; Jeremiah 31
29. Matthew 3; Isaiah 12
30. Revelation 1; Nahum 1
31. Isaiah 30